3/03

NORTH AMERICAN INDIANS

a

G. Catlin.

The Author painting a Chief at the base of the Rocky Mountains.

North American Indians

BEING LETTERS AND NOTES ON THEIR
MANNERS, CUSTOMS, AND CONDITIONS,
WRITTEN DURING EIGHT YEARS' TRAVEL
AMONGST THE WILDEST TRIBES OF
INDIANS IN NORTH AMERICA, 1832 - 1839

By GEORGE CATLIN

IN TWO VOLUMES–VOL. I.

WITH FOUR HUNDRED ILLUSTRATIONS, CAREFULLY ENGRAVED FROM
THE AUTHOR'S ORIGINAL, PAINTINGS

𝔈𝔡𝔦𝔫𝔟𝔲𝔯𝔤𝔥

JOHN GRANT

1903

NORTH AMERICAN INDIANS
Volume 1

By George Catlin
Originally Published in 1903 By John Grant

©2000 DSI digital reproduction
First DSI Printing: November 2000

Published by **DIGITAL SCANNING, INC.**
Scituate, MA 02066
www.digitalscanning.com

Trade Paperback ISBN: 1-58218-212-4
Hardcover ISBN: 1-58218-273-6
eBook ISBN: 1-58218-271-X

DIGITAL SCANNING
& PUBLISHING

Digital Scanning and Publishing is a leader in the electronic republication of historical books and documents. We publish our titles as eBooks, as well as traditional hardcover and trade paper editions. DSI is committed to bringing many traditional and little known books back to life, retaining the look and feel of the original work.

CONTENTS

a 2

LIST OF PLATES IN VOL. I.

The Author painting a Chief in an Indian Village   *Frontispiece*

Map of Indian Localities embraced within the Author's Travels   *to face page* 1

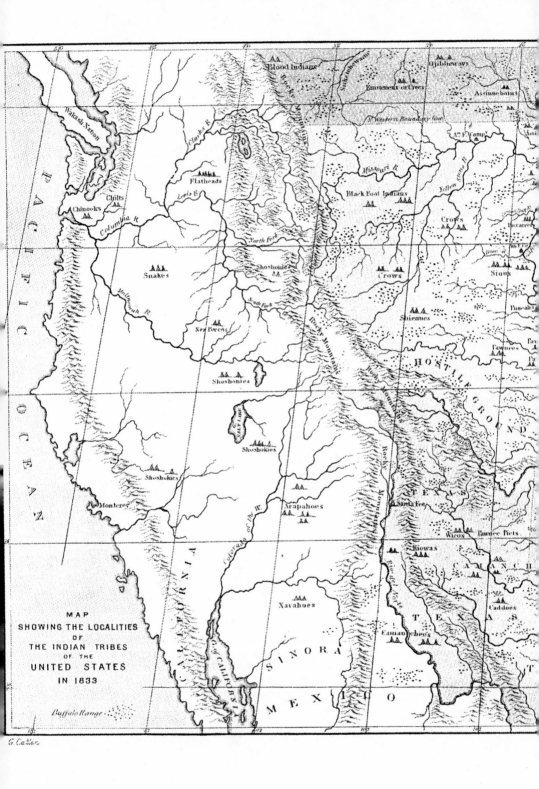

MAP
SHOWING THE LOCALITIES
OF
THE INDIAN TRIBES
OF THE
UNITED STATES
IN 1833

LETTERS AND NOTES

ON THE

NORTH AMERICAN INDIANS

LETTER—No. 1

As the following pages have been hastily compiled, at the urgent request of a number of my friends, from a series of Letters and Notes written by myself during several years' residence and travel amongst a number of the wildest and most remote tribes of the North American Indians, I have thought it best to make this page the beginning of my book; dispensing with Preface, and even with Dedication, other than that which I hereby make of it, with all my heart, to those who will take the pains to read it.

If it be necessary to render any apology for beginning thus unceremoniously, my readers will understand that I had no space in these, my first volumes, to throw away; nor much time at my disposal, which I could, in justice, use for introducing myself and my works to the world.

Having commenced thus abruptly then, I will venture to take upon myself the sin of calling this one of the series of Letters of which I have spoken; although I am writing it several years later, and placing it at the beginning of my book; by which means I will be enabled briefly to introduce myself to my readers (who, as yet, know little or nothing of me), and also the subjects of the following epistles, with such explanations of the customs described in them, as will serve for a key or glossary to the same, and prepare the reader's mind for the information they contain.

Amidst the multiplicity of books which are, in this enlightened age, flooding the world, I feel it my duty, as early as possible, to beg pardon for making a book at all; and in the next (if my readers should become so much interested in my narrations, as to censure me for the brevity of the work) to take some considerable credit for not having trespassed too long upon their time and patience.

Leaving my readers, therefore, to find out what is in the book, without promising them anything, I proceed to say—of *myself,* that I was born in Wyöming, in North America, some thirty or forty years since, of parents who entered that beautiful and famed valley soon after the close of the revolutionary war, and the disastrous event of the "Indian massacre."

The early part of my life was whiled away, apparently, somewhat in vain, with books reluctantly held in one hand, and a rifle or fishing-pole firmly and affectionately grasped in the other.

At the urgent request of my father, who was a practising lawyer, I was prevailed upon to abandon these favourite themes, and also my occasional dabblings with the brush, which had secured already a corner in my affections; and I commenced reading the law for a profession, under the direction of Reeve and Gould, of Connecticut. I attended the lectures of these learned judges for two years—was admitted to the bar—and practised the law, as a sort of *Nimrodical* lawyer, in my native land, for the term of two or three years; when I very deliberately sold my law library and all (save my rifle and fishing-tackle), and converting their proceeds into brushes and paint pots; I commenced the art of painting in Philadelphia, without teacher or adviser.

I there closely applied my hand to the labours of the art for several years; during which time my mind was continually reaching for some branch or enterprise of the art, on which to devote a whole lifetime of enthusiasm; when a delegation of some ten or fifteen noble and dignified-looking Indians, from the wilds of the "Far West," suddenly arrived in the city, arrayed and equipped in all their classic beauty,—with shield and helmet,—with tunic and manteau,—tinted and tasselled off, exactly for the painter's palette!

In silent and stoic dignity, these lords of the forest strutted about the city for a few days, wrapped in their pictured robes, with their brows plumed with the quills of the war-eagle, attracting the gaze and admiration of all who beheld them. After this they took their leave for Washington City, and I was left to reflect and regret, which I did long and deeply, until I came to the following deductions and conclusions.

Black and blue cloth and civilisation are destined, not only to veil, but to obliterate the grace and beauty of Nature. Man, in the simplicity and loftiness of his nature, unrestrained and unfettered by the disguises of art, is surely the most beautiful model for the painter,—and the country from which he hails is unquestionably the best study or school of the arts in the world: such I am sure, from the models I have seen, is the wilderness of North America. And the history and customs of such a people, preserved by pictorial illustrations, are themes worthy the lifetime of one man, and nothing short of the loss of my life, shall prevent me from visiting their country, and of becoming their historian.

There was something inexpressibly delightful in the above resolve, which was to bring me amidst such living models for my brush; and at the same time to place in my hands again, for my living and protection, the objects of my heart above-named; which had long been laid by to rust and decay in the city, without the remotest prospect of again contributing to my amusement.

I had fully resolved—I opened my views to my friends and relations, but got not one advocate or abettor. I tried fairly and faithfully, but it was in vain to reason with those whose anxieties were ready to fabricate every difficulty and danger that could be imagined, without being able to understand or appreciate the extent or importance of my designs, and I broke from them all,—from my wife and my aged parents,—myself my only adviser and protector.

With these views firmly fixed—armed, equipped, and supplied, I started out in the year 1832, and penetrated the vast and pathless wilds which are familiarly denominated the great "Far West" of the North American Continent, with a light heart, inspired with an enthusiastic hope and reliance that I could meet and overcome all the hazards and privations of a life devoted to the production of a literal and graphic delineation of the living manners, customs, and character of an interesting race of people, who are rapidly passing away from the face of the earth—lending a hand to a dying nation, who have no historians or biographers of their own to pourtray with fidelity their native looks and history; thus snatching from a hasty oblivion what could be saved for the benefit of posterity, and perpetuating it, as a fair and just monument, to the memory of a truly lofty and noble race.

I have spent about eight years already in the pursuit above-named, having been for the most of that time immersed in the Indian country, mingling with red men, and identifying myself with them as much as possible, in their games and amusements; in order the better to familiarise myself with their superstitions and mysteries, which are the keys to Indian life and character.

It was during the several years of my life just mentioned, and whilst I was in familiar participation with them in their sports and amusements, that I penned the following series of epistles; describing only such glowing or curious scenes and events as passed under my immediate observation; leaving their early history, and many of their traditions, language, etc., for a subsequent and much more elaborate work, for which I have procured the materials, and which I may eventually publish.

I set out on my arduous and perilous undertaking with the determination of reaching, ultimately, every tribe of Indians on the Continent of North America, and of bringing home faithful portraits of their principal personages, both men and women, from each tribe, views of their villages, games, etc., and full notes on their character and history. I designed, also, to procure their costumes, and a complete collection of their manufactures and weapons, and to perpetuate them in a *Gallery unique,* for the use and instruction of future ages.

I claim whatever merit there may have been in the originality of such a design, as I was undoubtedly the first artist who ever set out upon such a work, designing to carry his canvass to the Rocky Mountains; and a considerable part of the following Letters were written and published in the New York Papers, as early as the years 1832 and 1833; long before the Tours of Washington Irving and several others, whose interesting narratives are before the world.

I have, as yet, by no means visited *all* the tribes; but I have progressed a very great way with the enterprise, and with far greater and more complete success than I expected.

I have visited forty-eight different tribes, the greater part of which I found speaking different languages, and containing in all 400,000 souls. I have brought home safe, and in good order, 310 portraits in oil, all painted in their native dress, and in their own wigwams; and also 200 other paintings in oil, containing views of their villages—their wigwams—their games and religious ceremonies—their dances—their ball plays—their buffalo hunting, and other amusements (containing in all, over 3000 full-length figures); and the landscapes of the country they live in, as well as a very extensive and curious collection of their costumes, and all their other manufactures, from the size of a wigwam down to the size of a quill or a rattle.

A considerable part of the above-named paintings, and Indian manufactures, will be found amongst the very numerous illustrations in the following pages; having been, in every instance, faithfully copied and reduced by my own hand, for the engraver, from my original paintings; and the reader of this book who will take the pains to step in to "CATLIN'S NORTH AMERICAN INDIAN GALLERY," will find nearly every scene and custom which is described in this work, as well as many others, carefully and correctly delineated, and displayed upon the walls, and every weapon (and every "Sachem" and every "Sagamore" who has wielded them) according to the tenor of the tales herein recited.

So much of *myself* and of my *works,* which is all that I wish to say at present.

Of the INDIANS, I have much more to say, and to the following delineations of them, and their character and customs, I shall make no further apology for requesting the attention of my readers.

The Indians (as I shall call them), the savages or red men of the forests and prairies of North America, are at this time a subject of great interest and some importance to the civilised world; rendered more particularly so in this age, from their relative position to, and their rapid declension from, the civilised nations of the earth. A numerous nation of human beings, whose origin is beyond the reach of human investigation,—whose early history is lost—whose term of national existence is nearly expired—three-fourths of whose country has fallen into the possession of civilised man within the short space of 250 years—twelve millions of whose bodies have fattened the soil in the meantime; who have fallen victims to whiskey, the small-pox and the bayonet; leaving at this time but a meagre proportion to live a short time longer, in the certain apprehension of soon sharing a similar fate.

The writer who would undertake to embody the whole history of such a people, with all their misfortunes and calamities, must needs have much more space than I have allotted to this epitome; and he must needs begin also (as I am doing) with those who are *living,* or he would be very apt to dwell upon the preamble of his work, until the present living remnants of the race should have passed away; and their existence and customs, like those of ages gone bye, become subjects of doubt and incredulity to the world for whom his book was preparing. Such an historian also, to do them justice, must needs correct many theories and opinions which have, either ignorantly or maliciously, gone forth to the world in indelible characters; and gather and arrange a vast deal which has been but imperfectly recorded, or placed to the credit of a people who have not had the means of recording it themselves; but have entrusted it, from necessity, to the honesty and punctuality of their enemies.

In such an history should be embodied, also, a correct account of their treatment, and the causes which have led to their rapid destruction; and a plain and systematical prophecy as to the time and manner of their final extinction, based upon the causes and the ratio of their former and present declension.

So Herculean a task may fall to my lot at a future period, or it may not; but I send forth these volumes at this time, fresh and full of their living deeds and customs, as a familiar and unstudied introduction (at least) to them and their native character; which I confidently hope will repay the readers who read for information and historical facts, as well as those who read but for amusement.

The world know generally, that the Indians of North America are copper-coloured, that their eyes and their hair are black, etc.; that they are mostly uncivilised, and consequently unchristianised; that they are nevertheless human beings, with features, thoughts, reason, and sympathies like our own; but few yet know how they *live,* how they *dress,* how they *worship,* what are their actions, their customs, their religion, their amusements, etc., as they practise them in the uncivilised regions of their uninvaded country, which it is the main object of this work, clearly and distinctly to set forth.

It would be impossible at the same time, in a book of these dimensions, to explain *all* the manners and customs of these people; but as far as they are narrated, they have been described by my pen, upon the spot, as I have seen them transacted; and if some few of my narrations should seem a *little too highly coloured,* I trust the world will be ready to extend to me that pardon which it is customary to yield to all artists whose main faults exist in the vividness of their colouring, rather than in the drawing of their pictures; but there is nothing else in them, I think, that I should ask pardon for, even though some of them should stagger credulity, and incur for me the censure of those critics, who sometimes, unthinkingly, or unmercifully, sit at home at their desks, enjoying the luxury of wine and a good cigar, over the simple narration of the honest and weather-worn traveller (who shortens his half-starved life in catering for the world), to condemn him and his work to oblivion, and his wife and his little children to poverty and starvation; merely because he describes scenes which they have not beheld, and which, consequently, they are unable to believe.

The Indians of North America, as I have before said, are copper-coloured, with long black hair, black eyes, tall, straight, and elastic forms—are less than two millions in number—were originally the undisputed owners of the soil, and got their title to their lands from the Great Spirit who created them on it,—were once a happy and flourishing people, enjoying all the comforts and luxuries of life which they knew of, and consequently cared for;—were sixteen millions in numbers, and sent that number of daily prayers to the Almighty, and thanks for His goodness and protection. Their country was entered by white men, but a few hundred years since; and thirty millions of these are now scuffling for the goods and luxuries of life, over the bones and ashes of twelve millions of red men; six millions of whom have fallen victims to the small-pox, and the remainder to the sword, the bayonet, and whiskey; all of which means of their death and destruction have been introduced and visited upon them by acquisitive white men; and by white men, also, whose forefathers were welcomed and embraced in the land where the poor Indian met and fed them with "ears of green corn and with pemican." Of the two millions remaining alive at this time, about 1,400,000 are already the miserable living victims and dupes of white man's cupidity, degraded, discouraged, and lost in the bewildering maze that is produced by the use of whiskey and its concomitant vices; and the remaining number are yet unroused and unenticed from their wild haunts or their primitive modes, by the dread or love of white man and his allurements.

It has been with these, mostly, that I have spent my time, and of these, chiefly, and their customs, that the following Letters treat. Their habits (and theirs alone) as we can see them transacted, are native, and such as I have wished to fix and preserve for future ages.

Of the dead, and of those who are dying, of those who have suffered death, and of those who are now trodden and kicked through it, I may speak more fully in some deductions at the close of this book; or at some future time, when I may find more leisure, and may be able to speak of these scenes without giving offence to the world, or to any body in it.

Such a portrait then as I have set forth in the following pages (taken by myself from the free and vivid realities of life, instead of the vague and uncertain imagery of recollection, or from the haggard deformities and distortions of disease and death), I offer to the world for their amusement, as well as for their information; and I trust they will pardon me, if it should be thought that I have overestimated the Indian character, or at other times descended too much into the details and minutiæ of Indian mysteries and absurdities.

The reader, then, to understand me rightly, and draw from these Letters the information which they are intended to give, must follow me a vast way from the civilised world; he must needs wend his way from the city of New York, over the Alleghany, and far beyond the mighty Missouri, and even to the base and summit of the Rocky Mountains, some two or three thousand miles from the Atlantic coast. He should forget many theories he has read in the books of Indian barbarities, of wanton butcheries and murders; and divest himself, as far as possible, of the deadly prejudices which he has carried from his childhood, against this most unfortunate and most abused part of the race of his fellow-man.

He should consider, that if he has seen the savages of North America without making such a tour, he has fixed his eyes upon and drawn his conclusions (in all probability) only from those who inhabit the frontier; whose habits have been changed—whose pride has been cut down—whose country has been ransacked—whose wives and daughters have been shamefully abused—whose lands have been wrested from them—whose limbs have become enervated and naked by the excessive use of whiskey—whose friends and relations have been prematurely thrown into their graves—whose native pride and dignity have at last given way to the unnatural vices which civilised cupidity has engrafted upon them, to be silently nurtured and magnified by a burning sense of injury and injustice, and ready for that cruel vengeance which often falls from the hand that is palsied by refined abuses, and yet unrestrained by the glorious influences of refined and moral cultivation.—That if he has laid up, what he considers well-founded knowledge of these people, from books which he has read, and from newspapers only, he should pause at least, and withhold his sentence before he passes it upon the character of a people, who are dying at the hands of their enemies, without the means of recording their own annals —struggling in their nakedness with their simple weapons, against guns and gunpowder—against whiskey and steel, and disease, and mailed warriors who are continually trampling them to the earth, and at last exultingly promulgating from the very soil which they have wrested from the poor savage, the history of his cruelties and barbarities, whilst his bones are quietly resting under the very furrows which their ploughs are turning.

So great and unfortunate are the disparities between savage and civil, in numbers—in weapons and defences—in enterprise, in craft, and in education, that the former is almost universally the sufferer either in peace or in war; and not less so after his pipe and his tomahawk have retired to the grave with him, and his character is left to be entered upon the pages of history, and that justice done to his memory which, from necessity, he has entrusted to his enemy.

Amongst the numerous historians, however, of these strange people, they have had some friends who have done them justice; yet as a part of all systems of justice, whenever it is meted to the poor Indian, it comes invariably too late, or is administered at an ineffectual distance; and that too when his enemies are continually about him, and effectually applying the means of his destruction.

Some writers, I have been grieved to see, have written down the character of the North American Indian, as dark, relentless, cruel and murderous in the last degree; with scarce a quality to stamp his existence of a higher order than that of the brutes:—whilst others have given them a high rank, as I feel myself authorised to do, as honourable and highly-intellectual beings; and others, both friends and foes to the red man, have spoken of them as an "anomaly in nature!"

In this place I have no time or inclination to reply to so unaccountable an assertion as this; contenting myself with the belief that the term would be far more correctly applied to that part of the human family who have strayed farthest from nature, than it could be to those who are simply moving in, and filling the sphere for which they were designed by the Great Spirit who made them.

From what I have seen of these people I feel authorised to say, that there is nothing very strange or unaccountable in their character; but that it is a simple one, and easy to be learned and understood, if the right means be taken to familiarise ourselves with it. Although it has its dark spots; yet there is much in it to be applauded, and much to recommend it to the admiration of the enlightened world. And I trust that the reader, who looks through these volumes with care, will be disposed to join me in the conclusion: that the North American Indian in his native state is an honest, hospitable, faithful, brave, warlike, cruel, revengeful, relentless,—yet honourable, contemplative and religious being.

If such be the case, I am sure there is enough in it to recommend it to the fair perusal of the world, and charity enough in all civilised countries, in this enlightened age, to extend a helping hand to a dying race; provided that prejudice and fear can be removed, which have heretofore constantly held the civilised portions in dread of the savage—and away from that familiar and friendly embrace, in which alone his true native character can be justly appreciated.

I am fully convinced, from a long familiarity with these people, that the Indian's misfortune has consisted chiefly in our ignorance of their true native character and disposition, which has always held us at a distrustful distance from them; inducing us to look upon them in no other light than that of a hostile foe, and worthy only of that system of continued warfare and abuse that has been for ever waged against them.

There is no difficulty in approaching the Indian and getting acquainted with him in his wild and unsophisticated state, and finding him an honest and honourable man; with feelings to meet feelings, if the above prejudice and dread can be laid aside, and any one will take the pains, as I have done, to go and see him in the simplicity of his native state, smoking his pipe under his own humble roof, with his wife and children around him, and his faithful dogs and horses hanging about his hospitable tenement.—So the world *may* see him and smoke his friendly pipe, which is invariably extended to them; and share, with a hearty welcome, the best that his wigwam affords for the appetite, which is always set out to a stranger the next moment after he enters.

But so the mass of the world, most assuredly will *not* see these people; for they are too far off, and approachable to those only whose avarice or cupidity alone lead them to those remote regions, and whose shame prevents them from publishing to the world the virtues which they have thrown down and trampled under foot.

The very use of the word savage, as it is applied in its general sense, I am inclined to believe is an abuse of the word, and the people to whom it is applied. The word, in its true definition, means no more than *wild,* or *wild man;* and a wild man may have been endowed by his Maker with all the humane and noble traits that inhabit the heart of a tame man. Our ignorance and dread or fear of these people, therefore, have given a new definition to the adjective; and nearly the whole civilised world apply the word *savage,* as expressive of the most ferocious, cruel, and murderous character that can be described.

The grisly bear is called savage, because he is blood-thirsty, ravenous and cruel; and so is the tiger, and they, like the poor red man, have been feared and dreaded (from the distance at which ignorance and prejudice have kept us from them, or from resented abuses which we have practised when we have come in close contact with them), until Van Amburgh showed the world, that even these ferocious and unreasoning animals wanted only the friendship and close embrace of their master, to respect and to love him.

As evidence of the hospitality of these ignorant and benighted people, and also of their honesty and honour, there will be found recorded many striking instances in the following pages. And also, as an offset to these, many evidences of the dark and cruel, as well as ignorant and disgusting excesses of passions, unrestrained by the salutary influences of laws and Christianity.

I have roamed about from time to time during seven or eight years, visiting and associating with some three or four hundred thousand of these people, under an almost infinite variety of circumstances; and from the very many and decided voluntary acts of their hospitality and kindness, I feel bound to pronounce them, by nature, a kind and hospitable people. I have been welcomed generally in their country, and treated to the best that they could give me, without any charges made for my board; they have often escorted me through their enemies' country at some hazard to their own lives, and aided me in passing mountains and rivers with my awkward baggage; and under all of these circumstances of exposure, no Indian ever betrayed me, struck me a blow, or stole from me a shilling's worth of my property that I am aware of.

This is saying a great deal (and proving it too, if the reader will believe me) in favour of the virtues of these people; when it is borne in mind, as it should be, that there is no law in their land to punish a man for theft—that the commandments have never been divulged amongst them; nor can any human retribution fall upon the head of a thief, save the disgrace which attaches as a stigma to his character, in the eyes of his people about him.

And thus in these little communities, strange as it may seem, in the absence of all systems of jurisprudence, I have often beheld peace and happiness, and quiet, reigning supreme, for which even kings and emperors might envy them. I have seen rights and virtue protected, and wrongs redressed; and I have seen conjugal, filial and paternal affection in the simplicity and contentedness of nature. I have, unavoidably, formed warm and enduring attachments to some of these men which I do not wish to forget—who have brought me near to their hearts, and in our final separation have embraced me in their arms, and commended me and my affairs to the keeping of the Great Spirit.

For the above reasons, the reader will be disposed to forgive me for dwelling so long and so strong on the justness of the claims of these people; and for my occasional expressions of sadness, when my heart bleeds for the fate that awaits the remainder of their unlucky race; which is long to be outlived by the rocks, by the beasts, and even birds and reptiles of the country they live in;—set upon by their fellow-man, whose cupidity, it is feared, will fix no bounds to the Indian's earthly calamity, short of the grave.

I cannot help but repeat, before I close this Letter, that the tribes of the red men of North America, as a nation of human beings, are on their wane; that (to use their own very beautiful figure) "they are fast travelling to the shades of their fathers, towards the setting sun;" and that the traveller, who would see these people in their native simplicity and beauty, must needs be hastily on his way to the prairies and Rocky Mountains, or he will see them only as they are now seen on the frontiers, as a basket of *dead game,*—harassed, chased, bleeding and dead; with their plumage and colours despoiled, to be gazed amongst in vain for some system or moral, or for some scale by which to estimate their true native character, other than that which has too often recorded them; but a dark and unintelligible mass of cruelty and barbarity.

Without further comments I close this Letter, introducing my readers at once to the heart of the Indian country, only asking their forgiveness for having made it so long, and their patience whilst travelling through the following pages (as I journeyed through those remote realms) in search of information and rational amusement; in tracing out the true character of that *"strange anomaly"* of man in the simple elements of his nature, undissolved or compounded into the mysteries of enlightened and fashionable life.

NOTE

As the singular manners of the Country set forth in the following pages, and the extraordinary scenes represented in the very numerous illustrations are of such a character as to require all possible aids for the satisfaction of the reader; I hope they will excuse me for intruding in this place the numerous Certificates which follow, and which have been voluntarily furnished me by men whose lives, it will be seen, have been spent, in great part, in the Indian Country, and in familiarity with the men and manners set forth in the work:

CERTIFICATES

"I hereby certify, that the persons whose signatures are affixed to the certificates used below, by Mr CATLIN, are officers in the service of the United States, as herein set forth; and that their opinions of the accuracy of the likenesses, and correctness of the views, etc., exhibited by him in his 'INDIAN GALLERY,' are entitled to full credit.
"J. R. POINSETT, *Secretary of War, Washington.*"

"With regard to the gentlemen whose names are affixed to certificates below, I am fully warranted in saying, that no individuals have had better opportunities of acquiring a knowledge of the persons, habits, costumes, and sports of the Indian tribes, or possess stronger claims upon the public confidence in the statements they make, respecting the correctness of delineations, etc., of Mr CATLIN'S INDIAN GALLERY; and I may add my own testimony, with regard to many of those Indians whom I have seen, and whose likenesses are in the collection, and sketched with fidelity and correctness.
"C. A. HARRIS, *Commissioner of Indian Affairs, Washington.*"

"I have seen Mr CATLIN'S Collection of Portraits of Indians, east of the Rocky Mountains, many of which were familiar to me, and painted in my presence: and as far as they have included Indians of my acquaintance, the *likenesses* are easily recognised, bearing the most striking resemblance to the originals, as well as faithful representations of their costumes.

"W. CLARK, *Superintendent of Indian Affairs, St Louis.*"

"I have examined Mr CATLIN'S Collection of the Upper Missouri Indians to the Rocky Mountains, all of which I am acquainted with; and indeed most of them were painted when I was present, and I do not hesitate to pronounce them correct likenesses, and readily to be recognised. And I consider the *costumes,* as painted by him, to be the *only correct representations* I have ever seen.

"JOHN F. A. SANFORD,
*"U. SS. Indian Agent for Mandans, Rickarees, Minatarees,
Crows, Knisteneaux, Assineboins, Blackfeet, etc."*

"We have seen Mr CATLIN'S Portraits of Indians east of the Rocky Mountains, many of which are familiar to us; the likenesses are easily recognised, bearing a strong resemblance to the originals, as well as a faithful representation of their costumes.   "J. DOUGHERTY, *Indian Agent.*
"November 27th, 1837.   J. GANTT."

"We hereby certify, that the Portraits of the Grand Pawnees, Republican Pawnees, Pawnee Loups, Tappage Pawnees, Otoes, Omahaws, and Missouries, which are in Mr CATLIN'S INDIAN GALLERY, were painted from life by Mr GEO. CATLIN, and that the individuals sat to him in the costumes precisely in which they are painted.   "J. DOUGHERTY, *I. A. for Pawnees, Omahaws, and Otoes.*
"J. GANTT.
"New York, 1837."

"I have seen Mr CATLIN'S Collection of Indian Portraits, many of which were familiar to me, and painted in my presence at their own villages. I have spent the greater part of my life amongst the tribes and individuals he has represented, and I do not hesitate to pronounce them correct likenesses, and easily recognised; also his sketches of their *manners* and *customs,* I think, are excellent; and the *landscape views* on the Missouri and Mississippi, are correct representations.

"K. M'KENZIE, *of the Am. Fur Co. Mouth of Yellow Stone.*"

"We hereby certify that the Portraits of Seminoles and Euchees, in Mr CATLIN'S GALLERY were painted by him, from the life, at Fort Moultrie; that the Indians sat or stood in the costumes precisely in which they are painted, and that the likenesses are remarkably good.
"P. MORRISON, Capt. 4th Inft.   H. WHARTON, 2d Lieut. 6th Inft.
J. S. HATHAWAY, 2d Lieut. 1st Art. F. WEEDON, Assistant Surgeon.
"Fort Moultrie, January 26th, 1838."

"Having examined Mr CATLIN'S Collection of Portraits of Indians of the Missouri to the Rocky Mountains, I have no hesitation in pronouncing them, so far as I am acquainted with the individuals, to be the best I have ever seen, both as regards the expression of countenance, and the exact and complete manner in which the costume has been painted by him.

"J. L. BEAN, *S. Agent for Indian Affairs.*"

"I have been for many years past in familiar acquaintance with the Indian tribes of the Upper Missouri to the Rocky Mountains, and also with the landscape and other scenes represented in Mr CATLIN'S Collection; and it gives me great pleasure to assure the world, that on looking them over, I found the likenesses of my old friends easily to be recognised; and his sketches of Manners and Customs to be pourtrayed with singular truth and correctness.

"J. PILCHER, *Agent for Upper Missouri Indians.*"

"It gives me great pleasure in being enabled to add my name to the list of those who have spontaneously expressed their approbation of Mr CATLIN'S Collection of Indian Paintings. His Collection of materials place it in his power to throw much light on the Indian character, and his portraits, so far as I have seen them, are drawn with great fidelity as to character and likeness.

"H. SCHOOLCRAFT, *Indian Agent for Wisconsin Territory.*'

"Having lived and dealt with the Blackfeet Indians for five years past, I was enabled to recognise *every one* of the Portraits of those people, and of the Crows also, which Mr CATLIN has in his Collection, from the faithful likenesses they bore to the originals.

"*St Louis,* 1835.   "J. E. BRAZEAU."

"Having spent sixteen years in the continual acquaintance with the Indians of the several tribes of the Missouri, represented in Mr CATLIN'S Gallery of Indian Paintings, I was enabled to judge of the correctness of the likenesses, and I *instantly recognised every one of them,* when I looked them over, from the striking resemblance they bore to the originals—so also, of the Landscapes on the Missouri.

"HONORE   PICOTTE."

"The Portraits, in the possession of Mr CATLIN, of Pawnee Picts, Kioways, Camanches, Wecos, and Osages, were painted by him *from life,* when on a tour to their country, with the United States Dragoons. The *likenesses* are good, very easily to be recognised, and the *costumes* faithfully represented.

"HENRY DODGE, Col. of Drag.   D. PERKINS, Capt. of Drag.
R. H. MASON, Major of Ditto.   M. DUNCAN,   Ditto.
D. HUNTER, Capt.   Ditto.   T. B. WHEELOCK, Lieut. Drag."

"The Landscapes, Buffalo-Hunting scenes, etc., above-mentioned, I have seen, and although it has been thirty years since I travelled over that country; yet a considerable number of them I recognised as faithful representations, and the remainder of them are so much in the peculiar character of that country as to seem entirely familiar to me.   "WM. CLARK, *Superintendent of Indian Affairs.*"

"The Landscape Views on the Missouri, Buffalo Hunts, and other scenes, taken by my friend Mr CATLIN, are correct delineations of the scenes they profess to represent, as I am perfectly well acquainted with the country, having passed through it more than a dozen times. And further, I know, that they were taken on the spot, from nature, as I was present when Mr CATLIN visited that country.

"JOHN F. A. SANFORD, *U. SS. Indian Agent.*"

"It gives me great pleasure to be able to pronounce the Landscape Views, Views of Hunting, and other scenes, taken on the Upper Missouri by Mr CATLIN, to be correct delineations of the scenery they profess to represent; and although I was not present when they were taken in the field, I was able to identify almost every one between St Louis and the grand bend of the Missouri.

"J. L. BEAN, *S. Agent of Indian Affairs.*"

"I have examined a series of paintings by Mr CATLIN, representing *Indian Buffalo Hunts, Landscapes, etc.,* and from an acquaintance of twenty-seven years with such scenes as are represented, I feel qualified to judge them, and do unhesitatingly pronounce them good and unexaggerated representations.

"JNO. DOUGHERTY, *Indian Agent for Pawnees, Omahaws, and Otoes.*"

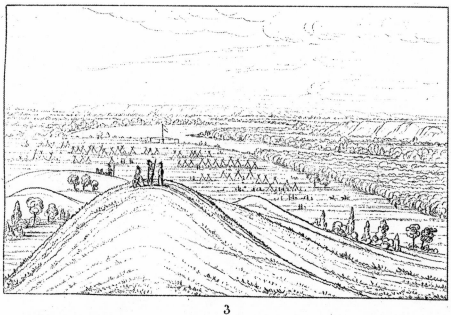

3

4

G Catlin

LETTER—No. 2

MOUTH OF YELLOW STONE, *UPPER MISSOURI*, 1832

I ARRIVED at this place yesterday in the steamer *Yellow Stone,* after a voyage of nearly three months from St Louis, a distance of two thousand miles, the greater part of which has never before been navigated by steam; and the almost insurmountable difficulties which continually oppose the *voyageur* on this turbid stream, have been by degrees overcome by the indefatigable zeal of Mr Chouteau, a gentleman of great perseverance, and part proprietor of the boat. To the politeness of this gentleman I am indebted for my passage from St Louis to this place, and I had also the pleasure of his *company,* with that of Major Sanford, the government agent for the Missouri Indians.

The American Fur Company have erected here, for their protection against the savages, a very substantial Fort, 300 feet square, with bastions armed with ordnance (Fig. 3); and our approach to it under the continued roar of cannon for half an hour, and the shrill yells of the half-affrighted savages who lined the shores, presented a scene of the most thrilling and picturesque appearance. A voyage so full of incident, and furnishing so many novel scenes of the picturesque and romantic, as we have passed the numerous villages of the "astonished natives," saluting them with the puffing of steam and the thunder of artillery, would afford subject for many epistles; and I cannot deny myself the pleasure of occasionally giving you some little sketches of scenes that I have witnessed, and *am witnessing;* and of the singular feelings that are excited in the breast of the stranger travelling through this interesting country. Interesting (as I have said) and *luxurious,* for this is truly the land of Epicures; we are invited by the savages to feasts of *dogs' meat,* as the most honourable food that can be presented to a stranger, and glutted with the more delicious food of beavers' tails, and buffaloes' tongues. You will, no doubt, be somewhat surprised on the receipt of a Letter from me, so far strayed into the Western World; and still more startled, when I tell you that I am here in the full enthusiasm and practice of my art. That enthusiasm alone has brought me into this remote region, 3500 miles from my native soil; the last two thousand of which have furnished me with almost unlimited models, both in landscape and the human figure, exactly suited to my feelings. I am now in the full possession and enjoyments of those conditions, on which alone I was induced to pursue the art as a profession; and in anticipation of which alone, my admiration for the art could ever have been kindled into a pure flame. I mean the free use of nature's undisguised models, with the privilege of selecting for myself. If I am here losing the benefit of the fleeting fashions of the day, and neglecting that elegant polish, which the world say an artist should draw from a continual intercourse with the polite world; yet have I this consolation, that in this country, I am entirely divested of those dangerous steps and allurements which beset an artist in fashionable life; and have little to steal my thoughts away from the contemplation of the beautiful models that are about me. If, also, I have not here the benefit of that feeling of emulation, which is the life and spur to the arts, where artists are associates together; yet am I surrounded by living models of such elegance and beauty, that I [?] an unceasing excitement of a much higher order—the certainty that I am drawing knowledge from the true source. My enthusiastic admiration of man in the honest and elegant simplicity of nature, has always fed the warmest feelings of my bosom, and shut half the avenues to my heart against the specious refinements of the accomplished world. This feeling, together with the desire to study my art, independently of the embarrassments which the ridiculous fashions of civilised society have thrown in its way, has led me to the wilderness for a while, as the true school of the arts.

I have for a long time been of opinion, that the wilderness of our country afforded models equal to those from which the Grecian sculptors transferred to the marble such inimitable grace and beauty; and I am now more confirmed in this opinion, since I have immersed myself in the midst of thousands and tens of thousands of these knights of the forest; whose whole lives are lives of chivalry, and whose daily feats, with their naked limbs, might vie with those of the Grecian youths in the beautiful rivalry of the Olympian games.

No man's imagination, with all the aids of description that can be given to it, can ever picture the beauty and wildness of scenes that may be daily witnessed in this romantic country; of hundreds of these graceful youths, without a care to wrinkle, or a fear to disturb the full expression of pleasure and enjoyment that beams upon their faces—their long black hair mingling with their horses' tails, floating in the wind, while they are flying over the carpeted prairie, and dealing death with their spears and arrows to a band of infuriated buffaloes; or their splendid procession in a war parade, arrayed in all their gorgeous colours and trappings, moving with most exquisite grace and manly beauty, added to that bold defiance which man carries on his front, who acknowledges no superior on earth, and who is amenable to no laws except the laws of God and honour.

In addition to the knowledge of human nature and of my art, which I hope to acquire by this toilsome and expensive undertaking, I have another in view, which, if it should not be of equal service to me, will be of no less interest and value to posterity. I have, for many years past, contemplated the noble races of red men, who are now spread over these trackless forests and boundless prairies, melting away at the approach of civilisation. Their rights invaded, their morals corrupted, their lands wrested from them, their customs changed, and therefore lost to the world; and they at last sunk into the earth, and the plough-share turning the sod over their graves, and I have flown to their rescue—not of their lives or of their race (for they are *"doomed"* and must perish), but to the rescue of their looks and their modes, at which the acquisitive world may hurl their poison and every besom of destruction, and trample them down and crush them to death; yet, phœnix-like, they may rise from the "stain on a painter's palette," and live again upon canvas, and stand forth for centuries yet to come, the living monuments of a noble race. For this purpose, I have designed to visit every tribe of Indians on the Continent, if my life should be spared; for the purpose of procuring portraits of distinguished Indians, of both sexes in each tribe, painted in their native costume; accompanied with pictures of their villages, domestic habits, games, mysteries, religious ceremonies, etc., with anecdotes, traditions, and history of their respective nations.

If I should live to accomplish my design, the result of my labours will doubtless be interesting to future ages; who will have little else left from which to judge of the original inhabitants of this noble race of beings, who require but a few years more of the march of civilisation and death, to deprive them of all their native customs and character. I have been kindly supplied by the Commander-in-Chief of the Army and the Secretary of War, with letters to the commander of every military post, and every Indian agent on the Western Frontier, with instructions to render me all the facilities in their power, which will be of great service to me in so arduous an undertaking. The opportunity afforded me by familiarity with so many tribes of human beings in the simplicity of nature, devoid of the deformities of art, of drawing fair conclusions in the interesting

B

sciences of physiognomy and phrenology, of their manners and customs, rites, ceremonies, etc.; and the opportunity of examining the geology and mineralogy of this western, and yet unexplored country, will enable me occasionally to entertain you with much new and interesting information, which I shall take equal pleasure in communicating by an occasional Letter in my clumsy way.

MOUTH OF YELLOW STONE

SINCE the date of my former Letter, I have been so much engaged in the amusements of the country, and the use of my brush, that I have scarcely been able to drop you a line until the present moment.

Before I let you into the amusements and customs of this delightful country, however (and which, as yet, are secrets to most of the world), I must hastily travel with you over the tedious journey of 2000 miles, from St Louis to this place; over which distance one is obliged to pass, before he can reach this wild and lovely spot.

The Missouri is, perhaps, different in appearance and character from all other rivers in the world; there is a terror in its manner which is sensibly felt, the moment we enter its muddy waters from the Mississippi. From the mouth of the Yellow Stone River, which is the place from whence I am now writing, to its junction with the Mississippi, a distance of 2000 miles, the Missouri, with its boiling, turbid waters, sweeps off, in one unceasing current; and in the whole distance there is scarcely an eddy or resting-place for a canoe. Owing to the continual falling in of its rich alluvial banks, its water is always turbid and opaque; having, at all seasons of the year, the colour of a cup of chocolate or coffee, with sugar and cream stirred into it. To give a better definition of its density and opacity, I have tried a number of simple experiments with it at this place, and at other points below, at the results of which I was exceedingly surprised. By placing a piece of silver (and afterwards a piece of shell, which is a much whiter substance) in a tumbler of this water, and looking through the side of the glass, I ascertained that those substances could not be seen through the eighth part of an inch; this, however, is in the spring of the year, when the freshet is upon the river, rendering the water, undoubtedly, much more turbid than it would be at other seasons; though it is always muddy and yellow, and from its boiling and wild character and uncommon colour, a stranger would think, even in its lowest state, that there was a freshet upon it.

For the distance of 1000 miles above St Louis, the shores of this river (and, in many places, the whole bed of the stream) are filled with snags and raft, formed of trees of the largest size, which have been undermined by the falling banks and cast into the stream; their roots becoming fastened in the bottom of the river, with their tops floating on the surface of the water, and pointing down the stream, forming the most frightful and discouraging prospect for the adventurous voyageur. (See Fig. 4.)

Almost every island and sand-bar is covered with huge piles of these floating trees, and when the river is flooded, its surface is almost literally covered with floating raft and drift wood; which bids positive defiance to keel-boats and steamers, on their way up the river.

With what propriety this "Hell of waters" might be denominated the "River Styx," I will not undertake to decide; but nothing could be more appropriate or innocent than to call it the River *of Sticks*.

The scene is not, however, all so dreary; there is a redeeming beauty in the green and carpeted shores, which hem in this huge and terrible deformity of waters. There is much of the way though, where the mighty forests of stately cotton wood stand, and frown in horrid dark and coolness over the filthy abyss below; into which they are ready to plunge headlong, when the mud and soil in which they were germed and reared has been washed out from underneath them, and is with the rolling current mixed, and on its way to the ocean.

The greater part of the shores of this river, however, are without timber, where the eye is delightfully relieved by wandering over the beautiful prairies; most of the way gracefully sloping down to the water's edge, carpeted with the deepest green, and, in distance, softening into velvet of the richest hues, entirely beyond the reach of the artist's pencil. Such is the character of the upper part of the river especially; and as one advances towards its source, and through its upper half, it becomes more pleasing to the eye, for snags and raft are no longer to be seen; yet the current holds its stiff and onward, turbid character.

It has been, heretofore, very erroneously represented to the world, that the scenery on this river was monotonous, and wanting in picturesque beauty. This intelligence is surely incorrect, and that because it has been brought perhaps, by men who are not the best judges in the world of Nature's beautiful works; and if they were, they always pass them by, in pain or desperate distress, in toil and trembling fear for the safety of their furs and peltries, or for their lives, which are at the mercy of the yelling savages who inhabit this delightful country.

One thousand miles or more, of the upper part of the river, was, to my eye, like fairy-land; and during our transit through that part of our voyage, I was most of the time rivetted to the deck of the boat, indulging my eyes in the boundless and tireless pleasure of roaming over the thousand hills, and bluffs, and dales, and ravines; where the astonished herds of buffaloes, of elks, and antelopes, and sneaking wolves, and mountain-goats, were to be seen bounding up and down and over the green fields; each one and each tribe, band, and gang, taking their own way, and using their own means to the greatest advantage possible, to leave the sight and sound of the puffing of our boat; which was, for the first time, saluting the green and wild shores of the Missouri with the din of mighty steam.

From St Louis to the falls of the Missouri, a distance of 2600 miles, is one continued prairie; with the exception of a few of the bottoms formed along the bank of the river, and the streams which are falling into it, which are often covered with the most luxuriant growth of forest timber.

The summit level of the great prairies stretching off to the west and the east from the river, to an almost boundless extent, is from two to three hundred feet above the level of the river; which has formed a bed or valley for its course, varying in width from two to twenty miles. This channel or valley has been evidently produced by the force of the current, which has gradually excavated, in its floods and gorges, this immense space, and sent its débris into the ocean. By the continual overflowing of the river, its deposits have been lodged and left with a horizontal surface, spreading the deepest and richest alluvion over the surface of its meadows on either side; through which the river winds its serpentine course, alternately running from one bluff to the other; which present themselves to its shores in all the most picturesque and beautiful shapes and colours imaginable—some with their green sides gracefully slope down in the most lovely groups to the water's edge (Fig. 5); whilst others, divested of their verdure, present themselves in immense masses of clay of different colours, which arrest the eye of the traveller, with the most curious views in the world.

These strange and picturesque appearances have been produced by the rains and frosts, which are continually changing the dimensions, and varying the thousand shapes of these denuded hills, by washing down their sides and carrying them into the river.

Amongst these groups may be seen tens and hundreds of thousands of different forms and figures, of the sublime and the picturesque; in many places for miles together, as the boat glides along, there is one continued appearance, before and behind us, of some ancient and boundless city in ruins—ramparts, terraces, domes, towers, citadels and castles may be seen,—cupolas, and magnificent porticoes, and here and there a solitary column and crumbling pedestal, and even spires of clay which stand alone—and glistening in distance, as the sun's rays are refracted back by the thousand crystals of gypsum which are embedded in the clay of which they are formed (Fig. 6). Over and through these groups of domes and battlements (as one is compelled to imagine them), the sun sends his long and gilding rays, at morn or in the evening; giving life and light, by aid of shadows cast to the different glowing colours of these clay-built ruins; shedding a glory over the solitude of this wild and pictured country, which no one can realise unless he travels here and looks upon it.

It is amidst these wild and quiet haunts that the mountain-sheep, and the fleet-bounding antelope sport and live in herds, secure from their enemies, to whom the sides and slopes of these bluffs (around which they fearlessly bound) are nearly inaccessible.

The grizzly bear also has chosen these places for his abode; he sullenly sneaks through the gulphs and chasms, and ravines, and frowns away the lurking Indian; whilst the mountain-sheep and antelope are bounding over and around the hill tops, safe and free from harm of man and beast.

Such is a hasty sketch of the river scenes and scenery for 2000 miles, over which we tugged, and puffed, and blowed, and toiled for three months, before we reached this place. Since we arrived here, the steamer has returned, and left me here to explore the country and visit the tribes in this vicinity, and then descend the river from this place to St Louis; which Tour, if I live through it, will furnish material for many a story and curious incident, which I may give you in detail in future epistles, and when I have more leisure than I have at the present moment. I will then undertake to tell how we astonished the natives, in many an instance, which I can in this Letter but just hint at and say adieu. If anything did ever literally and completely "astonish (and astound) the natives," it was the appearance of our steamer, puffing and blowing, and paddling and rushing by their villages which were on the banks of the river.

These poor and ignorant people, for the distance of 2000 miles, had never before seen or heard of a steam-boat, and in some places they seemed at a loss to know what to do, or how to act; they could not, as the Dutch did at Newburgh, on the Hudson River, take it to be a floating saw-mill—and they had no name for it—so it was, like everything else (with them), which is mysterious and unaccountable,

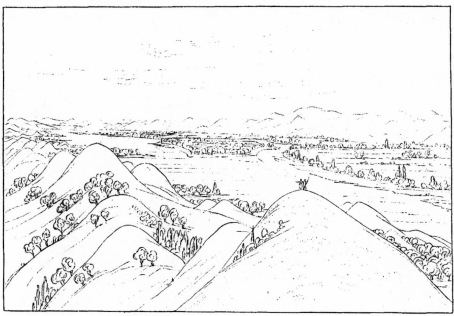

5

6

G Catlin.

called *medicine* (mystery). We had on board one twelve-pound cannon and three or four eight-pound swivels, which we were taking up to arm the Fur Company's Fort at the mouth of Yellow Stone; and at the approach to every village they were all discharged several times in rapid succession, which threw the inhabitants into utter confusion and amazement—some of them threw their faces to the ground, and cried to the Great Spirit—some shot their horses and dogs, and sacrificed them to appease the Great Spirit, whom they conceived was offended—some deserted their villages, and ran to the tops of the bluffs some miles distant; and others, in some places, as the boat landed in front of their villages, came with great caution, and peeped over the bank of the river to see the fate of their chiefs; whose duty it was (from the nature of their office) to approach us, whether friends or foes, and to go on board. Sometimes, in this plight, they were instantly thrown neck and heels over each other's heads and shoulders—men, women and children, and dogs—sage, sachem, old and young—all in a mass, at the frightful discharge of the steam from the escape-pipe, which the captain of the boat let loose upon them for his own fun and amusement.

There were many curious conjectures amongst their wise men, with regard to the nature and powers of the steam-boat. Amongst the Mandans, some called it the "big thunder canoe;" for, when in distance below the village, they saw the lightning flash from its sides, and heard the thunder come from it; others called it the "big medicine canoe with eyes;" it was *medicine* (mystery) because they could not understand it; and it must have eyes, for said they, "it sees its own way, and takes the deep water in the middle of the channel."

They had no idea of the boat being steered by the man at the wheel, and well they might have been astonished at its taking the deepest water. I may (if I do not forget it) hereafter give you an account of some other curious incidents of this kind, which we met with in this voyage; for we met many, and some of them were really laughable.

The Fort in which I am now residing was built by Mr M'Kenzie, who now occupies it; and it is the largest and best-built establishment of the kind on the river, being the great or principal headquarters and depôt of the Fur Company's business in this region. A vast stock of goods is kept on hand at this place; and at certain times of the year the numerous out-posts concentrate here with the returns of their season's trade, and refit out with a fresh supply of goods to trade with the Indians.

The site for the Fort is well selected, being a beautiful prairie on the bank near the junction of the Missouri with the Yellow Stone rivers; and its inmates and its stores well protected from Indian assaults.

Mr M'Kenzie is a kind-hearted and high-minded Scotchman; and seems to have charge of all the Fur Company's business in this region, and from this to the Rocky Mountains. He lives in good and comfortable style, inside of the Fort, which contains some eight or ten log-houses and stores, and has generally forty or fifty men, and one hundred and fifty horses about him.

He has, with the same spirit of liberality and politeness with which Mons. Pierre Chouteau treated me on my passage up the river, pronounced me welcome at his table, which groans under the luxuries of the country; with buffalo meat and tongues, with beavers' tails and marrow fat; but *sans* coffee, *sans* bread and butter. Good cheer and good living we get at it however, and good wine also; for a bottle of Madeira and one of excellent Port are set in a pail of ice every day, and exhausted at dinner.

At the hospitable board of this gentleman I found also another, who forms a happy companion for *mine host;* and whose intellectual and polished society has added not a little to *my* pleasure and amusement since I arrived here.

The gentleman of whom I am speaking is an Englishman, by the name of Hamilton, of the most pleasing and entertaining conversation, whose mind seems to be a complete store-house of ancient and modern literature and art; and whose free and familiar acquaintance with the manners and men of his country give him the stamp of a gentleman; who has had the curiosity to bring the embellishments of the enlightened world, to contrast with the rude and the wild of these remote regions.

We three *bons vivants* form the group about the dinner-table, of which I have before spoken, and crack our jokes and fun over the bottles of Port and Madeira, which I have named; and a considerable part of which, this gentleman has brought with great and precious care from his own country.

This post is the general rendezvous of a great number of Indian tribes in these regions, who are continually concentrating here for the purpose of trade; sometimes coming, the whole tribe together, in a mass. There are now here, and encamped about the Fort, a great many, and I am continually at work with my brush; we have now around us the Knisteneaux, Crows, Assinneboins, and Blackfeet, and in a few days are to have large accessions.

The finest specimen of Indians on the Continent are in these regions; and before I leave these parts, I shall make excursions into their respective countries, to their own native fire-sides; and there study their looks and peculiar customs; enabling me to drop you now and then an interesting Letter. The tribes which I shall be enabled to see and study by my visit to this region, are the Ojibbeways, the Assinneboins, Knisteneaux, Blackfeet, Crows, Shiennes, Grosventres, Mandans, and others; of whom and their customs, their history, traditions, costumes, etc., I shall in due season, give you further and minute accounts.

LETTER—No. 4

THE several tribes of Indians inhabiting the regions of the Upper Missouri, and of whom I spoke in my last Letter, are undoubtedly the finest looking, best equipped, and most beautifully costumed of any on the Continent. They live in a country well-stocked with buffaloes and wild horses, which furnish them an excellent and easy living; their atmosphere is pure, which produces good health and long life; and they are the most independent and the happiest races of Indians I have met with: they are all entirely in a state of primitive rudeness and wildness, and consequently are picturesque and handsome, almost beyond description. Nothing in the world, of its kind, can possibly surpass in beauty and grace, some of their games and amusements—their gambols and parades, of which I shall speak and paint hereafter.

As far as my travels have yet led me into the Indian country, I have more than realised my former predictions; that those Indians who could be found most entirely in a state of nature, with the least knowledge of civilised society, would be found to be the most cleanly in their persons, elegant in their dress and manners, and enjoying life to the greatest perfection. Of such tribes, perhaps the Crows and Blackfeet stand first; and no one would be able to appreciate the richness and elegance (and even taste too), with which some of these people dress, without seeing them in their own country. I will do all I can, however, to make their looks as well as customs known to the world; I will paint with my brush and scribble with my pen, and bring their plumes and plumage, dresses, weapons, etc., and every thing but the Indian himself, to prove to the world the assertions which I have made above.

Every one of these red sons of the forest (or rather of the prairie) is a knight and a lord—his squaws are his slaves; the only things which he deems worthy of his exertions are to mount his snorting steed, with his bow and quiver slung, his arrow shield upon his arm, and his long lance glistening in the war parade; or, divested of all his plumes and trappings, armed with a simple bow and quiver, to plunge his steed amongst the flying herds of buffaloes, and with his

7

8

G Catlin.

sinewy bow, which he seldom bends in vain, to drive deep to life's fountain the whizzing arrow.

The buffalo herds, which graze in almost countless numbers on these beautiful prairies, afford them an abundance of meat; and so much is it preferred to all other, that the deer, the elk, and the antelope sport upon the prairies in herds in the greatest security; as the Indians seldom kill them, unless they want their skins for a dress. The buffalo (or more correctly speaking bisom) is a noble animal, that roams over the vast prairies, from the borders of Mexico on the south, to Hudson's Bay on the north. Their size is somewhat above that of our common bullock, and their flesh of a delicious flavour, resembling and equalling that of fat beef. Their flesh, which is easily procured, furnishes the savages of these vast regions the means of a wholesome and good subsistence, and they live almost exclusively upon it—converting the skins, horns, hoofs and bones, to the construction of dresses, shields, bows, etc. The buffalo bull is one of the most formidable and frightful looking animals in the world when excited to resistance; his long shaggy mane hangs in great profusion over his neck and shoulders, and often extends quite down to the ground (Fig. 7). The cow is less in stature, and less ferocious; though not much less wild and frightful in her appearance (Fig. 8).

The mode in which these Indians kill this noble animal is spirited and thrilling in the extreme; and I must in a future epistle, give you a minute account of it. I have almost daily accompanied parties of Indians to see the fun, and have often shared in it myself; but much oftener ran my horse by their sides, to see how the thing was done— to study the modes and expressions of these splendid scenes, which I am industriously putting upon the canvas.

They are all (or nearly so) killed with arrows and the lance, while at full speed; and the reader may easily imagine, that these scenes afford the most spirited and picturesque views of the sporting kind that can possibly be seen.

At present, I will give a little sketch of a bit of fun I joined in yesterday, with Mr M'Kenzie and a number of his men, without the company or aid of Indians.

I mentioned the other day, that M'Kenzie's table from day to day groans under the weight of buffalo tongues and beavers' tails, and other luxuries of this western land. He has within his Fort a spacious ice-house, in which he preserves his meat fresh for any length of time required; and sometimes, when his larder runs low, he starts out, rallying some five or six of his best hunters (not to hunt, but to "go for meat"). He leads the party, mounted on his favourite buffalo horse (*i.e.* the horse amongst his whole group which is best trained to run the buffalo), trailing a light and short gun in his hand, such an one as he can most easily reload whilst his horse is at full speed.

Such was the condition of the ice-house yesterday morning, which caused these self-catering gentlemen to cast their eyes with a wishful look over the prairies; and such was the plight in which our host took the lead, and I, and then Mons. Chardon, and Ba'tiste, Défonde and Tullock (who is a trader amongst the Crows, and is here at this time, with a large party of that tribe), and there were several others whose names I do not know.

As we were mounted and ready to start, M'Kenzie called up some four or five of his men, and told them to start immediately on our trail, with as many one-horse carts; which they were to harness up, to bring home the meat; "ferry them across the river in the scow," said he, "and following our trail through the bottom, you will find us on the plain yonder, between the Yellow Stone and the Missouri rivers, with meat enough to load you home. My watch on yonder bluff has just told us by his signals, that there are cattle a plenty on that spot, and we are going there as fast as possible." We all crossed the river, and galloped away a couple of miles or so, when we mounted the bluff; and to be sure, as was said, there was in full view of us a fine herd of some four or five hundred buffaloes, perfectly at rest, and in their own estimation (probably) perfectly secure. Some were grazing, and others were lying down and sleeping; we advanced within a mile or so of them in full view, and came to a halt. Mons. Chardon "tossed the feather" (a custom always observed, to try the course of the wind), and we commenced "stripping," as it is termed (*i.e.* every man strips himself and his horse of every extraneous and unnecessary appendage of dress, etc., that might be an incumbrance in running): hats are laid off, and coats— and bullet pouches; sleeves are rolled up, a handkerchief tied lightly around the head, and another around the waist—cartridges are prepared and placed in the waistcoat pocket, or a half dozen bullets "throwed into the mouth," etc., etc., all of which takes up some ten or fifteen minutes, and is not, in appearance or in effect, unlike a council of war. Our leader lays the whole plan of the chase, and preliminaries all fixed, guns charged and ramrods in our hands, we mount and start for the onset. The horses are all trained for this business, and seem to enter into it with as much enthusiasm, and with as restless a spirit as their riders themselves. While "stripping" and mounting, they exhibit the most restless impaticnce; and when "approaching"—(which is, all of us abreast, upon a slow walk, and in a straight line towards the herd, until they discover us and run), they all seem to have caught entirely the spirit of the chase, for the laziest nag amongst them prances with an elasticity in his step—champing his bit—his ears erect—his eyes strained out of his head, and fixed upon the game before him, whilst he trembles under the saddle of his rider. In this way we carefully and silently marched, until within some forty or fifty rods; when the herd discovering us, wheeled and laid their course in a mass. At this instant we started! (and all must start, for no one could check the fury of those steeds at that moment of excitement), and away all sailed, and over the prairie flew, in a cloud of dust which was raised by their trampling hoofs. M'Kenzie was foremost in the throng, and soon dashed off amidst the dust and was out of sight—he was after the fattest and the fastest. I had discovered a huge bull whose shoulders towered above the whole band, and I picked my way through the crowd to get alongside of him. I went not for "meat," but for a trophy; I wanted his head and horns. I dashed along through the thundering mass, as they swept away over the plain, scarcely able to tell whether I was on a buffalo's back or my horse— hit, and hooked, and jostled about, till at length I found myself alongside of my game, when I gave him a shot, as I passed him. I saw guns flash in several directions about me, but I heard them not. Amidst the trampling throng, Mons. Chardon had wounded a stately bull, and at this moment was passing him again with his piece levelled for another shot; they were both at full speed and I also, within the reach of the muzzle of my gun, when the bull instantly turned and receiving the horse upon his horns, and the ground received poor Chardon, who made a frog's leap of some twenty feet or more over the bull's back (Fig. 9), and almost under my horse's heels. I wheeled my horse as soon as possible and rode back, where lay poor Chardon, gasping to start his breath again; and within a few paces of him his huge victim, with his heels high in the air, and the horse lying across him. I dismounted instantly, but Chardon was raising himself on his hands, with his eyes and mouth full of dirt, and feeling for his gun, which lay about thirty feet in advance of him. "Heaven spare you! are you hurt, Chardon?" "Hi—hic——hic——hic——hic——hic————————no,———hic———no—no, I believe not. Oh! this is not much, Mons. Cataline—this is nothing new—but this is a damned hard piece of ground here—hic—oh, hic!" At this the poor fellow fainted, but in a few moments arose, picked up his gun, took his horse by the bit; which then opened its eyes, and *h e* with a *hic,* and a *u g h*—UGHK! sprang upon his feet—shook off the dirt—and here we were, all upon our legs again, save the bull, whose fate had been more sad than that of either.

I turned my eyes in the direction where the herd had gone, and our companions in pursuit, and nothing could be seen of them, nor indication, except the cloud of dust which they left behind them. At a little distance on the right, however, I beheld my huge victim endeavouring to make as much head—way as he possibly could, from this dangerous ground, upon three legs. I galloped off to him, and at my approach he wheeled around—and bristled up for battle; he seemed to know perfectly well that he could not escape from me, and resolved to meet his enemy and death as bravely as possible.

I found that my shot had entered him a little too far forward, breaking one of his shoulders, and lodging in his breast, and from his very great weight it was impossible for him to make much advance upon me. As I rode up within a few paces of him, he would bristle up with fury enough in his *looks* alone, almost to annihilate me; (Fig. 10) and making one lunge at me, would fall upon his neck and nose, so that I found the sagacity of my horse alone enough to keep me out of reach of danger; and I drew from my pocket my sketch-book, laid my gun across my lap, and commenced taking his likeness. He stood stiffened up, and swelling with awful vengeance, which was sublime for a picture, but which he could not vent upon me. I rode around him and sketched him in numerous attitudes, sometimes he would lie down, and I would then sketch him; then throw my cap at him, and rousing him on his legs, rally a new expression, and sketch him again.

In this way I added to my sketch-book some invaluable sketches of this grim-visaged monster, who knew not that he was standing for his likeness.

No man on earth can imagine what is the look and expression of such a subject before him as this was. I defy the world to produce another animal that can look so frightful as a huge buffalo bull, when wounded as he was, turned around for battle, and swelling with rage;—his eyes bloodshot, and his long shaggy mane hanging to the ground,—his mouth open, and his horrid rage hissing in streams of smoke and blood from his mouth and through his nostrils, as he is bending forward to spring upon his assailant.

After I had had the requisite time and opportunity for using my pencil, M'Kenzie and his companions came walking their exhausted horses back from the chase, and in our rear came four or five carts

6

9

G Catlin.

10

to carry home the meat. The party met from all quarters around me and my buffalo bull, whom I then shot in the head and finished. And being seated together for a few minutes, each one took a smoke of the pipe, and recited his exploits, and his "coups" or deaths; when all parties had a hearty laugh at me, as a novice, for having aimed at an old bull, whose flesh was not suitable for food, and the carts were escorted on the trail, to bring away the meat. I rode back with Mr M'Kenzie, who pointed out five cows which he had killed, and all of them selected as the fattest and slickest of the herd. This astonishing feat was all performed within the distance of one mile—all were killed at full speed, and every one shot through the heart. In the short space of time required for a horse under full whip to run the distance of one mile, he had discharged his gun five, and loaded it four, times—selected his animals, and killed at every shot! There were six or eight others killed at the same time, which altogether furnished, as will be seen, abundance of freight for the carts; which returned, as well as several pack-horses, loaded with the choicest parts which were cut from the animals, and the remainder of the carcasses left a prey for the wolves.

Such is the mode by which white men live in this country—such the way in which they get their food, and such is one of their delightful amusements—at the hazard of every bone in one's body, to feel the fine and thrilling exhilaration of the chase for a moment, and then as often to upbraid and blame himself for his folly and imprudence.

From this scene we commenced leisurely wending our way back; and dismounting at the place where we had stripped, each man dressed himself again, or slung his extra articles of dress, etc., across his saddle, astride of which he sat; and we rode back to the Fort, reciting as we rode, and for twenty-four hours afterwards, deeds of chivalry and chase, and hair's-breadth escapes which each and either had fought and run on former occasions. M'Kenzie, with all the true character, and dignity of a leader, was silent on these subjects; but smiled, while those in his train were reciting for him the astonishing and almost incredible deeds of his sinewy arms, which they had witnessed in similar scenes; from which I learned (as well as from my own observations), that he was reputed (and actually was) the most distinguished of all the white men who had flourished in those regions, in the pursuit and death of the buffalo.

On our return to the Fort, a bottle or two of wine were set forth upon the table, and around them a half dozen parched throats were soon moistened, and good cheer ensued. Ba'tiste, Défonde, Chardon, etc., retired to their quarters, enlarging smoothly upon the events of our morning's work; which they were reciting to their wives and sweethearts; when about this time the gate of the Fort was thrown open, and the procession of carts and packhorses laden with buffalo meat made its entrée; gladdening the hearts of a hundred women and children, and tickling the noses of as many hungry dogs and puppies, who were stealing in and smelling at the tail of the procession. The door of the ice-house was thrown open, the meat was discharged into it, and I being fatigued went to sleep.

7

11

IN my former epistle I told you there were encamped about the
Fort a host of wild, incongruous spirits—chiefs and sachems—
warriors, braves, and women and children of different tribes—of
Crows and Blackfeet—Ojibbeways—Assinneboins—and Crees or
Knisteneaux. Amongst and in the midst of them am I, with my
paint pots and canvas, snugly ensconced in one of the bastions of
the Fort, which I occupy as a painting-room. My easel stands
before me, and the cool breech of a twelve-pounder makes me a
comfortable seat, whilst her muzzle is looking out at one of the
port-holes. The operations of my brush are mysteries of the highest
order to these red sons of the prairie, and my room the earliest and
latest place of concentration of these wild and jealous spirits; who
all meet here to be amused, and pay me signal honours; but gaze
upon each other, sending their sidelong looks of deep-rooted hatred
and revenge around the group. However, whilst in the Fort, their
weapons are placed within the arsenal, and naught but looks and
thoughts can be breathed here; but death and grim destruction will
visit back those looks upon each other, when these wild spirits again
are loose and free to breathe and act upon the plains.

I have this day been painting a portrait of the head chief
of the Blackfoot nation; he is a good-looking and dignified Indian,
about fifty years of age, and superbly dressed (Fig. 11); whilst
sitting for his picture he has been surrounded by his own braves
and warriors, and also gazed at by his enemies, the Crows and the
Knisteneaux, Assinneboins and Ojibbeways; a number of distinguished personages of each of which tribes, have laid all day
around the sides of my room; reciting to each other the battles they
have fought, and pointing to the scalp-locks, worn as proofs of their
victories, and attached to the seams of their shirts and leggings.
This is a curious scene to witness, when one sits in the midst of such
inflammable and combustible materials, brought together, unarmed,
for the first time in their lives; peaceably and calmly recounting
over the deeds of their lives, and smoking their pipes upon it, when
a few weeks or days will bring them on the plains again, where the

war-cry will be raised, and their deadly bows will again be drawn on each other.

The name of this dignitary, of whom I have just spoken, is Stumick-o-sucks (the buffalo's back fat), *i.e.* the "hump" or "fleece," the most delicious part of the buffalo's flesh. I have also painted, of the Blackfeet, Pe-toh-pee-kiss (the eagle ribs), and Mix-ke-mote-skin-na (the iron horn), and Wun-nes-tou (the white buffalo), and Tcha-aes-sa-ko-mah-pee (the bear's child), and In-ne-o-cose (the buffalo's child), and half-a-dozen others, and all in rich and costly dresses.

There is no tribe, perhaps, on the Continent, who dress more comfortably, and more gaudily, than the Blackfeet, unless it be the tribe of Crows. There is no great difference, however, in the costliness or elegance of their costumes; nor in the materials of which they are formed; though there is a distinctive mode in each tribe, of stitching or ornamenting with the porcupine quills, which constitute one of the principal ornaments to all their fine dresses; and which can be easily recognised, by any one a little familiar with their modes, as belonging to such or such a tribe. The dress, for instance of the chief whom I have just mentioned, and whose portrait I have just painted, consists of a shirt or tunic, made of two deer skins finely dressed, and so placed together with the necks of the skins downwards, and the skins of the hind legs stitched together, the seams running down on each arm, from the neck to the knuckles of the hand; this seam is covered with a band of two inches in width, of very beautiful embroidery of porcupine quills, and suspended from the under edge of this, from the shoulders to the hands, is a fringe of the locks of black hair, which he has taken from the heads of victims slain by his own hand in battle. The leggings are made also of the same material; and down the outer side of the leg, from the hip to the feet, extends also a similar band or belt of the same width; and wrought in the same manner, with porcupine quills, and fringed with scalp-locks. These locks of hair are procured from scalps, and worn as trophies.

The wife (or squaw) of this dignitary Eeh-nis-kim (the crystal stone), I have also placed upon my canvas (Fig. 13); her countenance is rather pleasing, which is an uncommon thing amongst the Blackfeet—her dress is made of skins, and being the youngest of a bevy of six or eight, and the last one taken under his guardianship, was smiled upon with great satisfaction, whilst he exempted her from the drudgeries of the camp; and keeping her continually in the halo of his own person, watched and guarded her as the apple of his eye. The grandson also of this sachem, a boy of six years of age,

12

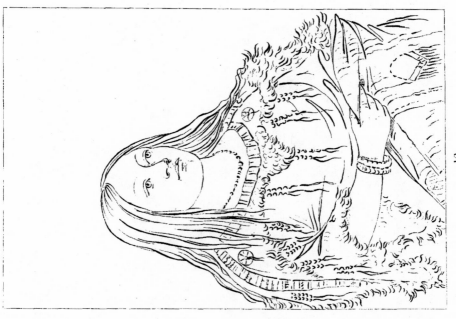

13

and too young as yet to have acquired a name, has stood forth like a tried warrior; and I have painted him at full length (Fig. 12), with his bow and quiver slung, and his robe made of a racoon skin. The history of this child is somewhat curious and interesting; his father is dead, and in case of the death of the chief of whom I have spoken, he becomes hereditary chief of the tribe. This boy has been twice stolen away by the Crows by ingenious stratagems, and twice re-captured by the Blackfeet, at considerable sacrifice of life, and at present he is lodged with Mr M'Kenzie, for safe keeping and protection, until he shall arrive at the proper age to take the office to which he is to succeed, and to protect himself.

The scalp of which I spoke above, is procured by cutting out a piece of the skin of the head, the size of the palm of the hand or less, containing the very centre or crown of the head, the place where the hair radiates from a point, and exactly over what the phrenologists call self-esteem. This patch then is kept and dried with great care, as proof positive of the death of an enemy, and evidence of a man's claims as a warrior; and after having been formally "danced," as the saying is (*i.e.* after it has been stuck up upon a pole or held up by an "old woman," and the warriors have danced around it for two or three weeks at intervals), it is fastened to the handle of a lance, or the end of a war club, or divided into a great many small locks and used to fringe and ornament the victor's dress. When these dresses are seen bearing such trophies, it is of course a difficult matter to purchase them of the Indian, for they often hold them above all price. I shall hereafter take occasion to speak of the scalp dance; describing it in all its parts, and giving a long Letter, at the same time on scalps and scalping, an interesting and general custom amongst all the North American Indians.

In the chief's dress, which I am describing, there are his moccasins, made also of buckskin, and ornamented in a corresponding manner. And over all, his robe, made of the skin of a young buffalo bull, with the hair remaining on; and on the inner or flesh side, beautifully garnished with porcupine quills, and the battles of his life very ingeniously, though rudely, pourtrayed in pictorial representations. In his hand he holds a very beautiful pipe, the stem of which is four or five feet long, and two inches wide, curiously wound with braids of the porcupine quills of various colours; and the bowl of the pipe ingeniously carved by himself from a piece of red steatite of an interesting character, and which they all tell me is procured somewhere between this place and the Falls of St Anthony, on the head waters of the Mississippi.

This curious stone has many peculiar qualities, and has, undoubtedly, but one origin in this country, and perhaps in the world. It is found but in the hands of the savage, and every tribe, and nearly every individual in the tribe has his pipe made of it. I consider this stone a subject of great interest, and curiosity to the world; and I shall most assuredly make it a point, during my Indian rambles, to visit the place from whence it is brought. I have already got a number of most remarkable traditions and stories relating to the "sacred quarry;" of pilgrimages performed there to procure the stone, and of curious transactions that have taken place on that ground. It seems, from all I can learn, that all the tribes in these regions, and also of the Mississippi and the Lakes, have been in the habit of going to that place, and meeting their enemies there, whom they are obliged to treat as friends, under an injunction of the Great Spirit.

So then is this sachem (the buffalo's back fat) dressed; and in a very similar manner, and almost the same, is each of the others above named; and all are armed with bow and quiver, lance and shield. These north western tribes are all armed with the bow and lance, and protected with the shield or arrow-fender, which is carried outside of the left arm, exactly as the Roman and Grecian shield was carried, and for the same purpose.

There is an appearance purely classic in the plight and equipment of these warriors and "knights of the lance." They are almost literally always on their horses' backs, and they wield these weapons with desperate effect upon the open plains; where they kill their game while at full speed, and contend in like manner in battles with their enemy. There is one prevailing custom in these respects, amongst all the tribes who inhabit the great plains or prairies of these western regions. These plains afford them an abundance of wild and fleet horses, which are easily procured; and on their backs, at full speed, they can come alongside of any animal, which they can easily destroy.

The bow with which they are armed is small, and apparently an insignificant weapon, though one of great and almost incredible power in the hands of its owner, whose sinews have been from childhood habituated to its use and service. The length of these bows is generally about three feet, and sometimes not more than two and a half (Fig. 18, a). They have, no doubt, studied to get the requisite power in the smallest compass possible, as it is more easily and handily used on horseback than one of greater length. The greater part of these bows are made of ash, or of "bois d'arc" (as the French call it), and lined on the back with layers of buffalo or deer's sinews, which are

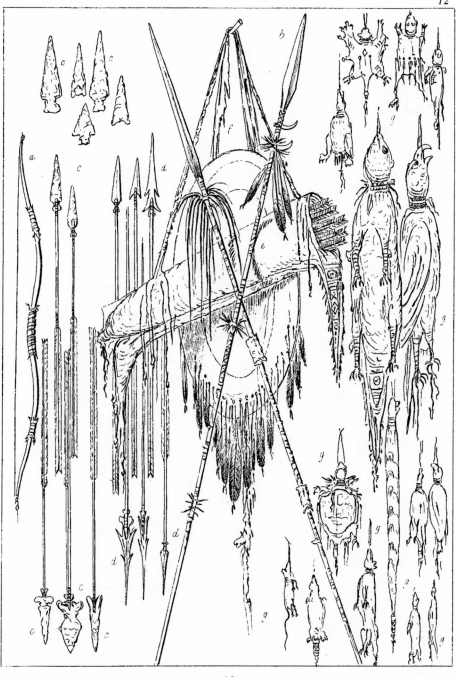

G. Catlin.

18

inseparably attached to it, and give it great elasticity. There are very many also (amongst the Blackfeet and the Crows) which are made of bone, and others of the horn of the mountain-sheep. Those made of bone are decidedly the most valuable, and cannot in this country, be procured of a good quality short of the price of one or two horses. About these there is a mystery yet to be solved, and I advance my opinion against all theories that I have heard in the country where they are used and made. I have procured several very fine specimens, and when purchasing them have inquired of the Indians, what bone they were made of? and in every instance, the answer was, "That's medicine," meaning that it was a mystery to them, or that they did not wish to be questioned about them. The bone of which they are made is certainly not the bone of any animal now grazing on the prairies, or in the mountains between this place and the Pacific Ocean; for some of these bows are three feet in length, of a solid piece of bone, and that as close-grained—as hard— as white, and as highly polished as any ivory; it cannot, therefore, be made from the elks' horn (as some have supposed), which is of a dark colour and porous: nor can it come from the buffalo. It is my opinion, therefore, that the Indians on the Pacific coast procure the bone from the jaw of the sperm whale, which is often stranded on that coast, and bringing the bone into the mountains, trade it to the Blackfeet and Crows, who manufacture it into these bows without knowing any more than we do, from what source it has been procured.

One of these little bows in the hands of an Indian, on a fleet and well-trained horse, with a quiver of arrows slung on his back, is a most effective and powerful weapon in the open plains. No one can easily credit the force with which these missiles are thrown, and the sanguinary effects produced by their wounds, until he has rode by the side of a party of Indians in chase of a herd of buffaloes; and wit- nessed the apparent ease and grace with which their supple arms have drawn the bow, and seen these huge animals tumbling down and gushing out their hearts' blood from their mouths and nostrils.

Their bows are often made of bone and sinews, and their arrows headed with flints or with bones, of their own construction (Fig. 18, c), or with steel, as they are now chiefly furnished by the Fur Traders quite to the Rocky Mountains (Fig. 18, d). The quiver, which is uniformly carried on the back, and made of the panther or otter skins (Fig. 18, e), is a magazine of these deadly weapons, and generally contains two varieties. The one to be drawn upon an enemy, gene- rally poisoned, and with long flukes or barbs, which are designed to hang the blade in the wound after the shaft is withdrawn, in which they are but slightly glued;—the other to be used for their game, with the blade firmly fastened to the shaft, and the flukes inverted; that it may easily be drawn from the wound, and used on future occasions.

Such is the training of men and horses in this country, that this work of death and slaughter is simple and easy. The horse is trained to approach the animals on the right side, enabling his rider to throw his arrows to the left; he runs and approaches without the use of the halter, which is hanging loose upon his neck, bringing his rider within three or four paces of the animal, when the arrow is thrown with great ease and certainty to the heart; and instances sometimes occur, where the arrow passes entirely through the animal's body.

An Indian, therefore, mounted on a fleet and well-trained horse, with his bow in his hand, and his quiver slung on his back, containing an hundred arrows, of which he can throw fifteen or twenty in a minute, is a formidable and dangerous enemy. Many of them also ride with a lance of twelve or fourteen feet in length (Fig. 18, *b*), with a blade of polished steel; and all of them (as a protection for their vital parts), with a shield or arrow-fender made of the skin of the buffalo's neck, which has been smoked and hardened with glue extracted from the hoofs (Fig. 18). These shields are arrow-proof, and will glance off a rifle-shot with perfect effect by being turned obliquely, which they do with great skill.

This shield or arrow-fender is, in my opinion, made of similar materials, and used in the same way, and for the same purpose, as was the clypeus or small shield in the Roman and Grecian cavalry. They were made in those days as a means of defence on horseback only—made small and light, of bulls' hides; sometimes single, sometimes double and tripled. Such was Hector's shield, and of most of the Homeric heroes of the Greek and Trojan wars. In those days also were darts or javelins and lances; the same were also used by the Ancient Britons; and such exactly are now in use amongst the Arabs and the North American Indians.

In this wise then, are all of these wild red knights of the prairie, armed and equipped,—and while nothing can possibly be more picturesque and thrilling than a troop or war party of these fellows galloping over these green and endless prairies; there can be no set of mounted men, of equal numbers, so effective and so invincible in this country as they would be, could they be inspired with confidence of their own powers and their own superiority; yet this never can be done;—for the Indian, as far as the name of white man has travelled, and long before he has to try his strength with him, is trembling with

G. Catlin.

14

G. Catlin.

16

17

G. Catlin

fright and fear of his approach; he hears of white man's arts and artifice—his tricks and cunning, and his hundred instruments of death and destruction—he dreads his approach, shrinks from him with fear and trembling—his heart sickens, and his pride and courage wither, at the thoughts of contending with an enemy, whom he thinks may war and destroy with weapons of *medicine* and mystery.

Of the Blackfeet, whom I mentioned in the beginning of this Letter, and whose portraits are now standing in my room, there is another of whom I must say a few words; Pe-toh-pee-kiss, the eagle ribs (Fig. 14). This man is one of the extraordinary men of the Blackfoot tribe; though not a chief he stands here in the Fort, and deliberately boasts of eight scalps, which he says he has taken from the heads of trappers and traders with his own hand. His dress is really superb, almost literally covered with scalp-locks, of savage and civil.

I have painted him at full length, with a head-dress made entirely of ermine skins and horns of the buffalo. This custom of wearing horns beautifully polished and surmounting the head-dress, is a very curious one, being worn only by the bravest of the brave; by the most extraordinary men in the nation. Of their importance and meaning, I shall say more in a future epistle. When he stood for his picture, he also held a lance and two "medicine-bags" in his hand; of lances I have spoken,—but "medicine-bags" and "medicine" will be the text for my next Letter.

Besides the chiefs and warriors above-named, I have also trans-ferred to my canvas the "looks and very resemblance" of an aged chief, who combines with his high office, the envied title of mystery or medicine-man, *i.e.* doctor—magician—prophet—soothsayer—jong-leur—and high priest, all combined in one person, who necessarily is looked upon as "Sir Oracle" of the nation. The name of this dis-tinguished functionary is Wun-nes-tou, the white buffalo (Fig. 15); and on his left arm he presents his mystery-drum or tambour, in which are concealed the hidden and sacred mysteries of his healing art.

And there is also In-ne-o-cose, the iron horn (Fig. 16), at full length, in a splendid dress, with his "medicine-bag" in his hand; and Ah-kay-ee-pix-en, the woman who strikes many (Fig. 17), in a beautiful dress of the mountain-goats' skin, and her robe of the young buffalo's hide.

LETTER—No. 6

MOUTH OF YELLOW STONE

Now for medicines or mysteries—for doctors, high priests, for hocus pocus, witchcraft, and animal magnetism!

In the last Letter I spoke of Pe-toh-pee-kiss (the eagle ribs), a Blackfoot brave, whose portrait I had just painted at full length, in a splendid dress. I mentioned also, that he held two medicine-bags in his hand; as they are represented in the picture; both of them made of the skins of otters, and curiously ornamented with ermine, and other strange things.

I must needs stop here—my painting and everything else, until I can explain the word *"medicine,"* and *"medicine-bag;"* and also some *medicine operations,* which I have seen transacted at this place within a few days past. "Medicine," is a great word in this country; and it is very necessary that one should know the meaning of it, whilst he is scanning and estimating the Indian character; which is made up, in a great degree, of mysteries and superstition.

The word medicine, in its common acceptation here, means *mystery,* and nothing else; and in that sense I *shall* use it very frequently in my notes on Indian manners and customs.

The Fur Traders in this country, are nearly all French; and in their language, a doctor or physician, is called *"Medecin."* The Indian country is full of doctors; and as they are all magicians, and skilled, or profess to be skilled, in many mysteries, the word "medecin" has become habitually applied to every thing mysterious or unaccountable; and the English and Americans, who are also trading and passing through this country, have easily and familiarly adopted the same word, with a slight alteration, conveying the same meaning; and to be a little more explicit, they have denominated these personages "medicine-men," which means something more than merely a doctor or physician. These physicians, however, are all *medicine-men,* as they are all supposed to deal more or less in mysteries and charms, which are aids and handmaids in their practice. Yet it was necessary to give the word or phrase a still more comprehensive meaning—as there were many personages amongst them; and also amongst the white men who visit the

40

country, who could deal in mysteries, though not skilled in the application of drugs and medicines; and they all range now, under the comprehensive and accommodating phrase of "medicine-men." For instance, I am a "medicine-man" of the highest order amongst these superstitious people, on account of the art which I practice; which is a strange and unaccountable thing to them, and of course, called the greatest of "medicine." My gun and pistols, which have percussion locks, are great medicine; and no Indian can be prevailed on to fire them off, for they say they have nothing to do with white man's medicine.

The Indians do not use the word medicine, however; but in each tribe they have a word of their own construction, synonymous with mystery or mystery-man.

The "medicine-bag" then, is a mystery-bag; and its meaning and importance necessary to be understood, as it may be said to be the key of Indian life and Indian character. These bags are constructed of the skins of animals, of birds, or of reptiles, and ornamented and preserved in a thousand different ways, as suits the taste or freak of the person who constructs them. These skins are generally attached to some part of the clothing of the Indian, or carried in his hand—they are oftentimes decorated in such a manner as to be exceedingly ornamental to his person, and always are stuffed with grass, or moss, or something of the kind; and generally without drugs or medicines within them, as they are religiously closed and sealed, and seldom, if ever, to be opened. I find that every Indian in his primitive state, carries his medicine-bag in some form or other, to which he pays the greatest homage, and to which he looks for safety and protection through life—and in fact, it might almost be called a species of idolatry; for it would seem in some instances, as if he actually worshipped it. Feasts are often made, and dogs and horses sacrificed, to a man's medicine; and days, and even weeks, of fasting and penance of various kinds are often suffered, to appease his medicine, which he imagines he has in some way offended.

This curious custom has principally been done away with along the frontier, where white men laugh at the Indian for the observance of so ridiculous and useless a form: but in this country it is in full force, and every male in the tribe carries this, his supernatural charm or guardian, to which he looks for the preservation of his life, in battle or in other danger; at which times it would be considered ominous of bad luck and an ill fate to be without it.

The manner in which this curious and important article is

instituted is this: a boy, at the age of fourteen or fifteen years, is said to be making or "forming his medicine," when he wanders away from his father's lodge, and absents himself for the space of two or three, and sometimes even four or five, days; lying on the ground in some remote or secluded spot, crying to the Great Spirit, and fasting the whole time. During this period of peril and abstinence, when he falls asleep, the first animal, bird, or reptile, of which he dreams (or pretends to have dreamed, perhaps), he considers the Great Spirit has designated for his mysterious protector through life. He then returns home to his father's lodge, and relates his success; and after allaying his thirst, and satiating his appetite, he sallies forth with weapons or traps, until he can procure the animal or bird, the skin of which he preserves entire, and ornaments it according to his own fancy, and carries it with him through life, for "good luck" (as he calls it); as his strength in battle—and in death his guardian *Spirit,* that is buried with him; and which is to conduct him safe to the beautiful hunting grounds, which he contemplates in the world to come.

The value of the medicine-bag to the Indian is beyond all price; for to sell it, or give it away, would subject him to such signal disgrace in his tribe, that he could never rise above it; and again, his superstition would stand in the way of any such disposition of it, for he considers it the gift of the Great Spirit. An Indian carries his *medicine-bag* into battle, and trusts to it for his protection; and if he loses it thus, when fighting ever so bravely for his country, he suffers a disgrace scarcely less than that which occurs in case he sells or gives it away; his enemy carries it off and displays it to his own people as a trophy; whilst the loser is cut short of the respect that is due to other young men of his tribe, and for ever subjected to the degrading epithet of "a man without medicine," or "he who has lost his medicine;" until he can replace it again, which can only be done, by rushing into battle and plundering one from an enemy whom he slays with his own hand. This done, his medicine is restored, and he is reinstated again in the estimation of his tribe; and even higher than before, for such is called the best of medicine, or *"medicine honourable."*

It is a singular fact, that a man can institute his mystery or medicine, but once in his life; and equally singular that he can reinstate himself by the adoption of the medicine of his enemy; both of which regulations are strong and violent inducements for him to fight bravely in battle: the first, that he may protect and preserve his medicine; and the second, in case he has been so unlucky as to lose it, that he may restore it, and his reputation also, while he is desperately contending for the protection of his community.

During my travels thus far, I have been unable to buy a medicine-bag of an Indian, although I have offered them extravagant prices for them; and even on the frontier, where they have been induced to abandon the practice, though a white man may induce an Indian to relinquish his medicine, yet he cannot *buy* it of him—the Indian in such case will bury it, to please a white man, and save it from his sacrilegious touch; and he will linger around the spot and at regular times visit it and pay it his devotions, as long as he lives.

These curious appendages to the persons or wardrobe of an Indian (Fig. 18, *g*), are sometimes made of the skin of an otter, a beaver, a musk-rat, a weazel, a racoon, a polecat, a snake, a frog, a toad, a bat, a mouse, a mole, a hawk, an eagle, a magpie, or a sparrow:—sometimes of the skin of an animal so large as a wolf; and at others, of the skins of the lesser animals, so small that they are hidden under the dress, and very difficult to be found, even if searched for.

Such then is the medicine-bag—such its meaning and importance; and when its owner dies, it is placed in his grave and decays with his body.

In the case of the portrait of which I spoke in the beginning of this Letter, there are seen two medicine-bags in the hand of Pe-toh-pee-kiss; the one was of his own instituting, and the other was taken from his enemy, whom he had slain in battle; both of these he has a right to display and boast of on such an occasion. This is but the beginning or incipient stage of "medicines," however, in this strange and superstitious country; and if you have patience, I will carry you a few degrees further into the mysteries of conjurations, before I close this Letter. Sit still then and read, until I relate a scene of a tragic, and yet of the most grotesque character, which took place in this Fort a few days since, and to all of which I was an eye-witness. The scene I will relate as it transpired precisely; and call it the story of the "doctor," or the "Blackfoot medicine-man."

Not many weeks since, a party of Knisteneaux came here from the north, for the purpose of making their summer's trade with the Fur Company; and, whilst here, a party of Blackfeet their natural enemies (the same who are here now), came from the west, also to trade. These two belligerent tribes encamped on different sides of the Fort, and had spent some weeks here in the Fort and about it, in apparently good feeling and fellowship; unable in fact to act otherwise, for, according to a regulation of the Fort, their arms and weapons were all locked up by M'Kenzie in his "arsenal," for the purpose of preserving the peace amongst these fighting-cocks.

The Knisteneaux had completed their trade, and loitered about the premises, until all, both Indians and white men, were getting tired of their company, wishing them quietly off. When they were ready to start, with their goods packed upon their backs, their arms were given them, and they started; bidding everybody, both friends and foes, a hearty farewell. They went out of the Fort, and though the party gradually moved off, one of them undiscovered, loitered about the Fort, until he got an opportunity to poke the muzzle of his gun through between the piquets; when he fired it at one of the chiefs of the Blackfeet, who stood within a few paces, talking with Mr M'Kenzie, and shot him with two musket bullets through the centre of his body! The Blackfoot fell, and rolled about upon the ground in the agonies of death. The Blackfeet who were in the Fort, seized their weapons and ran in a mass, out of the Fort, in pursuit of the Knisteneaux, who were rapidly retreating to the bluffs. The Frenchmen in the Fort, also, at so flagrant and cowardly an insult, seized their guns and ran out, joining the Blackfeet in the pursuit. I, at that moment, ran to my painting-room in one of the bastions overlooking the plain, where I had a fair view of the affair; many shots were exchanged back and forward, and a skirmish ensued which lasted half-an-hour; the parties, however, were so far apart that little effect was produced; the Knisteneaux were driven off over the bluffs, having lost one man and had several others wounded. The Blackfeet and Frenchmen returned into the Fort, and then, I saw what I never before saw in my life—I saw a *"medicine-man"* performing his mysteries over a dying man. The man who had been shot was still living, though two bullets had passed through the centre of his body, about two inches apart from each other; he was lying on the ground in the agonies of death, and no one could indulge the slightest hope of his recovery; yet the *medicine-man* must needs be called (for such a personage they had in their party), and hocus pocus applied to him, as the dernier resort, when all drugs and all specifics were useless, and after all possibility of recovery was extinct!

I have mentioned that all tribes have their physicians, who are also medicine (or mystery men). These professional gentlemen are worthies of the highest order in all tribes. They are regularly called and paid as physicians, to prescribe for the sick; and many of them acquire great skill in the medicinal world, and gain much celebrity in their nation. Their first prescriptions are roots and herbs, of which they have a great variety of species; and when these have all failed, their last resort is to *"medicine"* or mystery; and for this purpose, each one of them has a strange and unaccountable dress, conjured up and constructed during a life-time of practice, in the wildest fancy imaginable, in which he arrays himself, and makes his last visit to his dying patient,—dancing over him, shaking his frightful rattles, and singing songs of incantation, in hopes to cure him by a charm. There are some instances, of course, where the exhausted patient unaccountably recovers, under the application of these absurd forms; and in such cases, this ingenious son of *Indian* Esculapius will be seen for several days after on the top of a wigwam, with his right arm extended, and waving over the gaping multitude, to whom he is vaunting forth, without modesty, the surprising skill he has acquired in his art, and the undoubted efficacy of his medicine or mystery. But if, on the contrary, the patient dies, he soon changes his dress, and joins in doleful lamentations with the mourners; and easily, with his craft, and the ignorance and superstition of his people, protects his reputation and maintains his influence over them; by assuring them, that it was the will of the Great Spirit that his patient should die, and when sent for, his feeble efforts must cease.

Such was the case, and such the extraordinary means resorted to in the instance I am now relating. Several hundred spectators, including Indians and traders, were assembled around the dying man, when it was announced that the *"medicine-man"* was coming; we were required to "form a ring," leaving a space of some thirty or forty feet in diameter around the dying man, in which the doctor could perform his wonderful operations; and a space was also opened to allow him free room to pass through the crowd without touching any one. This being done, in a few moments his arrival was announced by the death-like "hush———sh——" through the crowd; and nothing was to be heard, save the light and casual tinkling of the rattles upon his dress, which was scarcely perceptible to the ear, as he cautiously and slowly moved through the avenue left for him; which at length brought him into the ring, in view of the pitiable object over whom his mysteries were to be performed.

Readers! you may have seen or read of the witch of Endor—or you may imagine all the ghosts, and spirits, and furies, that ever ranked amongst the "rank and file" of demonology; and yet you must see my painting of this strange scene before you can form a just conception of real frightful ugliness and Indian conjuration—

yes, and even more: you must see the magic *dress* of this Indian "big bug" (which I have this day procured in all its parts), placed upon the back of some person who can imitate the strides, and swells, the grunts, and spring the rattles of an Indian magician.

His entrée and his garb were somewhat thus:—he approached the ring with his body in a crouching position (Fig 19), with a slow and tilting step—his body and head were entirely covered with the skin of a yellow bear, the head of which (his own head being inside of it) served as a mask; the huge claws of which also, were dangling on his wrists and ankles; in one hand he shook a frightful rattle, and in the other brandished his medicine spear or magic wand; to the rattling din and discord of all of which, he added the wild and startling jumps and yelps of the Indian, and the horrid and appalling grunts, and snarls, and growls of the grizzly bear, in ejaculatory and gutteral incantations to the Good and Bad Spirits, in behalf of his patient; who was rolling and groaning in the agonies of death, whilst he was dancing around him, jumping over him, and pawing him about, and rolling him in every direction.

In this wise, this strange operation proceeded for half an hour, to the surprise of a numerous and death-like silent audience, until the man died; and the medicine-man danced off to his quarters, and packed up, and tied and secured from the sight of the world, his mystery dress and equipments.

This dress, in all its parts, is one of the greatest curiosities in the whole collection of Indian manufactures which I have yet obtained in the Indian country. It is the strangest medley and mixture, perhaps, of the mysteries of the animal and vegetable kingdoms that ever was seen. Besides the skin of the yellow bear (which being almost an anomaly in that country, is out of the regular order of nature, and, of course, great medicine, and converted to a medicine use), there are attached to it the skins of many animals, which are also anomalies or deformities, which render them, in their estimation, *medicine;* and there are also the skins of snakes, and frogs, and bats,—beaks and toes and tails of birds,—hoofs of deer, goats, and antelopes; and, in fact, the "odds and ends" and fag ends, and tails, and tips of almost everything that swims, flies, or runs, in this part of the wide world.

Such is a medicine-man or a physician, and such is one of his wild and ridiculous manœuvres, which I have just witnessed in this strange country.

These men, as I before remarked, are valued as dignitaries in the tribe, and the greatest respect is paid to them by the whole

G. Catlin.

19

community; not only for their skill in their "materia medica;" but more especially for their tact in magic and mysteries, in which they all deal to a very great extent. I shall have much more to say of these characters and their doings in future epistles, and barely observe in the present place, that no tribe is without them;—that in all tribes their doctors are conjurors—are magicians—are sooth-sayers, and I had like to have said, high priests, inasmuch as they superintend and conduct all their religious ceremonies;—they are looked upon by all, as oracles of the nation. In all councils of war and peace, they have a seat with the chiefs—are regularly consulted before any public step is taken, and the greatest deference and respect is paid to their opinions.

MOUTH OF YELLOW STONE

THE Letter which I gave you yesterday, on the subject of "medicines" and "medicine-men," has somewhat broken the 'thread of my discourse;" and left my painting-room (in the bastion), and all the Indians in it, and portraits, and buffalo hunts, and landscapes of these beautiful regions, to be taken up and discussed; which I will now endeavour to do, beginning just where I left (or digressed) off.

I was seated on the cool breech of a twelve-pounder, and had my easel before me, and Crows and Blackfeet, and Assinneboins, whom I was tracing upon the canvas. And so I have been doing to-day, and shall be, for several days to come. My painting-room has become so great a lounge, and I so great a "medicine-man," that all other amusements are left; and all other topics of conversation and gossip, are postponed for future consideration. The chiefs have had to place "soldiers" (as they are called) at my door, with spear in hand to protect me from the throng, who otherwise would press upon me; and none but the worthies are allowed to come into my medicine apartments, and none to be painted, except such as are decided by the chiefs to be worthy of so high an honour.

The Crows and Blackfeet who are here together, are enemies of the most deadly kind while out on the plains; but here they sit and smoke quietly together, yet with a studied and dignified reserve.

The Blackfeet are, perhaps, one of the most (if not entirely the most) numerous and warlike tribes on the Continent. They occupy the whole of the country about the sources of the Missouri, from this place to the Rocky Mountains; and their numbers, from the best computations, are something like forty or fifty thousand—they are (like all other tribes whose numbers are sufficiently large to give them boldness) warlike and ferocious, *i.e.* they are predatory, are roaming fearlessly about the country, even into and through every part of the Rocky Mountains, and carrying war amongst their enemies; who are, of course, every tribe who inhabit the country about them.

The Crows who live on the head waters of Yellow Stone, and

21

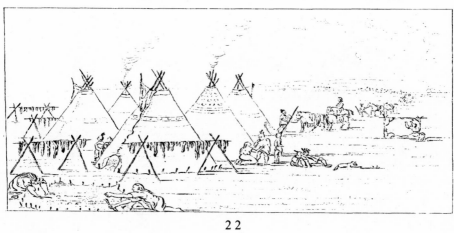

22

G. Catlin.

extend from this neighbourhood also to the base of the Rocky Mountains, are similar in the above respects to the Blackfeet; roaming about a great part of the year—and seeking their enemies wherever they can find them.

They are a much smaller tribe than the Blackfeet, with whom they are always at war, and from whose great numbers they suffer prodigiously in battle; and probably will be in a, few years entirely destroyed by them.

The Crows have not, perhaps, more than 7000 in their nation, and probably not more than eight hundred warriors or fighting men. Amongst the more powerful tribes, like the Sioux and Blackfeet, who have been enabled to preserve their warriors, it is a fair calculation to count one in five as warriors; but among the Crows, and Minatarees, and Puncahs, and several other small but warlike tribes, this proportion cannot exist; as in some of these I have found two or three women to a man in the nation; in consequence of the continual losses sustained amongst their men in war, and also whilst pursuing the buffalo on the plains for food, where their lives are exceedingly exposed.

The Blackfeet and the Crows, like the Sioux and Assinneboins, have nearly the same mode of' constructing their wigwam or lodge; in which tribes it is made of buffalo skins sewed together, after being dressed, and made into the form of a tent; supported within by some twenty or thirty pine poles of twenty-five feet in height, with an apex or aperture at the top, through which the smoke escapes and the light is admitted. These lodges, or tents, are taken down in a few minutes by the squaws, when they wish to change their location, and easily transported to any part of the country where they wish to encamp; and they generally move some six or eight times in the course of the summer; following the immense herds of buffaloes, as they range over these vast plains, from east to west, and north to south. The objects for which they do this are two-fold,—to procure and dress their skins, which are brought in, in the fall and winter, and sold to the Fur Company, for white man's luxury; and also for the purpose of killing and drying buffalo meat (Fig. 22), which they bring in from their hunts, packed on their horses' backs, in great quantities; making pemican, and preserving the marrow-fat for their winter quarters; which are generally taken up in some heavy-timbered bottom, on the banks of some stream, deep embedded within the surrounding bluffs, which break off the winds, and make their long and tedious winter tolerable and supportable. They then sometimes erect their skin lodges amongst the timber, and dwell in them during the winter months; but more frequently cut logs and make a miserable and rude sort of a log cabin; in which they can live much warmer and better protected from the assaults of their enemies, in case they are attacked; in which case a log cabin is a tolerable fort against Indian weapons.

The Crows, of all the tribes in this region, or on the Continent, make the most beautiful lodge. As I have before mentioned, they construct them as the Sioux do, and make them of the same material; yet they oftentimes dress the skins of which it is composed almost as white as linen, and beautifully garnish them with porcupine quills, and paint and ornament them in such a variety of ways, as renders them exceedingly picturesque and agreeable to the eye. I have procured a very beautiful one of this description (Fig. 20), highly-ornamented, and fringed with scalp-locks, and sufficiently large for forty men to dine under. The poles which support it are about thirty in number, of pine, and all cut in the Rocky Mountains, having been some hundred years, perhaps, in use. This tent, when erected, is about twenty-five feet high, and has a very pleasing effect; with the Great or Good Spirit painted on one side, and the Evil Spirit on the other. If I can ever succeed in transporting it to New York and other eastern cities, it will be looked upon as a beautiful and exceedingly interesting specimen.

The manner in which an encampment of Indians strike their tents and transport them is curious, and to the traveller in this country a very novel and unexpected sight, when he first beholds it. Whilst ascending the river to this place, I saw an encampment of Sioux, consisting of six hundred of these lodges, struck, and all things packed and on the move in a very few minutes. The chief sends his runners or criers (for such all chiefs keep in their employment) through the village, a few hours before they are to start; announcing his determination to move, and the hour fixed upon, and the necessary preparations are in the meantime making; and at the time announced, the lodge of the chief is seen flapping in the wind, a part of the poles having been taken out from under it; this is the signal, and in one minute, six hundred of them (on a level and beautiful prairie), which before had been strained tight and fixed, were seen waving and flapping in the wind, and in one minute more all were flat upon the ground. Their horses and dogs, of which they had a vast number, had all been secured upon the spot in readiness; and each one was speedily loaded with the burthen allotted to it, and ready to fall into the grand procession.

For this strange cavalcade, preparation is made in the following

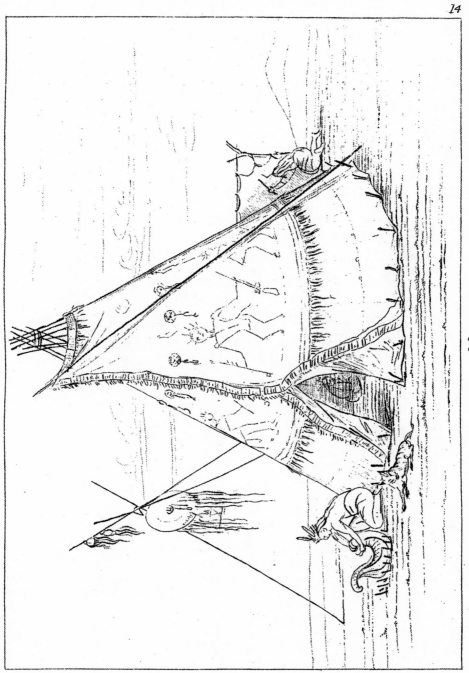

20

G. Catlin.

manner: the poles of a lodge are divided into two bunches, and the little ends of each bunch fastened upon the shoulders or withers of a horse, leaving the butt ends to drag behind on the ground on either side; just behind the horse, a brace or pole is tied across, which keeps the poles in their respective places; and then upon that and the poles behind the horse, is placed the lodge or tent, which is rolled up, and also numerous other articles of household and domestic furniture, and on the top of all, two, three, and even (sometimes) four women and children! Each one of these horses has a conductress, who sometimes walks before and leads him, with a tremendous pack upon her own back; and at others she sits astride of his back, with a child, perhaps, at her breast, and another astride of the horse's back behind her; clinging to her waist with one arm, while it affectionately embraces a sneaking dog-pup in the other.

In this way five or six hundred wigwams, with all their furniture (Fig. 21), may be seen drawn out for miles, creeping over the grass-covered plains of this country; and three times that number of men, on good horses, strolling along in front or on the flank, and, in some tribes, in the rear of this heterogeneous caravan; at least five times that number of dogs, which fall into the rank, and follow in the train and company of the women; and every cur of them, who is large enough, and not too cunning to be enslaved, is encumbered with a car or sled (or whatever it may be better called), on which he patiently drags his load—a part of the household goods and furniture of the lodge to which he belongs. Two poles, about fifteen feet long, are placed upon the dog's shoulder, in the same manner as the lodge poles are attached to the horses, leaving the larger ends to drag upon the ground behind him; on which is placed a bundle or wallet which is allotted to him to carry, and with which he trots off amid the throng of dogs and squaws; faithfully and cheerfully dragging his load 'till night, and by the way loitering and occasionally

"Catching at little bits of fun and glee
That's played on dogs enslaved by dog that's free."

The Crows, like the Blackfeet, are beautifully costumed, and perhaps with somewhat more of taste and elegance; inasmuch as (with their dresses and with their lodges), the skins of which they are made are more delicately and whitely dressed. The art of dressing skins belongs to the Indians in all countries; and the Crows surpass the civilised world in the beauty of their skin-dressing. The art of tanning is unknown to them, so far as civilised habits and arts have not been taught them; yet the art of dressing skins, so far as we have it in the civilised world, has been (like hundreds of other ornamental and useful customs which we are practising) borrowed from the savage; without our ever stopping to inquire from whence they come, or by whom invented.

The usual mode of dressing the buffalo, and other skins, is by immersing them for a few days under a lye from ashes and water, until the hair can be removed; when they are strained upon a frame or upon the ground, with stakes or pins driven through the edges into the earth; where they remain for several days, with the brains of the buffalo or elk spread upon and over them; and at last finished by "graining," as it is termed, by the squaws; who use a sharpened bone, the shoulder-blade or other large bone of the animal, sharpened at the edge, somewhat like an adze; with the edge of which they scrape the fleshy side of the skin; bearing on it with the weight of their bodies, thereby drying and softening the skin, and fitting it for use.

The greater part of these skins, however, go through still another operation afterwards, which gives them a greater value, and renders them much more serviceable—that is the process of smoking. For this, a small hole is dug in the ground, and a fire is built in it with rotten wood, which will produce a great quantity of smoke without much blaze; and several small poles of the proper length stuck in the ground around it, and drawn and fastened together at the top, around which a skin is wrapped in form of a tent, and generally sewed together at the edges to secure the smoke within it; within this the skins to be smoked are placed, and in this condition the tent will stand a day or so, enclosing the heated smoke; and by some chemical process or other, which I do not understand, the skins thus acquire a quality which enables them, after being ever so many times wet, to dry soft and pliant as they were before, which secret I have never yet seen practised in my own country; and for the lack of which, all of our dressed skins when once wet, are, I think, chiefly ruined.

An Indian's dress of deer skins, which is wet a hundred times upon his back, dries soft; and his lodge also, which stands in the rains, and even through the severity of winter, is taken down as soft and as clean as when it was first put up.

A Crow is known wherever he is met by his beautiful white dress, and his tall and elegant figure; the greater part of the men being six feet high. The Blackfeet, on the other hand, are more of the Herculean make—about middling stature, with broad shoulders, and great expansion of chest; and the skins, of which their dresses are made, are chiefly dressed black, or of a dark brown colour; from which circumstance, in all probability, they having black leggings or moccasins, have got the name of Blackfeet.

The Crows are very handsome and gentlemanly Indians in their personal appearance; and have been always reputed, since the first acquaintance made with them, very civil and friendly.

These people to be sure, have in some instances plundered and robbed trappers and travellers in their country; and for that I have sometimes heard them called rascals and thieves, and rogues of the first order, etc.; yet they do not consider themselves such; for thieving in their estimation is a high crime, and considered the most disgraceful act that a man can possibly do. They call this *capturing,* where they sometimes run off a Trader's horses and make their boast of it; considering it a kind of retaliation or summary justice, which they think it right and honourable that they should administer. And why not? for the unlicensed trespass committed through their country from one end to the other, by mercenary white men, who are destroying the game, and catching all the beaver and other rich and valuable furs out of their country, without paying them an equivalent, or, in fact, anything at all, for it; and this too, when they have been warned time and again of the danger they would be in, if they longer persisted in the practice. Reader, I look upon the Indian as the most honest and honourable race of people that I ever lived amongst in my life; and in their native state, I pledge you my honour they are the last of all the human family to pilfer or to steal, if you trust to their honour; and for this never-ending and boundless system of theft and plunder, and debauchery, that is practised off upon these rightful owners of the soil, by acquisitive white men, I consider the infliction, or retaliation, by driving off and appropriating a few horses, but a lenient punishment, which those persons at least should expect; and which, in fact, none but a very honourable and high-minded people could inflict, instead of a much severer one; which they could easily practise upon the few white men in their country, without rendering themselves amenable to any law.

Mr M'Kenzie has repeatedly told me, within the four last weeks, while in conversation relative to the Crows, that they were friendly and honourable in their dealing with the whites, and that he considered them the finest Indians of his acquaintance.

I recollect whilst in St Louis, and other places at the East, to have heard it often said, that the Crows were a rascally and thieving set of vagabonds, highway robbers, etc., etc.; and I have been told since, that this information has become current in the world; from the fact, that they made some depredations upon the camp of Messrs Crooke and Hunt of the Fur Company; and drove off a number of their horses, when they were passing through the Crow country, on their way to Astoria. This was no doubt true; and equally true, would these very Indians tell us, was the fact, that they had a good and sufficient reason for it.

These gentlemen, with their party, were crossing the Crow country with a large stock of goods, of guns, and ammunition, of knives, and spears, arrow-heads, etc.; and stopped for some time and encamped in the midst of the Crow country (and I think wintered there), when the Crows assembled in large numbers about them, and treated them in a kind and friendly manner; and at the same time proposed to trade with them for guns and ammunition, etc. (according to their own account), of which they were in great want, and for which they brought a great many horses, and offered them repeatedly in trade; which these gentlemen refused to take, persisting in their determination of carrying their goods to their destined place, across the mountains; thereby disappointing these Indians, by denying them the arms and weapons which were in their possession, whilst they were living upon them, and exhausting the game and food of their country. No doubt, these gentlemen told the Crows, that these goods were going to Astoria, of which place they knew nothing; and of course, it was enough for them that they were going to take them farther west; which they would at once suppose was to the Blackfeet, their principal enemy, having eight or ten warriors to one of the Crows; where they supposed the white men could get a greater price for their weapons, and arm their enemies in such a way as would enable them to turn upon the Crows, and cut them to pieces without mercy. Under these circumstances, the Crows rode off, and to show their indignation, drove off some of the Company's horses, for which they have ever since been denominated a band of thieves and highway robbers. It is a custom, and a part of the system of jurisprudence amongst all savages, to revenge upon the person or persons who give the offence, if they can; and if not, to let that punishment fall upon the head of the first white man who comes in their way, provided the offender was a white man. And I would not be surprised, therefore, if I get robbed of my horse; and you too, readers, if you go into that country, for that very (supposed) offence.

I have conversed often and much with Messrs Sublette and

Campbell, two gentlemen of the highest respectability, who have traded with the Crows for several years, and they tell me they are one of the most honourable, honest, and high-minded races of people on earth; and with Mr Tullock, also, a man of the strictest veracity, who is now here with a party of them; and, he says, they never steal,—have a high sense of honour,—and being fearless and proud, are quick to punish or retaliate.

So much for the character of the Crows for the present, a subject which I shall assuredly take up again, when I shall have seen more of them myself.

LETTER—No. 8

SINCE my last Letter, nothing of great moment has transpired at this place; but I have been continually employed in painting my portraits and making notes on the character and customs of the wild folks who are about me. I have just been painting a number of the Crows, fine looking and noble gentlemen. They are really a handsome and well-formed set of men as can be seen in any part of the world. There is a sort of ease and grace added to their dignity of manners, which gives them the air of gentlemen at once. I observed the other day, that most of them were over six feet high, and very many of these have cultivated their natural hair to such an almost incredible length, that it sweeps the ground as they walk: there are frequent instances of this kind amongst them, and in some cases, a foot or more of it will drag on the grass as they walk, giving exceeding grace and beauty to their movements. They usually oil their hair with a profusion of bear's grease every morning, which is no doubt one cause of the unusual length to which their hair extends; though it cannot be the sole cause of it, for the other tribes throughout this country use the bear's grease in equal profusion without producing the same results. The Mandans, however, and the Sioux, of whom I shall speak in future epistles, have cultivated a very great growth of the hair, as many of them are seen whose hair reaches near to the ground.

This extraordinary length of hair amongst the Crows is confined to the men alone; for the women, though all of them with glossy and beautiful hair, and a great profusion of it, are unable to cultivate it to so great a length; or else they are not allowed to compete with their lords in a fashion so ornamental (and on which the men so highly pride themselves), and are obliged to cut it short off.

The fashion of long hair amongst the men, prevails throughout all the Western and North Western tribes, after passing the Sacs and Foxes; and the Pawnees of the Platte, who, with two or three other tribes only, are in the habit of shaving nearly the whole head.

The present chief of the Crows, who is called "Long-hair," and

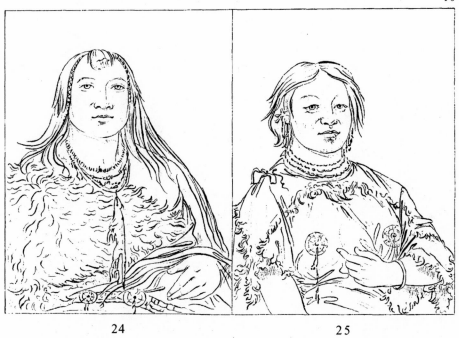

24

25

26

27

G. Catlin.

has received his name as well as his office from the circumstance of having the longest hair of any man in the nation, I have not yet seen; but I hope I yet may, ere I leave this part of the country. This extraordinary man is known to several gentlemen with whom I am acquainted, and particularly to Messrs Sublette and Campbell, of whom I have before spoken, who told me they had lived in his hospitable lodge, with him for months together; and assured me that they had measured his hair by a correct means, and found it to be ten feet and seven inches in length; closely inspecting every part of it at the same time, and satisfying themselves that it was the natural growth.

On ordinary occasions it is wound with a broad leather strap, from his head to its extreme end, and then folded up into a budget or block, of some ten or twelve inches in length, and of some pounds weight; which when he walks is carried under his arm, or placed in his bosom, within the folds of his robe; but on any great parade or similar occasion, his pride is to unfold it, oil it with bear's grease and let it drag behind him; some three or four feet of it spread out upon the grass, and black and shining like a raven's wing.

It is a common custom amongst most of these upper tribes, to splice or add on several lengths of hair, by fastening them with glue; probably for the purpose of imitating the Crows, upon whom alone Nature has bestowed this conspicuous and signal ornament.

Amongst the Crows of distinction now at this place, I have painted the portraits of several, who exhibit some striking peculiarities. Amongst whom is Chah-ee-chopes, the four wolves (Fig. 24); a fine looking fellow, six feet in stature, and whose natural hair sweeps the grass as he walks; he is beautifully clad, and carries himself with the most graceful and manly mien—he is in mourning for a brother; and, according to their custom, has cut off a number of locks of his long hair, which is as much as a man can well spare of so valued an ornament, which he has been for the greater part of his life cultivating; whilst a woman who mourns for a husband or child, is obliged to crop her hair short to her head, and so remain till it grows out again; ceasing gradually to mourn as her hair approaches to its former length.

Duhk-pits-a-ho-shee, the red bear (Fig. 26), a distinguished warrior; and Oo-je-en-a-he-ah, the woman who lives in the bear's den (Fig. 25). I have also painted Pa-ris-ka-roo-pa (two crows) the younger (Fig. 27), one of the most extraordinary men in the Crow nation; not only for his looks, from the form of his head, which seems to be distortion itself—and curtailed of all its fair proportions; but from his extraordinary sagacity as a councillor and orator, even at an early stage of his life.

There is something very uncommon in this outline, and sets forth the striking peculiarity of the Crow tribe, though rather in an exaggerated form. The semi-lunar outline of the Crow head, with an exceedingly low and retreating forehead, is certainly a very peculiar and striking characteristic; and though not so strongly marked in most of the tribe as in the present instance, is sufficient for their detection whenever they are met; and will be subject for further comment in another place.

The Crow women (and Blackfeet also) are not handsome, and I shall at present say but little of them. They are, like all other Indian women, the slaves of their husbands: being obliged to perform all the domestic duties and drudgeries of the tribe, and not allowed to join in their religious rites or ceremonies, nor in the dance or other amusements.

The women in all these upper and western tribes are decently dressed, and many of them with great beauty and taste; their dresses are all of deer or goat skins, extending from their chins quite down to the feet; these dresses are in many instances trimmed with ermine, and ornamented with porcupine quills and beads with exceeding ingenuity.

The Crow and Blackfeet women, like all others I ever saw in any Indian tribe, divide the hair on the forehead, and paint the separation or crease with vermilion or red earth. For what purpose this little, but universal, custom is observed, I never have been able to learn.

The men amongst the Blackfeet tribe, have a fashion equally simple, and probably of as little meaning, which seems strictly to be adhered to by every man in the tribe; they separate the hair in two places on the forehead, leaving a lock between the two, of an inch or two in width, which is carefully straightened down on to the bridge of the nose, and there cut square off. It is more than probable that this is done for the purpose of distinction; that they may thereby be free from the epithet of effeminacy, which might otherwise attach to them.

These two tribes, whom I have spoken of connectedly, speak two distinct and entirely dissimilar languages; and the language of each is different, and radically so, from that of all other tribes about them. As these people are always at war, and have been, time out of mind, they do not intermarry or hold converse with each other, by which any knowledge of each other's language could be acquired. It would be the work of a man's life-time to collect the languages of all the different tribes which I am visiting; and I shall, from necessity, leave this subject chiefly for others, who have the time to devote to them, to explain them to the world. I have, however, procured a brief vocabulary of their words and sentences in these tribes; and shall continue to do so amongst the tribes I shall visit, which will answer as a specimen or sample in each; and which, in the sequel to these Letters (if they should ever be published), will probably be arranged.

The Blackfeet are, perhaps, the most powerful tribe of Indians on the Continent; and being sensible of their strength, have stubbornly resisted the Traders in their country, who have been gradually forming an acquaintance with them, and endeavouring to establish a permanent and profitable system of trade. Their country abounds in beaver and buffalo, and most of the fur-bearing animals of North America; and the American Fur Company, with an unconquerable spirit of trade and enterprise, has pushed its establishments into their country; and the numerous parties of trappers are tracing up their streams and rivers, rapidly destroying the beavers which dwell in them. The Blackfeet have repeatedly informed the Traders of the Company, that if their men persisted in trapping beavers in their country, they should kill them whenever they met them. They have executed their threats in many instances, and the Company lose some fifteen or twenty men annually; who fall by the hands of these people, in defence of what they deem their property and their rights. Trinkets and whiskey, however, will soon spread their charms amongst these, as it has done amongst other tribes; and white man's voracity will sweep the prairies and the streams of their wealth, to the Rocky Mountains and the Pacific Ocean; leaving the Indians to inhabit, and at last to starve upon, a dreary and solitary waste.

The Blackfeet, therefore, having been less traded with, and less seen by white people than most of the other tribes, are more imperfectly understood; and it yet remains a question to be solved— whether there are twenty, or forty or fifty thousand of them? for no one, as yet, can correctly estimate their real strength. From all I can learn, however, which is the best information that can be got from the Traders, there are not far from 30,000 Indians (all together), who range under the general denomination of Blackfeet.

From our slight and imperfect knowledge of them, and other tribes occupying the country about the sources of the Missouri, there is no doubt in my mind, that we are in the habit of bringing more Indians into the computation, than are entitled justly to the appellation of "Blackfeet." Such, for instance, are the "Grosventres de Prairie" and Cotonnés, neither of which speak the Blackfeet language; but hunt, and eat, and fight, and intermarry with the Blackfeet; living therefore in a state of confederacy and friendship with them, but speaking their own language, and practising their own customs.

The Blackfeet proper are divided into four bands or families, as follow:—the "Pe-a-gans," of 500 lodges; the "Blackfoot" band, of 450 lodges; the "Blood" band, of 450 lodges; and the "Small Robes," of 250 lodges. These four bands constituting about 1650 lodges, averaging ten to the lodge, amount to about 16,500 souls.

There are then of the other tribes above-mentioned (and whom we, perhaps, incorrectly denominate Blackfeet), Grosventres des Prairies, 430 lodges, with language entirely distinct; Circes, of 220 lodges, and Cotonnés, of 250 lodges, with language also distinct from either.*

There is in this region a rich and interesting field for the linguist or the antiquarian; and stubborn facts, I think, if they could be well procured, that would do away the idea which many learned gentlemen entertain, that the Indian languages of North America can all be traced to two or three roots. The language of the Dohcotas is entirely and radically distinct from that of the Mandans, and theirs equally so from the Blackfoot and the Crows. And from the lips of Mr Brazeau, a gentleman of education and strict observation, who has lived several years with the Blackfeet and Shiennes, and who speaks the language of tribes on either side of them, assures me that these languages are radically distinct and dissimilar, as I have above stated: and also, that although he has been several years amongst those tribes, he has not been able to trace the slightest resemblance between the Circee, Cotonné, and Blackfoot, and Shienne, and Crow, and Mandan tongues; and from a great deal of corroborating information, which I have got from other persons acquainted with these tribes, I am fully convinced of the correctness of his statements.

Besides the Blackfeet and Crows, whom I told you were assembled at this place, are also the Knisteneaux (or Crees, as they are commonly called), a very pretty and pleasing tribe of Indians of about 3000 in number, living on the north of this, and also the Assinneboins and Ojibbeways; both of which tribes also inhabit the country to the north and north-east of the mouth of Yellow Stone.

The Knisteneaux are of small stature, but well-built for strength

* Several years since writing the above, I held a conversation with Major Pilcher (a strictly correct and honourable man, who was then the agent for these people, who has lived amongst them, and is at this time superintendent of Indian affairs at St Louis), who informed me, much to my surprise, that the Blackfeet were not far from 60,000 in numbers, including all the confederacy of which I have just spoken.

and activity combined; are a people of wonderful prowess for their numbers, and have waged an unceasing warfare with the Blackfeet, who are their neighbours and enemies on the west. From their disparity in numbers, they are rapidly thinning the ranks of their warriors, who bravely sacrifice their lives in contentions with their powerful neighbours. This tribe occupy the country from the mouth of the Yellow Stone, in a north-western direction, far into the British territory, and trade principally at the British N. W. Company's Posts.

The Assinneboins of seven thousand, and the Ojibbeways of six thousand, occupy a vast extent of country, in a north-eastern direction from this; extending also into the British possessions as high north as Lake Winnipeg; and trading principally with the British Company. These three tribes are in a state of nature, living as neighbours, and are also on terms of friendship with each other. This friendship, however, is probably but a temporary arrangement, brought about by the Traders amongst them; and which, like most Indian peace establishments, will be of short duration.

The Ojibbeways are, undoubtedly, a part of the tribe of Chippeways, with whom we are more familiarly acquainted, and who inhabit the south-west shore of Lake Superior. Their language is the same, though they are separated several hundred miles from any of them, and seem to have no knowledge of them, or traditions of the manner in which, or of the time when, they became severed from each other.

The Assinneboins are a part of the Dohcotas, or Sioux, undoubtedly; for their personal appearance as well as their language is very similar.

At what time, or in what manner, these two parts of a nation got strayed away from each other is a mystery; yet such cases have often occurred, of which I shall say more in future. Large parties, who are straying off in pursuit of game, or in the occupation of war, are oftentimes intercepted by their enemy; and being prevented from returning, are run off to a distant region, where they take up their residence and establish themselves as a nation.

There is a very curious custom amongst the Assinneboins, from which they have taken their name; a name given them by their neighbours, from a singular mode they have of boiling their meat, which is done in the following manner:—When they kill meat, a hole is dug in the ground about the size of a common pot, and a piece of the raw hide of the animal, as taken from the back, is put over the hole, and then pressed down with the hands close around the sides, and filled with water. The meat to be boiled is then put in this hole or pot of water; and in a fire, which is built near by, several large stones are heated to a red heat, which are successively dipped and held in the water until the meat is boiled; from which singular and peculiar custom, the Ojibbeways have given them the appellation of Assinneboins or stone-boilers.

This custom is a very awkward and tedious one, and used only as an ingenious means of boiling their meat, by a tribe who was too rude and ignorant to construct a kettle or pot.

The Traders have recently supplied these people with pots; and even long before that, the Mandans had instructed them in the secret of manufacturing very good and serviceable earthen pots; which together have entirely done away the custom, excepting at public festivals; where they seem, like all others of the human family, to take pleasure in cherishing and perpetuating their ancient customs.

Of these three tribes, I have also lined my painting-room with a number of very interesting portraits of the distinguished and brave men; and also representations of their games and ceremonies, which will be found in my INDIAN GALLERY, if I live, and they can be preserved until I get home.

The Assinneboins, or stone-boilers, are a fine and noble looking race of Indians; bearing, both in their looks and customs, a striking resemblance to the Dohcotas or Sioux, from whom they have undoubtedly sprung. The men are tall, and graceful in their movements; and wear their pictured robes of the buffalo hide with great skill and pleasing effect. They are good hunters, and tolerably supplied with horses; and living in a country abounding with buffaloes, are well supplied with the necessaries of Indian life, and may be said to live well. Their games and amusements are many, of which the most valued one is the ball-play; and in addition to which, they have the game of the moccasin, horse-racing, and dancing; some one of which, they seem to be almost continually practising, and of all of which I shall hereafter give the reader (as well as of many others of their amusements) a minute account.

Their dances, which were frequent and varied, were generally exactly the same as those of the Sioux, of which I have given a faithful account in my Notes on the Sioux, and which the reader will soon meet with. There was one of these scenes, however, that I witnessed the other day, which appeared to me to be peculiar to this tribe, and exceedingly picturesque in its effect; which was described to me as the *pipe-dance,* and was as follows:—On a hard trodden pavement in front of their village, which place is used for all their

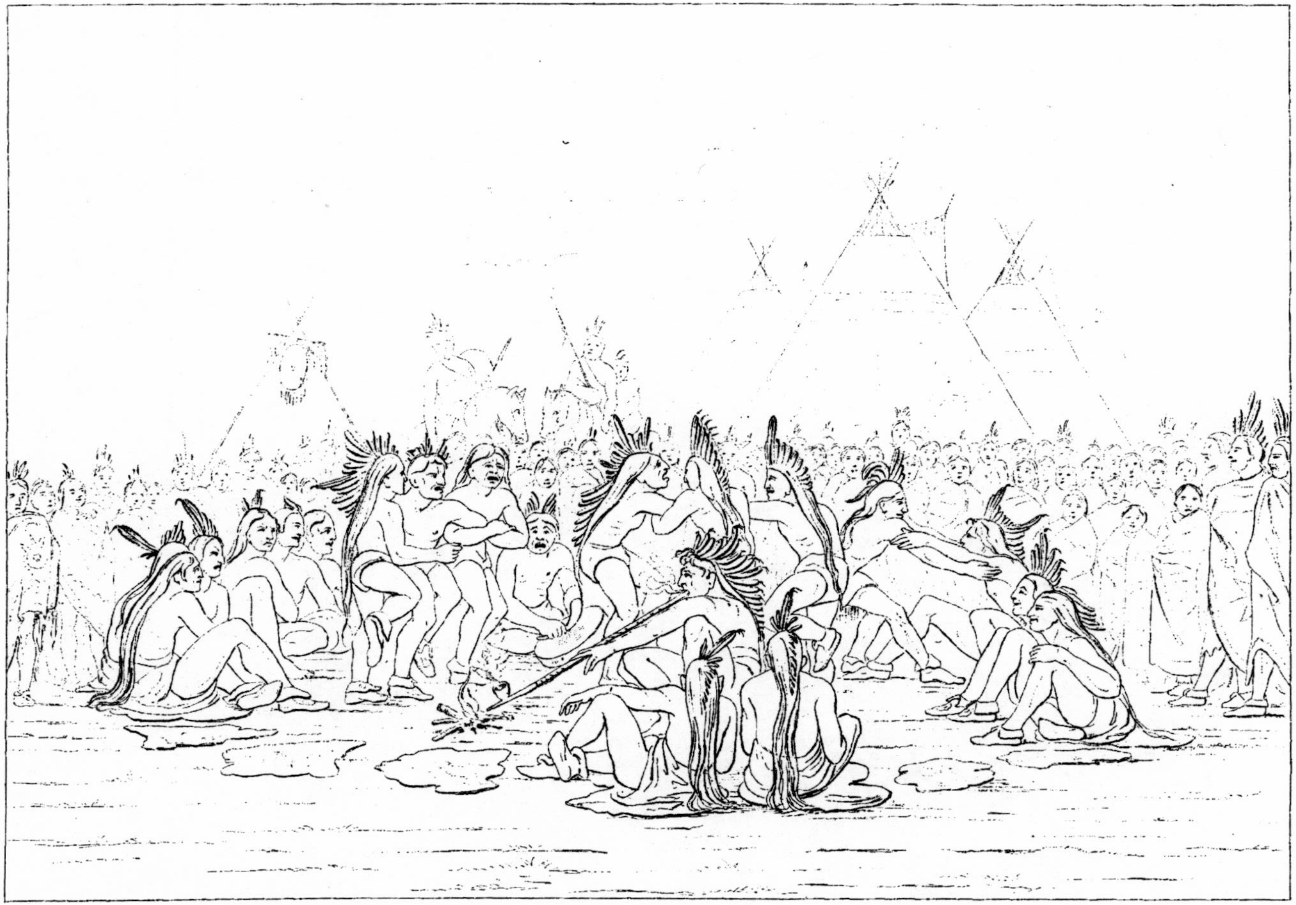

32

G. Catlin.

public meetings, and many of their amusements; the young men who were to compose the dance had gathered themselves around a small fire (Fig. 32), and each one seated on a buffalo-robe spread upon the ground. In the centre and by the fire, was seated a dignitary, who seemed to be a chief (perhaps a doctor or medicine-man), with a long pipe in his hand, which he lighted at the fire and smoked incessantly, grunting forth at the same time, in half-strangled gutturals, a sort of song, which I did not get translated to my satisfaction, and which might have been susceptible of none. While this was going on, another grim-visaged fellow in another part of the group, commenced beating on a drum or tambourine, accompanied by his voice; when one of the young men seated, sprang instantly on his feet, and commenced singing in time with the taps of the drum, and leaping about on one foot and the other in the most violent manner imaginable. In this way he went several times around the circle, bowing and brandishing his fists in the faces of each one who was seated, until at length he grasped one of them by the hands, and jerked him forcibly up upon his feet; who joined in the dance for a moment, leaving the one who had pulled him up, to continue his steps and his song in the centre of the ring; whilst he danced around in a similar manner, jerking up another, and then joining his companion in the centre; leaving the third and the fourth, and so on to drag into the ring, each one his man, until all were upon their feet; and at last joined in the most frightful gesticulations and yells that seemed almost to make the earth quake under our feet. This strange manœuvre, which I did but partially understand, lasted for half or three-quarters of an hour; to the great amusement of the gaping multitude who were assembled around, and broke up with the most piercing yells and barks like those of so many affrighted dogs.

The Assinneboins, somewhat like the Crows, cultivate their hair to a very great length, in many instances reaching down nearly to the ground; but in most instances of this kind, I find the great length is produced by splicing or adding on several lengths, which are fastened very ingeniously by means of glue, and the joints obscured by a sort of paste of red earth and glue, with which the hair is at intervals of every two or three inches filled, and divided into locks and slabs of an inch or so in breadth, and falling straight down over the back to the heels.

I have just painted the portrait of a very distinguished young man, and son of the chief (Fig. 28); his dress is a very handsome one, and in every respect answers well to the descriptions I have given above. The name of this man is Wi-jun-jon (the pigeon's egg head), and by the side of him (Fig. 29) will be seen the portrait of his wife, Chin-cha-pee (the fire bug that creeps), a fine looking squaw, in a handsome dress of the mountain-sheep skin, holding in her hand a stick curiously carved, with which every woman in this country is supplied; for the purpose of digging up the "Pomme Blanche," or prairie turnip, which is found in great quantities in these northern prairies, and furnishes the Indians with an abundant and nourishing food. The women collect these turnips by striking the end of the stick into the ground, and prying them out; after which they are dried and preserved in their wigwams for use during the season.

I have just had the satisfaction of seeing this travelled-gentleman (Wi-jun-jon) meet his tribe, his wife and his little children; after an absence of a year or more, on his journey of 6000 miles to Washington City, and back again (in company with Major Sanford, the Indian agent); where he has been spending the winter amongst the fashionables in the polished circles of civilised society. And I can assure you, readers, that his entrée amongst his own people, in the dress and with the airs of a civilised beau, was one of no ordinary occurrence; and produced no common sensation amongst the red-visaged Assinneboins, or in the minds of those who were travellers, and but spectators to the scene.

On his way home from St Louis to this place, a distance of 2000 miles, I travelled with this gentleman, on the steamer *Yellow Stone;* and saw him step ashore (on a beautiful prairie, where several thousands of his people were encamped), with a complete suit *en militaire,* a colonel's uniform of blue, presented to him by the President of the United States, with a beaver hat and feather, with epaulettes of gold—with sash and belt, and broad sword; with high-heeled boots—with a keg of whiskey under his arm, and a blue umbrella in his hand. In this plight and metamorphose, he took his position on the bank, amongst his friends—his wife and other relations; not one of whom exhibited, for an half-hour or more, the least symptoms of recognition, although they knew well who was before them. He also gazed upon them—upon his wife and parents, and little children, who were about, as if they were foreign to him, and he had not a feeling or thought to interchange with them. Thus the mutual gazings upon and from this would-be-stranger, lasted for full half an hour; when a gradual, but cold and exceedingly formal recognition began to take place, and an acquaintance ensued, which ultimately and smoothly resolved itself, without the least apparent emotion, into its former state; and the mutual kindred intercourse

29   28

30   31

G. Catlin.

seemed to flow on exactly where it had been broken off, as if it had been but for a moment, and nothing had transpired in the interim to check or change its character or expression.

Such is one of the stoic instances of a custom which belongs to all the North American Indians, forming one of the most striking features in their character; valued, cherished, and practised, like many others of their strange notions, for reasons which are difficult to be learned or understood; and which probably will never be justly appreciated by others than themselves.

This man, at this time, is creating a wonderful sensation amongst his tribe, who are daily and nightly gathered in gaping and listless crowds around him, whilst he is descanting upon what he has seen in the fashionable world; and which to them is unintelligible and beyond their comprehension; for which I find they are already setting him down as a liar and impostor. What may be the final results of his travels and initiation into the fashionable world, and to what disasters his incredible narrations may yet subject the poor fellow in this strange land, time only will develop.

He is now in disgrace, and spurned by the leading men of the tribe, and rather to be pitied than envied, for the advantages which one might have supposed would have flown from his fashionable tour. More of this curious occurrence and of this extraordinary man, I will surely give in some future epistles.

The women of this tribe are often comely, and sometimes pretty; in Fig. 34, will be seen a fair illustration of the dresses of the women and children, which are usually made of the skins of the mountain-goat, and ornamented with porcupine's quills and rows of elk's teeth.

The Knisteneaux (or Crees, as they are more familiarly called in this country) are a very numerous tribe, extending from this place as high north as the shores of Lake Winnipeg; and even much further in a north-westerly direction, towards, and even through, a great part of the Rocky Mountains.

I have before said of these, that they were about 3000 in numbers —by that, I meant but a small part of this extensive tribe, who are in the habit of visiting the American Fur Company's Establishment, at this place, to do their trading; and who themselves, scarcely know anything of the great extent of country over which this numerous and scattered family range. Their customs may properly be said to be primitive, as no inroads of civilised habits have been as yet successfully made amongst them. Like the other tribes in these regions, they dress in skins, and gain their food, and conduct their wars in a very similar manner. They are a very daring and most adventurous tribe; roaming vast distances over the prairies and carrying war into their enemy's country. With the numerous tribe of Blackfeet, they are always waging an uncompromising warfare; and though fewer in numbers and less in stature, they have shown themselves equal in sinew, and not less successful in mortal combats.

Amongst the foremost and most renowned of their warriors, is Bro-cas-sie, the broken arm (Fig. 30), in a handsome dress; and by the side of him (Fig. 31), his wife, a simple and comely looking woman. In Fig. 33, will be seen the full-length portrait of a young woman with a child on her back, showing fairly the fashion of cutting and ornamenting the dresses of the females in this tribe; which, without further comment, is all I shall say at this time of the valorous tribe of Crees or Knisteneaux.

The Ojibbeways I have briefly mentioned in a former place, and of them should say more; which will be done at a proper time, after I shall have visited other branches of this great and scattered family.

The chief of that part of the Ojibbeway tribe who inhabit these northern regions (Fig. 35), and whose name is Sha-co-pay (the Six), is a man of huge size; with dignity of manner, and pride and vanity, just about in proportion to his bulk. He sat for his portrait in a most beautiful dress, fringed with scalp-locks in profusion; which he had snatched, in his early life from his enemies' heads, and now wears as proud trophies and proofs of what his arm has accomplished in battles with his enemies. His shirt of buckskin is beautifully embroidered and painted in curious hieroglyphics, the history of his battles and charts of his life. This, and also each and every article of his varied dress, had been manufactured by his wives, of which he had several; and one, though not the most agreeable (Fig. 36), is seen represented by his side.

I have much to see of these people yet, and much consequently to write; so for the present I close my book.

34

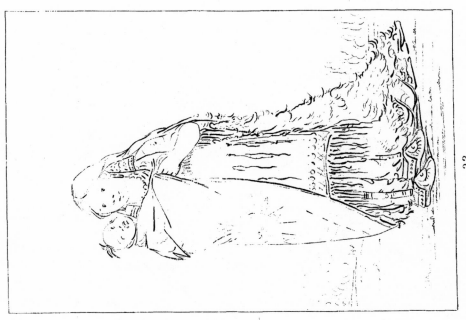

33

G. Catlin.

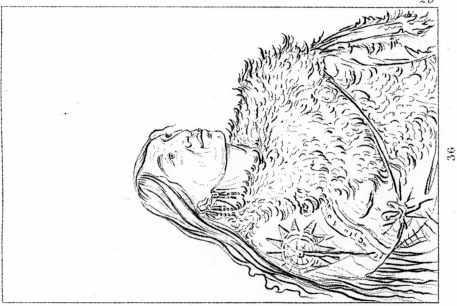

LETTER—No. 9

SINCE the dates of my other Letters from this place, I have been taking some wild rambles about this beautiful country of green fields; jolted and tossed about, on horseback and on foot, where pen, ink, and paper never thought of going; and of course the most that I saw and have learned, and would tell to the world, is yet to be written. It is not probable, however, that I shall again date a letter at this place, as I commence, in a few days, my voyage down the river in a canoe; but yet I may give you many a retrospective glance at this fairy land and its amusements.

A traveller on his tour through such a country as this, has no time to write, and scarcely time enough to moralise. It is as much as he can *well* do to "look out for his *scalp,*" and "for *something to eat.*" Impressions, however, of the most vivid kind, are rapidly and indelibly made by the fleeting incidents of savage life; and for the mind that can ruminate upon them with pleasure, there are abundant materials clinging to it for its endless entertainment in driving the quill when he gets back. The mind susceptible of such impressions catches volumes of incidents which are easy to write—it is but to unfold a web which the fascinations of this *shorn* country and its allurements have spun over the soul—it is but to paint the splendid panorama of a world entirely different from anything seen or painted before; with its thousands of miles, and tens of thousands of grassy hills and dales, where nought but silence reigns, and where the soul of a contemplative mould is seemingly lifted up to its Creator. What man in the world, I would ask, ever ascended to the pinnacle of one of Missouri's green-carpeted bluffs, a thousand miles severed from his own familiar land, and giddily gazed over the interminable and boundless ocean of grass-covered hills and valleys which lie beneath him, where the gloom of *silence* is complete—where not even the voice of the sparrow or cricket is heard—without feeling a sweet melancholy come over him, which seemed to drown his sense of everything beneath and on a level with him?

It is but to paint a vast country of green fields, where the *men* are all *red*—where *meat* is the staff of life—where no *laws,* but those of *honour,* are known—where the oak and the pine give way to the cotton-wood and peccan—where the buffalo range, the elk, mountain-sheep, and the fleet-bounding antelope—where the magpie and chattering parroquettes supply the place of the red-breast and the blue-bird—where wolves are white and bears grizzly—where pheasants are hens of the prairie, and frogs have horns!—where the rivers are yellow, and white men are turned savages in looks. Through the whole of this strange land the dogs are all wolves—women all slaves —men all lords. The *sun* and *rats* alone (of all the list of old acquaintance), could be recognised in this country of strange metamorphose. The former shed everywhere his familiar rays; and Monsr. Ratapon was hailed as an old acquaintance, which it gave me pleasure to meet; though he had grown a little more *savage* in his look.

In traversing the immense regions of the *classic* West, the mind of a philanthropist is filled to the brim, with feelings of admiration; but to reach this country, one is obliged to descend from the light and glow of civilised atmosphere, through the different grades of civilisation, which gradually sink to the most deplorable condition along the extreme frontier; thence through the most pitiable misery and wretchedness of savage degradation; where the genius of natural liberty and independence have been blasted and destroyed by the contaminating vices and dissipations introduced by the immoral part of *civilised* society. Through this dark and sunken vale of wretchedness one hurries, as through a pestilence, until he gradually rises again into the proud and chivalrous pale of savage society, in its state of original nature, beyond the reach of civilised contamination; here he finds much to fix his enthusiasm upon, and much to admire. Even here, the predominant passions of the savage breast, of ferocity and cruelty, are often found; yet *restrained,* and frequently *subdued,* by the noblest traits of honour and magnanimity,—a race of men who live and enjoy life and its luxuries, and practise its virtues, very far beyond the usual estimation of the world; who are apt to judge the savage and his virtues from the poor, degraded, and humbled specimens which alone can be seen along our frontiers. From the first settlements of our Atlantic coast to the present day, the bane of this *blasting frontier* has regularly crowded upon them, from the northern to the southern extremities of our country; and, like the fire in a prairie, which destroys everything where it passes, it has blasted and sunk them, and all but their names, into oblivion, wherever it has travelled. It is to this tainted class alone that the epithet of "poor, naked, and drunken savage," can be, with propriety, applied; for all those numerous tribes which I have visited, and are yet uncorrupted by the vices of civilised acquaintance, are well clad, in many instances cleanly, and in the full enjoyment of life and its luxuries. It is for the character and preservation of these noble fellows that I am an enthusiast; and it is for these uncontaminated people that I would be willing to devote the energies of my life. It is a sad and melancholy truth to contemplate, that all the numerous tribes who inhabited our vast Atlantic States *have not* "fled to the West;"—that they are not to be found here—that they have been blasted by the fire which has passed over them—have sunk into their graves, and everything but their names travelled into oblivion.

The distinctive character of all these Western Indians, as well as their traditions relative to their ancient locations, prove, beyond a doubt, that they have been for a very long time located on the soil which they now possess; and in most respects, distinct and unlike those nations who formerly inhabited the Atlantic coast, and who (according to the erroneous opinion of a great part of the world), have fled to the West.

It is for these inoffensive and unoffending people, yet unvisited by the vices of civilised society, that I would proclaim to the world, that it is time, for the honour of our country—for the honour of every citizen of the republic—and for the sake of humanity, that our government should raise her strong arm to save the remainder of them from the pestilence which is rapidly advancing upon them. We have gotten from them territory enough, and the country which they now inhabit is most of it too barren of timber for the use of civilised man; it affords them, however, the means and luxuries of savage life; and it is to be hoped that our government will not acquiesce in the continued wilful destruction of these happy people.

My heart has sometimes almost bled with pity for them, while amongst them, and witnessing their innocent amusements, as I have contemplated the inevitable bane that was rapidly advancing upon them; without that check from the protecting arm of government, and which alone could shield them from destruction.

What degree of happiness these sons of Nature may attain to in the world, in their own way; or in what proportion they may relish the pleasures of life, compared to the sum of happiness belonging to civilised society, has long been a subject of much doubt, and one which I cannot undertake to decide at this time. I would say thus much, however, that if the thirst for knowledge has entailed everlasting miseries on mankind from the beginning of the world; if refined and intellectual pains increase in proportion to our intellectual pleasures, I do not see that we gain much advantage over them on that score; and judging from the full-toned enjoyment which beams from their happy faces, I should give it as my opinion, that their lives were much more happy than ours; that is, if the word happiness is properly applied to the enjoyments of those who have not experienced the light of the Christian religion. I have long looked with the eye of a critic, into the jovial faces of these sons of the forest, unfurrowed with cares—where the agonising feeling of poverty had never stamped distress upon the brow. I have watched the bold, intrepid step—the proud, yet dignified deportment of Nature's man, in fearless freedom, with a soul unalloyed by mercenary lusts, too great to yield to laws or power except from God. As these independent fellows are all joint-tenants of the soil, they are all rich, and none of the steepings of comparative poverty can strangle their just claims to renown. Who (I would ask) can look without admiring, into a society where peace and harmony prevail—where virtue is cherished—where rights are protected, and wrongs are redressed —with no laws, but the laws of honour, which are the supreme laws of their land. Trust the boasted virtues of civilised society for awhile, with all its intellectual refinements, to such a tribunal, and then write down the degradation of the "lawless savage," and our transcendent virtues.

As these people have no laws, the sovereign right of summary redress lies in the breast of the party (or friends of the party) aggrieved; and infinitely more dreaded is the certainty of cruel revenge from the licensed hands of an offended savage, than the slow and uncertain vengeance of the law.

If you think me *enthusiast,* be it so; for I deny it not. It has ever been the predominant passion of my soul to seek Nature's wildest haunts, and give my hand to Nature's men. Legends of *these,* and visits to *those,* filled the earliest page of my juvenile impressions.

The tablet has stood, and I am an enthusiast for God's works as He left them.

The sad tale of my native "valley,"* has been beautifully sung; and from the flight of "Gertrude's" soul, my young imagination closely traced the savage to his deep retreats, and gazed upon him in dreadful horror, until pity pleaded, and admiration worked a charm.

A journey of 4000 miles from the Atlantic shore, regularly receding from the centre of civilised society to the extreme wilderness of Nature's original work, and back again, opens a book for many an interesting tale to be sketched; and the mind which lives, but to

* Wyóming.

relish the works of Nature, reaps a reward on such a tour of a much higher order than can arise from the selfish expectations of pecuniary emolument. Notwithstanding all that has been written and said, there is scarcely any subject on which the *knowing* people of the East, are yet less informed and instructed than on the character and amusements of the West: by this I mean the "Far West;"— the country whose fascinations spread a charm over the mind almost dangerous to civilised pursuits. Few people even know the true definition of the term "West;" and where is its location?—phantom-like it flies before us as we travel, and on our way is continually gilded, before us, as we approach the setting sun.

In the commencement of my Tour, several of my travelling companions from the city of New York, found themselves at a frightful distance to the West, when we arrived at Niagara Falls; and hastened back to amuse their friends with tales and scenes of the West. At Buffalo a steamboat was landing with 400 passengers, and twelve days out—"Where from?" "From the West." In the rich state of Ohio, hundreds were selling their farms and going—to the West. In the beautiful city of Cincinnati, people said to me "Our town has passed the days of its most rapid growth, it is not far enough West." —In St Louis, 1400 miles west of New York, my landlady assured me that I would be pleased with her boarders, for they were nearly all merchants from the "West." I there asked,—"Whence come those steamboats, laden with pork, honey, hides, etc.?"

From the West.

Whence those ponderous bars of silver, which those men have been for hours shouldering and putting on board that boat?

They come from Santa Fee, from the West.

Whence goes this steamboat so richly laden with dry-goods, steam engines, etc.?

She goes to Jefferson city.

Jefferson city?—Where is that?

Far to the West.

And where goes that boat laden down to her gunnels, the *Yellow Stone?*

She goes still farther to the West—"Then," said I, "I'll go to the West."

I went on the *Yellow Stone*—   *   *   *   *

*   *   *   Two thousand miles on her, and we were at the mouth of Yellow Stone river, at the West. What! invoices, bills of lading, etc., a wholesale establishment so far to the West! And those strange looking, long-haired gentlemen, who have just

arrived, and are relating the adventures of their long and tedious journey. Who are they?

Oh! they are some of our merchants just arrived from the West.

And that keel-boat, that Mackinaw-boat, and that formidable caravan, all of which are richly laden with goods.

These, Sir, are outfits starting for the *West.*

Going to the *West,* ha? "Then," said I, "I'll try it again. I will try and see if I can go to the West."   *   *   *   *

    *   *   *   What, a Fort here, too?

Oui, Monsieur—oui, Monsieur (as a dauntless and *semibarbarian-*looking, jolly fellow, dashed forth in advance of his party on his wild horse to meet me).

What distance are you west of Yellow Stone here, my good fellow?

Comment?

What   distance?—(stop)—quel   distance?

Pardón, Monsieur, je ne sais pas, Monsieur.

Ne parlez vous l'Anglais?

Non, Monsr. I speaks de French and de Americaine; mais je ne parle pas l'Anglais.

"Well, then, my good fellow, I will speak English, and you may speak Americaine."

Pardón, pardón, Monsieur.

Well, then, we will both speak Americaine.

Val, sare, je suis bien content, pour for I see dat you speaks putty coot Americaine.

What may I call your name?

Ba'tiste, Monsieur.

What Indians are those so splendidly dressed, and with such fine horses, encamped on the plain yonder?

Ils sont Corbeaux.

Crows, ha?

Yes, sare, Monsieur.

We are then in the Crow country?

Non, Monsieur, not putty éxact; we are in de coontrae of de dam Pieds noirs.

Blackfeet, ha?

Oui.

What blue mountain is that which we see in the distance yonder?

Ha, quel Montaigne? cela est la Montaigne du (pardón).

Du Rochers, I suppose?

Oui, Monsieur, de Rock Montaigne.

You live here, I suppose?

Non, Monsieur, I comes fair from de West.

What, from the West! Where under the heavens is that?

Wat, diable! de West? well you shall see, Monsieur, he is putty fair off, suppose. Monsieur Pierre Chouteau can give you the histoire de ma vie—il bien sait que je prends les castors, very fair in de West!

You carry goods, I suppose, to trade with the Snake Indians beyond the mountains, and trap beaver also?

Oui, Monsieur.

Do you see anything of the "Flat-heads" in your country?

Non, Monsieur, ils demeurent very, *very* fair to de West.

Well, Ba'tiste, I'll lay my course back again for the present, and at some future period, endeavour to go to the "West." But you say you trade with the Indians and trap beavers; you are in the employment of the American Fur Company, I suppose?

Non, Monsieur, not quite éxact; mais, suppose, I am *"free trappare,"* free, Mons. free!

Free trapper, what's that? I don't understand you, Ba'tiste.

Well, Mons. súppose he is easy pour understand—you shall know all. In de first place, I am enlist for tree year in de Fur Comp in St Louis—for bounté—pour bounté, eighty dóllare (understand, ha?) den I am go for wages, et I ave come de Missouri up, et I am trap castors putty much for six years, you see, until I am learn very much; and den you see, Mons. M'Kenzie is give me tree horse—one pour ride, et two pour pack (mais he is not buy, him not give, he is lend), and he is lend twelve trap; and I ave make start into de Rocky Montaigne, et I am live all álone on de leet rivares pour prendre les castors. Sometime six months—sometime five month, and I come back to Yel Stone, et Mons. M'Kenzie is give me coot price pour all.

So Mr M'Kenzie fits you out, and takes your beaver off you at a certain price?

Oui, Monsr. oui.

What price does he pay you for your beaver, Ba'tiste?

Ha! suppose one dollare pour one beavare.

A dollar a skin, ha?

Oui.

Well, you must live a lonesome and hazardous sort of life; can you make anything by it?

Oh, oui, Monsr. putty coot, mais if it is not pour for de dam rascalité Rickarree et de dam Pieds noirs, de Blackfoot Ingin, I am make very much monair, mais (sacré), I am rob—rob—rob too much!

What, do the Blackfeet rob you of your furs?

Oui, Monsr. rob, súppose, five time! I am been free trappare seven year, and I am rob five time—I am someting left not at all—he is take all; he is take all de horse—he is take my gun—he is take all my clothes—he is takee de castors—et I am come back with foot. So in de Fort, some cloths is cost putty much monnair, et some whiskey is give sixteen dollares pour gall; so you see I am owe de Fur Comp 600 dollare, by Gar!

Well, Ba'tiste, this then is what you call being a free trapper is it?

Oui, Mons. "free trappare," free!

You seem to be going down towards the Yellow Stone, and probably have been out on a trapping excursion.

Oui, Monsr. c'est vrai.

Have you been robbed this time, Ba'tiste?

Oui, Monsr. by de dam Pieds noirs—I am loose much; I am loose all—very all——eh bien—pour le dernier—c'est le dernier fois, Monsr. I am go to Yel Stone—I am go le Missouri down, I am go to St Louis.

Well, Ba'tiste, I am to figure about in this part of the world a few weeks longer, and then I shall descend the Missouri, from the mouth of Yellow Stone, to St Louis; and I should like exceedingly to employ just such a man as you are as a voyageur with me—I will give you good wages, and pay all your expenses; what say you?

Avec tout mon cour, Mons. remercie, remercie.

It's a bargain then, Ba'tiste; I will see you at the mouth of Yellow Stone.

Oui, Monsr. in de Yel Stone, bon soir, bon soir, Monsr.

But stop, Ba'tiste, you told me those were Crows encamped yonder.

Oui, Monsieur, oui, des Corbeaux.

And I suppose you are their interpreter?

Non, Monsieur.

But you speak the Crow language?

Ouis, Monsieur.

Well then, turn about; I am going to pay them a visit, and you can render me a service.—Bien, Monsieur, allons.

LETTER—No. 10

SOON after the writing of my last Letter, which was dated at the Mouth of Yellow Stone, I embarked on the River for this place, where I landed safely; and have resided for a couple of weeks, a guest in this almost subterraneous city—the strangest place in the world; where one sees in the most rapid succession, scenes which force him to mirth—to pity and compassion—to admiration—disgust; to fear and astonishment. But before I proceed to reveal them, I must give you a brief sketch of my voyage down the river from the Mouth of the Yellow Stone river to this place, a distance of 200 miles; and which my little note-book says, was performed somewhat in the following manner.

When I had completed my rambles and my sketches in those regions, and Ba'tiste and Bogard had taken their last spree, and fought their last battles, and forgotten them in the final and affectionate embrace and farewell (all of which are habitual with these game-fellows, when settling up their long-standing accounts with their fellow-trappers of the mountain streams); and after Mr M'Kenzie had procured for me a snug little craft, that was to waft us down the mighty torrent; we launched off one fine morning, taking our leave of the Fort, and the friends within it; and also, for ever, of the beautiful green fields, and hills, and dales, and prairie bluffs, that encompass the enchanting shores of the Yellow Stone.

Our canoe, which was made of green timber, was heavy and awkward; but our course being with the current, promised us a fair and successful voyage. Ammunition was laid in in abundance—a good stock of dried buffalo tongues—a dozen or two of beavers' tails —and a good supply of pemican. Bogard and Ba'tiste occupied the middle and bow, with their paddles in their hands; and I took my seat in the stern of the boat, at the steering oar. Our larder was as I have said; and added to that, some few pounds of fresh buffalo meat.

Besides which, and ourselves, our little craft carried several packs of Indian dresses and other articles, which I had purchased of the

Indians; and also my canvas and easel, and our culinary articles, which were few and simple; consisting of three tin cups, a coffee-pot —one plate—a frying-pan—and a tin-kettle.

Thus fitted out and embarked, we swept off at a rapid rate under the shouts of the savages, and the cheers of our friends, who lined the banks as we gradually lost sight of them, and turned our eyes towards St Louis, which was 2000 miles below us, with nought intervening, save the wide-spread and wild regions, inhabited by the roaming savage.

At the end of our first day's journey, we found ourselves handily encamping with several thousand Assinneboins, who had pitched their tents upon the bank of the river, and received us with every mark of esteem and friendship.

In the midst of this group, was my friend Wi-jun-jon (the pigeon's egg head), still lecturing on the manners and customs of the "pale faces." Continuing to relate without any appearance of exhaustion, the marvellous scenes which he had witnessed amongst the white people, on his tour to Washington City.

Many were the gazers who seemed to be the whole time crowding around him, to hear his recitals; and the plight which he was in rendered his appearance quite ridiculous. His beautiful military dress, of which I before spoke, had been so shockingly tattered and metamorphosed, that his appearance was truly laughable.

His keg of whiskey had dealt out to his friends all its charms— his frock-coat, which his wife had thought was of no earthly use below the waist, had been cut off at that place, and the nether half of it supplied her with a beautiful pair of leggings; and his silver-laced hat-band had been converted into a splendid pair of garters for the same. His umbrella the poor fellow still affectionately held on to, and kept spread at all times. As I before said, his theme seemed to be exhaustless, and he, in the estimation of his tribe, to be an unexampled liar.

Of the village of Assinneboins we took leave on the following morning, and rapidly made our way down the river. The rate of the current being four or five miles per hour, through one continued series of picturesque grass-covered bluffs and knolls, which everywhere had the appearance of an old and highly-cultivated country, with houses and fences removed.

There is, much of the way on one side or the other, a bold and abrupt precipice of three or four hundred feet in elevation, presenting itself in an exceedingly rough and picturesque form, to the shore of the river; sloping down from the summit level of the prairies above, which sweep off from the brink of the precipice, almost level, to an unknown distance.

It is along the rugged and wild fronts of these cliffs, whose sides are generally formed of hard clay, that the mountain-sheep dwell, and are often discovered in great numbers. Their habits are much like those of the goat; and in every respect they are like that animal, except in the horns, which resemble those of the ram; sometimes making two entire circles in their coil; and at the roots each horn is; in some instances, from five to six inches in breadth.

On the second day of our voyage we discovered a number of these animals skipping along the sides of the precipice, always keeping about equi-distant between the top and bottom of the ledge; leaping and vaulting in the most extraordinary manner from point to point, and seeming to cling actually, to the sides of the wall, where neither man nor beast could possibly follow them.

We landed our canoe, and endeavoured to shoot one of these sagacious animals; and after he had lead us a long and fruitless chase, amongst the cliffs, we thought we had fairly entrapped him in such a way as to be sure to bring him, at last, within the command of our rifles; when he suddenly bounded from his narrow foot-hold in the ledge, and tumbled down a distance of more than a hundred feet, amongst the fragments of rocks and clay, where I thought we must certainly find his carcass without further trouble; when, to my great surprise, I saw him bounding off, and he was almost instantly out of my sight.

Bogard, who was an old hunter, and well acquainted with these creatures, shouldered his rifle, and said to me—"the game is up; and you now see the use of those big horns; when they fall by accident, or find it necessary to quit their foot-hold in the crevice, they fall upon their head at a great distance unharmed, even though it should be on the solid rock."

Being on shore, and our canoe landed secure, we whiled away the greater part of this day amongst the wild and ragged cliffs, into which we had entered; and a part of our labours were vainly spent in the pursuit of a war-eagle. This noble bird is the one which the Indians in these regions, value so highly for their tail feathers, which are used as the most valued plumes for decorating the head and dresses of the warriors. It is a beautiful bird, and, the Indians tell me, conquers all other varieties of eagles in the country; from which circumstance, the Indians respect the bird, and hold it in the highest esteem, and value its quills. I am unable to say to what variety it belongs; but I am sure it is not to be seen in any of our museums;

nor is it to be found in America (I think), until one gets near to the base of the Rocky Mountains. This bird has often been called the calumet-eagle and war-eagle; the last of which appellations I have already accounted for; and the other has arisen from the fact, that the Indians almost invariably ornament their calumets or pipes of peace with its quills.

Our day's loitering brought us through many a wild scene; occasionally across the tracks of the grizzly bear, and, in sight merely, of a band of buffaloes; "which got the wind of us," and were out of the way, leaving us to return to our canoe at night, with a mere speck of good luck. Just before we reached the river, I heard the crack of a rifle, and in a few moments Bogard came in sight, and threw down from his shoulders a fine antelope; which added to our larder, and we were ready to proceed. We embarked and travelled until nightfall, when we encamped on a beautiful little prairie at the base of a series of grass-covered bluffs; and the next morning cooked our breakfast and ate it, and rowed on until late in the afternoon; when we stopped at the base of some huge clay bluffs, forming one of the most curious and romantic scenes imaginable. At this spot the river expands itself into the appearance somewhat of a beautiful lake; and in the midst of it, and on and about its sand-bars, floated and stood, hundreds and thousands of white swans and pelicans.

Though the scene in front of our encampment at this place was placid and beautiful; with its flowing water—its wild fowl—and its almost endless variety of gracefully sloping hills and green prairies in the distance; yet it was not less wild and picturesque in our rear, where the rugged and various coloured bluffs were grouped in all the wildest fancies and rudeness of Nature's accidental varieties.

The whole country behind us seemed to have been dug and thrown up into huge piles, as if some giant mason had been there mixing his mortar and paints, and throwing together his rude models for some sublime structure of a colossal city;—with its walls—its domes—its ramparts—its huge porticos and galleries—its castles—its fosses and ditches;—and in the midst of his progress, he had abandoned his works to the destroying hand of time, which had already done much to tumble them down, and deface their noble structure; by jostling them together, with all their vivid colours, into an unsystematic and unintelligible mass of sublime ruins.

To this group of clay bluffs, which line the river for many miles in distance, the voyageurs have very appropriately given the name of

37

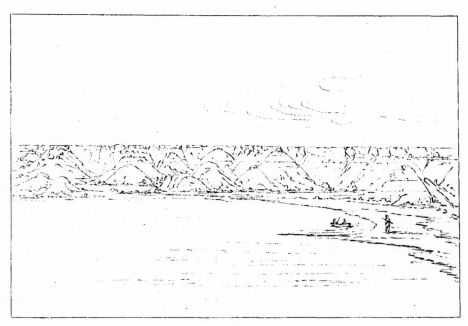

38

G. Catlin.

"the Brick-kilns;" owing to their red appearance, which may be discovered in a clear day at the distance of many leagues.

By the action of water, or other power, the country seems to have been graded away; leaving occasionally a solitary mound or bluff, rising in a conical form to the height of two or three hundred feet, generally pointed or rounded at the top, and in some places grouped together in great numbers; some of which having a tabular surface on the top, and covered with a green turf. This fact (as all of those which are horizontal on their tops, and corresponding exactly with the summit level of the wide-spreading prairies in distance) clearly shows, that their present isolated and rounded forms have been produced by the action of waters; which have carried away the intervening earth, and left them in the picturesque shapes in which they are now seen.

A similar formation (or *de*formation) may be seen in hundreds of places on the shores of the Missouri river, and the actual progress of the operation by which it is produced; leaving yet for the singularity of this place, the peculiar feature, that nowhere else (to my knowledge) occurs; that the superstratum, forming the tops of these mounds (where they remain high enough to support anything of the original surface) is composed, for the depth of fifteen feet, of red pumice; terminating at its bottom, in a layer of several feet of sedimentary deposit, which is formed into endless conglomerates of basaltic crystals.

This strange feature in the country arrests the eye of a traveller suddenly, and as instantly brings him to the conclusion, that he stands in the midst of the ruins of an extinguished volcano.

As will be seen in the drawings (Fig. 37, a near view, and Fig. 38, a distant view), the sides of these conical bluffs (which are composed of strata of different coloured clays), are continually washing down by the effect of the rains and melting of the frost; and the superincumbent masses of pumice and basalt are crumbling off, and falling down to their bases; and from thence, in vast quantities, by the force of the gorges of water which are often cutting their channels between them—carried into the river, which is close by; and wafted for thousands of miles, floating as light as a cork upon its surface, and lodging in every pile of drift-wood from this place to the ocean.

The upper part of this layer of pumice is of a brilliant red; and when the sun is shining upon it, is as bright and vivid as vermilion. It is porous and open, and its specific gravity but trifling. These curious bluffs must be seen as they are in nature; or else in a painting, where their colours are faithfully given, or they lose their picturesque beauty, which consists in the variety of their vivid tints. The strata of clay are alternating from red to yellow—white—brown and dark blue; and so curiously arranged, as to form the most pleasing and singular effects.

During the day that I loitered about this strange scene, I left my men stretched upon the grass, by the canoe; and taking my rifle and sketch-book in my hand, I wandered and clambered through the rugged defiles between the bluffs; passing over and under the immense blocks of the pumice, that had fallen to their bases; determined, if possible, to find the crater, or source, from whence these strange phenomena had sprung; but after clambering and squeezing about for some time, I unfortunately came upon the enormous tracks of a grizzly bear, which, apparently, was travelling in the same direction (probably for a very different purpose) but a few moments before me; and my ardour for exploring was instantly so cooled down, that I hastily retraced my steps, and was satisfied with making my drawings, and collecting specimens of the lava and other minerals in its vicinity.

After strolling about during the day, and contemplating the beauty of the scenes that were around me, while I sat upon the pinnacles of these pumice-capped mounds; most of which time, Bogard and Ba'tiste laid enjoying the pleasure of a "mountaineer's nap" we met together—took our coffee and dried buffalo tongues—spread our buffalo robes upon the grass, and enjoyed during the night the luxury of sleep, that belongs so peculiarly to the tired voyageur in these realms of pure air and dead silence.

In the morning, and before sunrise, as usual, Bogard (who was a Yankee, and a "wide-awake-fellow," just retiring from a ten years' siege of hunting and trapping in the Rocky Mountains), thrust his head out from under the robe, rubbing his eyes open, and exclaiming as he grasped for his gun, "By darn, look at old Cale! will you!" Ba'tiste, who was more fond of his dreams, snored away, muttering something that I could not understand, when Bogard seized him with a grip, that instantly shook off his iron slumbers. I rose at the same time, and all eyes were turned at once upon *Caleb* (as the grizzly bear is familiarly called by the trappers in the Rocky Mountains—or more often "Cale," for brevity's sake), who was sitting up in the dignity and fury of her sex, within a few rods, and gazing upon us, with her two little cubs at her side! here was a *"fix,"* and a subject for the painter; but I had no time to sketch it—I turned my eyes to the canoe which had been fastened at the shore a few paces from us; and saw that everything had been pawed out of it, and all eatables had been without ceremony devoured. My packages of dresses and Indian curiosities had been drawn out upon the bank, and deliberately opened and inspected. Every thing had been scraped and pawed out, to the bottom of the boat; and even the raw-hide thong, with which it was tied to a stake, had been chewed, and no doubt swallowed, as there was no trace of it remaining. Nor was this peep into the secrets of our luggage enough for her insatiable curiosity—we saw by the prints of her huge paws, that were left in the ground, that she had been perambulating our humble mattresses, smelling at our toes and our noses, without choosing to molest us; verifying a, trite saying of the country, "That man laying down is *medicine* to the grizzly bear;" though it is a well-known fact, that man and beast, upon their feet, are sure to be attacked when they cross the path of this grizzly and grim monster, which is the terror of all this country; often growing to the enormous size of eight hundred or one thousand pounds.

Well—whilst we sat in the dilemma which I have just described, each one was hastily preparing his weapons for defence, when I proposed the mode of attack; by which means I was in hopes to destroy her—capture her young ones, and bring her skin home as a trophy. My plans, however, entirely failed, though we were well armed; for Bogard and Ba'tiste both remonstrated with a vehemence that was irresistible; saying that the standing rule in the mountains was "never to fight Caleb, except in self-defence." I was almost induced, however, to attack her alone, with my rifle in hand, and a pair of heavy pistols; with a tomahawk and scalping-knife in my belt; when Ba'tiste suddenly thrust his arm over my shoulder and pointing in another direction, exclaimed in an empathic tone, "Voila! voila un corps de reserve—Monsr. Cataline—voila sa mari! allons—allons! déscendons la riviére, toute de suite! toute de suite! Monsr.," to which Bogard added, "these darned animals are too much for us, and we had better be off;" at which my courage cooled, and we packed up and re-embarked as fast as possible; giving each one of them the contents of our rifles as we drifted off in the current; which brought the she-monster, in all her rage and fury, to the spot where we, a moment before, had passed our most prudent resolve.

During the rest of this day, we passed on rapidly, gazing on and admiring the beautiful shores, which were continually changing, from the high and ragged cliffs, to the graceful and green slopes of the prairie bluffs; and then to the wide expanded meadows, with their long waving grass, enamelled with myriads of wild flowers.

The scene was one of enchantment the whole way; our chief

conversation was about grizzly bears and hair's-breadth escapes; of the histories of which my companions had volumes in store.—Our breakfast was a late one—cooked and eaten about five in the afternoon; at which time our demolished larder was luckily replenished by the unerring rifle of Bogard, which brought down a fine antelope, as it was innocently gazing at us, from the bank of the river. We landed our boat, and took in our prize; but there being no wood for our fire, we shoved off, and soon ran upon the head of an island, that was covered with immense quantities of raft and drift wood, where we easily kindled a huge fire and ate our delicious meal from a clean peeled log, astride of which we comfortably sat, making it answer admirably the double purpose of chairs and a table. After our meal was finished, we plied the paddles, and proceeded several miles further on our course; leaving our fire burning, and dragging our canoe upon the shore, in the dark, in a wild and unknown spot; and silently spreading our robes for our slumbers, which it is not generally considered prudent to do by the side of our fires, which might lead a war-party upon us, who often are prowling about and seeking an advantage over their enemy.

The scenery of this day's travel, as I have before said, was exceedingly beautiful; and our canoe was often run to the shore, upon which we stepped to admire the endless variety of wild flowers, "wasting their sweetness on the desert air," and the abundance of delicious fruits that were about us. Whilst wandering through the high grass, the wild sun-flowers and voluptuous lilies were constantly taunting us by striking our faces; whilst here and there, in every direction, there were little copses and clusters of plum trees and gooseberries, and wild currants, loaded down with their fruit; and amongst these, to sweeten the atmosphere and add a charm to the effect, the wild rose bushes seemed planted in beds and in hedges, and everywhere were decked out in all the glory of their delicate tints, and shedding sweet aroma to every breath of the air that passed over them.

In addition to these, we had the luxury of service-berries, without stint; and the buffalo bushes, which are peculiar to these northern regions, lined the banks of the river and defiles in the bluffs, sometimes for miles together; forming almost impassable hedges, so loaded with the weight of their fruit, that their boughs were everywhere gracefully bending down and resting on the ground.

This last shrub (*shepperdia*), which may be said to be the most beautiful ornament that decks out the wild prairies, forms a striking contrast to the rest of the foliage, from the blue appearance of its leaves, by which it can be distinguished for miles in distance. The fruit which it produces in such incredible profusion, hanging in clusters to every limb and to every twig, is about the size of ordinary currants, and not unlike them in colour and even in flavour; being exceedingly acid, and almost unpalatable, until they are bitten by the frosts of autumn, when they are sweetened, and their flavour delicious; having, to the taste, much the character of grapes, and I am inclined to think, would produce excellent wine.

The shrub which bears them resembles some varieties of the thorn, though (as I have said) differs entirely in the colour of its leaves. It generally grows to the height of six or seven feet, and often to ten or twelve; and in groves or hedges, in some places, for miles in extent. While gathering the fruit, and contemplating it as capable of producing good wine, I asked my men this question, "Suppose we three had ascended the river to this point in the spring of the year, and in a timbered bottom had pitched our little encampment; and one of you two had been a boat-builder, and the other a cooper—the one to have got out your staves and constructed the wine casks, and the other to have constructed a mackinaw-boat, capable of carrying fifty or a hundred casks; and I had been a good hunter, capable of supplying the little encampment with meat; and we should have started off about this time, to float down the current, stopping our boat wherever we saw the finest groves of the buffalo bush, collecting the berries and expressing the juice, and putting it into our casks for fermentation while on the water for two thousand miles; how many bushels of these berries could you two gather in a day, provided I watched the boat and cooked your meals? and how many barrels of good wine do you think we could offer for sale in St Louis when we arrived there?"

This idea startled my two men exceedingly, and Ba'tiste gabbled so fast in French, that I could not translate: and I am almost willing to believe, that but for the want of the requisite tools for the enterprise, I should have lost the company of Bogard and Ba'tiste; or that I should have been under the necessity of submitting to one of the unpleasant alternatives which are often regulated by the *majority* in this strange and singular wilderness.

I at length, however, got their opinions on the subject; when they mutually agreed that they could gather thirty bushels of this fruit per day; and I gave it then, and I offer it now, as my own also, that their estimate was not out of the way, and judged so from the experiments which we made in the following manner:—We several times took a large mackinaw blanket which I had in the canoe, and spreading it on the ground under the bushes, where they were the most abundantly loaded with fruit; and by striking the stalk of the tree with a club, we received the whole contents of its branches in an instant on the blanket, which was taken up by the corners, and not unfrequently would produce us, from one blow, the eighth part of a bushel of this fruit; when the boughs, relieved of their burden, instantly flew up to their native position.

Of this beautiful native, which I think would form one of the loveliest ornamental shrubs for a gentleman's park or pleasure grounds, I procured a number of the roots; but which, from the many accidents and incidents that our unlucky bark was subjected to on our rough passage, I lost them (and almost the recollection of them) as well as many other curiosities I had collected on our way down the river.

On the morning of the next day, and not long after we had stopped and taken our breakfast, and while our canoe was swiftly gliding along under the shore of a beautiful prairie, I saw in the grass, on the bank above me, what I supposed to be the back of a fine elk, busy at his grazing. I let our craft float silently by for a little distance, when I communicated the intelligence to my men, and slily ran in, to the shore. I pricked the priming of my firelock, and taking a bullet or two in my mouth, stepped ashore, and trailing my rifle in my hand, went back under the bank, carefully crawling up in a little ravine, quite sure of my game; when to my utter surprise and violent alarm, I found the elk to be no more nor less than an Indian pony, getting his breakfast! and a little beyond him, a number of others grazing; and nearer to me, on the left, a war-party reclining around a little fire; and yet nearer, and within twenty paces of the muzzle of my gun, the naked shoulders of a brawny Indian, who seemed busily engaged in cleaning his gun. From this critical dilemma, the reader can easily imagine that I vanished with all the suddenness and secrecy that was possible, bending my course towards my canoe. Bogard and Ba'tiste correctly construing the expression of my face, and the agitation of my hurried retreat, prematurely unmoored from the shore; and the force of the current carrying them around a huge pile of drift wood, threw me back for some distance upon my own resources; though they finally got in, near the shore, and I into the boat, with the steering oar in my hand; when we plied our sinews with effect and in silence, till we were wafted far from the ground which we deemed critical and dangerous to our lives; for we had been daily in dread of meeting a war-party of the revengeful Riccarees, which we had been told was

22

39

40

G. Catlin.

on the river, in search of the Mandans. From and after this exciting occurrence, the entries in my journal for the rest of the voyage to the village of the Mandans, were as follow:—

Saturday, fifth day of our voyage from the mouth of Yellow Stone, at eleven o'clock—Landed our canoe in the grand détour (or Big Bend) as it is called, at the base of a stately clay mound, and ascended, all hands, to the summit level, to take a glance at the picturesque and magnificent works of nature that were about us. Spent the remainder of the day in painting a view of this grand scene; for which purpose Ba'tiste and Bogard carried my easel and canvas to the top of a huge mound, where they left me at my work; and I painted my picture (Fig. 39), whilst they amused themselves with their rifles, decoying a flock of antelopes, of which they killed several, and abundantly added to the stock of our provisions.

Scarcely anything in nature can be found, I am sure, more exceedingly picturesque than the view from this place; exhibiting the wonderful manner in which the gorges of the river have cut out its deep channel through these walls of clay on either side, of two or three hundred feet in elevation; and the imposing features of the high table-lands in distance, standing as a perpetual anomaly in the country, and producing the indisputable, though astounding evidence of the fact, that there has been at some ancient period, a *super* surface to this country, corresponding with the elevation of these tabular hills, whose surface, for half a mile or more, on their tops, is perfectly level; being covered with a green turf, and yet one hundred and fifty or two hundred feet elevated above what may now be properly termed the summit level of all this section of country; as will be seen stretching off at their base, without furnishing other instances in hundreds of miles, of anything rising one foot above its surface, excepting the solitary group which is shown in the painting.

The fact, that *there* was once the summit level of this great valley, is a stubborn one, however difficult it may be to reconcile it with reasonable causes and results; and the mind of feeble man is at once almost paralysed in endeavouring to comprehend the process by which the adjacent country, from this to the base of the Rocky Mountains, as well as in other directions, could have been swept away; and equally so, for knowledge of the place where its mighty deposits have been carried.

I recollect to have seen on my way up the river, at the distance of six or eight hundred miles below, a place called "the Square Hills." and another denominated "the Bijou Hills;" which are the only features on the river, seeming to correspond with this strange *remain,* and which, on my way down, I shall carefully examine; and not fail to add their testimonies (if I am not mistaken in their character) to further speculations on this interesting feature of the geology of the great valley of the Missouri. Whilst my men were yet engaged in their sporting excursions, I left my easel and travelled to the base and summit of these tabular hills; which, to my great surprise, I found to be several miles from the river, and a severe journey to accomplish getting back to our encampment at nightfall. I found by their sides that they were evidently of an alluvial deposit, composed of a great variety of horizontal layers of clays of different colours—of granitic sand and pebbles (many of which furnished me beautiful specimens of agate, jasper and carnelians), and here and there large fragments of pumice and cinders, which gave, as instances above-mentioned, evidences of volcanic remains.

The mode by which Bogard and Ba'tiste had been entrapping the timid and sagacious antelopes was one which is frequently and successfully practised in this country; and on this day had afforded them fine sport.

The antelope of this country, I believe to be different from all other known varieties, and forms one of the most pleasing, living ornaments to this western world. They are seen in some places in great numbers sporting and playing about the hills and dales; and often, in flocks of fifty or a hundred, will follow the boat of the descending voyageur, or the travelling caravan, for hours together; keeping off at a safe distance, on the right or left, galloping up and down the hills, snuffing their noses and stamping their feet; as if they were endeavouring to remind the traveller of the wicked trespass he was making on their own hallowed ground.

This little animal seems to be endowed, like many other gentle and sweet breathing creatures, with an undue share of curiosity, which often leads them to destruction; and the hunter who wishes to entrap them, saves himself the trouble of travelling after them, When he has been discovered, he has only to elevate above the tops of the grass, his red or yellow handkerchief on the end of his gun-rod (Fig. 40), which he sticks in the ground, and to which they are sure to advance, though with great coyness and caution; whilst he lies close, at a little distance, with his rifle in hand; when it is quite an easy matter to make sure of two or three at a shot, which he gets in range of his eye, to be pierced with one bullet.

On Sunday, departed from our encampment in the Grand Détour; and having passed for many miles, through a series of winding and ever-varying bluffs and fancied ruins, like such as have

41

42

already been described, our attention was more than usually excited by the stupendous scene (Fig. 41), called by the voyageurs "the Grand Dome," which was lying in full view before us.

Our canoe was here hauled ashore, and a day whiled away again, amongst these clay-built ruins.

We clambered to their summits and enjoyed the distant view of the Missouri for many miles below, wending its way through the countless groups of clay and grass-covered hills; and we wandered back on the plains, in a toilsome and unsuccessful pursuit of a herd of buffaloes, which we discovered at some distance. Though we were disappointed in the results of the chase; yet we were in a measure repaid in amusements, which we found in paying a visit to an extensive village of prairie dogs, and of which I should render some account.

I have subjoined a sketch (Fig. 42) of one of these *sub-terra* communities; though it was taken in a former excursion, when my party was on horseback, and near the mouth of the Yellow Stone River; yet it answers for this place as well as any other, for their habits are one and the same wherever they are found; their houses or burrows are all alike, and as their location is uniformly on a level and desolate prairie, without timber, there is little room for variety or dissimilarity.

The prairie dog of the American Prairies is undoubtedly a variety of the marmot; and probably not unlike those which inhabit the vast Steppes of Asia. It bears no resemblance to any variety of dogs, except in the sound of its voice, when excited by the approach of danger, which is something like that of a very small dog, and still much more resembling the barking of a grey squirrel.

The size of these curious little animals is not far from that of a very large rat, and they are not unlike them in their appearance. As I have said, their burrows are uniformly built in a lonely desert; and away, both from the proximity of timber and water. Each individual, or each family, dig their hole in the prairie, to the depth of eight or ten feet, throwing up the dirt from the excavation, in a little pile, in the form of a cone, which forms the only elevation for them to ascend; where they sit, to bark and chatter when an enemy is approaching their village. These villages are sometimes of several miles in extent; containing (I would almost say) myriads of their excavations and little dirt hillocks, and to the ears of their visitors, the din of their barkings is too confused and too peculiar to be described.

In the present instance, we made many fruitless endeavours to shoot them; but found our efforts to be entirely in vain. As we were approaching them at a distance, every one seemed to be perched up on his hind feet, on his appropriate domicile, with a significant jerk of his tail at every bark, positively disputing our right of approach. I made several attempts to get near enough to "draw a bead" upon one of them; and just before I was ready to fire (and as if they knew the limits of their safety), they sprang down into their holes, and instantly turning their bodies, showed their ears and the ends of their noses, as they were peeping out at me; which position they would hold, until the shortness of the distance subjected their scalps to danger again, from the aim of a rifle; when they instantly disappeared from our sight, and all was silence thereafter, about their premises as I passed them over; until I had so far advanced by them, that their ears were again discovered, and at length themselves, at full length, perched on the tops of their little hillocks and threatening as before; thus gradually sinking and rising like a wave before and behind me.

The holes leading down to their burrows, are four or five inches in diameter, and run down nearly perpendicular; where they undoubtedly communicate into something like a subterraneous city (as I have formerly learned from fruitless endeavours to dig them out), undermined and vaulted; by which means, they can travel for a great distance under the ground, without danger from pursuit.

Their food is simply the grass in the immediate vicinity of their burrows, which is cut close to the ground by their flat shovel teeth; and, as they sometimes live twenty miles from any water, it is to be supposed that they get moisture enough from the dew on the grass, on which they feed chiefly at night; or that (as is generally supposed) they sink wells from their under-ground habitations, by which they descend low enough to get their supply. In the winter, they are for several months invisible; existing, undoubtedly, in a torpid state, as they certainly lay by no food for that season—nor can they procure any. These curious little animals belong to almost every latitude in the vast plains of prairie in North America; and their villages, which I have sometimes encountered in my travels, have compelled my party to ride several miles out of our way to get by them; for their burrows are generally within a few feet of each other, and dangerous to the feet and the limbs of our horses.

The sketch of the bluffs denominated "the Grand Dome," of which I spoke but a few moments since, is a faithful delineatian of the lines and character of that wonderful scene; and the reader has here a just and striking illustration of the ruin-like appearances, as

24

43

44

G. Catlin

I have formerly described, that are so often met with on the banks of this mighty river.

This is, perhaps, one of the most grand and beautiful scenes of the kind to be met with in this country, owing to the perfect appearance of its several huge domes, turrets, and towers, which were everywhere as precise and as perfect in their forms as they are represented in the illustration. These stupendous works are produced by the continual washing down of the sides of these clay-formed hills; and although, in many instances, their sides, by exposure, have become so hardened, that their change is very slow; yet they are mostly subjected to continual phases, more or less, until ultimately their decomposition ceases, and their sides becoming seeded and covered with a green turf, which protects and holds them (and will hold them) unalterable; with carpets of green, and enamelled with flowers, to be gazed upon with admiration, by the hardy voyageur and the tourist, for ages and centuries to come.

On Monday, the seventh day from the mouth of the Yellow Stone River, we floated away from this noble scene; looking back again and again upon it, wondering at its curious and endless changes, as the swift current of the river hurried us by, and gradually out of sight of it. We took a sort of melancholy leave of it—but at every bend and turn in the stream, we were introduced to others—and others—and yet others, almost as strange and curious. At the base of one of these, although we had passed it, we with difficulty landed our canoe, and I ascended to its top, with some hours' labour; having to cut a foot-hold in the clay with my hatchet for each step, a great part of the way up its sides. So curious was this solitary bluff, standing alone as it did, to the height of 250 feet (Fig. 43), with its sides washed down into hundreds of variegated forms—with large blocks of indurated clay, remaining upon pedestals and columns as it were, and with such a variety of tints; that I looked upon it as a beautiful picture, and devoted an hour or two with my brush, in transferring it to my canvas.

In the after part of this day we passed another extraordinary scene which is denominated "the Three Domes" (Fig. 44), forming an exceedingly pleasing group, though requiring no further description for the reader, who is now sufficiently acquainted with these scenes to understand them.

On this day, just before night, we landed our little boat in front of the Mandan village; and amongst the hundreds and thousands who flocked towards the river to meet and to greet us, was Mr Kipp, the agent of the American Fur Company, who has charge of their

Establishment at this place. He kindly ordered my canoe to be taken care of, and my things to be carried to his quarters, which was at once done; and I am at this time reaping the benefits of his genuine politeness, and gathering the pleasures of his amusing and interesting society.

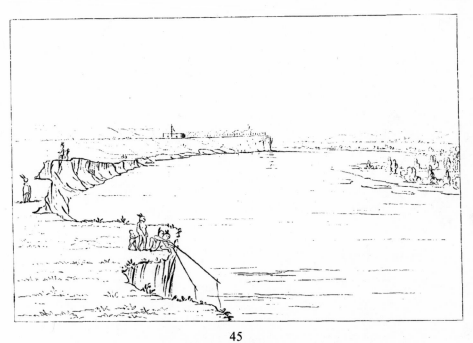

25

45

46

G. Catlin.

MANDAN VILLAGE, UPPER MISSOURI

I SAID that I was here in the midst of a strange people, which is literally true; and I find myself surrounded by subjects and scenes worthy the pens of Irving or Cooper; or the pencils of Raphael or Hogarth; rich in legends and romances, which would require no aid of the imagination for a book. or a picture.

The Mandans (or See-pohs-ka-nu-mah-kah-kee, "people of the pheasants"), as they call themselves, are perhaps one of the most ancient tribes of Indians in our country. Their origin, like that of all the other tribes is, from necessity, involved in mystery and obscurity. Their traditions and peculiarities I shall casually recite in this or future epistles; which, when understood, will at once, I think, denominate them a peculiar and distinct race. They take great pride in relating their traditions, with regard to their origin; contending that they were the *first* people created on earth. Their existence in these regions has, undoubtedly, been from a very ancient period; and, from what I could learn of their traditions, they have, at a former period, been a very numerous and powerful nation; but by the continual wars which have existed between them and their neighbours, they have been reduced to their present numbers.

This tribe is at present located on the west bank of the Missouri, about 1800 miles above St Louis, and 200 below the mouth of Yellow Stone River. They have two villages only, which are about two miles distant from each other; and number in all (as near as I can learn), about 2000 souls. Their present villages are beautifully located, and judiciously also, for defence against the assaults of their enemies. The site of the lower (or principal) town, in particular (Fig. 45), is one of the most beautiful and pleasing that can be seen in the world, and even more beautiful than imagination could ever create. In the very midst of an extensive valley (embraced within a thousand graceful swells and parapets or mounds of interminable green, changing to blue, as they vanish in distance) is built the city, or principal town of the Mandans. On an extensive plain (which is covered with a green turf, as well as the hills and dales, as far as the eye can possibly range, without tree or bush to be seen) are to

91

be seen rising from the ground, and towards the heavens, domes—
(not "of gold," but) of dirt—and the thousand spears (not "spires")
and scalp-poles, etc., etc., of the semi-subterraneous village of the
hospitable and gentlemanly Mandans.

These people formerly (and within the recollection of many of
their oldest men) lived fifteen or twenty miles farther down the river
in ten contiguous villages; the marks or ruins of which are yet
plainly to be seen. At that period, it is evident, as well from the
number of lodges which their villages contained, as from their traditions, that their numbers were much greater than at the present day.

There are other, and very interesting, traditions and historical
facts relative to a still prior location and condition of these people,
of which I shall speak more fully on a future occasion. From these,
when they are promulged, I think there may be a pretty fair deduction drawn, that they formerly occupied the lower part of the
Missouri, and even the Ohio and Muskingum, and have gradually
made their way up the Missouri to where they now are.

There are many remains on the river below this place (and, in
fact, to be seen nearly as low down as St Louis), which show clearly
the peculiar construction of Mandan lodges, and consequently carry
a strong proof of the above position. While descending the river,
however, which I shall commence in a few weeks, in a canoe, this
will be a subject of interest; and I shall give it close examination.

The ground on which the Mandan village is at present built, was
admirably selected for defence; being on a bank forty or fifty feet
above the bed of the river. The greater part of this bank is nearly
perpendicular, and of solid rock. The river, suddenly changing its
course to a right-angle, protects two sides of the village, which is
built upon this promontory or angle; they have therefore but one
side to protect, which is effectually done by a strong piquet, and a
ditch inside of it, of three or four feet in depth. The piquet is
composed of timbers of a foot or more in diameter, and eighteen feet
high, set firmly in the ground at sufficient distances from each other
to admit of guns and other missiles to be fired between them. The
ditch (unlike that of civilised modes of fortifications) is inside of the
piquet, in which their warriors screen their bodies from the view and
weapons of their enemies, whilst they are reloading and discharging
their weapons through the piquets.

The Mandans are undoubtedly secure in their villages, from the
attacks of any Indian nation, and have nothing to fear, except when
they meet their enemy on the prairie. Their village has a most
novel appearance to the eye of a stranger; their lodges are closely

grouped together, leaving but just room enough for walking and riding between them; and appear from without, to be built entirely of dirt; but one is surprised when he enters them, to see the neatness, comfort, and spacious dimensions of these earth-covered dwellings. They all have a circular form, and are from forty to sixty feet in diameter. Their foundations are prepared by digging some two feet in the ground, and forming the floor of earth, by levelling the requisite size for the lodge. These floors or foundations are all perfectly circular, and varying in size in proportion to the number of inmates, or of the quality or standing of the families which are to occupy them. The superstructure is then produced, by arranging, inside of this circular excavation, firmly fixed in the ground and resting against the bank, a barrier or wall of timbers, some eight or nine inches in diameter, of equal height (about six feet) placed on end, and resting against each other, supported by a formidable embankment of earth raised against them outside; then, resting upon the tops of these timbers or piles, are others of equal size and equal in numbers, of twenty or twenty-five feet in length, resting firmly against each other, and sending their upper or smaller ends towards the centre and top of the lodge; rising at an angle of forty-five degrees to the apex or sky-light, which is about three or four feet in diameter, answering as a chimney and a sky-light at the same time. The roof of the lodge being thus formed, is supported by beams passing around the inner part of the lodge about the middle of these poles or timbers, and themselves upheld by four or five large posts passing down to the floor of the lodge. On the top of, and over the poles forming the roof, is placed a complete mat of willow-boughs, of half a foot or more in thickness, which protects the timbers from the dampness of the earth, with which the lodge is covered from bottom to top, to the depth of two or three feet; and then with a hard or tough clay, which is impervious to water, and which with long use becomes quite hard, and a lounging place for the whole family in pleasant weather -for sage-for wooing lovers-for dogs and all; an airing place-a look-out-a place for gossip and mirth-a seat for the solitary gaze and meditations of the stern. warrior, who sits and contemplates the peaceful mirth and happiness that is breathed beneath him, fruits of his hard-fought battles, on fields of desperate combat with bristling Red Men.

The floors of these dwellings are of earth, but so hardened by use, and swept so clean, and tracked by bare and moccasined feet, that they have almost a polish, and would scarcely soil the whitest linen. In the centre, and immediately under the sky-light (Fig. 46) is the fire-place—a hole of four or five feet in diameter, of a circular form, sunk a foot or more below the surface, and curbed around with stone. Over the fire-place, and suspended from the apex of diverging props or poles, is generally seen the pot or kettle, filled with buffalo meat; and around it are the family, reclining in all the most picturesque attitudes and groups, resting on their buffalo-robes and beautiful mats of rushes. These cabins are so spacious, that they hold from twenty to forty persons—a family and all their connections. They all sleep on bedsteads similar in form to ours, but generally not quite so high; made of round poles rudely lashed together with thongs. A buffalo skin, fresh stripped from the animal, is stretched across the bottom poles, and about two feet from the floor; which, when it dries, becomes much contracted, and forms a perfect sacking-bottom. The fur side of this skin is placed uppermost, on which they lie with great comfort, with a buffalo-robe folded up for a pillow, and others drawn over them instead of blankets. These beds, as far as I have seen them (and I have visited almost every lodge in the village), are uniformly screened with a covering of buffalo or elk skins, oftentimes beautifully dressed and placed over the upright poles or frame, like a suit of curtains; leaving a hole in front, sufficiently spacious for the occupant to pass in and out, to and from his or her bed. Some of these coverings or curtains are exceedingly beautiful, being cut tastefully into fringe, and handsomely ornamented with porcupines' quills and picture writings or hieroglyphics.

From the great number of inmates in these lodges, they are necessarily very spacious, and the number of beds considerable. It is no uncommon thing to see these lodges fifty feet in diameter inside (which is an immense room), with a row of these curtained beds extending quite around their sides, being some ten or twelve of them, placed four or five feet apart, and the space between them occupied by a large post, fixed quite firm in the ground, and six or seven feet high, with large wooden pegs or bolts in it, on which are hung and grouped, with a wild and startling taste, the arms and armour of the respective proprietor; consisting of his whitened shield, embossed and emblazoned with a figure of his protecting *medicine* (or mystery), his bow and quiver, his war-club or battle-axe, his dart or javelin— his tobacco pouch and pipe—his medicine-bag—and his eagle— ermine or raven head-dress; and over all, and on the top of the post (as if placed by some conjuror or Indian magician, to guard and protect the spell of wildness that reigns in this strange place), stands forth and in full relief the head and horns of a buffalo, which is, by a village regulation, owned and possessed by every man in the nation, and hung at the head of his bed, which he uses as a mask when called upon by the chiefs, to join in the buffalo-dance, of which I shall say more in a future epistle.

This arrangement of beds, of arms, etc., combining the most vivid display and arrangement of colours, of furs, of trinkets—of barbed and glistening points and steel—of mysteries and hocus pocus, together with the sombre and smoked colour of the roof and sides of the lodge; and the wild, and rude and red—the graceful (though uncivil) conversational, garrulous, story-telling and happy, though ignorant and untutored groups, that are smoking their pipes—wooing their sweethearts, and embracing their little ones about their peaceful and endeared fire-sides; together with their pots and kettles, spoons, and other culinary articles of their own manufacture, around them; present altogether, one of the most picturesque scenes to the eye of a stranger, that can be possibly seen; and far more wild and vivid than could ever be imagined.

Reader, I said these people were garrulous, story-telling and happy; this is true, and literally so; and it belongs to me to establish the fact, and correct the error which seems to have gone forth to the world on this subject.

As I have before observed, there is no subject that I know of, within the scope and reach of human wisdom, on which the civilised world in this enlightened age are more incorrectly informed, than upon that of the true manners and customs, and moral condition, rights and abuses, of the North American Indians; and that, as I have also before remarked, chiefly on account of the difficulty of our cultivating a fair and honourable acquaintance with them, and doing them the justice, and ourselves the credit, of a fair and impartial investigation of their true character. The present age of refinement and research has brought every thing else that I know of (and a vast deal more than the most enthusiastic mind ever dreamed of) within the scope and fair estimation of refined intellect and of science; while the wild and timid savage, with his interesting customs and modes has vanished, or his character has become changed, at the approach of the enlightened and intellectual world; who follow him like a phantom for awhile, and in ignorance of his true character, at last turn back to the common business and social transactions of life.

Owing to the above difficulties, which have stood in the way, the world have fallen into many egregious errors with regard to the true modes and meaning of the savage, which I am striving to set forth and correct in the course of these epistles. And amongst them all, there is none more common, nor more entirely erroneous, nor more easily refuted, than the current one, that "the Indian is a sour, morose, reserved and taciturn man." I have heard this opinion advanced a thousand times and I believed it; but such certainly, is not uniformly nor generally the case.

I have observed in all my travels amongst the Indian tribes, and more particularly amongst these unassuming people, that they are a far more talkative and conversational race than can easily be seen in the civilised world. This assertion, like many others I shall occasionally make, will somewhat startle the folks at the East, yet it is true. No one can look into the wigwams of these people, or into any little momentary group of them, without being at once struck with the conviction that small-talk, gossip, garrulity, and story-telling, are the leading passions with them, who have little else to do in the world, but to while away their lives in the innocent and endless amusement of the exercise of those talents with which Nature has liberally endowed them, for their mirth and enjoyment.

One has but to walk or ride about this little town and its environs for a few hours in a pleasant day, and overlook the numerous games and gambols, where their notes and yelps of exultation are unceasingly vibrating in the atmosphere; or peep into their wigwams (and watch the glistening fun that's beaming from the noses, cheeks, and chins, of the crouching, cross-legged, and prostrate groups around the fire; where the pipe is passed, and jokes and anecdote, and laughter are excessive) to become convinced that it is natural to laugh and be merry. Indeed it would be strange if a race of people like these, who have little else to do or relish in life, should be curtailed in that source of pleasure and amusement; and it would be also strange, if a life-time of indulgence and practice in so innocent and productive a mode of amusement, free from the cares and anxieties of business or professions, should not advance them in their modes, and enable them to draw far greater pleasure from such sources, than we in the civilised and business world can possibly feel. If the uncultivated condition of their minds curtails the number of their enjoyments; yet they are free from, and independent of, a thousand cares and jealousies, which arise from mercenary motives in the civilised world; and are yet far a-head of us (in my opinion) in the real and uninterrupted enjoyment of their simple natural faculties.

They live in a country and in communities, where it is not customary to look forward into the future with concern, for they live without incurring the expenses of life, which are absolutely necessary and unavoidable in the enlightened world; and of course their inclinations and faculties are solely directed to the enjoyment of the present day, without the sober reflections on the past or apprehensions of the future.

With minds thus unexpanded and uninfluenced by the thousand passions and ambitions of civilised life, it is easy and natural to concentrate their thoughts and their conversation upon the little and trifling occurrences of their lives. They are fond of fun and good cheer, and can laugh easily and heartily at a slight joke, of which their peculiar modes of life furnish them an inexhaustible fund, and enable them to cheer their little circle about the wigwam fire-side with endless laughter and garrulity.

It may be thought, that I am taking a great deal of pains to establish this fact, and I am dwelling longer upon it than I otherwise should, inasmuch as I am opposing an error that seems to have become current through the world; and which, if it be once corrected, removes a material difficulty, which has always stood in the way of a fair and just estimation of the Indian character. For the purpose of placing the Indian in a proper light before the world, as I hope to do in many respects, it is of importance to me—it is but justice to the savage—and justice to my readers also, that such points should be cleared up as I proceed; and for the world who inquire for correct and just information, they must take my words for the truth, or else come to this country and look for themselves, into these grotesque circles of never-ending laughter and fun, instead of going to Washington City to gaze on the poor embarrassed Indian who is called there by his "Great Father," to contend with the sophistry of the learned and acquisitive world, in bartering away his lands with the graves and the hunting grounds of his ancestors. There is not the proper place to study the Indian character; yet it is the place where the sycophant and the scribbler go to gaze and frown upon him—to learn his character, and write his history! and because he does not speak, and quaffs the delicious beverage which he receives from white men's hands, "he's a speechless brute and a drunkard." An Indian is a beggar in Washington City, and a white man is almost equally so in the Mandan village. An Indian in Washington is mute, is dumb and embarrassed; and so is a white man (and for the very same reasons) in this place—he has nobody to talk to.

A wild Indian, to reach the civilised world, must needs travel some thousands of miles in vehicles of conveyance, to which he is unaccustomed—through latitudes and longitudes which are new to him—living on food that he is unused to—stared and gazed at by the thousands and tens of thousands whom he cannot talk to—his heart grieving and his body sickening at the exhibition of white men's wealth and luxuries, which are enjoyed on the land, and over the bones of his ancestors. And at the end of his journey he stands (like a caged animal) to be scanned—to be criticised—to be pitied—and heralded to the world as a mute—as a brute, and a beggar.

A white man, to reach this village, must travel by steam-boat—by canoes—on horseback and on foot; swim rivers—wade quagmires—fight mosquitoes—patch his moccasins, and patch them again and again, and his breeches; live on meat alone—sleep on the ground the whole way, and think and dream of his friends he has left behind; and when he gets here, half-starved, and half-naked, and more than half sick, he finds himself a beggar for a place to sleep, and for something to eat; a mute amongst thousands who flock about him, to look and to criticise, and to laugh at him for his jaded appearance, and to speak of him as they do of all white men (without distinction) as liars. These people are in the habit of seeing no white men in their country but Traders, and know of no other; deeming us all alike, and receiving us all under the presumption that we come to trade or barter; applying to us all, indiscriminately, the epithet of "liars" or Traders.

The reader will therefore see, that we mutually suffer in each other's estimation from the unfortunate ignorance, which distance has chained us in; and (as I can vouch, and the Indian also, who has visited the civilised world) that the historian who would record justly and correctly the character and customs of a people, must go and live among them.

47

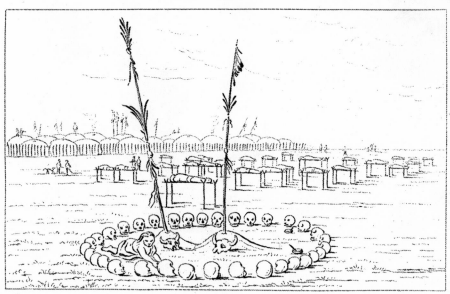

48

G. Catlin.

MANDAN VILLAGE, UPPER MISSOURI

IN my last, I gave some account of the village, and the customs, and appearances of this strange people—and I will now proceed to give further details on that subject.

I have this morning, perched myself upon the top of one of the earth-covered lodges, which I have before described, and having the whole village beneath and about me (Fig. 47), with its sachems—its warriors—its dogs—and its horses in motion—its medicines (or mysteries) and scalp-poles waving over my head—its piquets—its green fields and prairies, and river in full view, with the din and bustle of the thrilling panorama that is about me. I shall be able, I hope, to give some sketches more to the life than I could have done from any effort of recollection.

I said that the lodges or wigwams were covered with earth— were of forty or sixty feet in diameter, and so closely grouped that there was but just room enough to walk and ride between them,— that they had a door by which to enter them, and a hole in the top for the admission of light, and for the smoke to escape,—that the inmates were at times grouped upon their tops, in conversations and other amusements, etc.; and yet you know not exactly how they look, nor what is the precise appearance of the strange world that is about me. There is really a newness and rudeness in everything that is to be seen. There are several hundred houses or dwellings about me, and they are purely unique—they are all covered with dirt—the people are all red, and yet distinct from all other red folks I have seen. The horses are wild—every dog is a wolf—the whole moving mass are strangers to me: the living, in everything, carry an air of intractable wildness about them, and the dead are not buried, but dried upon scaffolds.

The groups of lodges around me present a very curious and pleasing appearance, resembling in shape (more nearly than anything else I can compare them to) so many potash-kettles inverted. On the tops of these are to be seen groups standing and reclining, whose wild and picturesque appearance it would be difficult to describe. Stern warriors, like statues, standing in dignified groups, wrapped in their painted robes, with their heads decked and plumed with quills of the war-eagle; extending their long arms to the east or the west, the scenes of their battles, which they are recounting over to each other. In another direction, the wooing lover, softening the heart of his fair Taih-nah-tai-a with the notes of his simple lute. On other lodges, and beyond these, groups are engaged in games of the "moccasin," or the "platter." Some are to be seen manufacturing robes and dresses, and others, fatigued with amusements or occupations, have stretched their limbs to enjoy the luxury of sleep, whilst basking in the sun. With all this wild and varied medley of living beings are mixed their dogs, which seem to be so near an Indian's heart, as almost to constitute a material link of his existence.

In the centre of the village is an open space, or public area, of 150 feet in diameter, and circular in form, which is used for all public games and festivals, shows and exhibitions; and also for their "annual religious ceremonies," which are soon to take place, and of which I shall hereafter give some account. The lodges around this open space front in, with their doors towards the centre; and in the middle of this circle stands an object of great religious veneration, as I am told, on account of the importance it has in the conduction of those annual religious rites.

This object is in form of a large hogshead, some eight or ten feet high, made of planks and hoops, containing within it some of their choicest medicines or mysteries, and religiously preserved, unhacked or scratched, as a symbol of the "Big Canoe," as they call it.

One of the lodges fronting on this circular area, and facing this strange object of their superstition, is called the "Medicine Lodge," or council house. It is in this sacred building that these wonderful ceremonies, in commemoration of the Flood, take place. I am told by the Traders that the cruelties of these scenes are frightful and abhorrent in the extreme; and that this huge wigwam, which is now closed, has been built exclusively for this grand celebration. I am every day reminded of the near approach of the season for this strange affair, and as I have not yet seen anything of it I cannot describe it; I know it only from the relations of the Traders who have witnessed parts of it; and their descriptions are of so extraordinary a character, that I would not be willing to describe until I can see for myself,—which will, in all probability, be in a few days,

In ranging the eye over the village from where I am writing, there is presented to the view the strangest mixture and medley of unintelligible trash (independent of the living beings that are in motion), that can possibly be imagined. On the roofs of the lodges, besides the groups of living, are buffaloes' skulls, skin canoes, pots and pottery; sleds and sledges—and suspended on poles, erected some twenty feet above the doors of their wigwams, are displayed in a pleasant day, the scalps of warriors, preserved as trophies; and thus proudly exposed as evidence of their warlike deeds. In other parts are raised on poles the warriors' pure and whitened shields and quivers, with medicine-bags attached; and here and there a sacrifice of red cloth, or other costly stuff, offered up to the Great Spirit, over the door of some benignant chief, in humble gratitude for the blessings which he is enjoying. Such is a part of the strange medley that is before and around me; and amidst them and the blue streams of smoke that are rising from the tops of these hundred "coal-pits," can be seen in distance, the green and boundless, treeless, bushless prairie; and on it, and contiguous to the piquet which encloses the village, a hundred scaffolds, on which their "dead live," as they term it.

These people never bury the dead, but place the bodies on slight scaffolds just above the reach of human hands, and out of the way of wolves and dogs; and they are there left to moulder and decay. This cemetery, or place of deposit for the dead, is just back of the village, on a level prairie (Fig. 48); and with all its appearances, history, forms, ceremonies, etc., is one of the strangest and most interesting objects to be described in the vicinity of this peculiar race.

Whenever a person dies in the Mandan village, and the customary honours and condolence are paid to his remains, and the body dressed in its best attire, painted, oiled, feasted, and supplied with bow and quiver, shield, pipe and tobacco—knife, flint and steel, and provisions enough to last him a few days on the journey which he is to perform; a fresh buffalo's skin, just taken from the animal's back, is wrapped around the body, and tightly bound and wound with thongs of raw hide from head to foot. Then other robes are soaked in water, till they are quite soft and elastic, which are also bandaged around the body in the same manner, and tied fast with thongs, which are wound with great care and exactness, so as to exclude the action of the air from all parts of the body.

There is then a separate scaffold erected for it, constructed of four upright posts, a little higher than human hands can reach; and on the tops of these are small poles passing around from one post to the others; across which a number of willow-rods just strong enough to support the body, which is laid upon them on its back, with its feet carefully presented towards the rising sun.

There are a great number of these bodies resting exactly in a similar way; excepting in some instances where a chief, or medicine-man, may be seen with a few yards of scarlet or blue cloth spread over his remains, as a mark of public respect and esteem. Some hundreds of these bodies may be seen reposing in this manner in this curious place, which the Indians call, "the village of the dead;" and the traveller, who visits this country to study and learn, will not only be struck with the novel appearance of the scene; but if he will give attention to the respect and devotions that are paid to this sacred place, he will draw many a moral deduction that will last him through life; he will learn, at least, that filial, conjugal, and paternal affection are not necessarily the results of civilisation; but that the Great Spirit has given them to man in his native state; and that the spices and improvements of the enlightened world have never refined upon them.

There is not a day in the year in which one may not see in this place evidences of this fact, that will wring tears from his eyes, and kindle in his bosom a spark of respect and sympathy for the poor Indian, if he never felt it before. Fathers, mothers, wives, and children, may be seen lying under these scaffolds, prostrated upon the ground, with their faces in the dirt, howling forth incessantly the most piteous and heart-broken cries and lamentations for the misfortunes of their kindred; tearing their hair—cutting their flesh with their knives, and doing other penance to appease the spirits of the dead, whose misfortunes they attribute to some sin or omission of their own, for which they sometimes inflict the most excruciating self-torture.

When the scaffolds on which the bodies rest, decay and fall to the ground, the nearest relations having buried the rest of the bones, take the skulls, which are perfectly bleached and purified, and place them in circles of a hundred or more on the prairie—placed at equal distances apart (some eight or nine inches from each other), with the faces all looking to the centre; where they are religiously protected and preserved in their precise positions from year to year, as objects of religious and affectionate veneration (Fig. 48).

There are several of these "Golgothas" or circles of twenty or thirty feet in diameter, and in the centre of each ring or circle is a little mound of three feet high, on which uniformly rests two buffalo skulls (a male and female); and in the centre of the little mound is erected a "medicine pole," about twenty feet high, supporting many curious articles of mystery and superstition, which they suppose have the power of guarding and protecting this sacred arrangement,

Here then, to this strange place do these people again resort, to evince their further affections for the dead—not in groans and lamentations however, for several years have cured the anguish; but fond affections and endearments are here renewed, and conversations are here held and cherished with the dead.

Every one of these skulls is placed upon a bunch of wild sage, which has been pulled and placed under it. The wife knows (by some mark or resemblance) the skull of her husband or her child, which lies in this group; and there seldom passes a day that she does not visit it, with a dish of the best cooked food that her wigwam affords, which she sets before the skull at night, and returns for the dish in the morning. As soon as it is discovered that the sage on which the skull rests is beginning to decay, the woman cuts a fresh bunch, and places the skull carefully upon it, removing that which was under it.

Independent of the above-named duties, which draw the women to this spot, they visit it from inclination, and linger upon it to hold converse and company with the dead. There is scarcely an hour in a pleasant day, but more or less of these women may be seen sitting or lying by the skull of their child or husband—talking to it in the most pleasant and endearing language that they can use (as they were wont to do in former days) and seemingly getting an answer back. It is not unfrequently the case, that the woman brings her needle-work with her, spending the greater part of the day, sitting by the side of the skull of her child, chatting incessantly with it, while she is embroidering or garnishing a pair of moccasins; and, perhaps, overcome with fatigue, falls asleep, with her arms encircled around it, forgetting herself for hours; after which she gathers up her things and returns to the village.

There is something exceedingly interesting and impressive in these scenes, which are so strikingly dissimilar, and yet within a few rods of each other; the one is the place where they pour forth the frantic anguish of their souls—and afterwards pay their visits to the other, to jest and gossip with the dead.

The great variety of shapes and characters exhibited in these groups of crania, render them a very interesting study for the craniologist and phrenologist; but I apprehend that it would be a matter of great difficulty (if not of impossibility) to procure them at this time, for the use and benefit of the scientific world.

LETTER—No. 13

IN several of my former Letters I have given sketches of the village, and some few of the customs of these peculiar people; and I have many more yet in store; some of which will induce the readers to laugh, and others almost dispose them to weep. But at present, I drop them, and introduce a few of the wild and gentlemanly Mandans themselves; and first, Ha-na-tah-au-mauh, the wolf chief (Fig. 49). This man is head-chief of the nation, and familiarly known by the name of "Chef de Loup," as the French Traders call him; a haughty, austere, and overbearing man, respected and feared by his people rather than loved. The tenure by which this man hold his office, is that by which the head-chiefs of most of the tribes claim, that of inheritance. It is a general, though not an infallible rule amongst the numerous tribes of North American Indians, that the office of chief belongs to the eldest son of a chief; provided he shows himself, by his conduct, to be equally worthy of it as any other in the nation; making it hereditary on a very proper condition—in default of which requisites, or others which may happen, the office is elective.

The dress of this chief was one of great extravagance, and some beauty; manufactured of skins, and a great number of quills of the raven, forming his stylish head-dress.

The next and second chief of the tribe, is Mah-to-toh-pa (the four bears). This extraordinary man, though second in office is un-doubtedly the first and most popular man in the nation. Free, generous, elegant, and gentlemanly in his deportment—handsome, brave and valiant; wearing a robe on his back, with the history of his battles emblazoned on it; which would fill a book of themselves, if properly translated. This, readers, is the most extraordinary man, perhaps, who lives at this day, in the atmosphere of Nature's noble-men; and I shall certainly tell you more of him anon.

After him, there are Mah-tahp-ta-ha, he who rushes through the middle (Fig. 50); Seehk-hee-da, the mouse-coloured feather (Fig. 51); San-ja-ka-ko-kah (the deceiving wolf); Mah-to-he-ha (the old bear), and others, distinguished as chiefs and warriors—and there are belles also; such as Mi-neek-e-sunk-te-ca, the mink (Fig. 53); and the

G. Catlin.

50

51

52

53

G. Catlin.

little grey-haired Sha-ko-ka, mint (Fig. 52); and fifty others, who are famous for their conquests, not with the bow or the javelin, but with their small black eyes, which shoot out from under their un-fledged brows, and pierce the boldest, fiercest chieftain to the heart.

The Mandans are certainly a very interesting and pleasing people in their personal appearance and manners; differing in many respects, both in looks and customs, from all other tribes which I have seen. They are not a warlike people; for they seldom, if ever, carry war into their enemies' country; but when invaded, show their valour and courage to be equal to that of any people on earth. Being a small tribe, and unable to contend on the wide prairies with the Sioux and other roaming tribes, who are ten times more numerous; they have very judiciously located themselves in a per-manent village, which is strongly fortified, and ensures their pre-servation. By this means they have advanced further in the arts of manufacture; have supplied their lodges more abundantly with the comforts, and even luxuries of life, than any Indian nation I know of. The consequence of this is, that this tribe have taken many steps ahead of other tribes in manners and refinements (if I may be allowed to apply the word refinement to Indian life); and are there-fore familiarly (and correctly) denominated, by the Traders and others, who have been amongst them, "the polite and friendly Mandans."

There is certainly great justice in the remark; and so forcibly have I been struck with the peculiar ease and elegance of these people, together with the diversity of complexions, the various colours of their hair and eyes; the singularity of their language, and their peculiar and unaccountable customs, that I am fully convinced that they have sprung from some other origin than that of the other North American tribes, or that they are an amalgam of natives with some civilised race.

Here arises a question of very great interest and importance for discussion; and, after further familiarity with their character, customs, and traditions, if I forget it not, I will eventually give it further consideration. Suffice it then, for the present, that their *personal appearance* alone, independent of their modes and customs, pronounces them at once, as more or less, than savage.

A stranger in the Mandan village is first struck with the different shades of complexion, and various colours of hair which he sees in a crowd about him; and is at once almost disposed to exclaim that "these are not Indians."

There are a great many of these people whose complexions appear as light as half breeds; and amongst the women particularly, there are many whose skins are almost white, with the most pleasing symmetry and proportion of features; with hazel, with grey, and with blue eyes,—with mildness and sweetness of expression, and excessive modesty of demeanour, which render them exceedingly pleasing and beautiful.

Why this diversity of complexion I cannot tell, nor can they themselves account for it. Their traditions, so far as I have yet learned them, afford us no information of their having had any knowledge of white men before the visit of Lewis and Clarke, made to their village thirty-three years ago. Since that time there have been but very few visits from white men to this place, and surely not enough to have changed the complexions and the customs of a nation. And I recollect perfectly well that Governor Clarke told me, before I started for this place, that I would find the Mandans a strange people and half white.

The diversity in the colour of hair is also equally as great as that in the complexion; for in a numerous group of these people (and more particularly amongst the females, who never take pains to change its natural colour, as the men often do), there may be seen every shade and colour of hair that can be seen in our own country, with the exception of red or auburn, which is not to be found.

And there is yet one more strange and unaccountable peculiarity, which can probably be seen nowhere else on earth; nor on any rational grounds accounted for,—other than it is a freak or order of Nature, for which she has not seen fit to assign a reason. There are very many, of both sexes, and of every age, from infancy to manhood and old age, with hair of a bright silvery grey; and in some instances almost perfectly white.

This singular and eccentric appearance is much oftener seen among the women than it is with the men; for many of the latter who have it, seem ashamed of it, and artfully conceal it, by filling their hair with glue and black and red earth. The women, on the other hand, seem proud of it, and display it often in an almost incredible profusion, which spreads over their shoulders and falls as low as the knee. I have ascertained, on a careful inquiry, that about one in ten or twelve of the whole tribe are what the French call "cheveux gris," or greyhairs; and that this strange and unaccountable phenomenon is not the result of disease or habit; but that it is unquestionably a hereditary character which runs in families, and indicates no inequality in disposition or intellect. And by passing this hair through my hands, as I often have, I have found

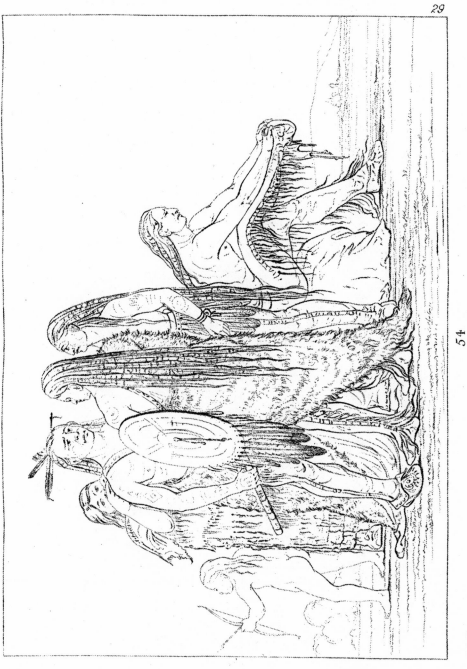

29

54

G. Catlin.

it uniformly to be as coarse and harsh as a horse's mane; differing materially from the hair of other colours, which amongst the Mandans, is generally as fine and as soft as silk.

The reader will at once see, by the above facts, that there is enough upon the faces and heads of these people to stamp them peculiar,—when he meets them in the heart of this almost boundless wilderness, presenting such diversities of colour in the complexion and hair; when he knows from what he has seen, and what he has read, that all other primitive tribes known in America, are dark copper-coloured, with jet black hair.

From these few facts alone, the reader will see that I am amongst a strange and interesting people, and know how to pardon me, if I lead him through a maze of novelty and mysteries to the knowledge of a strange, yet kind and hospitable, people, whose fate, like that of all their race, is sealed;—whose doom is fixed to live just long enough to be imperfectly known, and then to fall before the fell disease or sword of civilising devastation.

The stature of the Mandans is rather below the ordinary size of man, with beautiful symmetry of form and proportion, and wonderful suppleness and elasticity; they are pleasingly erect and graceful, both in their walk and their attitudes; and the hair of the men, which generally spreads over their backs, falling down to the hams, and sometimes to the ground, is divided into plaits or slabs of two inches in width, and filled with a profusion of glue and red earth or vermilion, at intervals of an inch or two, which becoming very hard, remains in and unchanged from year to year.

This mode of dressing the hair is curious, and gives to the Mandans the most singular appearance. The hair of the men is uniformly all laid over from the forehead backwards; carefully kept above and resting on the ear, and thence falling down over the back, in these flattened bunches, and painted red, extending oftentimes quite on to the calf of the leg, and sometimes in such profusion as almost to conceal the whole figure from the person walking behind them. In the portrait of San-ja-ka-ko-kah, the deceiving wolf (Fig. 54), where he is represented at full length, with several others of his family around him in a group, there will be seen a fair illustration of these and other customs of these people.

The hair of the women is also worn as long as they can possibly cultivate it, oiled very often, which preserves on it a beautiful gloss and shows its natural colour. They often braid it in two large plaits, one falling down just back of the ear, on each side of the head; and on any occasion which requires them to "put on their best looks," they pass their fingers through it, drawing it out of braid, and spreading it over their shoulders. The Mandan women observe strictly the same custom which I observed amongst the Crows and Blackfeet (and, in fact, all other tribes I have seen, without a single exception), of parting the hair on the forehead, and always keeping the crease or separation filled with vermilion or other red paint. This is one of the very few little (and apparently trivial) customs which I have found amongst the Indians, without being able to assign any cause for it, other than that "they are Indians," and that this is an Indian fashion.

In mourning, like the Crows and most other tribes, the women are obliged to crop their hair all off; and the usual term of that condolence is until the hair has grown again to its former length.

When a man mourns for the death of a near relation the case is quite different; his long, valued tresses, are of much greater importance, and only a lock or two can be spared. Just enough to tell of his grief to his friends, without destroying his most valued ornament, is doing just reverence and respect to the dead.

To repeat what I have said before, the Mandans are a pleasing and friendly race of people, of whom it is proverbial amongst the Traders and all who ever have known them, that their treatment of white men in their country has been friendly and kind ever since their first acquaintance with them—they have ever met and received them, on the prairie or in their villages, with hospitality and honour.

They are handsome, straight and elegant in their forms—not tall, but quick and graceful; easy and polite in their manners, neat in their persons and beautifully clad. When I say "neat in person and beautifully clad," however, I do not intend my readers to understand that such is the case with them all, for among them and most other tribes, as with the enlightened world, there are different grades of society—those who care but little for their personal appearance, and those who take great pains to please themselves and their friends. Amongst this class of personages, such as chiefs and braves, or warriors of distinction, and their families, and dandies or exquisites (a class of beings of whom I shall take due time to speak in a future Letter), the strictest regard to decency, and cleanliness and elegance of dress is observed; and there are few people, perhaps, who take more pains to keep their persons neat and cleanly than they do.

At the distance of half a mile or so above the village, is the customary place where the women and girls resort every morning in the summer months, to bathe in the river. To this spot they repair by hundreds, every morning at sunrise, where, on a beautiful beach, they can be seen running and glistening in the sun, whilst they are playing their innocent gambols and leaping into the stream. They all learn to swim well, and the poorest swimmer amongst them will dash fearlessly into the boiling and eddying current of the Missouri, and cross it with perfect ease. At the distance of a quarter of a mile back from the river, extends a terrace or elevated prairie, running north from the village, and forming a kind of semicircle around this bathing-place; and on this terrace, which is some twenty or thirty feet higher than the meadow between it and the river, are stationed every morning several sentinels, with their bows and arrows in hand, to guard and protect this sacred ground from the approach of boys or men from any directions.

At a little distance below the village, also, is the place where the men and boys go to bathe and learn to swim After this morning ablution, they return to their village, wipe their limbs dry, and use a profusion of bear's grease through their hair and over their bodies.

The art of swimming is known to all the American Indians; and perhaps no people on earth have taken more pains to learn it, nor any who turn it to better account. There certainly are no people whose avocations of life more often call for the use of their limbs in this way; as many of the tribes spend their lives on the shores of our vast lakes and rivers, paddling about from their childhood in their fragile bark canoes, which are liable to continual accidents, which often throw the Indian upon his natural resources for the preservation of his life.

There are many times also, when out upon their long marches in the prosecution of their almost continued warfare, when it becomes necessary to plunge into and swim across the wildest streams and rivers, at times when they have no canoes or craft in which to cross them. I have as yet seen no tribe where this art is neglected. It is learned at a very early age by both sexes, and enables the strong and hardy muscles of the squaws to take their child upon the back, and successfully to pass any river that lies in their way.

The mode of swimming amongst the Mandans, as well as amongst most of the other tribes, is quite different from that practised in those parts of the civilised world, which I have had the pleasure yet to visit. The Indian, instead of parting his hands simultaneously under the chin, and making the stroke outward, in a horizontal direction, causing thereby a serious strain upon the chest; throws his body alternately upon the left and the right side, raising one arm entirely above the water and reaching as far forward as he can, to dip it, whilst his whole weight and force are spent upon the one that is passing under him, and like a paddle propelling him along; whilst this arm is making a half circle, and is being raised out of the water behind him, the opposite arm is describing a similar arch in the air over his head, to be dipped in the water as far as he can reach before him, with the hand turned under, forming a sort of bucket, to act most effectively as it passes in its turn underneath him.

By this bold and powerful mode of swimming, which may want the grace that many would wish to see, I am quite sure, from the experience I have had, that much of the fatigue and strain upon the breast and spine are avoided, and that a man will preserve his strength and his breath much longer in this alternate and rolling motion, than he can in the usual mode of swimming in the polished world.

In addition to the modes of bathing which I have above described, the Mandans have another, which is a much greater luxury, and often resorted to by the sick, but far more often by the well and sound, as a matter of luxury only, or perhaps for the purpose of hardening their limbs and preparing them for the thousand exposures and vicissitudes of life to which they are continually liable. I allude to their vapour baths, or *sudatories,* of which each village has several, and which seem to be a kind of public property— accessible to all, and resorted to by all, male and female, old and young, sick and well.

In every Mandan lodge is to be seen a crib or basket, much in the shape of a bathing-tub, curiously woven with willow boughs, and sufficiently large to receive any person of the family in a reclining or recumbent posture; which, when any one is to take a bath, is carried by the squaw to the sudatory for the purpose, and brought back to the wigwam again after it has been used.

These sudatories are always near the village, above or below it, on the bank of the river. They are generally built of skins (in form of a Crow or Sioux lodge which I have before described), covered with buffalo skins sewed tight together, with a kind of furnace in the centre; or in other words, in the centre of the lodge are two walls of stone about six feet long and two and a half apart, and about three feet high; across and over this space, between the two walls, are laid a number of round sticks, on which the bathing crib is placed (*vide* Fig. 71). Contiguous to the lodge, and outside of it, is a little furnace something similar, in the side of the bank, where the woman kindles a hot fire, and heats to a red heat a number of large stones, which are kept at these places for this particular purpose; and having them all in readiness, she goes home or sends word to inform her husband or other one who is waiting, that all is ready; when he makes his appearance entirely naked, though with a large buffalo robe wrapped around him. He then enters the lodge and places himself in the crib or basket, either on his back or in a sitting posture (the latter of which is generally preferred), with his back towards the door of the lodge; when the squaw brings in a large stone red hot, between two sticks (lashed together somewhat in the form of a pair of tongs) and, placing it under him, throws cold water upon it, which raises a profusion of vapour about him. He is at once enveloped in a cloud of' steam, and a woman or child will sit at a little distance and continue to dash water upon the stone, whilst the matron of the lodge is out, and preparing to make her appearance with another heated stone: or he will sit and dip from a wooden bowl, with a ladle made of the mountain-sheep's horn, and throw upon the heated stones, with his own hands, the water which he is drawing through his lungs and pores, in the next moment, in the most delectable and exhilarating vapours, as it distils through the mat of wild sage and other medicinal and aromatic herbs, which he has strewed over the bottom of his basket, and on which he reclines.

During all this time the lodge is shut perfectly tight, and he quaffs this delicious and renovating draught to his lungs with deep drawn sighs, and with extended nostrils, until he is drenched in the most profuse degree of perspiration that can be produced; when he makes a kind of strangled signal, at which the lodge is opened, and he darts forth with the speed of a frightened deer, and plunges headlong into the river, from which he instantly escapes again, wraps his robe around him and "leans" as fast as possible for home. Here his limbs are wiped dry, and wrapped close and tight within the fur of the buffalo robes, in which he takes his nap, with his feet to the fire; then oils his limbs and hair with bear's grease, dresses and plumes himself for a visit—a feast—a parade, or a council; or slicks down his long hair, and rubs his oiled limbs to a polish, with a piece of soft buckskin, prepared to join in games of ball or Tchung-kee.

Such is the sudatory or the vapour bath of the Mandans, and, as I before observed, it is resorted to both as an everyday luxury by those who have the time and energy or industry to indulge in it; and also used by the sick as a remedy for nearly all the diseases which are known amongst them. Fevers are very rare, and in fact almost unknown amongst these people: but in the few cases of fever which have been known, this treatment has been applied, and without the fatal consequences which we would naturally predict. The greater part of their diseases are inflammatory rheumatisms, and other chronic diseases; and for these, this mode of treatment, with their modes of life, does admirably well. This custom is similar amongst nearly all of these Missouri Indians, and amongst the Pawnees, Omahas, and Punchas and other tribes, who have suffered with the small-pox (the dread destroyer of the Indian race), this mode was practised by the poor creatures, who fled by hundreds to the river's edge, and by hundreds died before they could escape from the waves, into which they had plunged in the heat and rage of a burning fever. Such will yet be the scourge, and such the misery of these poor unthinking people, and each tribe to the Rocky Mountains, as it has been with every tribe between here and the Atlantic Ocean. White men — whiskey — tomahawks — scalping knives—guns, powder and ball—small-pox—debauchery—extermination.

LETTER—No. 14

THE Mandans in many instances dress very neatly, and some of them splendidly. As they are in their native state, their dresses are all of their own manufacture; and of course, altogether made of skins of different animals belonging to those regions. There is, certainly, a reigning and striking similarity of costume amongst most of the North-Western tribes; and I cannot say that the dress of the Mandans is decidedly distinct from that of the Crows or the Blackfeet, the Assinneboins or the Sioux; yet there are modes of stitching or embroidering, in every tribe, which may at once enable the traveller, who is familiar with their modes, to detect or distinguish the dress of any tribe. These differences consist generally in the fashions of constructing the head-dress, or of garnishing their dresses with the porcupine quills, which they use in great profusion.

Amongst so many different and distinct nations, always at war with each other, and knowing nothing at all of each other's languages; and amongst whom, fashions in dress seldom if ever change; it may seem somewhat strange that we should find these people so nearly following, or imitating each other, in the forms and modes of their dress and ornaments. This must however, be admitted, and I think may be accounted for in a manner, without raising the least argument in favour of the theory of their having all sprung from one stock or one family; for in their continual warfare, when chiefs or warriors fall, their clothes and weapons usually fall into the possession of the victors, who wear them; and the rest of the tribe would naturally more or less often copy from or imitate them; and so also in their repeated councils or treaties of peace, such articles of dress and other manufactures are customarily exchanged, which are equally adopted by the other tribe; and consequently, eventually lead to the similarity which we find amongst the modes of dress, etc., of the different tribes.

The tunic or shirt of the Mandan men is very similar in shape to that of the Blackfeet—made of two skins of deer or mountain-sheep, strung with scalp-locks, beads, and ermine. The leggings, like those of the other tribes, of whom I have spoken, are made of deer skins, and shaped to fit the leg, embroidered with porcupine quills, and fringed with scalps from their enemies' heads. Their moccasins are made of buckskin, and neatly ornamented with porcupine quills—over their shoulders (or in other words, over one shoulder and passing under the other), they very gracefully wear a robe from the young buffalo's back, oftentimes cut down to about half its original size, to make it handy and easy for use. Many of these are also fringed on one side with scalp-locks; and the flesh side of the skin curiously ornamented with pictured representations of the creditable events and battles of their lives.

Their head-dresses are of various sorts, and many of them exceedingly picturesque and handsome; generally made of war-eagles' or ravens' quills and ermine. These are the most costly part of an Indian's dress in all this country, owing to the difficulty of procuring the quills and the fur. The war-eagle being the *"rara avis,"* and the ermine the rarest animal that is found in the country. The tail of a war-eagle in this village, provided it is a perfect one, containing some six or eight quills, which are denominated first-rate plumes, and suitable to arrange in a head-dress, will purchase a tolerable good horse (horses, however, are much cheaper here than they are in most other countries). I have had abundant oppor-tunities of learning the great value which these people sometimes attach to such articles of dress and ornament, as I have been pur-chasing a great many, which I intend to place in my Gallery of Indian Paintings, that the world may examine them for themselves, and thereby be enabled to judge of the fidelity of my works, and the ingenuity of Indian manufactures.

In these purchases I have often been surprised at the prices demanded by them; and perhaps I could not recite a better instance of the kind, than one which occurred here a few days since:—One of the chiefs, whom I had painted at full length, in a beautiful costume, with head-dress of war-eagle's quills and ermine, extending quite down to his feet; and whom I was soliciting for the purchase of his dress complete, was willing to sell to me all but the head-dress; saying, that "he could not part with that, as he would never be able to get quills and ermine of so good a quality to make another like it." I agreed with him, however, for the rest of the dress, and importuned him, from day to day, for the head-dress, until he at length replied, that, if I must have it, he must have two horses for it; the bargain was instantly struck—the horses were procured of the Traders at twenty-five dollars each, and the head-dress secured for my Collection.

There is occasionally, a chief or a warrior of so extraordinary renown, that he is allowed to wear horns on his head-dress, which give to his aspect a strange and majestic effect. These are made of about a third part of the horn of a buffalo bull; the horn having been split from end to end, and a third part of it taken and shaved thin and light, and highly polished. These are attached to the top of the head-dress on each side, in the same place that they rise and stand on the head of a buffalo; rising out of a mat of ermine skins and tails, which hang over the top of the head-dress, somewhat in the form that the large and profuse locks of hair hang and fall over the head of a buffalo bull. See head-dress in Figs. 14, 64, and 91, of three different tribes.

The same custom I have found observed amongst the Sioux,—the Crows—the Blackfeet and Assinneboins, and it is one of so striking a character as needs a few more words of observation, There is a peculiar meaning or importance (in their estimation) to this and many other curious and unaccountable appearances in the habits of Indians; upon which the world generally look as things that are absurd and ridiculous, merely because they are beyond the world's comprehensions, or because we do not stop to inquire or learn their uses or meaning.

I find that the principal cause why we underrate and despise the savage, is generally because we do not understand him; and the reason why we are ignorant of him and his modes, is that we do not stop to investigate—the world have been too much in the habit of looking upon him as altogether inferior—as a beast, a brute; and unworthy of more than a passing notice. If they stop long enough to form an acquaintance, it is but to take advantage of his ignorance and credulities—to rob him of the wealth and resources of his country;—to make him drunk with whiskey, and visit him with abuses which in his ignorance he never thought of. By this method his first visitors entirely overlook and never understand the meaning of his thousand interesting and characteristic customs; and at the same time, by changing his native modes and habits of life, blot them out from the view of the inquiring world for ever.

It is from the observance of a thousand little and apparently trivial modes and tricks of Indian life, that the Indian character must be learned; and, in fact, it is just the same with us if the subject were reversed: excepting that the system of civilised life would furnish ten apparently useless and ridiculous trifles to one which is found in Indian life; and at least twenty to one which are purely nonsensical and unmeaning.

The civilised world look upon a group of Indians, in their classic dress, with their few and simple oddities, all of which have their moral or meaning, and laugh at them excessively, because they are not like ourselves—we ask, "why do the silly creatures wear such great bunches of quills on their heads?—Such loads and streaks of paint upon their bodies—and bear's grease? abominable!" and a thousand other equally silly questions, without ever stopping to think that Nature taught them to do so—and that they all have some definite importance or meaning which an Indian could explain to us at once, if he were asked and felt disposed to do so—that each quill in his head stood, in the eyes of his whole tribe, as the symbol of an enemy who had fallen by his hand—that every streak of red paint covered a wound which he had got in honourable combat—and that the bear's grease with which he carefully anoints his body every morning, from head to foot, cleanses and purifies the body, and protects his skin from the bite of mosquitoes, and at the same time preserves him from colds and coughs which are usually taken through the pores of the skin.

At the same time, an Indian looks among the civilised world, no doubt, with equal, if not much greater, astonishment, at our apparently, as well as *really,* ridiculous customs and fashions; but he laughs not, nor ridicules, nor questions,—for his natural good sense and good manners forbid him,—until he is reclining about the fireside of his wigwam companions, when he vents forth his just criticisms upon the learned world, who are a rich and just theme for Indian criticism and Indian gossip.

An Indian will not ask a white man the reason why he does not oil his skin with bear's grease, or why he does not paint his body— or why he wears a hat on his head, or why he has buttons on the back part of his coat, where they never can be used—or why he wears whiskers, and a shirt collar up to his eyes—or why he sleeps with his head towards the fire instead of his feet—why he walks with his toes out instead of turning them in—or why it is that hundreds of white folk will flocks and crowd round a table to see an Indian eat—but he will go home to his wigwam fire-side, and "make the welkin ring" with jokes and fun upon the ignorance and folly of the knowing world.

A wild Indian thrown into the civilised atmosphere will see a man occasionally moving in society, wearing a cocked hat; and another with a laced coat and gold or silver epaulettes upon his shoulders, without knowing or inquiring the meaning of them, or the objects for which they are worn. Just so a white man travels amongst a wild and untaught tribe of Indians, and sees occasionally one of them parading about their village, with a head-dress of eagle's quills and ermine, and elevated above it a pair of beautifully polished buffalo horns; and just as ignorant is he also, of their meaning or importance; and more so, for the first will admit the presumption that epaulettes and cocked hats amongst the civilised world, are made for some important purpose,—but the latter will presume that horns on an Indian's head are nothing more nor less (nor can they ·be in their estimation), than Indian nonsense and stupidity.

This brings us to the "corned crest" again, and if the poor Indian scans epaulettes and cocked hats, without inquiring their meaning, and explaining them to his tribe, it is no reason why I should have associated with the noble dignitaries of these western regions, with horns and ermine on their heads, and then to have introduced the subject without giving some further clue to their importance and meaning. For me, this negligence would be doubly unpardonable, as I travel, not to *trade,* but to *herald* the Indian and his dying customs to posterity.

This custom then, which I have before observed belongs to all the North-Western tribes, is one no doubt of very ancient origin, having a purely classic meaning. No one wears the head-dress surmounted with horns except the dignitaries who are very high in authority, and whose exceeding valour, worth, and power is admitted by all the nation.

He may wear them, however, who is not a *chief;* but a brave, or warrior of such remarkable character, that he is esteemed universally in the tribe, as a man whose "voice is as loud in council" as that of a chief of the first grade, and consequently his *power* as great.

This head-dress with horns is used only on certain occasions, and they are very seldom. When foreign chiefs, Indian agents, or other important personages visit a tribe; or at war parades, at the celebration of a victory, at public festivals, etc., they are worn; but on no other occasions—unless, sometimes, when a chief sees fit to lead a war-party to battle, he decorates his head with this symbol of power, to stimulate his men; and throws himself into the foremost of the battle, inviting his enemy to concentrate their shafts upon him.

The horns on these head-dresses are but loosely attached at the bottom, so that they easily fall back or forward, according as the head is inclined forward or backward; and by an ingenious motion of the head, which is so slight as to be almost imperceptible— they are made to balance to and fro, and sometimes, one backward and the other forward like a horse's ears, giving a vast deal of expression and force of character, to the appearance of the chief who is wearing them. This, reader, is a remarkable instance (like hundreds of others), for its striking similarity to *Jewish customs,* to the kerns (or keren, in Hebrew), the horns worn by the Abyssinian chiefs and Hebrews, as a *symbol of power* and command; worn at great parades and celebrations of victories.

"The false prophet Zedekiah, made him horns of iron" (1 Kings xxii. 11). "Lift not your horns on high; speak not with a stiff neck" (Ps. lxxv. 5).

This last citation seems so exactly to convey to my mind the mode of raising and changing the position of the horns by a motion of the head, as I have above described, that I am irresistibly led to believe that this custom is now practised amongst these tribes very nearly as it was amongst the Jews; and that it has been, like many other customs of which I shall speak more in future epistles, handed down and preserved with very little innovation or change from that ancient people.

The reader will see this custom exemplified in the portrait of Mah-to-toh-pa (Fig. 64). This man, although the second chief, was the only man in the nation who was allowed to wear the horns; and all, I found, looked upon him as the leader, who had the power to lead all the warriors in time of war; and that, in consequence of the extraordinary battles which he had fought.

MANDAN VILLAGE, UPPER MISSOURI

A WEEK or more has elapsed since the date of my last Letter, and nothing as yet of the great and curious event—of the *Mandan religious ceremony*. There is evidently much preparation making for it, however; and from what I can learn, no one in the nation, save the *medicine-men,* have any knowledge of the exact day on which it is to commence. I am informed by the chiefs, that it takes place as soon as the willow-tree is in full leaf; for, say they, "the twig which the bird brought in was a willow bough, and had full-grown leaves on it." So it seems that this celebration has some relation to the Flood.

This great occasion is close at hand, and will, undoubtedly, commence in a few days; in the meantime I will give a few notes and memorandums, which I have made since my last.

I have been continually at work with my brush, with fine and picturesque subjects before me; and from the strange, whimsical, and superstitious notions which they have of an art so novel and unaccountable to them, I have been initiated into many of their mysteries—have witnessed many very curious incidents, and preserved several anecdotes, some of which I must relate.

Perhaps nothing ever more completely astonished these people than the operations of my *brush.* The art of portrait-painting was a subject entirely new to them, and of course, unthought of; and my appearance here has commenced a new era in the arcana of *medicine* or mystery. Soon after arriving here, I commenced and finished the portraits of the two principal chiefs. This was done without having awakened the curiosity of the villagers, as they had heard nothing of what was going on, and even the chiefs themselves seemed to be ignorant of my designs, until the pictures were completed. No one else was admitted into my lodge during the operation; and when finished, it was exceedingly amusing to see them mutually recognising each other's likeness, and assuring each other of the striking resemblance which they bore to the originals. Both of these pressed their hand over their mouths awhile in dead silence (a custom amongst most tribes, when anything surprises them very much); looking attentively upon the portraits and myself, and upon the palette and colours with which these unaccountable effects had been produced.

They then walked up to me in the most gentle manner, taking me in turn by the hand, with a firm grip; with head and eyes inclined downwards, and in a tone a little above a whisper—pronounced the words "te-ho-pe-nee Wash-ee!" and walked off.

Readers, at that moment I was christened with a new and a great name—one by which I am now familiarly hailed, and talked of in this village; and no doubt will be, as long as traditions last in this strange community.

That moment conferred an honour on me, which you as yet do not understand. I took the degree (not of Doctor of Laws, nor Bachelor of Arts) of Master of Arts—of mysteries—of magic, and of hocus pocus. I was recognised in that short sentence as a "great *medicine white man;*" and since that time, have been regularly installed *medicine* or mystery, which is the most honourable degree that could be conferred upon me here; and I now hold a place amongst the most eminent and envied personages, the doctors and conjurati of this titled community.

Te-ho-pe-nee Wash-ee (or medicine white man) is the name I now go by, and it will prove to me, no doubt, of more value than gold, for I have been called upon and feasted by the doctors, who are all mystery-men; and it has been an easy and successful passport already to many strange and mysterious places; and has put me in possession of a vast deal of curious and interesting information, which I am sure I never should have otherwise learned. I am daily growing in the estimation of the medicine-men and the chiefs; and by assuming all the gravity and circumspection due from so high a dignitary (and even considerably more); and endeavouring to perform now and then some art or trick that is unfathomable, I am in hopes of supporting my standing, until the great annual ceremony commences; on which occasion, I may possibly be allowed a seat in the *medicine-lodge* by the doctors, who are the sole conductors of this great source and fountain of all priestcraft and conjuration in this country.

After I had finished the portraits of the two chiefs, and they had returned to their wigwams, and deliberately seated themselves by their respective fire-sides, and silently smoked a pipe or two (according to an universal custom), they gradually began to tell what had taken place; and at length crowds of gaping listeners, with mouths wide open, thronged their lodges; and a throng of women and girls were about my house, and through every crack and crevice I could see their glistening eyes, which were piercing my hut in a hundred places, from a natural and restless propensity, a curiosity to see what was going on within. An hour or more passed in this way, and the soft and silken throng continually increased, until some hundreds of them were clung, and piled about my wigwam like a swarm of bees hanging on the front and sides of their hive.

During this time, not a man made his appearance about the premises—after awhile, however, they could be seen, folded in their robes, gradually *siding* up towards the lodge, with a silly look upon their faces, which confessed at once that curiosity was leading them reluctantly, where their pride checked and forbade them to go. The rush soon after became general, and the chiefs and medicine-men took possession of my room, placing *soldiers* (braves with spears in their hands) at the door, admitting no one, but such as were allowed by the chiefs, to come in.

Monsr. Kipp (the agent of the Fur Company, who has lived here eight years, and to whom, for his politeness and hospitality, I am much indebted), at this time took a seat with the chiefs, and, speaking their language fluently, he explained to them my views and the objects for which I was painting these portraits; and also expounded to them the manner in which they were made,—at which they seemed all to be very much pleased. The necessity at this time of exposing the portraits to the view of the crowds who were assembled around the house, became imperative, and they were held up together over the door, so that the whole village had a chance to see and recognise their chiefs. The effect upon so mixed a multitude, who as yet had heard no way of accounting for them, was novel and really laughable. The likenesses were instantly reeognised, and many of the gaping multitude commenced yelping; some were stamping off in the jarring dance—others were singing, and others again were crying—hundreds covered their mouths with their hands and were mute; others, indignant, drove their spears frightfully into the ground, and some threw a reddened arrow at the sun, and went home to their wigwams.

The pictures seen,—the next curiosity was to see the man who made them, and I was called forth. Readers! if you have any imagination, save me the trouble of painting this scene. * * * * * * I stepped forth, and was instantly hemmed in in the throng. Women were gaping and gazing—and warriors and braves were offering me their hands,—whilst little boys and girls, by dozens, were struggling through the crowd to touch me with the ends of their fingers; and whilst I was engaged, from the waist upwards, in fending off the throng and shaking hands, my legs were assailed (not unlike the nibbling of little fish, when I have been standing in deep water) by children who were creeping between the legs of the by-standers for the curiosity or honour of touching me with the end of their finger. The eager curiosity and expression of astonishment with which they gazed upon me, plainly showed that they looked upon me as some strange and unaccountable being. They pronounced me the greatest *medicine-man* in the world; for they said I had made *living beings*,—they said they could see their chiefs alive, in two places—those that I had made were a *little* alive—they could see their eyes move—could see them smile and laugh, and that if they could laugh they could certainly speak, if they should try, and they must therefore have *some life* in them.

The squaws generally agreed, that they had discovered life enough in them to render my *medicine* too great for the Mandans; saying that such an operation could not be performed without taking away from the original something of his existence, which I put in the picture, and they could see it move, could see it stir.

This curtailing of the natural existence, for the purpose of in-stilling life into the secondary one, they decided to be an useless and destructive operation, and one which was calculated to do great mis-chief in their happy community; and they commenced a mournful and doleful chaunt against me, crying and weeping bitterly through the village, proclaiming me a most "dangerous man; one who could make living persons by looking at them; and at the same time, could, as a matter of course, destroy life in the same way, if I chose. That my medicine was dangerous to their lives, and that I must leave the village immediately. That bad luck would happen to those whom I painted—that I was to take a part of the existence of those whom I painted, and carry it home with me amongst the white people, and that when they died they would never sleep quiet in their graves."

In this way the women and some old quack medicine-men together, had succeeded in raising an opposition against me; and the reasons they assigned were so plausible and so exactly suited for their superstitious feelings, that they completely succeeded in exciting fears and a general panic in the minds of a number of chiefs who had agreed to sit for their portraits, and my operations were, of course, for several days completely at a stand. A grave council was held on the subject from day to day, and there seemed great difficulty in deciding what was to be done with me and the dangerous art which I was practising; and which had far exceeded their original expecta-tions. I finally got admittance to their sacred conclave, and assured them that I was but a man like themselves,—that my art had no *medicine* or mystery about it, but could be learned by any of them if they would practice it as long as I had—that my intentions towards them were of the most friendly kind, and that in the country where I lived, brave men never allowed their squaws to frighten them with their foolish whims and stories. They all immediately arose, shook me by the hand, and dressed themselves for their pictures. After this, there was no further difficulty about sitting; all were ready to be painted,—the squaws were silent, and my painting-room a continual resort for the chiefs, and braves, and medicine-men; where they waited with impatience for the completion of each one's picture, —that they could decide as to the likeness as it came from under the brush; that they could laugh, and yell, and sing a new song, and smoke a fresh pipe to the health and success of him who had just been safely delivered from the hands and the mystic operation of the *"white medicine."*

In each of these operations, as they successfully took place, I observed that a pipe or two were well filled, and as soon as I commenced painting, the chiefs and braves, who sat around the sides of the lodge, commenced smoking for the success of the picture (and probably as much or more so for the safe deliverance of the sitter from harm while under the operation); and so they continued to pass the pipe around until the portrait was completed.

In this way I progressed with my portraits, stopping occasionally very suddenly as if something was wrong, and taking a tremendous puff or two at the pipe, and streaming the smoke through my nostrils, exhibiting in my looks and actions an evident relief; enabling me to proceed with more facility and success,—by flattering and complimenting each one on his good looks after I had got it done, and taking them according to rank, or standing, making it a matter of honour with them, which pleased them exceedingly, and give me and my art the stamp of respectability at once.

I was then taken by the arm by the chiefs, and led to their lodges, where feasts were prepared for me in elegant style, *i.e.* in the best manner which this country affords; and being led by the arm, and welcomed to them by *gentlemen* of high and exalted feelings, rendered them in my estimation truly elegant.

I was waited upon in due form and ceremony by the *medicine-men,* who received me upon the old adage, "Similis simili gaudet." I was invited to a feast, and they presented me a *she-shee-quoi,* or a doctor's rattle, and also a magical wand, or a doctor's staff, strung with claws of the grizzly bear, with hoofs of the antelope—with ermine—with wild sage and bat's wings—and perfumed withal with the *choice* and *savoury* odour of the pole-cat—a dog was sacrificed and hung by the legs over my wigwam, and I was therefore and thereby initiated into (and countenanced in the practice of) the arcana of medicine or mystery, and considered a Fellow of the Extraordinary Society of *Conjurati.*

Since this signal success and good fortune in my operations, things have gone on very pleasantly, and I have had a great deal of amusement. Some altercation has taken place, however, amongst the chiefs and braves, with regard to standing or rank, of which they are exceedingly jealous; and they must sit (if at all) in regular order, according to that rank; the trouble is all settled at last, however, and I have had no want of subjects, though a great many have become again alarmed, and are unwilling to sit, for fear, as some say, that they will die prematurely if painted; and as others say, that if they are painted, the picture will live after they are dead, and they cannot sleep quiet in their graves.

I have had several most remarkable occurrences in my painting-room, of this kind, which have made me some everlasting enemies here; though the minds and feelings of the chiefs and medicine-men have not been affected by them. There has been three or four instances where proud and aspiring young men have been in my lodge, and after gazing at the portraits of the head-chief across the room (which sits looking them in the eyes), have raised their hands before their faces and walked around to the side of the lodge, on the right or left, from whence to take a long and fair side look at the chief, instead of staring him full in the face (which is a most unpardonable offence in all Indian tribes); and after having got in that position, and cast their eyes again upon the portrait which was yet looking them full in the face, have thrown their robes over their heads and bolted out of the wigwam, filled equally with astonishment and indignation; averring, as they always will in a sullen mood, that they "saw the eyes move,"—that as they walk around the room "the eyes of the portrait followed them." With these unfortunate gentlemen, repeated efforts have been made by the Traders, and also by the chiefs and doctors, who understand the illusion, to convince them of their error, by explaining the mystery; but they will not hear to any explanation whatever; saying, that "what they see with their eyes is always evidence enough for them;" that they always "believe their own eyes sooner than a hundred tongues," and all efforts to get them a second time to my room, or into my company in any place, have proved entirely unsuccessful.

30

55

G Catlin.

I had trouble brewing also the other day from another source; one of the *"medicines"* commenced howling and haranguing around my domicile, amongst the throng that was outside, proclaiming that all who were inside and being painted were fools and would soon die; and very materially affecting thereby my popularity. I however sent for him and called him in the next morning, when I was alone, having only the interpreter with me; telling him that I had had my eye upon him for several days, and had been so well pleased with his looks, that I had taken great pains to find out his history, which had been explained by all as one of a most extraordinary kind, and his character and standing in his tribe as worthy of my particular notice; and that I had several days since resolved that as soon as I had practised my hand long enough upon the others, to get the stiffness out of it (after paddling my canoe so far as I had) and make it to work easily and successfully, I would begin on his portrait, which I was then prepared to commence on that day, and that I felt as if I could do him justice. He shook me by the hand, giving me the "Doctor's grip," and beckoned me to sit down, which I did, and we smoked a pipe together. After this was over, he told me, that "he had no inimical feelings towards me, although he had been telling the chiefs that they were all fools, and all would die who had their portraits painted—that although he had set the old women and children all crying, and even made some of the young warriors tremble, yet he had no unfriendly feelings towards me, nor any fear or dread of my art." "I know your are a good man (said he), I know you will do no harm to any one, your medicine is great, and you are a great 'medicine-man.' I would like to see myself very well—and so would all of the chiefs; but they have all been many days in this medicine-house, and they all know me well, and they have not asked me to come in and be *made alive* with paints—my friend, I am glad that my people have told you who I am—my heart is glad—I will go to my wigwam and eat, and in a little while I will come, and you may go to work;"—another pipe was lit and smoked, and he got up and went off. I prepared my canvas and palette and whistled away the time until twelve o'clock, before he made his appearance; having used the whole of the fore-part of the day at his toilette, arranging his dress and ornamenting his body for his picture.

At that hour then, bedaubed and streaked with paints of various colours, with bear's grease and charcoal, with medicine-pipes in his hands and foxes' tails attached to his heels, entered Mah-to-he-hah, the old bear (Fig. 55), with a train of his own profession, who seated themselves around him; and also a number of boys, whom it was requested should remain with him, and whom I supposed it possible might have been pupils, whom he was instructing in the mysteries of *materia medica* and *hoca poca*. He took his position in the middle of the room, waving his eagle calumets in each hand, and singing his medicine-song which he sings over his dying patient, looking me full in the face until I completed his picture, which I painted at full length. His vanity has been completely gratified in the operation; he lies for hours together, day after day, in my room, in front of his picture, gazing intensely upon it; lights my pipe for me while I am painting—shakes hands with me a dozen times on each day, and talks of me, and enlarges upon my *medicine* virtues and my talents, wherever he goes; so that this new difficulty is now removed, and instead of preaching against me, he is one of my strongest and most enthusiastic friends and aids in the country.

There is yet to be described another sort of personage, that is often seen stalking about in all Indian communities, a kind of nondescript, with whom I have been somewhat annoyed, and still more amused, since I came to this village, of whom (or of *which*) I shall give some account in my next epistle.

BESIDES chiefs, and braves and doctors, of whom I have heretofore spoken, there is yet another character of whom I must say a few words before I proceed to other topics. The person I allude to, is the one mentioned at the close of my last Letter, and familiarly known and countenanced in every tribe as an Indian *beau* or *dandy*. Such personages may be seen on every pleasant day, strutting and parading around the village in the most beautiful and unsoiled dresses, without the honourable trophies however of scalp-locks and claws of the grizzly bear, attached to their costume, for with such things they deal not. They are not peculiarly anxious to hazard their lives in equal and honourable combat with the one, or disposed to cross the path of the other; but generally remain about the village, to take care of the women, and attire themselves in the skins of such animals as they can easily kill, without seeking the rugged cliffs for the war-eagle, or visiting the haunts of the grizzly bear. They plume themselves with swan's-down and quills of ducks, with braids and plaits of sweet-scented grass and other harmless and unmeaning ornaments which have no other merit than they themselves have, that of looking pretty and ornamental.

These clean and elegant gentlemen, who are very few in each tribe, are held in very little estimation by the chiefs and braves; inasmuch as it is known by all, that they have a most horrible aversion to arms, and are denominated "faint hearts" or "old women" by the whole tribe, and are therefore but little respected. They seem, however, to be tolerably well contented with the appellation, together with the celebrity they have acquired amongst the women and children for the beauty and elegance of their personal appearance; and most of them seem to take and enjoy their share of the world's pleasures, although they are looked upon as drones in society.

These gay and tinselled bucks may be seen in a pleasant day in all their plumes, astride of their pied or dappled ponies, with a fan in the right hand, made of a turkey's tail—with whip and a fly-brush attached to the wrist of the same hand, and underneath them a white and beautiful and soft pleasure-saddle, ornamented with porcupine quills and ermine, parading through and lounging about the village for an hour or so, when they will cautiously bend their course to the suburbs of the town, where they will sit or recline upon their horses for an hour or two, overlooking the beautiful games where the braves and the young aspirants are contending in manly and athletic amusements;—when they are fatigued with this severe effort, they wend their way back again, lift off their fine white saddle of doe's-skin, which is wadded with buffalo's hair, turn out their pony—take a little refreshment, smoke a pipe, fan themselves to sleep, and doze away the rest of the day.

Whilst I have been painting, from day to day, there have been two or three of these fops continually strutting and taking their attitudes in front of my door; decked out in all their finery, without receiving other benefit or other information, than such as they could discover through the cracks and seams of my cabin. The chiefs, I observed, passed them by without notice, and of course, without inviting them in; and they seemed to figure about my door from day to day in their best dresses and best attitudes, as if in hopes that I would select them as models, for my canvas. It was natural that I should do so, for their costume and personal appearance was entirely more beautiful that anything else to be seen in the village. My plans were laid, and one day when I had got through with all of the head men, who were willing to sit to be painted, and there were two or three of the chiefs lounging in my room, I stepped to the door and tapped one of these fellows on the shoulder, who took the hint, and stepped in, well-pleased and delighted with the signal and honourable notice I had at length taken of him and his beautiful dress. Readers, you cannot imagine what was the expression of gratitude which beamed forth in this poor fellow's face, and how high his heart beat with joy and pride at the idea of my selecting him to be immortal, alongside of the chiefs and worthies whose portraits he saw arranged around the room; and by which honour he, undoubtedly, considered himself well paid for two or three weeks of regular painting, and greasing, and dressing, and standing alternately on one leg and the other at the door of my premises.

Well, I placed him before me, and a canvas on my easel, and "chalked him out" at full length. He was truly a beautiful subject for the brush, and I was filled with enthusiasm—his dress from head to foot was of the skins of the mountain-goat, and dressed so neatly, that they were almost as soft and as white as Canton crape—around the bottom and the sides it was trimmed with ermine, and porcupine quills of beautiful dyes garnished it in a hundred parts; his hair, which was long, and spread over his back and shoulders, extending nearly to the ground, was all combed back and parted on his forehead like that of a woman. He was a tall and fine figure, with ease and grace in his movements, that were well worthy of a man of better caste. In his left hand he held a beautiful pipe—and in his right hand he plied his fan, and on his wrist was still attached his whip of elk's horn, and his fly-brush, made of the buffalo's tail. There was nought about him of the terrible, and nought to shock the finest, chastest intellect.

I had thus far progressed, with high-wrought feelings of pleasure, when the two or three chiefs, who had been seated around the lodge, and whose portraits I had before painted, arose suddenly, and wrapping themselves tightly in their robes, crossed my room with a quick and heavy step, and took an informal leave of my cabin. I was apprehensive of their displeasure, though I continued my work; and in a few moments the interpreter came furiously into my room, addressing me thus:—"My God, sir! this never will do; you have given great offence to the chiefs—they have made complaint of your conduct to me—they tell me this is a worthless fellow—a man of no account in the nation, and if you paint his picture, you must instantly destroy theirs; you have no alternative, my dear sir—and the quicker this chap is out of your lodge the better."

The same matter was explained to my sitter by the interpreter, when he picked up his robe, wrapped himself in it, plied his fan nimbly about his face, and walked out of the lodge in silence, but with quite a consequential smile, taking his old position in front of the door for awhile, after which he drew himself quietly off without further exhibition. So highly do Mandan braves and worthies value the honour of being painted; and so little do they value a man, however lavishly Nature may have bestowed her master touches upon him, who has not the pride and noble bearing of a warrior.

I spoke in a former Letter of Mah-to-toh-pa (the four bears), the second chief of the nation, and the most popular man of the Mandans—a high-minded and gallant warrior, as well as a polite and polished gentleman. Since I painted his portrait, as I before described, I have received at his hands many marked and signal attentions; some of which I must name to you, as the very relation of them will put you in possession of many little forms and modes of Indian life, that otherwise might not have been noted.

About a week since, this noble fellow stepped into my painting-room about twelve o'clock in the day, in full and splendid dress, and passing his arm through mine, pointed the way, and led me in the most gentlemanly manner, through the village and into his own lodge, where a feast was prepared in a careful manner and waiting our arrival. The lodge in which he dwelt was a room of immense size, some forty or fifty feet in diameter, in a circular form, and about twenty feet high—with a sunken curb of stone in the centre, of five or six feet in diameter and one foot deep, which contained the fire over which the pot was boiling. I was led near the edge of this curb, and seated on a very handsome robe, most ingeniously garnished and painted with hieroglyphics; and he seated himself gracefully on another one at a little distance from me; with the feast prepared in several dishes, resting on a beautiful rush mat, which was placed between us (Fig. 62).

The simple feast which was spread before us consisted of three dishes only, two of which were served in wooden bowls, and the third in an earthen vessel of their own manufacture, somewhat in shape of a bread-tray in our own country. This last contained a quantity of *pem-i-can* and *marrow-fat;* and one of the former held a fine brace of buffalo ribs, delightfully roasted; and the other was filled with a kind of paste or pudding, made of the flour of the *"pomme blanche,"* as the French call it, a delicious turnip of the prairie, finely flavoured with the buffalo berries, which are collected in great quantities in this country, and used with divers dishes in cooking, as we in civilised countries use dried currants, which they very much resemble.

A handsome pipe and a tobacco-pouch made of the otter skin, filled with k'nick-k'neck (Indian tobacco), laid by the side of the feast; and when we were seated, mine host took up his pipe, and deliberately filled it; and instead of lighting it by the fire, which he could easily have done, he drew from his pouch his flint and steel, and raised a spark with which he kindled it. He drew a few strong whiffs through it, and presented the stem of it to my mouth, through which I drew a whiff or two while he held the stem in his hands. This done, he laid down the pipe, and drawing his knife from his belt, cut off a very small piece of the meat from the ribs, and pronouncing the words "Ho-pe-ne-chee wa-pa-shee" (meaning a *medicine* sacrifice), threw it into the fire.

He then (by signals) requested me to eat, and I commenced, after drawing out from my belt my knife (which it is supposed that every man in this country carries about him, for at an Indian feast a knife is never offered to a guest). Reader, be not astonished that I sat and ate my dinner *alone,* for such is the custom of this strange land. In all tribes in these western regions it is an invariable rule that a chief never eats with his guests invited to a feast; but while they eat, he sits by, at their service, and ready to wait upon them; deliber-

31

56

G. Catlin

ately charging and lighting the pipe which is to be passed around after the feast is over. Such was the case in the present instance, and while I was eating, Mah-to-toh-pa sat cross-legged before me, cleaning his pipe and preparing it for a cheerful smoke when I had finished my meal. To this ceremony I observed he was making unusual preparation, and I observed as I ate, that after he had taken enough of the k'nick-k'neck or bark of the red willow, from his pouch, he rolled out of it also a piece of the *"castor,"* which it is customary amongst these folks to carry in their tobacco-sack to give it a flavour; and, shaving off a small quantity of it, mixed it with the bark, with which he charged his pipe. This done, he drew also from his sack a small parcel containing a fine powder, which was made of dried buffalo dung, a little of which he spread over the top (according also to custom), which was like tinder, having no other effect than that of lighting the pipe with ease and satisfaction. My appetite satiated, I straightened up, and with a whiff the pipe was lit, and we enjoyed together for a quarter of an hour the most delightful exchange of good feelings, amid clouds of smoke and pantomimic signs and gesticulations.

The dish of "pemican and marrow-fat," of which I spoke, was thus:—The first, an article of food used throughout this country, as familiarly as we use bread in the civilised world. It is made of buffalo meat dried very hard, and afterwards pounded in a large wooden mortar until it is made nearly as fine as sawdust, then packed in this dry state in bladders or sacks of skin, and is easily carried to any part of the world in good order. "Marrow-fat" is collected by the Indians from the buffalo bones which they break to pieces, yielding a prodigious quantity of marrow, which is boiled out and put into buffalo bladders which have been distended; and after it cools, becomes quite hard like tallow, and has the appearance, and very nearly the flavour, of the richest yellow butter. At a feast, chunks of this marrow-fat are cut off and placed in a tray or bowl, with the pemican, and eaten together; which we civilised folks in these regions consider a very good substitute for (and indeed we generally so denominate it) "bread and butter." In this dish laid a spoon made of the buffalo's horn, which was black as jet, and beautifully polished; in one of the others there was another of still more ingenious and beautiful workmanship, made of the horn of the mountain-sheep, or "Gros corn," as the French trappers call them; it was large enough to hold of itself two or three pints, and was almost entirely transparent.

I spoke also of the earthen dishes or bowls in which these viands

were served out; they are a familiar part of the culinary furniture
of every Mandan lodge, and are manufactured by the women of this
tribe in great quantities, and modelled into a thousand forms and
tastes. They are made by the hands of the women, from a tough
black clay, and baked in kilns which are made for the purpose, and
are nearly equal in hardness to our own manufacture of pottery;
though they have not yet got the art of glazing, which would be to
them a most valuable secret. They make them so strong and serviceable, however, that they hang them over the fire as we do our iron
pots, and boil their meat in them with perfect success. I have seen
some few specimens of such manufacture, which have been dug up
in Indian mounds and tombs in the southern and middle states,
placed in our Eastern Museum and looked upon as a great wonder,
when here this novelty is at once done away with, and the whole
mystery; where women can be seen handling and using them by
hundreds, and they can be seen every day in the summer also,
moulding them into many fanciful forms, and passing them through
the kiln where they are hardened.

Whilst sitting at this feast the wigwam was as silent as death,
although we were not alone in it. This chief, like most others, had
a plurality of wives, and all of them (some six or seven) were seated
around the sides of the lodge, upon robes or mats placed upon the
ground, and not allowed to speak, though they were in readiness to
obey his orders or commands, which were uniformly given by signs-
manual, and executed in the neatest and most silent manner.

When I arose to return, the pipe through which we had smoked
was presented to me; and the robe on which I had sat, he gracefully
raised by the corners and tendered it to me, explaining by signs that
the paintings which were on it were the representations of the
battles of his life, where he had fought and killed with his own hand
fourteen of his enemies; that he had been two weeks engaged in
painting it for me, and that he had invited me here on this occasion
to present it to me. The robe, readers, which I shall describe in a
future epistle, I took upon my shoulder, and he took me by the arm
and led me back to my painting-room.

MANDAN VILLAGE, UPPER MISSOURI

I MENTIONED in the foregoing epistle, that the chiefs of the Mandans frequently have a plurality of wives. Such is the custom amongst all of these North-Western tribes, and a few general remarks on this subject will apply to them all, and save the trouble of repeating them.

Polygamy is countenanced amongst all of the North American Indians, so far as I have visited them; and it is no uncommon thing to find a chief with six, eight, or ten, and some with twelve or fourteen wives in his lodge. Such is an ancient custom, and in their estimation is right as well as necessary. Women in a savage state, I believe, are always held in a rank inferior to that of the men, in relation to whom in many respects they stand rather in the light of menials and slaves than otherwise; and as they are the "hewers of wood and drawers of water," it becomes a matter of necessity for a chief (who must be liberal, keep open doors, and entertain, for the support of his popularity) to have in his wigwam a sufficient number of such handmaids or menials to perform the numerous duties and drudgeries of so large and expensive an establishment.

There are two other reasons for this custom which operate with equal, if not with greater force than the one above assigned. In the first place, these people, though far behind the civilised world in acquisitiveness, have still more or less passion for the accumulation ef wealth, or, in other words, for the luxuries of life; and a chief, excited by a desire of this kind, together with a wish to be able to furnish his lodge with something more than ordinary for the entertainment of his own people, as well as strangers who fall upon his hospitality, sees fit to marry a number of wives, who are kept at hard labour during most of the year; and the avails of that labour enable him to procure those luxuries, and give to his lodge the appearance of respectability which is not ordinarily seen. Amongst those tribes who trade with the Fur Companies, this system is carried out to a great extent, and the women are kept for the greater part of the year, dressing buffalo robes and other skins for the market; and the brave or chief, who has the greatest number of wives, is considered the most affluent and envied man in the tribe; for his table is most bountifully supplied, and his lodge the most abundantly furnished with the luxuries of civilised manufacture, who has at the year's end the greatest number of robes to vend to the Fur Company.

The manual labour amongst savages is all done by the women; and as there are no daily labourers or persons who will *"hire out"* to labour for another, it becomes necessary for him who requires more than the labour or services of one, to add to the number by legalising and compromising by the ceremony of marriage, his stock of labourers; who can thus, and thus alone, be easily enslaved, and the results of their labour turned to good account.

There is yet the other inducement, which probably is more effective than either; the natural inclination which belongs to man, who stands high in the estimation of his people and wields the sceptre of power—surrounded by temptations which he considers it would be unnatural to resist, where no law or regulation of society stands in the way of his enjoyment. Such a custom amongst savage nations can easily be excused too, and we are bound to excuse it, when we behold man in a state of nature, as he was made, following a natural inclination, which is sanctioned by ancient custom and by their religion, without a law or regulation of their society to discountenance it; and when, at the same time, such an accumulation of a man's household, instead of quadrupling his expenses (as would be the case in the civilised world), actually becomes his wealth, as the results of their labour abundantly secure to him all the necessaries and luxuries of life.

There are other and very rational grounds on which the propriety of such a custom may be urged, one of which is as follows:—as all nations of Indians in their natural condition are unceasingly at war with the tribes that are about them, for the adjustment of ancient and never-ending feuds, as well as from a love of glory, to which in Indian life the battle-field is almost the only road, their warriors are killed off to that extent, that in many instances two and sometimes three women to a man are found in a tribe. In such instances I have found that the custom of polygamy has kindly helped the community to an evident relief from a cruel and prodigious calamity.

The instances of which I have above spoken, are generally confined to the chiefs and medicine-men; though there is no regulation prohibiting a poor or obscure individual from marrying several wives, other than the personal difficulties which lie between him and the hand which he wishes in vain to get, for want of sufficient celebrity in society, or from a still more frequent objection, that of his inability (from want of worldly goods) to deal in the customary way with the fathers of the girls whom he would appropriate to his own household.

There are very few instances indeed, to be seen in these regions, where a poor or ordinary citizen has more than one wife; but amongst chiefs and braves of great reputation, and doctors, it is common to see some six or eight living under one roof, and all apparently quiet and contented; seemingly harmonising, and enjoying the modes of life and treatment that falls to their lot.

Wives in this country are mostly treated for with the father, as in all instances they are regularly bought and sold. In many cases the bargain is made with the father alone without ever consulting the inclinations of the girl, and seems to be conducted on his part as a mercenary contract entirely, where he stands out for the highest price he can possibly command for her. There are other instances to be sure, where the parties approach each other, and from the expression of a mutual fondness, make their own arrangements, and pass their own mutual vows, which are quite as sacred and inviolable as similar assurances when made in the civilised world. Yet even in such cases, the marriage is never consummated without the necessary form of making presents to the father of the girl.

It becomes a matter of policy and almost of absolute necessity, for the white men who are Traders in these regions to connect themselves in this way, to one or more of the most influential families in the tribe, which in a measure identifies their interest with that of the nation, and enables them, with the influence of their new family connections, to carry on successfully their business transactions with them. The young women of the best families only can aspire to such an elevation; and the most of them are exceedingly ambitious for such a connection, inasmuch as they are certain of a delightful exemption from the slavish duties that devolve upon them when married under other circumstances; and expect to be, as they generally are, allowed to lead a life of ease and idleness, covered with mantles of blue and scarlet cloth—with beads and trinkets, and ribbons, in which they flounce and flirt about, the envied and tinselled belles of every tribe.

These connections, however, can scarcely be called marriages, for I believe they are generally entered into without the form or solemnising ceremony of a marriage, and on the part of the father of the girls, conducted purely as a mercenary or business transaction; in which they are very expert, and practise a deal of shrewdness in exacting an adequate price from a purchaser whom they consider possessed of so large and so rich a stock of the world's goods; and who they deem abundantly able to pay liberally for so delightful a commodity.

Almost every Trader and every clerk who commences in the business of this country, speedily enters into such an arrangement, which is done with as little ceremony as he would bargain for a horse, and just as unceremoniously do they annul and abolish this connection when they wish to leave the country, or change their positions from one tribe to another; at which time the woman is left, a fair and proper candidate for matrimony or speculation, when another applicant comes along, and her father equally desirous for another horse or gun, etc., which he can easily command at her second espousal.

From the enslaved and degraded condition in which the women are held in the Indian country, the world would naturally think that theirs must be a community formed of incongruous and unharmonising materials; and consequently destitute of the fine, reciprocal feelings and attachments which flow from the domestic relations in the civilised world; yet it would be untrue, and doing injustice to the Indians, to say that they were in the least behind us in conjugal, in filial, and in paternal affection. There is no trait in the human character which is more universal than the attachments which flow from these relations, and there is no part of the human species who have a stronger affection and a higher regard for them than the North American Indians.

There is no subject in the Indian character of more importance to be rightly understood than this, and none either that has furnished me more numerous instances and more striking proofs, of which I shall make use on a future occasion, when I shall say a vast deal more of marriage—of divorce—of polygamy—and of Indian domestic relations. For the present I am scribbling about the looks and usages of the Indians who are about me and under my eye; and I must not digress too much into general remarks, lest I lose sight of those who are near me, and the first to be heralded.

Such then, are the Mandans—their women are beautiful and modest,—and amongst the respectable families, virtue is as highly cherished and as inapproachable, as in any society whatever; yet at the same time a chief may marry a dozen wives if he pleases, and so may a white man; and if either wishes to marry the most beautiful and modest girl in the tribe, she is valued only equal, perhaps to two horses, a gun with powder and ball for a year, five or six pounds of beads, a couple of gallons of whiskey, and a handful of awls.

The girls of this tribe, like those of most of these North-Western tribes, marry at the age of twelve or fourteen, and some at the age of eleven years; and their beauty, from this fact, as well as from the slavish life they lead, soon after marriage vanishes. Their occupations are almost continual, and they seem to go industriously at them, as if from choice or inclination, without a murmur.

The principal occupations of the women in this village, consist in procuring wood and water, in cooking, dressing robes and other skins, in drying meat and wild fruit, and raising corn (maize). The Mandans are somewhat of agriculturists, as they raise a great deal of corn and some pumpkins and squashes. This is all done by the women, who make their hoes of the shoulder-blade of the buffalo or the elk, and dig the ground over instead of ploughing it, which is consequently done with a vast deal of labour. They raise a very small sort of corn, the ears of which are not longer than a man's thumb. This variety is well adapted to their climate, as it ripens sooner than other varieties, which would not mature in so cold a latitude. The green corn season is one of great festivity with them, and one of much importance. The greater part of their crop is eaten during these festivals, and the remainder is gathered and dried on the cob, before it has ripened, and packed away in *"caches"* (as the French call them), holes dug in the ground, some six or seven feet deep, the insides of which are somewhat in the form of a jug, and tightly closed at the top. The corn, and even dried meat and pemican, are placed in these *caches,* being packed tight around the sides, with prairie grass, and effectually preserved through the severest winters.

Corn and dried meat are generally laid in, in the fall, in sufficient quantities to support them through the winter. These are the principal articles of food during that long and inclement season; and in addition to them, they oftentimes have in store great quantities of dried squashes and dried *pommes blanches,* a kind of turnip which grows in great abundance in these regions, and of which I have before spoken. These are dried in great quantities, and pounded into a sort of meal, and cooked with the dried meat and corn. Great quantities also of wild fruit of different kinds are dried and laid away in store for the winter season, such as buffalo berries, service berries, strawberries, and wild plums.

The buffalo meat, however, is the great staple and "staff of life" in this country, and seldom (if ever) fails to afford them an abundant and wholesome means of subsistence. There are, from a fair computation, something like 250,000 Indians in these western regions, who live almost exclusively on the flesh of these animals, through every part of the year. During the summer and fall months they use the meat fresh, and cook it in a great variety of ways, by roasting, broiling, boiling, stewing, smoking, etc.; and by boiling the ribs and joints with the marrow in them, make a delicious soup, which is universally used, and in vast quantities. The Mandans, I find, have no regular or stated times for their meals, but generally eat about twice in the twenty-four hours. The pot is always boiling over the fire, and any one who is hungry (either of the household or from any other part of the village) has a right to order it taken off, and to fall to eating as he pleases. Such is an unvarying custom amongst the North American Indians, and I very much doubt, whether the civilised world have in their institutions any system which can properly be called more humane and charitable. Every man, woman, or child in Indian communities is allowed to enter any one's lodge, and even that of the chief of the nation, and eat when they are hungry, provided misfortune or necessity has driven them to it. Even so can the poorest and most worthless drone of the nation; if he is too lazy to hunt or to supply himself, he can walk into any lodge, and any one will share with him as long as there is anything to eat. He, however, who thus begs when he is able to hunt, pays dear for his meat, for he is stigmatised with the disgraceful epithet of a poltroon and a beggar.

The Mandans, like all other tribes, sit at their meals cross-legged, or rather with their ankles crossed in front of them, and both feet drawn close under their bodies; or, which is very often the case also, take their meals in a reclining posture, with the legs thrown out, and the body resting on one elbow and fore-arm, which are under them. The dishes from which they eat are invariably on the ground or floor of the lodge, and the group resting on buffalo robes or mats of various structure and manufacture.

The position in which the women sit at their meals and on other occasions is different from that of the men, and one which they take and rise from again, with great ease and much grace, by merely bending the knees both together, inclining the body back and the head and shoulders quite forward, they squat entirely down to the ground, inclining both feet either to the right or the left. In this position they always rest while eating, and it is both modest and graceful, for they seem, with apparent ease, to assume the position and rise out of it, without using their hands in any way to assist them.

These women, however, although graceful and civil, and ever so beautiful or ever so hungry, are not allowed to sit in the same group with the men while at their meals. So far as I have yet travelled in Indian country, I never have seen an Indian woman eating with her husband. Men form the first group at the banquet, and women, and children and dogs all come together at the next, and these gormandise and glut themselves to an enormous extent, though the men very seldom do.

It is time that an error on this subject, which has gone generally abroad in the world, was corrected. It is everywhere asserted, and almost universally believed, that the Indians are "enormous eaters;" but comparatively speaking, I assure my readers that this is an error. I venture to say that there are no persons on earth who practise greater prudence and self-denial, than the men do (amongst the wild Indians), who are constantly in war and in the chase, or in their athletic sports and exercises; for all of which they are excited by the highest ideas of pride and honour, and every kind of excess is studiously avoided; and for a very great part of their lives, the most painful abstinence is enforced upon themselves, for the purpose of preparing their bodies and their limbs for these extravagant exertions. Many a man who has been a few weeks along the frontier, amongst the drunken, naked and beggared part of the Indian race, and run home and written a book on Indians, has, no doubt, often seen them eat to beastly excess; and he has seen them also guzzle whiskey (and perhaps *sold* it to them) till he has seen them glutted and besotted without will or energy to move; and many and thousands of such things can always be seen, where white people have made beggars of them, and they have nothing to do but lie under a fence and beg a whole week to get meat and whiskey enough for one feast and one carouse; but amongst the wild Indians in this country there are no beggars—no drunkards—and every man, from a beautiful natural precept, studies to keep his body and mind in such a healthy shape and condition as will at all times enable him to use his weapons in self-defence, or struggle for the prize in their manly games.

As I before observed, these men generally eat but twice a day, and many times not more than once, and those meals are light and simple compared with the meals that are swallowed in the civilised world; and by the very people also, who sit at the festive board three times a day, making a jest of the Indian for his eating, when they actually guzzle more liquids, besides their eating, than would fill the stomach of an Indian.

There are, however, many seasons and occasions in the year with all Indians, when they fast for several days in succession; and others where they can *get* nothing to eat; and at such times (their habits are such) they may be seen to commence with an enormous meal, and because they do so, it is an insufficient reason why we should for ever remain under so egregious an error with regard to a single custom of these people.

I have seen so many of these, and lived with them, and travelled with them, and oftentimes felt as if I should starve to death on an equal allowance, that I am fully convinced I am correct in saying that the North American Indians, taking them in the aggregate, even where they have an abundance to subsist on, eat less than any civilised population of equal numbers, that I ever travelled amongst.

Their mode of curing and preserving the buffalo meat is somewhat curious, and in fact it is almost incredible also; for it is all cured or dried in the sun, without the aid of salt or smoke! The method of doing this is the same amongst all the tribes, from this to the Mexican Provinces, and is as follows:—The choicest parts of the flesh from the buffalo are cut out by the squaws, and carried home on their backs or on horses, and there cut *"across the grain,"* in such a manner as will take alternately the layers of lean and fat; and having prepared it all in this way, in strips about half an inch in thickness, it is hung up by hundreds and thousands of pounds on poles resting on crotches, out of the reach of dogs or wolves, and exposed to the rays of the sun for several days, when it becomes so effectually dried, that it can be carried to any part of the world without damage. This seems almost an unaccountable thing, and the more so, as it is done in the hottest months of the year, and also in all the different latitudes of an Indian country.

So singular a fact as this can only be accounted for, I consider, on the ground of the extraordinary rarity and purity of the air which we meet with in these vast tracts of country, which are now properly denominated "the great buffalo plains," a series of exceedingly elevated plateaus of *steppes* or *prairies,* lying at and near the base of the Rocky Mountains.

It is a fact then, which I presume will be new to most of the world, that meat can be cured in the sun without the aid of smoke or salt; and it is a fact equally true and equally surprising also, that none of these tribes use salt in any way, although their country abounds in salt springs; and in many places, in the frequent walks of the Indian, the prairie may be seen, for miles together, covered with an incrustation of salt as white as the drifted snow.

I have, in travelling with Indians, encamped by such places, where they have cooked and eaten their meat, when I have been unable to prevail on them to use salt in any quantity whatever.

The Indians cook their meat more than the civilised people do, and I have long since learned, from necessity, that meat thus cooked can easily be eaten and relished too, without salt or other condiment.

The fact above asserted applies exclusively to those tribes of Indians which I have found in their primitive state, living entirely on meat; but everywhere along our frontier, where the game of the country has long since been chiefly destroyed, and these people have become semi-civilised, raising and eating, as we do, a variety of vegetable food, they use (and no doubt require) a great deal of salt; and in many instances use it even to destructive excess.

LETTER—No. 18

THE Mandans, like all other tribes, lead lives of idleness and leisure; and of course, devote a great deal of time to their sports and amusements, of which they have a great variety. Of these, dancing is one of the principal, and may be seen in a variety of forms: such as the buffalo dance, the boasting dance, the begging dance, the scalp dance, and a dozen other kinds of dances, all of which have their peculiar characters and meanings or objects.

These exercises are exceedingly grotesque in their appearance, and to the eye of a traveller who knows not their meaning or importance, they are an uncouth and frightful display of starts, and jumps, and yelps, and jarring gutturals, which are sometimes truly terrifying. But when one gives them a little attention, and has been lucky enough to be initiated into their mysterious meaning, they become a subject of the most intense and exciting interest. Every dance has its peculiar step, and every step has its meaning; every dance also has its peculiar song, and that is so intricate and mysterious oftentimes, that not one in ten of the young men who are dancing and singing it, know the meaning of the song which they are chanting over. None but the medicine-men are allowed to understand them; and even they are generally only initiated into these secret arcana, on the payment of a liberal stipend for their tuition, which requires much application and study. There is evidently a set song and sentiment for every dance, for the songs are perfectly measured, and sung in exact time with the beat of the drum; and always with an uniform and invariable set of sounds and expressions, which clearly indicate certain sentiments, which are expressed by the voice, though sometimes not given in any known language whatever.

They have other dances and songs which are not so mystified, but which are sung and understood by every person in the tribe, being sung in their own language, with much poetry in them, and perfectly metred, but without rhyme. On these subjects I shall take another occasion to say more; and will for the present turn your attention to the style and modes in which some of these curious transactions are conducted.

My ears have been almost continually ringing since I came here, with the din of yelping and beating of the drums; but I have for several days past been peculiarly engrossed, and my senses almost confounded with the stamping, and grunting, and bellowing of the *buffalo dance,* which closed a few days since at sunrise (thank Heaven), and which I must needs describe to you.

Buffaloes, it is known, are a sort of roaming creatures, congregating occasionally in huge masses, and strolling away about the country from east to west, or from north to south, or just where their whims or strange fancies may lead them; and the Mandans are sometimes, by this means, most unceremoniously left without any thing to eat; and being a small tribe, and unwilling to risk their lives by going far from home in the face of their more powerful enemies, are oftentimes left almost in a state of starvation. In any emergency of this kind, every man musters and brings out of his lodge his mask (the skin of a buffalo's head with the horns on), which he is obliged to keep in readiness for this occasion; and then commences the buffalo dance, of which I have above spoken, which is held for the purpose of making "buffalo come" (as they term it), of inducing the buffalo herds to change the direction of their wanderings, and bend their course towards the Mandan village, and graze about on the beautiful hills and bluffs in its vicinity, where the Mandans can shoot them down and cook them as they want them for food.

For the most part of the year, the young warriors and hunters, by riding out a mile or two from the village, can kill meat in abundance; and sometimes large herds of these animals may be seen grazing in full view of the village. There are other seasons also when the young men have ranged about the country as far as they are willing to risk their lives, on account of their enemies, without finding meat. This sad intelligence is brought back to the chiefs and doctors, who sit in solemn council, and consult on the most expedient measures to be taken, until they are sure to decide upon the old and only expedient which "never has failed."

The chief issues his order to his runners or criers, who proclaim it through the village—and in a few minutes the dance begins. The place where this strange operation is carried on is in the public area in the centre of the village, and in front of the great medicine or mystery lodge. About ten or fifteen Mandans at a time join in the dance, each one with the skin of the buffalo's head (or mask) with the horns on, placed over his head, and in his hand his favourite bow or lance, with which he is used to slay the buffalo.

I mentioned that this dance always had the desired effect, that it

never fails, nor can it, for it cannot be stopped (but is going incessantly day and night) until "buffalo come." Drums are beating and
rattles are shaken, and songs and yells incessantly are shouted, and
lookers-on stand ready with masks on their heads, and weapons in
hand, to take the place of each one as he becomes fatigued, and jumps
out of the ring.

During this time of general excitement, spies or *lookers* are kept
on the hills in the neighbourhood of the village, who, when they
discover buffaloes in sight, give the appropriate signal, by "throwing
their robes," which is instantly seen in the village, and understood
by the whole tribe. At this joyful intelligence there is a shout of
thanks to the Great Spirit, and more especially to the mystery-man,
and the dancers, who *have been the immediate cause of their success!*
There is then a brisk preparation for the chase—a grand hunt takes
place. The choicest pieces of the victims are sacrificed to the Great
Spirit, and then a surfeit and a carouse.

These dances have sometimes been continued in this village two
and three weeks without stopping an instant, until the joyful moment
when buffaloes made their appearance. So they *never fail;* and they
think they have been the means of bringing them in.

Every man in the Mandan village (as I have before said) is obliged
by a village regulation, to keep the mask of the buffalo, hanging on
a post at the head of his bed, which he can use on his head whenever
he is called upon by the chiefs, to dance for the coming of buffaloes.
The mask is put over the head, and generally has a strip of the skin
hanging to it, of the whole length of the animal, with the tail attached
to it, which, passing down over the back of the dancer, is dragging on
the ground (Fig. 56). When one becomes fatigued of the exercise,
he signifies it by bending quite forward, and sinking his body towards
the ground; when another draws a bow upon him and hits him with
a blunt arrow, and he falls like a buffalo—is seized by the bystanders,
who drag him out of the ring by the heels, brandishing their knives
about him; and having gone through the motions of skinning and
cutting him up, they let him off, and his place is at once supplied by
another, who dances into the ring with his mask on; and by this
taking of places, the scene is easily kept up night and day, until the
desired effect has been produced, that of "making buffalo come."

The day before yesterday however, readers, which, though it
commenced in joy and thanksgiving to the Great Spirit for the signal
success which had attended their several days of dancing and suppli-
cation, ended in a calamity which threw the village of the Mandans
into mourning and repentant tears, and that at a time of scarcity and

32

57

G.Catlin.

great distress. The signal was given into the village on that morning from the top of a distant bluff, that a band of buffaloes were in sight, though at a considerable distance off, and every heart beat with joy, and every eye watered and glistened with gladness.

The dance had lasted some three or four days, and now, instead of the doleful tap of the drum and the begging chants of the dancers, the stamping of horses was heard as they were led and galloped through the village—young men were throwing off their robes and their shirts—were seen snatching a handful of arrows from their quivers, and stringing their sinewy bows, glancing their eyes and their smiles at their sweethearts, and mounting their ponies.   *

*   *   *   *   A few minutes there had been of bustle and boasting, whilst bows were twanging, and spears were polishing by running their blades into the ground—every face and every eye was filled with joy and gladness—horses were pawing and snuffing in fury for the outset, when Louison Frénié, an interpreter of the Fur Company, galloped through the village with his rifle in his hand and his powder-horn at his side; his head and his waist were bandaged with handkerchiefs, and his shirt sleeves rolled up to his shoulders—the hunter's yell issued from his lips and was repeated through the village; he flew to the bluffs, and behind him and over the graceful swells of the prairie, galloped the emulous youths, whose hearts were beating high and quick for the onset.

In the village, where hunger had reigned, and starvation was almost ready to look them in the face, all was instantly turned to joy and gladness. The chiefs and doctors who had been for some days dealing out minimum rations to the community from the public crib, now spread before their subjects the contents of their own private *caches,* and the last of everything that could be mustered, that they might eat a thanksgiving to the Great Spirit for his goodness in sending them a supply of buffalo meat. A general carouse of banqueting ensued, which occupied the greater part of the day; and their hidden stores, which might have fed an emergency for several weeks, were pretty nearly used up on the occasion—bones were half picked, and dishes half emptied, and then handed to the dogs. *I* was not forgotten neither, in the general surfeit; several large and generous wooden bowls of pemican and other palatable food were sent to my painting-room, and I received them in this time of scarcity with great pleasure.

After this general indulgence was over, and the dogs had licked the dishes, their usual games and amusements ensued—and hilarity, and mirth, and joy took possession of, and reigned in, every nook and corner of the village; and in the midst of this, screams and shrieks were heard! and echoed everywhere.—Women and children scrambled to the tops of their wigwams, with their eyes and their hands stretched in agonising earnestness to the prairie, whilst blackened warriors ran furiously through every winding maze of the village, and issuing their jarring gutturals of vengeance, as they snatched their deadly weapons from their lodges, and struck the reddened post as they furiously passed it by! Two of their hunters were bending their course down the sides of the bluff towards the village, and another broke suddenly out of a deep ravine, and yet another was seen dashing over and down the green hills, and all were goading on their horses at full speed! and then came another, and another, and all entered the village amid shouts and groans of the villagers who crowded around them; the story was told in their looks, for one was bleeding, and the blood that flowed from his naked breast had crimsoned his milk-white steed as it had dripped over him; another grasped in his left hand a scalp that was reeking in blood— and in the other his whip—another grasped nothing, save the reins in one hand and the mane of the horse in the other, having thrown his bow and his arrows away and trusted to the fleetness of his horse for his safety; yet the story was audibly told, and the fatal tragedy recited in irregular and almost suffocating ejaculations—the names of the dead were in turns pronounced, and screams and shrieks burst forth at their recital—murmurs and groans ran through the village, and this happy little community were in a moment smitten with sorrow and distraction.

Their proud band of hunters who had started full of glee and mirth in the morning, had been surrounded by their enemy, the Sioux, and eight of them killed. The Sioux, who had probably reconnoitred their village during the night, and ascertained that they were dancing for buffaloes, laid a stratagem to entrap them in the following manner:— Some six or eight of them appeared the next morning (on a distant bluff, in sight of their sentinel) under the skins of buffaloes, imitating the movements of those animals whilst grazing; and being discovered by the sentinel, the intelligence was telegraphed to the village, which brought out their hunters as I have described. The masked buffaloes were seen grazing on the top of a high bluff, and when the hunters had approached within half a mile or so of them, they suddenly disappeared over the hill. Louison Frénié, who was leading the little band of hunters, became at that moment suspicious of so strange a movement, and came to a halt   *   *   *   *   *   "Look!" (said a Mandan, pointing to a little ravine to the right, and at the foot of the hill, from which suddenly broke some forty or fifty furious Sioux, on fleet horses and under full whip, who were rushing upon them); they wheeled, and in front of them came another band more furious from the other side of the hill! they started for home (poor fellows), and strained every nerve; but the Sioux were too fleet for them; and every now and then, the whizzing arrow and the lance were heard to rip the flesh of their naked backs, and a grunt and a groan, as they tumbled from their horses. Several miles were run in this desperate race; and Frénié got home, and several of the Mandans, though eight of them were killed and scalped by the way.

So ended that day, and the hunt; but many a day and sad, will last the grief of those whose hearts were broken on that unlucky occasion.

This day, though, my readers, has been one of a more joyful kind, for the Great Spirit, who was indignant at so flagrant an injustice, has sent the Mandans an abundance of buffaloes; and all hearts have joined in a general thanksgiving to Him for his goodness and justice.

MANDAN VILLAGE, UPPER MISSOURI

In my last Letter I gave an account of the buffalo dance, and in future epistles may give some descriptions of a dozen other kinds of dance, which these people have in common with other tribes; but in the present Letter I shall make an endeavour to confine my observations to several other customs and forms, which are very curious and peculiar to the Mandans.

Of these, one of the most pleasing is the *sham-fight* and sham scalp-dance of the Mandan boys, which is a part of their regular exercise, and constitutes a material branch of their education. During the pleasant mornings of the summer, the little boys between the age of seven and fifteen are called out, to the number of several hundred, and being divided into two companies, each of which is headed by some experienced warrior, who leads them on, in the character of a teacher; they are led out into the prairie at sunrise, where this curious discipline is regularly taught them (Fig. 57). Their bodies are naked, and each one has a little bow in his left hand and a number of arrows made of large spears of grass, which are harmless in their effects. Each one has also a little belt or girdle around his waist, in which he carries a knife made of a piece of wood and equally harmless—on the tops of their heads are slightly attached small tufts of grass, which answer as scalps, and in this plight they follow the dictates of their experienced leaders, who lead them through the judicious evolutions of Indian warfare—of feints —of retreats—of attacks—and at last to a general fight. Many manœuvres are gone through, and eventually they are brought up face to face, within fifteen or twenty feet of each other, with their leaders at their head stimulating them on. Their bows are bent upon each other and their missiles flying, whilst they are dodging and fending them off.

If any one is struck with an arrow on any vital part of his body, he is obliged to fall, and his adversary rushes up to him, places his foot upon him, and snatching from his belt his wooden knife, grasps hold of his victim's scalp-lock of grass, and making a feint at it with

58

59

G. Catlin.

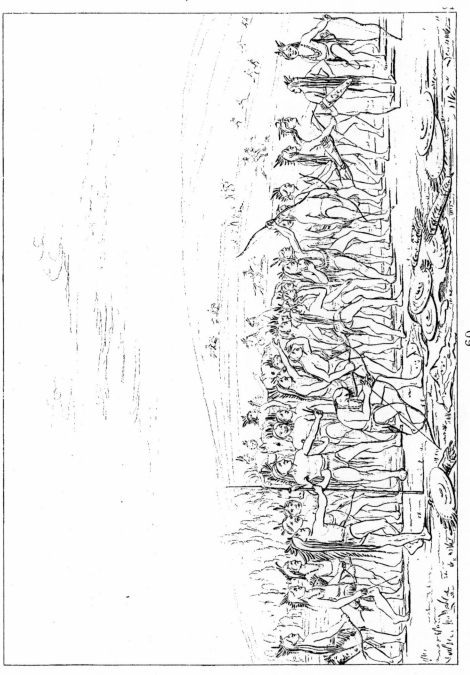

60

G. Catlin.

his wooden knife, twitches it off and puts its into his belt, and enters again into the ranks and front of battle.

This mode of training generally lasts an hour or more in the morning, and is performed on an empty stomach affording them a rigid and wholesome exercise, whilst they are instructed in the important science of war. Some five or six miles of ground are run over during these evolutions, giving suppleness to their limbs and strength to their muscles, which last and benefit them through life.

After this exciting exhibition is ended, they all return to their village, where the chiefs and braves pay profound attention to their vaunting, and applaud them for their artifice and valour.

Those who have taken scalps then step forward, brandishing them and making their boast as they enter into the *scalp-dance* (in which they are also instructed by their leaders or teachers), jumping and yelling—brandishing their scalps, and reciting their *sanguinary deeds,* to the great astonishment of their tender-aged sweethearts, who are gazing with wonder upon them.

The games and amusements of these people are in most respects like those of the other tribes, consisting of ball plays—game of the moccasin, of the platter—feats of archery—horse-racing, etc.; and they have yet another, which may be said to be their favourite amusement and unknown to the other tribes about them. The game of Tchung-kee, a beautiful athletic exercise, which they seem to be almost unceasingly practising whilst the weather is fair, and they have nothing else of moment to demand their attention. This game is decidedly their favourite amusement, and is played near to the village on a pavement of clay, which has been used for that purpose until it has become as smooth and hard as a floor. For this game, two champions form their respective parties, by choosing alternately the most famous players, until their requisite numbers are made up. Their bettings are then made, and their stakes are held by some of the chiefs or others present. The play commences (Fig. 59) with two (one from each party), who start off upon a trot, abreast of each other, and one of them rolls in advance of them, on the pavement, a little ring of two or three inches in diameter, cut out of a stone; and each one follows it up with his "tchung-kee" (a stick of six feet in length, with little bits of leather projecting from its sides of an inch or more in length), which he throws before him as he runs, sliding it along upon the ground after the ring, endeavouring to place it in such a position when it stops, that the ring may fall upon it, and receive one of the little projections of leather through it, which counts for game, one, or two, or four, according to the position of the leather on which the ring is lodged. The last winner always has the rolling of the ring, and both start and throw the tchung-kee together; if either fails to receive the ring or to lie in a certain position, it is a forfeiture of the amount of the number he was nearest to, and he loses his throw; when another steps into his place. This game is a very difficult one to describe, so as to give an exact idea of it, unless one can see it played—it is a game of great beauty and fine bodily exercise, and these people become excessively fascinated with it; often gambling away everything they possess, and even sometimes, when everything else was gone, have been known to stake their liberty upon the issue of these games, offering themselves as slaves to their opponents in case they get beaten.

Feasting and *fasting* are important customs observed by the Mandans, as well as by most other tribes, at stated times and for particular purposes. These observances are strictly religious, and rigidly observed. There are many of these forms practised amongst the Mandans, some of which are exceedingly interesting, and important also, in forming a correct estimate of the Indian character; and I shall at a future period take particular pains to lay them before my readers.

Sacrificing is also a religious custom with these people, and is performed in many different modes, and on numerous occasions. Of this custom I shall also speak more fully hereafter, merely noticing at present, some few of the hundred modes in which these offerings are made to the Good and Evil Spirits. Human sacrifices have never been made by the Mandans, nor by any of the North-Western tribes (so far as I can learn), excepting the Pawnees of the Platte; who have, undoubtedly, observed such an inhuman practice in former times, though they have relinquished it of late. The Mandans sacrifice their fingers to the Great Spirit, and of their worldly goods, the best and the most costly; if a horse or a dog, it must be the favourite one; if it is an arrow from their quiver, they will select the most perfect one as the most effective gift; if it is meat, it is the choicest piece cut from the buffalo or other animal; if it is anything from the stores of the Traders, it is the most costly—it is blue or scarlet cloth, which costs them in this country an enormous price, and is chiefly used for the purpose of hanging over their wigwams to decay, or to cover the scaffolds where rest the bones of their departed relations.

Of these kinds of sacrifices there are three of an interesting nature, erected over the great medicine-lodge in the centre of the village—they consist of ten or fifteen yards of blue and black cloth each, purchased from the Fur Company at fifteen or twenty dollars per yard, which are folded up so as to resemble human figures, with quills on their heads and masks on their faces. These singular-looking figures, like *"scare crows"* (Fig. 47), are erected on poles about thirty feet high, over the door of the mystery-lodge, and there are left to decay. There hangs now by the side of them another, which was added to the number a few days since, of the skin of a white buffalo, which will remain there until it decays and falls to pieces.

This beautiful and costly skin, when its history is known, will furnish a striking proof of the importance which they attach to these propitiatory offerings. But a few weeks since, a party of Mandans returned from the Mouth of the Yellow Stone, two hundred miles above, with information that a party of Blackfeet were visiting that place on business with the American Fur Company; and that they had with them a white buffalo robe for sale. This was looked upon as a subject of great importance by the chiefs, and one worthy of public consideration. A white buffalo robe is a great curiosity, even in the country of buffaloes, and will always command an almost incredible price, from its extreme scarcity; and then, from its being the most costly article of traffic in these regions, it is usually converted into a *sacrifice,* being offered to the Great Spirit, as the most acceptable gift that can be procured. Amongst the vast herds of buffaloes which graze on these boundless prairies, there is not one in a hundred thousand, perhaps, that is white; and when such an one is obtained, it is considered great *medicine* or mystery.

On the receipt of the intelligence above mentioned, the chiefs convened in council, and deliberated on the expediency of procuring the white robe from the Blackfeet; and also of appropriating the requisite means, and devising the proper mode of procedure for effecting the purchase. At the close of their deliberations, eight men were fitted out on eight of their best horses, who took from the Fur Company's store, on the credit of the chiefs, goods exceeding even the value of their eight horses; and they started for the Mouth of the Yellow Stone, where they arrived in due time, and made the purchase, by leaving the eight horses and all the goods which they carried; returning on foot to their own village, bringing home with them the white robe, which was looked upon by all eyes of the villagers as a thing that was vastly curious, and containing (as they express it) something of the Great Spirit. This wonderful anomaly lay several days in the chief's lodge, until public curiosity was gratified; and then it was taken by the doctors or high-priests, and with a great deal of form and mystery consecrated, and raised on the top of a long pole over the *medicine-lodge;* where it now stands in a group with the others, and will stand as an offering to the Great Spirit, until it decays and falls to the ground.

This Letter, as I promised in its commencement, being devoted to some of the customs peculiar to the Mandans, and all of which will be new to the world, I shall close, after recording in it an account of a laughable farce, which was enacted in this village when I was on my journey up the river, and had stopped on the way to spend a day or two in the Mandan village.

Readers, did you ever hear of *"Rain Makers?"* If not, sit still, and read on; but laugh not—keep cool and sober, or else you may laugh in the *beginning,* and cry at the *end* of my story. Well, I introduce to you a new character—not a *doctor* or a *high-priest,* yet a *medicine-man,* and one of the highest and most respectable order, a *"Rain Maker!"* Such dignitaries live in the Mandan nation, ay, and *"rain stoppers"* too; and even those also amongst their *conjurati* who, like Joshua of old, have even essayed to stop the sun in his course; but, from the inefficiency of their medicine or mystery, have long since descended into insignificance.

Well, the story begins thus:—The Mandans, as I have said in a former Letter, raise a great deal of corn; and sometimes a most disastrous drought will be visited on the land, destructive to their promised harvest. Such was the case when I arrived at the Mandan village on the steamboat *Yellow Stone.* Rain had not fallen for many a day, and the dear little girls and the ugly old squaws, altogether (all of whom had fields of corn), were groaning and crying to their lords, and imploring them to intercede for rain, that their little respective patches, which were now turning pale and yellow, might not be withered, and they be deprived of the pleasure of their customary annual festivity, and the joyful occasion of the "roasting ears," and the "green corn dance."

The chiefs and doctors sympathised with the plaints of the women, and recommended patience. Great deliberation, they said, was necessary in these cases; and though they resolved on making the attempt to produce rain for the benefit of the corn; yet they very wisely resolved that to begin too soon might ensure their entire defeat in the endeavour; and that the longer they put it off, the more certain they would feel of ultimate success. So, after a few days of further delay, when the importunities of the women had become clamorous, and even mournful, and almost insupportable, the *medicine-men* assembled in the council-house, with all their mystery apparatus about them—with an abundance of wild sage, and other aromatic herbs, with a fire prepared to burn them, that their savoury odours might be sent forth to the Great Spirit. The lodge was closed to all the villagers, except some ten or fifteen young men, who were willing to hazard the dreadful alternative of making it rain, or suffer the everlasting disgrace of having made a fruitless essay.

They, only, were allowed as witnesses to the *hocus pocus* and *conjuration* devised by the doctors inside of the medicine-lodge; and they were called up by lot, each one in his turn, to spend a day upon the top of the lodge, to test the potency of his medicine; or, in other words, to see how far his voice might be heard and obeyed amongst the clouds of the heavens; whilst the doctors were burning incense in the wigwam below, and with their songs and prayers to the Great Spirit for success, were sending forth grateful fumes and odours to Him "who lives in the sun and commands the thunders of Heaven." Wah-kee (the shield) was the first who ascended the wigwam at sunrise; and he stood all day, and looked foolish, as he was counting over and over his string of mystery-beads—the whole village were assembled around him, and praying for his success. Not a cloud appeared—the day was calm and hot; and at the setting of the sun, he descended from the lodge and went home—"his *medicine* was not good," nor can he ever be a *medicine-man*.

Om-pah (the elk) was the next; he ascended the lodge at sunrise the next morning. His body was entirely naked, being covered with yellow clay. On his left arm he carried a beautiful shield, and a long lance in his right; and on his head the skin of a raven, the bird that soars amidst the clouds, and above the lightning's glare—he flourished his shield and brandished his lance, and raised his voice, but in vain; for at sunset the ground was dry and the sky was clear; the squaws were crying, and their corn was withering at its roots.

War-rah-pa (the beaver) was the next; he also spent his breath in vain upon the empty air, and came down at night—and Wak-a-dah-ha-hee (the white buffalo's hair) took the stand the next morning. He is a small but beautifully proportioned young man. He was dressed in a tunic and leggings of the skins of the mountain-sheep, splendidly garnished with quills of the porcupine, and fringed with locks of hair taken by his own hand from the heads of his enemies. On his arm he carried his shield, made of the buffalo's hide—its boss was the head of the war-eagle—and its front was ornamented with "red chains of lightning." In his left hand he clenched his sinewy bow and one single arrow. The villagers were all gathered about him; when he threw up a feather to decide on the course of the wind, and he commenced thus:—"My friends! people of the pheasants! you see me here a sacrifice—I shall this day relieve you from great distress, and bring joy amongst you; or I shall descend from this lodge when the sun goes down, and live amongst the dogs and old women all my days. My friends! you saw which way the feather flew, and I hold my shield this day in the direction where the wind comes—the lightning on my shield will draw a great cloud, and this arrow, which is selected from my quiver, and which is feathered with the quill of the white swan, will make a hole in it, My friends! this hole in the lodge at my feet, shows me the medicine-men, who are seated in the lodge below me and crying to the Great Spirit; and through it comes and passes into my nose delightful odours, which you see rising in the smoke to the Great Spirit above, who rides in the clouds and commands the winds! Three days they have sat here, my friends, and nothing has been done to relieve your distress. On the first day was Wah-kee (the shield), he could do nothing; he counted his beads and came down—his medicine was not good—his name was bad, and it kept off the rain. The next was Om-pah (the elk); on his head the raven was seen, who flies *above* the storm, and he failed. War-rah-pa (the beaver) was the next, my friends; the beaver lives *under* the *water,* and he never wants it to rain. My friends! I see you are in great distress, and nothing has yet been done; this shield belonged to my father, the White Buffalo; and the lightning you see on it is red; it was taken from a black cloud, and that cloud will come over us to-day. I am the White Buffalo's Hair—and I am the son of my father."

In this manner flourished and manœuvred Wak-a-dah-ha-hee (the white buffalo's hair), alternately addressing the audience and the heavens—and holding converse with the winds and the *"je-bi"* (Spirits) that are floating about in them—stamping his foot over the heads of the *magi,* who were involved in mysteries beneath him, and invoking the spirits of darkness and light to send rain, to gladden the hearts of the Mandans.

It happened on this memorable day about noon, that the steam-boat *Yellow Stone,* on her first trip up the Missouri River, approached and landed at the Mandan village, as I have described in a former epistle. I was lucky enough to be a passenger on this boat, and helped to fire a salute of twenty guns of twelve pounds calibre, when we first came in sight of the village, some three or four miles below. These guns introduced a *new sound* into this strange country, which the Mandans at first supposed to be thunder; and the young man upon the lodge, who turned it to good account, was gathering fame in rounds of applause, which were repeated and echoed through the whole village; all eyes were centred upon him—chiefs envied him—mothers' hearts were beating high whilst they were decorating and leading up their fair daughters to offer him in marriage, on his signal success. The medicine-men had left the lodge, and came out to bestow upon him the envied title of *"medicine-man"* or *"doctor,"* which he had so deservedly won—wreaths were prepared to decorate his brows, and eagle's plumes and calumets were in readiness for him; his friends were all rejoiced—his enemies wore on their faces a silent gloom and hatred; and his old sweethearts, who had formerly cast him off, gazed intensely upon him, as they glowed with the burning fever of repentance.

During all this excitement, Wak-a-dah-ha-hee kept his position, assuming the most commanding and threatening attitudes; brandishing his shield in the direction of the thunder (Fig. 58), although there was not a cloud to be seen, until he (poor fellow), being elevated above the rest of the village, espied, to his inexpressible amazement, the steamboat ploughing its way up the windings of the river below; puffing her steam from her pipes, and sending forth the thunder from a twelve-pounder on her deck! * * * The White Buffalo's Hair stood motionless and turned pale; he looked awhile, and turned to the chief and to the multitude, and addressed them with a trembling lip—"My friends, we will get no rain!—there are, you see, no clouds; but my medicine is great—I have brought a *thunder-boat!* look and see it! the thunder you hear is out of her mouth, and the lightning which you see is on the waters!"

At this intelligence, the whole village flew to the tops of their wigwams, or to the bank of the river, from whence the steamer was in full view, and ploughing along, to their utter dismay and confusion.

In this promiscuous throng of chiefs, doctors, women, children and dogs, was mingled Wak-a-dah-ha-hee (the white buffalo's hair), having descended from his high place to mingle with the frightened throng.

Dismayed at the approach of so strange and unaccountable an object, the Mandans stood their ground but a few moments; when, by an order of the chiefs, all hands were ensconced within the piquets of their village, and all the warriors armed for desperate defence. A few moments brought the boat in front of the village, and all was still and quiet as death; not a Mandan was to be seen upon the banks. The steamer was moored; and three or four of the chiefs soon after walked boldly down the bank and on to her deck, with a spear in one hand and the calumet or pipe of peace in the other. The moment they stepped on board they met (to their great surprise and joy) their old friend Major Sanford, their agent, which circumstance put an instant end to all their fears. The villagers were soon apprised of the fact, and the whole race of the beautiful and friendly Mandans was paraded on the bank of the river, in front of the steamer.

The "rain maker," whose apprehensions of a public calamity brought upon the nation by his extraordinary *medicine,* had, for the better security of his person from apprehended vengeance, secreted himself in some secure place, and was the last to come forward, and the last to be convinced that this visitation was a friendly one from the white people; and that his *medicine* had not in the least been instrumental in bringing it about. This information, though received by him with much caution and suspicion, at length gave him great relief, and quieted his mind as to his danger. Yet still in his breast there was a rankling thorn, though he escaped the dreaded vengeance which he had a few moments before apprehended as at hand; as he had the mortification and disgrace of having failed in his mysterious operations. He set up, however (during the day, in his conversation about the strange arrival), his *medicines,* as the cause of its approach; asserting everywhere and to everybody, that he knew of its coming, and that he had by his magic brought the occurrence about. This plea, however, did not get him much audience; and in fact, everything else was pretty much swallowed up in the guttural talk, and bustle, and gossip about the mysteries of the "thunder-boat;" and so passed the day, until just at the approach of evening, when the "White Buffalo's Hair" (more watchful of such matters on this occasion than most others) observed that a black cloud had been jutting up in the horizon, and was almost directly over the village! In an instant his shield was on his arm, and his bow in his hand, and he again upon the lodge! stiffened and braced to the last sinew, he stood, with his face and his shield presented to the cloud, and his bow drawn. He drew the eyes of the whole village upon him as he vaunted forth his superhuman powers, and at the same time commanding the cloud to come nearer, that he might draw down its contents upon the heads and the corn-fields of the Mandans! In this wise he stood, waving his shield over his head, stamping his foot and frowning as he drew his bow and threatened the heavens, commanding it to rain—his bow was bent, and the arrow drawn to its head, was sent to the cloud, and he exclaimed, "My friends, it is done! Wak-a-dah-ha-hee's arrow has entered that black cloud, and the Mandans will be wet with the water of the skies!" His predictions were true;—in a few moments the cloud was over the village, and the rain fell in torrents, He stood for some time wielding his weapons and presenting his shield to the sky, while he boasted of his power and the efficacy of his *medicine* to those who had been about him, but were now driven to the shelter of their wigwams. He, at length, finished his vaunts and his threats, and descended from his high place (in which he had been perfectly drenched), prepared to receive the honours and the homage that were due to one so potent in his mysteries; and to receive the style and title of *"medicine-man."* This is one of a hundred different modes in which a man in Indian countries acquires this honourable appellation.

This man had "made it rain," and of course was to receive more than usual honours, as he had done much more than ordinary men could do. All eyes were upon him, and all were ready to admit that he was skilled in the magic art; and must be so nearly allied to the Great or Evil Spirit, that he must needs be a man of great and powerful influence in the nation, and well entitled to the style of doctor or *medicine-man.*

Readers, there are two facts relative to these strange transactions, which are infallibly true, and should needs be made known. The first is, that when the Mandans undertake to make it rain, *they never fail to succeed,* for their ceremonies never stop until rain begins to fall. The second is equally true, and is this:—that he who has once *made it rain,* never attempts it again; his medicine is undoubted— and on future occasions of the kind, he stands aloof, who has once done it in presence of the whole village, giving an opportunity to other young men who are ambitious to signalise themselves in the same way.

During the memorable night of which I have just spoken, the steamboat remained by the side of the Mandan village, and the rain that had commenced falling continued to pour down its torrents until midnight; black thunder roared, and livid lightning flashed until the heavens appeared to be lit up with one unceasing and appalling glare. In this frightful moment of consternation, a flash of lightning buried itself in one of the earth-covered lodges of the Mandans, and killed a beautiful girl. Here was food and fuel fresh for their superstitions; and a night of vast tumult and excitement ensued. The dreams of the new-made medicine-man were troubled, and he had dreadful apprehensions for the coming day—for he knew that he was subject to the irrevocable decree of the chiefs and doctors, who canvass every strange and unaccountable event with close and superstitious scrutiny, and let their vengeance fall without mercy upon its immediate cause.

He looked upon his well-earned fame as likely to be withheld from him; and also considered that his life might perhaps be demanded as the forfeit for this girl's death, which would certainly be charged upon him. He looked upon himself as culpable, and supposed the accident to have been occasioned by his criminal desertion of his post, when the steamboat was approaching the village. Morning came, and he soon learned from some of his friends, the opinions of the wise men; and also the nature of the tribunal that was preparing for him; he sent to the prairie for his three horses, which were brought in, and he mounted. the *medicine-lodge,* around which, in a few moments, the villagers were all assembled. "My friends! (said he) I see you all around me, and I am before you; my medicine, you see, is great—it is *too great*—I am young, and I was too fast—I knew not when to stop. The wigwam of Mah-sish is laid low, and many are the eyes that weep for Ko-ka (the antelope); Wak-a-dah-ha-hee gives three horses to gladden the hearts of those who weep for Ko-ka; his medicine was great—his arrow pierced the black cloud, and the lightning came, and the *thunder-boat* also! who says the medicine of Wak-a-dah-ha-hee is not strong?"

At the end of this sentence an unanimous shout of approbation ran through the crowd, and the "Hair of the White Buffalo" descended amongst them, where he was greeted by shakes of the hand; and amongst whom he now lives and thrives under the familiar and honourable appellation of the "BIG DOUBLE MEDICINE."

35

G. Catlin.

LETTER—No. 20

THIS day has been one of unusual mirth and amusement amongst the Mandans, and whether on account of some annual celebration or not, I am as yet unable to say, though I think such is the case; for these people have many days which, like this, are devoted to festivities and amusements.

Their lives, however, are lives of idleness and ease, and almost all their days and hours are spent in innocent amusements. Amongst a people who have no office hours to attend to—no professions to study, and of whom but very little time is required in the chase, to supply their families with food, it would be strange if they did not practice many games and amusements, and also become exceedingly expert in them.

I have this day been a spectator of games and plays until I am fatigued with looking on; and also by lending a hand, which I have done; but with so little success as only to attract general observation, and as generally to excite the criticisms and laughter of the squaws and little children.

I have seen a fair exhibition of their archery this day, in a favourite amusement which they call the *game of the arrow* (see Fig. 60), where the young men who are the most distinguished in this exercise, assemble on the prairie at a little distance from the village, and having paid, each one, his "entrance-fee," such as a shield, a robe, a pipe, or other article, step forward in turn, shooting their arrows into the air, endeavouring to see who can get the greatest number flying in the air at one time, thrown from the same bow. For this, the number of eight or ten arrows are clenched in the left hand with the bow, and the first one which is thrown is elevated to such a degree as will enable it to remain the longest time possible in the air, and while it is flying, the others are discharged as rapidly as possible; and he who succeeds in getting the greatest number up at once, is "best," and takes the goods staked.

In looking on at this amusement, the spectator is surprised; not at the great distance to which the arrows are actually sent; but at the quickness of fixing them on the string, and discharging them in succession; which is, no doubt, the result of great practice, and enables the most expert of them to get as many as eight arrows up before the first one reaches the ground.

For the successful use of the bow, as it is used through all this region of country on horseback, and that invariably at full speed, the great object of practice is to enable the bowman to draw the bow with suddenness and instant effect; and also to repeat the shots in the most rapid manner. As their game is killed from their horses' backs while at the swiftest rate—and their enemies fought in the same way; and as the horse is the swiftest animal of the prairie, and always able to bring his rider alongside, within a few paces of his victim; it will easily be seen that the Indian has little use in throwing his arrow more than a few paces; when he leans quite low on his horse's side, and drives it with astonishing force, capable of producing instant death to the buffalo, or any other animal in the country. The bows which are generally in use in these regions, I have described in a former Letter, and the effects produced by them at the distance of a few paces is almost beyond belief, considering their length, which is not often over three—and sometimes not exceeding two and a half feet. It can easily be seen, from what has been said, that the Indian has little use or object in throwing the arrow to any great distance. And as it is very seldom that they can be seen shooting at a target, I doubt very much whether their skill in such practice would compare with that attained to in many parts of the civilised world; but with the same weapon, and dashing forward at fullest speed on the wild horse, without the use of the rein, when the shot is required to be made with the most instantaneous effect, I scarcely think it possible that any people can be found more skilled, and capable of producing more deadly effects with the bow.

The horses which the Indians ride in this country are invariably the wild horses, which are found in great numbers on the prairies; and have, unquestionably, strayed from the Mexican borders, into which they were introduced by the Spanish invaders of that country; and now range and subsist themselves, in winter and summer, over the vast plains of prairie that stretch from the Mexican frontiers to Lake Winnipeg on the north, a distance of 3000 miles. These horses are all of small stature, of the pony order; but a very hardy and tough animal, being able to perform for the Indians a continual and essential service. They are taken with the *lasso*, which is a long halter or thong, made of raw-hide, of some fifteen or twenty yards in length, and which the Indians throw with great dexterity; with a

36

62

G. Catlin

noose at one end of it, which drops over the head of the animal they wish to catch, whilst running at full speed—when the Indian dismounts from his own horse, and holding to the end of the lasso, chokes the animal down, and afterwards tames and converts him to his own use.

Scarcely a man in these regions is to be found, who is not the owner of one or more of these horses; and in many instances of eight, ten, or even twenty, which he values as his own personal property.

The Indians are hard and cruel masters; and, added to their cruelties is the sin that is familiar in the Christian world, of sporting with the limbs and the lives of these noble animals. *Horse-racing* here, as in all more enlightened communities, is one of the most exciting amusements, and one of the most extravagant modes of gambling.

I have been this day a spectator to scenes of this kind, which have been enacted in abundance, on a course which they have, just back of their village; and although I never had the least taste for this cruel amusement in my own country, yet, I must say, I have been not a little amused and pleased with the thrilling effect which these exciting scenes have produced amongst so wild and picturesque a group.

I have made a sketch of the ground and the group, as near as I could (Fig. 61). Showing the manner of "starting" and "coming out," which vary a little from. the customs of the *knowing* world; but in other respects, I believe, a horse-race is the same all the world over.

Besides these, many have been the amusements of this day, to which I have been an eye-witness; and since writing the above, I have learned the cause of this unusual expression of hilarity and mirth; which was no more nor less than the safe return of a small war-party, who had been so long out without any tidings having been received of them—that they had long since been looked upon as sacrificed to the fates of war and lost. This party was made up of the most distinguished and desperate young men of the tribe, who had sallied out against the Riccarees, and taken the most solemn oath amongst themselves never to return without achieving a victory. They had wandered long and faithfully about the country, following the trails of their enemy; when they were attacked by a numerous party, and lost several of their men and all their horses. In this condition, to evade the scrutiny of their enemy, who were closely investing the natural route to their village; they took a circuitous range of the country, to enable them to return with their lives, to their village.

In this plight, it seems, I had dropped my little canoe alongside of them, while descending from the Mouth of Yellow Stone to this place, not many weeks since; where they had bivouacked or halted, to smoke and consult on the best and safest mode of procedure. At the time of meeting them, not knowing anything of their language, they were unable to communicate their condition to me, and more probably were afraid to do so even if they could have done it, from apprehension that we might have given some account of them to their enemies. I rested my canoe an hour or so with them, during which time they treated us with an indifferent reserve, yet respectfully; and we passed on our way, without further information of them or their plans than the sketch that I there made (Fig. 63), and which I shall preserve and value as one of the most pleasing groups I ever have had the pleasure to see. Seated on their buffalo robes, which were spread upon the grass, with their respective weapons lying about them, and lighting their pipes at a little fire which was kindled in the centre—the chief or leader of the party, with his arms stacked behind him, and his long head-dress of war-eagle's quills and ermine falling down over his back, whilst he sat in a contemplative and almost desponding mood, was surely one of the most striking and beautiful illustrations of a natural hero that I ever looked upon.

These gallant fellows got safely home to their village, and the numerous expressions of joy for their return, which I have this day witnessed, have so much fatigued me that I write brief, and close my Letter here.

37

G Catlin

LETTER—No. 21

IN a former Letter I gave some account of Mah-to-toh-pa (the four bears), second chief of the Mandans, whom I said I had painted at full length, in a splendid costume. I therein said, also, that "this extraordinary man, though second in office, is undoubtedly the first and most popular man in the nation. Free, generous, elegant, and gentlemanly in his deportment—handsome, brave and valiant; wearing a robe on his back, with the history of all his battles painted on it, which would fill a book of themselves if they were properly enlarged and translated."

I gave you also, in another epistle, an account of the manner in which he invited me to a feast in his hospitable wigwam, at the same time presenting me a beautifully garnished robe; and I promised to say more of him on a future occasion. My readers will therefore pardon me for devoting a Letter or two at this time, to a sketch of this extraordinary man, which I will give in as brief a manner as possible, by describing the costume in which I painted his portrait; and afterwards reciting the most remarkable incidents of his life, as I had them from the Traders and the Indian agents, and afterwards corroborated by his own words, translated to me as he spoke, whilst I was writing them down.

The dress of Mah-to-toh-pa then, the greater part of which I have represented in his full-length portrait, and which I shall now describe, was purchased of him after I had painted his picture; and every article of it can be seen in my Indian Gallery by the side of the portrait, provided I succeed in getting them home to the civilised world without injury.

Mah-to-toh-pa had agreed to stand before me for his portrait at an early hour of the next morning, and on that day I sat with my palette of colours prepared, and waited till twelve o'clock, before he could leave his toilette with feelings of satisfaction as to the propriety of his looks and the arrangement of his equipments; and at that time it was announced, that "Mah-to-toh-pa was coming in full dress!" I looked out of the door of the wigwam, and saw him approaching with a firm and elastic step, accompanied by a great crowd of women and children, who were gazing on him with admiration, and escorting him to my room. No tragedian ever trod the stage, nor gladiator ever entered the Roman Forum, with more grace and manly dignity than did Mah-to-toh-pa enter the wigwam, where I was in readiness to receive him. He took his attitude before me (Fig. 64), and with the sternness of a Brutus and the stillness of a statue, he stood until the darkness of night broke upon the solitary stillness. His dress, which was a very splendid one, was complete in all its parts, and consisted of a shirt or tunic, leggings, moccasins, head-dress, necklace, shield, bow and quiver, lance, tobacco-sack, and pipe; robe, belt, and knife; medicine-bag, tomahawk, and war-club, or *po-ko-mo-kon.*

The shirt, of which I have spoken, was made of two skins of the mountain-sheep, beautifully dressed, and sewed together by seams which rested upon the arms; one skin hanging in front, upon the breast, and the other falling down upon the back; the head being passed between them, and they falling over and resting on the shoulders. Across each shoulder, and somewhat in the form of an epaulette, was a beautiful band; and down each arm from the neck to the hand was a similar one, of two inches in width (and crossing the other at right angles on the shoulder) beautifully embroidered with porcupine quills worked on the dress, and covering the seams. To the lower edge of these bands the whole way, at intervals of half an inch, were attached long locks of black hair, which he had taken with his own hand from the heads of his enemies whom he had slain in battle, and which he thus wore as a trophy, and also as an ornament to his dress. The front and back of the shirt were curiously garnished in several parts with porcupine quills and paintings of the battles he had fought, and also with representations of the victims that had fallen by his hand. The bottom of the dress was bound or hemmed with ermine skins, and tassels of ermine's tails were suspended from the arms and the shoulders.

The *Leggings,* which were made of deer skins, beautifully dressed, and fitting tight to the leg, extended from the feet to the hips, and were fastened to a belt which was passed around the waist. These; like the shirt, had a similar band, worked with porcupine quills of richest dyes, passing down the seam on the outer part of the leg, and fringed also the whole length of the leg, with the scalp-locks taken from his enemies' heads.

The *Moccasins* were of buckskin, and covered in almost every part with the beautiful embroidery of porcupine's quills.

The *Head-dress,* which was superb and truly magnificent, con-

38

G Catlin.

sisted of a crest of war-eagle's quills, gracefully falling back from the forehead over the back part of the head, and extending quite down to his feet; set the whole way in a profusion of ermine, and surmounted on the top of the head, with the horns of the buffalo, shaved thin and highly polished.

The *Necklace* was made of fifty huge claws or nails of the grizzly bear, ingeniously arranged on the skin of an otter, and worn, like the scalp-locks, as a trophy—as an evidence unquestionable, that he had contended with and overcome that desperate enemy in open combat.

His *Shield* was made of the hide of the buffalo's neck, and hardened with the glue that was taken from its hoofs; its boss was the skin of a pole-cat, and its edges were fringed with rows of eagle's quills and hoofs of the antelope.

His *Bow* was of bone, and as white and beautiful as ivory; over its back was laid, and firmly attached to it, a coating of deer's sinews, which gave it its elasticity, and of course death to all that stood inimically before it. Its string was three stranded and twisted of sinews, which many a time had twanged and sent the whizzing death to animal and to human victims.

The *Quiver* was made of a panther's skin and hung upon his back, charged with its deadly arrows; some were poisoned and some were not; they were feathered with hawk's and eagle's quills; some were clean and innocent, and pure, and others were stained all over, with animal and human blood that was dried upon them. Their blades or points were of flints, and some of steel; and altogether were a deadly magazine.

The *Lance* or spear was held in his left hand; its blade was two-edged and of polished steel, and the blood of several human victims was seen dried upon it, one over the other; its shaft was of the toughest ash, and ornamented at intervals with tufts of war-eagle's quills.

His *Tobacco-sack* was made of the skin of an otter, and tastefully garnished with quills of the porcupine; in it was carried his *k'nick-k'neck* (the bark of the red willow, which is smoked as a substitute for tobacco), it contained also his flint and steel, and spunk for lighting————

His *Pipe,* which was ingeniously carved out of the red steatite (or pipestone), the stem of which was three feet long and two inches wide, made from the stalk of the young ash; about half its length was wound with delicate braids of the porcupine quills, so ingeniously wrought as to represent figures of men and animals upon it. It was also ornamented with the skins and beaks of wood-pecker's heads, and the hair of the white buffalo's tail. The lower half of the stem was painted red, and on its edges it bore the notches he had recorded for the snows (or years) of his life.

His *Robe* was made of the skin of a young buffalo bull, with the fur on one side, and the other finely and delicately dressed; with all the battles of his life emblazoned on it by his own hand.

His *Belt,* which was of a substantial piece of buckskin, was firmly girded around his waist; and in it were worn his tomahawk and scalping-knife.

His *Medicine-bag* was the skin of a beaver, curiously ornamented with hawk's bills and ermine. It was held in his right hand, and his *po-ko-mo-kon* (or war-club) which was made of a round stone, tied up in a piece of rawhide, and attached to the end of a stick, somewhat in the form of a sling, was laid with others of his weapons at his feet.

Such was the dress of Mah-to-toh-pa when he entered my wigwam to stand for his picture; but such I have not entirely represented it in his portrait; having rejected such trappings and ornaments as interfered with the grace and simplicity of the figure. He was beautifully and extravagantly dressed; and in this he was not alone, for hundreds of others are equally elegant. In plumes, and arms, and ornaments, he is not singular; but in laurels and wreaths he stands unparalleled. His breast has been bared and scarred in defence of his country, and his brows crowned with honours that elevate him conspicuous above all of his nation. There is no man amongst the Mandans so generally loved, nor any one who wears a robe so justly famed and honourable as that of Mah-to-toh-pa.

I said his robe was of the skin of a young buffalo bull, and that the battles of his life were emblazoned on it; and on a former occasion, that he presented me a beautiful robe, containing all the battles of his life, which he had spent two weeks' time in copying from his original one, which he wore on his shoulders.

This robe, with his tracings on it, is the chart of his military life; and when explained, will tell more of Mah-to-toh-pa.

Some days after this robe was presented, he called upon me with Mr Kipp, the trader and interpreter for the Mandans, and gave me of each battle there pourtrayed the following history, which was interpreted by Mr Kipp, from his own lips, and written down by me, as we three sat upon the robe. Mr Kipp, who is a gentleman of respectability and truth; and who has lived with these people ten years, assured me, that nearly every one of these narrations were of events that had happened whilst he had lived with them, and had

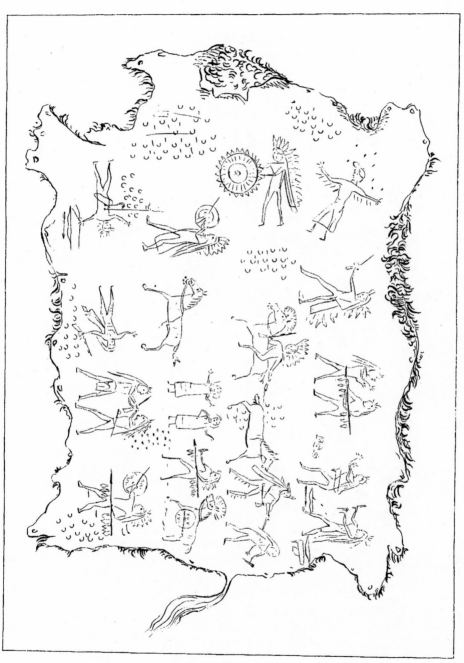

G. Catlin.

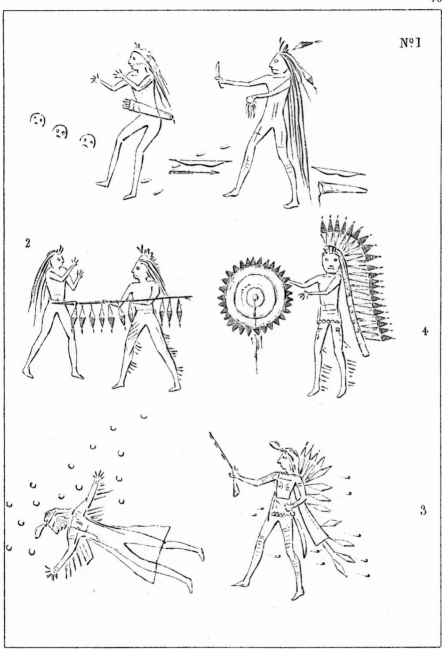

№ I

2

4

3

G. Catlin.

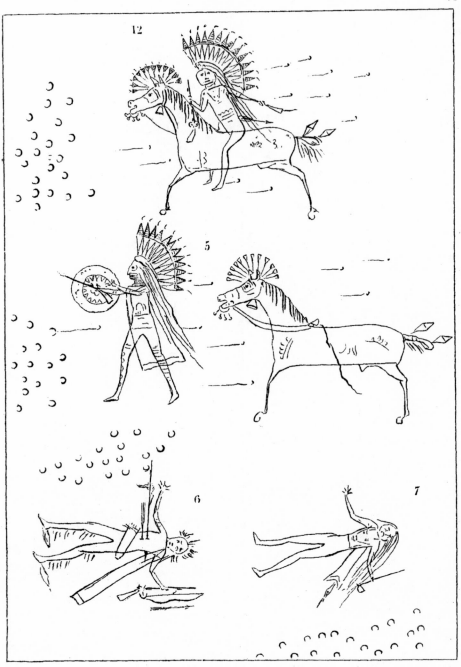

G. Caltin.

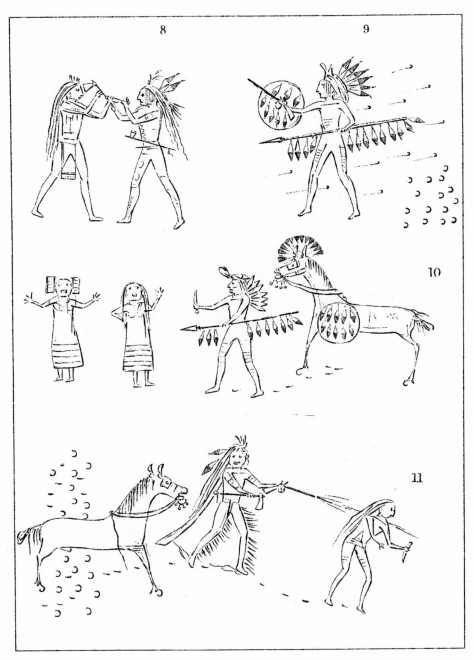

G. Catlin.

been familiarly known to him; and that every word that he asserted was true.

And again, reader, in this country where, of all countries I ever was in, men are the most jealous of rank and of standing, and in a community so small also, that every man's deeds of honour and chivalry are familiarly known to all; it would not be reputable, or even safe to life, for a warrior to wear upon his back the representations of battles he never had fought; professing to have done what every child in the village would know he never had done.

So then I take the records of battles on the robe of Mah-to-toh-pa to be matter of historical fact; and I proceed to give them as I wrote them down from his own lips. Twelve battle-scenes are there represented, where he has contended with his enemy, and in which he has taken fourteen of their scalps. The groups are drawn according to his own rude ideas of the arts; and I proceed to describe them in turn, as they were explained to me.

ROBE OF MAH-TO-TOH-PA (FIG. 65).

1. Mah-to-toh-pa kills a Sioux chief—the three heads represent the three Riccarees, whom the Sioux chief had previously killed. The Sioux chief is seen with war-paint black on his face. Mah-to-toh-pa is seen with the scalp of the Sioux in one hand, and his knife in the other, and his bow and quiver lying behind him.*

2. A Shienne chief, who sent word to Mah-to-toh-pa that he wished to fight him—was killed by Mah-to-toh-pa with a lance, in presence of a large party of Mandans and Shiennes. Mah-to-toh-pa is here known by his lance with eagle's quills on it.

3. A Shienne killed by Mah-to-toh-pa after Mah-to-toh-pa had been left by his party, badly wounded and bleeding; the twenty-five or thirty foot-tracks around, represent the number of Shiennes, who were present when the battle took place; and the bullets from their guns represented as flying all around the head of Mah-to-toh-pa.

4. Shienne chief with war-eagle head-dress, and a beautiful shield, ornamented with eagle's quills, killed by Mah-to-toh-pa. In this battle the wife of the Shienne rushed forward in a desperate manner to his assistance; but arriving too late, fell a victim. In this battle Mah-to-toh-pa obtained two scalps.

5. Mah-to-toh-pa, with a party of Riccarees, fired at by a party of Sioux; the Riccarees fled—Mah-to-toh-pa dismounted and drove his

* The reader will see in Fig. 65, an accurate drawing of this curious robe, and on the following pages, each group numbered, and delineated on a larger scale, which are *facsimiles* of the drawings on the robe.

horse back, facing the enemy alone and killing one of them. Mah-to-toh-pa is here represented with a beautiful head-dress of war-eagle's quills, and one on his horse's head of equal beauty; his shield is on his arm, and the party of Sioux is represented in front of him by the number of horse tracks.

6. The brother of Mah-to-toh-pa killed by a Riccaree, who shot him with an arrow, and then running a lance through his body, left it there. Mah-to-toh-pa was the first to find his brother's body with the lance in it; he drew the lance from the body, kept it four years with the blood dried on its blade, and then, according to his oath, killed the same Riccaree with the same lance; the dead body of his brother is here seen with the arrow and lance remaining in it, and the tracks of the Riccaree's horses in front.

The following was, perhaps, one of the most extraordinary exploits of this remarkable man's life, and is well attested by Mr Kipp, and several white men, who were living in the Mandan village at the time of its occurrence. In a skirmish, near the Mandan village, when they were set upon by their enemies, the Riccarees, the brother of Mah-to-toh-pa was missing for several days, when Mah-to-toh-pa found the body shockingly mangled, and a handsome spear left piercing the body through the heart. The spear was by him brought into the Mandan village, where it was recognised by many as a famous weapon belonging to a noted brave of the Riccarees, by the name of Won-ga-tap. This spear was brandished through the Mandan village by Mah-to-toh-pa (with the blood of his brother dried on its blade), crying most piteously, and swearing that he would some day revenge the death of his brother with the same weapon.

It is almost an incredible fact, that he kept this spear with great care in his wigwam for the space of four years, in the fruitless expectation of an opportunity to use it upon the breast of its owner; when his indignant soul, impatient of further delay, burst forth in the most uncontrollable frenzy and fury; he again brandished it through the village, and said, that the blood of his brother's heart which was seen on its blade was yet fresh, and called loudly for revenge. "Let every Mandan (said he) be silent, and let no one sound the name of Mah-to-toh-pa—let no one ask for him, nor where he has gone, until you hear him sound the war-cry in front of the village, when he will enter it and show you the blood of Won-ga-tap. The blade of this lance shall drink the heart's blood of Won-ga-tap, or Mah-to-toh-pa mingles his shadow with that of his brother."

With this he sallied forth from the village, and over the plains,

with the lance in his hand; his direction was towards the Riccaree
village, and all eyes were upon him, though none dared to speak till
he disappeared over the distant grassy bluffs. He travelled the
distance of two hundred miles entirely alone, with a little parched
corn in his pouch, making his marches by night, and lying secreted
by days, until he reached the Riccaree village; where (being
acquainted with its shapes and its habits, and knowing the position
of the wigwam of his doomed enemy) he loitered about in disguise,
mingling himself in the obscure throng; and at last, silently and
alone, observed through the rents of the wigwam, the last motions
and movements of his victim, as he retired to bed with his wife: he
saw him light his last pipe and smoke it "to its end"—he saw the
last whiff, and saw the last curl of blue smoke that faintly steeped
from its bowl—he saw the village awhile in darkness and silence,
and the embers that were covered in the middle of the wigwam gone
nearly out, and the last flickering light which had been gently playing over them, when he walked softly, but not slyly, into the wigwam
and seated himself by the fire, over which was hanging a large pot,
with a quantity of cooked meat remaining in it; and by the side of
the fire, the pipe and tobacco-pouch which had just been used; and
knowing that the twilight of the wigwam was not sufficient to dis-
close the features of his face to his enemy, he very deliberately
turned to the pot and completely satiated the desperate appetite
which he had got in a journey of six or seven days, with little or
nothing to eat; and then, as deliberately, charged and lighted the
pipe, and sent (no doubt, in every whiff that he drew through its
stem) a prayer to the Great Spirit for a moment longer for the consummation of his design. Whilst eating and smoking, the wife of his
victim, while lying in bed, several times inquired of her husband, what
man it was who was eating in their lodge? to which, he as many
times replied, "It's no matter; let him eat, for he is probably hungry."

Mah-to-toh-pa knew full well that his appearance would cause no
other reply than this, from the dignitary of the nation; for, from an
invariable custom amongst these Northern Indians, any one who is
hungry is allowed to walk into any man's lodge and eat. Whilst
smoking his last gentle and tremulous whiffs on the pipe, Mah-to-toh-
pa (leaning back, and turning gradually on his side, to get a better
view of the position of his enemy, and to see a little more distinctly
the shapes of things) stirred the embers with his toes (readers, I had
every word of this from his own lips, and every attitude and gesture
acted out with his own limbs), until he saw his way was clear; at
which moment, with his lance in his hands, he rose and drove it

through the body of his enemy, and snatching the scalp from his head, he darted from the lodge—and quick as lightning, with the lance in one hand, and the scalp in the other, made his way to the prairie! The village was in an uproar, but he was off, and no one knew the enemy who had struck the blow. Mah-to-toh-pa ran all night, and lay close during the days; thanking the Great Spirit for strengthening his heart and his arm to this noble revenge; and prayed fervently for a continuance of his aid and protection till he should get back to his own village. His prayers were heard; and on the sixth morning, at sunrise, Mah-to-toh-pa descended the bluffs, and entered the village amidst deafening shouts of applause, while he brandished and showed to his people the blade of his lance, with the blood of his victim dried upon it, over that of his brother; and the scalp of Won-ga-tap suspended from its handle!

Such was the feat represented by Mah-to-toh-pa on his robe—and the lance, of which I have just spoken, is seen in the hand of his portrait, which will stand in my Gallery, and of which I have thus formerly spoken:—"The lance or spear of Mah-to-toh-pa, when he stood for his portrait, was held in his left hand; its blade was two-edged, and of polished steel, and the blood of several human victims was seen dried upon its surface, one over the other; its shaft was of the toughest ash, and ornamented at intervals with tufts of war-eagle's quills."

In the portrait, of which I am speaking, there will be seen an eagle's quill balanced on the hilt of the lance, severed from its original position, and loose from the weapon. When I painted his portrait, he brought that quill to my wigwam in his left hand, and carefully balancing it on the lance, as seen in the painting; he desired me to be very exact with it, to have it appear as separate from, and unconnected with, the lance; and to represent a spot of blood which was visible upon it. I indulged him in his request, and then got from him the following explanation:—"That quill (said he) is great *medicine!* it belongs to the Great Spirit, and not to me—when I was running out of the lodge of Won-ga-tap, I looked back and saw that quill hanging to the wound in his side; I ran back and pulling it out, brought it home in my left hand, and I have kept it for the Great Spirit to this day!"

"Why do you not then tie it on to the lance again, where it came off?"

"Hush-sh (said he), if the Great Spirit had wished it to be tied on in that place, it never would have come off; he has been kind to me, and I will not offend him."

7. A Riccaree killed by Mah-to-toh-pa in revenge of the death of a white man killed by a Riccaree in the Fur Traders' Fort, a short time previous.

8. Mah-to-toh-pa, or four bears, kills a Shienne chief, who challenged him to single combat, in presence of the two war-parties; they fought on horseback with guns, until Mah-to-toh-pa's powder-horn was shot away; they then fought with bows and arrows, until their quivers were emptied, when they dismounted and fought single-handed. The Shienne drew his knife, and Mah-to-toh-pa had left his; they struggled for the knife, which Mah-to-toh-pa wrested from the Shienne, and killed him with it; in the struggle, the blade of the knife was several times drawn through the hand of Mah-to-toh-pa, and the blood is seen running from the wound.

This extraordinary occurrence also, was one which admits of, and deserves a more elaborate description, which I will here give as it was translated from his own lips, while he sat upon the robe, pointing to his painting of it; and at the same time brandishing the identical knife which he drew from his belt, as he was showing how the fatal blow was given; and exhibiting the wounds inflicted in his hand, as the blade of the knife was several times drawn through it before he wrested it from his antagonist.

A party of about 150 Shienne warriors had made an assault upon the Mandan village at an early hour in the morning, and driven off a considerable number of horses, and taken one scalp. Mah-to-toh-pa, who was then a young man, but famed as one of the most valiant of the Mandans, took the lead of a party of fifty warriors, all he could at that time muster, and went in pursuit of the enemy; about noon of the second day, they came in sight of the Shiennes; and the Mandans, seeing their enemy much more numerous than they had expected, were generally disposed to turn about and return without attacking them. They started to go back, when Mah-to-toh-pa galloped out in front upon the prairie, and plunged his lance into the ground; the blade was driven into the earth to its hilt—he made another circuit around, and in that circuit tore from his breast his reddened sash, which he hung upon its handle as a flag, calling out to the Mandans, "What! have we come to this? we have dogged our enemy two days, and now when we have found them, are we to turn about and go back like cowards? Mah-to-toh-pa's lance, which is red with the blood of brave men, has led you to the sight of your enemy, and you have followed it; it now stands firm in the ground, where the earth will drink the blood of Mah-to-toh-pa! you may all go back, and Mah-to-toh-pa will fight them alone!"

During this manœuvre, the Shiennes, who had discovered the Mandans behind them, had turned about and were gradually approaching, in order to give them battle; the chief of the Shienne war-party seeing and understanding the difficulty, and admiring the gallant conduct of Mah-to-toh-pa, galloped his horse forward within hailing distance in front of the Mandans, and called out to know "who he was who had stuck down his lance and defied the whole enemy alone?"

"I am Mah-to-toh-pa, second in command of the brave and valiant Mandans."

"I have heard often of Mah-to-toh-pa, he is a great warrior—dares Mah-to-toh-pa to come forward and fight this battle with me alone, and our warriors will look on?"

"Is he a chief who speaks to Mah-to-toh-pa?"

"My scalps you see hanging to my horse's bits, and here is my lance with the ermine skins and the war-eagle's tail!"

"You have said enough."

The Shienne chief made a circuit or two at full gallop on a beautiful white horse, when he struck his lance into the ground, and left it standing by the side of the lance of Mah-to-toh-pa, both of which were waving together their little red flags, tokens of blood and defiance.

The two parties then drew nearer, on a beautiful prairie, and the two full-plumed chiefs, at full speed, drove furiously upon each other! both firing their guns at the same moment. They passed each other a little distance and wheeled, when Mah-to-toh-pa drew off his powder-horn, and by holding it up, showed his adversary that the bullet had shattered it to pieces and destroyed his ammunition; he then threw it from him, and his gun also—drew his bow from his quiver, and an arrow, and his shield upon his left arm! The Shienne instantly did the same; *his* horn was thrown off, and his gun was thrown into the air—his shield was balanced on his arm—his bow drawn, and quick as lightning, they were both on the wing for a deadly combat! Like two soaring eagles in the open air, they made their circuits around, and the twangs of their sinewy bows were heard, and the war-whoop, as they dashed by each other, parrying off the whizzing arrows with their shields! Some lodged in their legs and others in their arms; but both protected their *bodies* with their bucklers of bull's hide. Deadly and many were the shafts that fled from their murderous bows. At length the horse of Mah-to-toh-pa fell to the ground with an arrow in his heart! his rider sprang upon his feet prepared to renew the combat; but the Shienne, seeing his adversary dismounted, sprang from his horse, and driving him back, presented the face of his shield towards his enemy, inviting him to come on!—a few shots more were exchanged thus, when the Shienne, having discharged all his arrows, held up his empty quiver, and dashing it furiously to the ground, with his bow and his shield, drew and brandished his naked knife.

"Yes!" said Mah-to-toh-pa, as he threw *his* shield and quiver to the earth, and was rushing up—*he* grasped for his knife, but his belt had it not; he had left it at home! his bow was in his hand, with which he parried his antagonist's blow and felled him to the ground! A desperate struggle now ensued for the knife—the blade of it was several times drawn through the right hand of Mah-to-toh-pa, inflicting the most frightful wounds, while he was severely wounded in several parts of the body. He at length succeeded, however, in wresting it from his adversary's hand, and plunged it to his heart!

By this time the two parties had drawn up in close view of each other, and at the close of the battle, Mah-to-toh-pa held up, and claimed in deadly silence the knife and scalp of the noble Shienne chief.

9. Several hundred Minatarees and Mandans attacked by a party of Assinneboins—all fled but Mah-to-toh-pa, who stood his ground, fired, and killed one of the enemy, putting the rest of them to flight, and driving off sixty horses! He is here seen with his lance and shield—foot-tracks of his enemy in front and his own party's horse-tracks behind him, and a shower of bullets flying around his head; here he got the name of *"the four bears,"* as the Assinneboins said he rushed on like four bears.

10. Mah-to-toh-pa gets from his horse and kills two Ojibbeway women, and takes their scalps; done by the side of an Ojibbeway village, where they went to the river for water. He is here seen with his lance in one hand and his knife in the other—an eagle's plume head-dress on his horse, and his shield left on his horse's back. I incurred his ill-will for a while by asking him, whether it was manly to boast of taking the scalps of women? and his pride prevented him from giving me any explanation or apology. The interpreter, however, explained to me that he had secreted himself in the most daring manner, in full sight of the Ojibbeway village, seeking to revenge a murder, where he remained six days without sustenance, and then killed the two women in full view of the tribe, and made his escape, which entitled him to the credit of a victory, though his victims were women.

11. A large party of Assinneboins entrenched near the Mandan

village attacked by the Mandans and Minatarees, who were driven back—Mah-to-toh-pa rushes into the entrenchment alone—an Indian fires at him and burns his face with the muzzle of his gun, which burst—the Indian retreats, leaving his exploded gun, and Mah-to-toh-pa shoots him through the shoulders as he runs, and kills him with his tomahawk; the gun of the Assinneboin is seen falling to the ground, and in front of him the heads of the Assinneboins in the entrenchment; the horse of Mah-to-toh-pa is seen behind him.

12. Mah-to-toh-pa between his enemy the Sioux, and his own people, with an arrow shot through him, after standing the fire of the Sioux for a long time alone. In this battle he took no scalps, yet his valour was so extraordinary that the chiefs and braves awarded him the honour of a victory.

This feat is seen in the centre of the robe—head-dress of war-eagle's quills on his own and his horse's head—the tracks of his enemies' horses are seen in front of him, and bullets flying both ways all around him. With his whip in his hand, he is seen urging his horse forward, and an arrow is seen flying, and bloody, as it has passed through his body. For this wound, and the several others mentioned above, he bears the honourable scars on his body, which he generally keeps covered with red paint.

Such are the battles traced upon the robe of Mah-to-toh-pa or four bears, interpreted by J. Kipp from the words of the hero while sitting upon the robe, explaining each battle as represented.

LETTER—No. 22

MANDAN VILLAGE, UPPER MISSOURI

OH: *"horribile visu—et mirabile dictu!"* Thank God, it is over, that I have seen it, and am able to tell it to the world.

The *annual religious ceremony,* of four days, of which I have so often spoken, and which I have so long been wishing to see, has at last been enacted in this village; and I have, fortunately, been able to see and to understand it in most of its bearings, which was more than I had reason to expect; for no white man, in all probability, has ever been before admitted to the *medicine-lodge* during these most remarkable and appalling scenes.

Well and truly has it been said, that the Mandans are a strange and peculiar people; and most correctly had I been informed, that this was an important and interesting scene, by those who had, on former occasions, witnessed such parts of it as are transacted out of doors, and in front of the *medicine-lodge.*

Since the date of my last Letter, I was lucky enough to have painted the *medicine-man,* who was high-priest on this grand occasion, or conductor of the ceremonies, who had me regularly installed doctor or *"medicine;"* and who, on the morning when these grand refinements in mysteries commenced, took me by the arm, and led me into the *medicine-lodge,* where the Fur Trader, Mr Kipp, and his two clerks accompanied me in close attendance for four days; all of us going to our own quarters at sun-down, and returning again at sunrise the next morning.

I took my sketch-book with me, and have made many and faithful drawings of what we saw, and full notes of everything as translated to me by the interpreter; and since the close of that horrid and frightful scene, which was a week ago or more, I have been closely ensconced in an earth-covered wigwam, with a fine sky-light over my head, with my palette and brushes, endeavouring faithfully to put the whole of what we saw upon canvas, which my companions all agree to be critically correct, and of the fidelity of which they have attached their certificates to the backs of the paintings. I have made four paintings of these strange scenes, containing several hundred figures, representing the transactions of each day; and if I live to

175

get them home, they will be found to be exceedingly curious and interesting.

I shudder at the relation, or even at the thought of these barbarous and cruel scenes, and am almost ready to shrink from the task of reciting them after I have so long promised some account of them. I entered the *medicine-house* of these scenes, as I would have entered a church, and expected to see something extraordinary and strange, but yet in the form of worship or devotion; but alas! little did I expect to see the interior of their holy temple turned into a *slaughter-house,* and its floor strewed with the blood of its fanatic devotees. Little did I think that I was entering a house of God, where His blinded worshippers were to pollute its sacred interior with their blood, and propitiatory suffering and tortures—surpassing, if possible, the cruelty of the rack or the inquisition; but such the scene has been, and as such I will endeavour to describe it.

The *"Mandan religious ceremony"* then, as I believe it is very justly denominated, is an annual transaction, held in their *medicine-lodge* once a year, as a great religious anniversary, and for several distinct objects, as I shall in a few minutes describe; during and after which, they look with implicit reliance for the justification and approval of the Great Spirit.

All of the Indian tribes, as I have before observed, are religious— are worshipful—and many of them go to almost incredible lengths (as will be seen in the present instance, and many others I may recite) in worshipping the Great Spirit; denying and humbling themselves before Him for the same purpose, and in the same hope as we do, perhaps in a more rational and acceptable way.

The tribes, so far as I have visited them, all distinctly believe in the existence of a Great (or Good) Spirit, an Evil (or Bad) Spirit, and also in a future existence and future accountability, according to their virtues and vices in this world. So far the North American Indians would seem to be one family and such an unbroken theory amongst them; yet with regard to the manner and form, and time and place of that accountability—to the constructions of virtues and vices, and the modes of appeasing and propitiating the Good and Evil Spirits, they are found with all the changes and variety which fortuitous circumstances, and fictions, and fables have wrought upon them.

If from their superstitions and their ignorance, there are often-times obscurities and mysteries thrown over and around their system, yet these affect not the theory itself, which is everywhere essentially the same—and which, if it be not correct, has this much to command the admiration of the enlightened world, that they worship with great sincerity, and all according to one creed.

The Mandans believe in the existence of a Great (or Good) Spirit, and also of an Evil Spirit, who they say existed long before the Good Spirit, and is far superior in power. They all believe also in a future state of existence, and a future administration of rewards and punishments, and (as do all other tribes that I have yet visited) they believe those punishments are not eternal, but commensurate with their sins.

These people, living in a climate where they suffer from cold in the severity of their winters, have very naturally reversed our ideas of Heaven and Hell. The latter they describe to be a country very far to the north, of barren and hideous aspect, and covered with eternal snows and ice. The torments of this freezing place they describe as most excruciating; whilst Heaven they suppose to be in a warmer and delightful latitude, where nothing is felt but the keenest enjoyment, and where the country abounds in buffaloes and other luxuries of life. The Great or Good Spirit they believe dwells in the former place, for the purpose of there meeting those who have offended him; increasing the agony of their sufferings, by being himself present, administering the penalties. The Bad or Evil Spirit they at the same time suppose to reside in Paradise, still tempting the happy; and those who have gone to the regions of punishment they believe to be tortured for a time proportioned to the amount of their transgressions, and that they are then to be transferred to the land of the happy, where they are again liable to the temptations of the Evil Spirit, and answerable again at a future period for their new offences.

Such is the religious creed of the Mandans, and for the purpose of appeasing the Good and Evil Spirits, and to secure their entrance into those "fields Elysian," or beautiful hunting grounds, do the young men subject themselves to the horrid and sickening cruelties to be described in the following pages.

There are other three distinct objects (yet to be named) for which these religious ceremonies are held, which are as follows:—

First, they are held annually as a celebration of the event of the subsiding of the Flood, which they call *Mee-nee-ro-ka-ha-sha* (sinking down or settling of the waters).

Secondly, for the purpose of dancing what they call, *Bel-lohck-na-pick* (the bull-dance); to the strict observance of which they attribute the coming of buffaloes to supply them with food during the season; and

Thirdly and lastly, for the purpose of conducting all the young men of the tribe, as they annually arrive to the age of manhood, through an ordeal of privation and torture, which, while it is supposed to harden their muscles and prepare them for extreme endurance, enables the chiefs who are spectators to the scene, to decide upon their comparative bodily strength and ability to endure the extreme privations and sufferings that often fall to the lots of Indian warriors; and that they may decide who is the most hardy and best able to lead a war-party in case of extreme exigency.

This part of the ceremony, as I have just witnessed it, is truly shocking to behold, and will almost stagger the belief of the world when they read of it. The scene is too terrible and too revolting to be seen or to be told, were it not an essential part of a whole, which will be new to the civilised world, and therefore worth their knowing.

The bull-dance, and many other parts of these ceremonies are exceedingly grotesque and amusing, and that part of them which has a relation to the Deluge is harmless and full of interest.

In the centre of the Mandan village is an open, circular area of 150 feet diameter, kept always clear, as a public ground, for the display of all their public feasts, parades, etc., and around it are their wigwams placed as near to each other as they can well stand, their doors facing the centre of this public area.

In the middle of this ground, which is trodden like a hard pavement, is a curb (somewhat like a large hogshead standing on its end) made of planks (and bound with hoops), some eight or nine feet high, which they religiously preserve and protect from year to year, free from mark or scratch, and which they call the "big canoe"—it is undoubtedly a symbolic representation of a part of their traditional history of the Flood; which it is very evident, from this and numerous other features of this grand ceremony, they have in some way or other received, and are here endeavouring to perpetuate by vividly impressing it on the minds of the whole nation. This object of superstition, from its position as the very centre of the village, is the rallying point of the whole nation. To it their devotions are paid on various occasions of feasts and religious exercises during the year; and in this extraordinary scene it was often the nucleus of their mysteries and cruelties, as I shall shortly describe them, and becomes an object worth bearing in mind, and worthy of being understood.

This exciting and appalling scene, then, which is familiarly (and no doubt correctly) called the "Mandan religious ceremony," commences, not on a particular day of the year (for these people keep no record of days or weeks), but at a particular season, which is designated by the full expansion of the willow leaves under the bank of the river; for according to their tradition, "the twig that the bird brought home was a willow bough, and had full-grown leaves on it," and the bird to which they allude, is the mourning or turtle-dove, which they took great pains to point out to me, as it is often to be seen feeding on the sides of their earth-covered lodges, and which, being, as they call it, a *medicine-bird,* is not to be destroyed or harmed by any one, and even their dogs are instructed not to do it injury.

On the morning on which this strange transaction commenced, I was sitting at breakfast in the house of the Trader, Mr Kipp, when at sunrise, we were suddenly startled by the shrieking and screaming of the women, and barking and howling of dogs, as if an enemy were actually storming their village.

"Now we have it! (exclaimed *mine host,* as he sprang from the table,) the grand ceremony has commenced!—drop your knife and fork, Monsr., and get your sketch-book as soon as possible, that you may lose nothing, for the very moment of *commencing* is as curious as anything else of this strange affair." I seized my sketch-book, and all hands of us were in an instant in front of the medicine-lodge, ready to see and to hear all that was to take place. Groups of women and children were gathered on the tops of their earth-covered wigwams, and all were screaming, and dogs were howling, and all eyes directed to the prairies in the West, where was beheld at a mile distant a solitary individual descending a prairie bluff, and making his way in a direct line towards the village!

The whole community joined in the general expression of great alarm, as if they were in danger of instant destruction; bows were strung and thrummed to test their elasticity—their horses were caught upon the prairie and run into the village—warriors were blackening their faces, and dogs were muzzled, and every preparation made, as if for instant combat.

During this deafening din and confusion within the piquets of the village of the Mandans, the figure discovered on the prairie continued to approach with a dignified step and in a right line towards the village; all eyes were upon him, and he at length made his appearance (without opposition) within the piquets, and proceeded towards the centre of the village, where all the chiefs and braves stood ready to receive him, which they did in a cordial manner, by shaking hands with him, recognising him as an old acquaintance, and pronouncing his name *Nu-mohk-muck-a-nah* (the first or only man). The body of this strange personage, which was chiefly naked, was painted with white clay, so as to resemble at a little distance, a white man; he wore a robe of four white wolf skins falling back over his shoulders; on his head he had a splendid head-dress made of two ravens' skins, and in his left hand he cautiously carried a large pipe, which he seemed to watch and guard as something of great importance. After passing the chiefs and braves as described, he approached the *medicine* or mystery lodge, which he had the means of opening, and which had been religiously closed during the year except for the performance of these religious rites.

Having opened and entered it, he called in four men whom he appointed to clean it out, and put it in readiness for the ceremonies, by sweeping it and strewing a profusion of green willow boughs over its floor, and with them decorating its sides. Wild sage also, and many other aromatic herbs they gathered from the prairies, and scattered over its floor; and over these were arranged a curious group of buffalo and human skulls, and other articles, which were to be used during this strange and unaccountable transaction.

During the whole of this day, and while these preparations were making in the *medicine-lodge,* Nu-mohk-muck-a-nah (the first or only man) travelled through the village, stopping in front of every man's lodge, and crying until the owner of the lodge came out, and asked who he was, and what was the matter? to which he replied by relating the sad catastrophe which had happened on the earth's surface by the overflowing of the waters, saying that "he was the only person saved from the universal calamity; that he landed his big canoe on a high mountain in the west, where he now resides; that he had come to open the *medicine-lodge,* which must needs receive a present of some edged-tool from the owner of every wigwam, that it may be sacrificed to the water; for he says, "if this is not done, there will be another flood, and no one will be saved, as it was with such tools that the big canoe was made."

Having visited every lodge or wigwam in the village, during the day, and having received such a present at each, as a hatchet, a knife, etc. (which is undoubtedly always prepared and ready for the occasion), he returned at evening and deposited them in the *medicine-lodge,* where they remained until the afternoon of the last day of the ceremony, when, as the final or closing scene, they were thrown into the river in a deep place, from a bank thirty feet high, and in presence of the whole village; from whence they can never be recovered, and where they were, undoubtedly, *sacrificed* to the Spirit of the Water.

During the first night of this strange character in the village, no one could tell where he slept; and every person, both old and young, and dogs, and all living things were kept within doors, and dead silence reigned everywhere. On the next morning at sunrise, however, he made his appearance again, and entered the *medicine-lodge;* and at his heels (in *"Indian file,"* *i.e.* single file, one following in another's tracks) all the young men who were candidates for the self-tortures which were to be inflicted, and for the honours that were to be bestowed by the chiefs on those who could most manfully endure them. There were on this occasion about fifty young men who entered the lists, and as they went into the sacred lodge, each one's body was chiefly naked, and covered with clay of different colours; some were red, others were yellow, and some were covered with white clay, giving them the appearance of white men. Each one of them carried in his right hand his *medicine-bag*—on his left arm, his shield of the bull's hide—in his left hand, his bow and arrows, with his quiver slung on his back.

When all had entered the lodge, they placed themselves in reclining postures around its sides, and each one had suspended over his head his respective weapons and *medicine,* presenting altogether, one of the most wild and picturesque scenes imaginable.

Nu-mohk-muck-a-nah (the first or only man) was in the midst of them, and having lit and smoked his medicine-pipe for their success; and having addressed them in a short speech, stimulating and encouraging them to trust to the Great Spirit for his protection during the severe ordeal they were about to pass through; he called into the lodge an old medicine or mystery-man, whose body was painted yellow, and whom he appointed master of ceremonies during this occasion, whom they denominated in their language *O-kee-pah Ka-se-kah* (keeper or conductor of the ceremonies). He was appointed, and the authority passed by the presentation of the medicine-pipe, on which they consider hangs all the power of holding and conducting all these rites.

After this delegated authority had thus passed over to the medicine-man, Nu-mohk-muck-a-nah shook hands with him, and bade him good-bye, saying "that he was going back to the mountains in the west, from whence he should assuredly return in just a year from that time, to open the lodge again." He then went out of the lodge, and passing through the village, took formal leave of the chiefs in the same manner, and soon disappeared over the bluffs from whence he came. No more was seen of this surprising character during the occasion; but I shall have something yet to say of him and his strange office before I get through the Letter.

To return to the lodge,—the medicine or mystery-man just

appointed, and who had received his injunctions from Nu-mohk-muck-a-nah, was left sole conductor and keeper; and according to those injunctions, it was his duty to lie by a small fire in the centre of the lodge, with his medicine-pipe in his hand, crying to the Great Spirit incessantly, watching the young men, and preventing entirely their escape from the lodge, and all communication whatever with people outside, for the space of four days and nights, during which time they were not allowed to *eat,* to *drink,* or to *sleep,* preparatory to the excruciating self-tortures which they were to endure on the fourth day.

I mentioned that I had made four paintings of these strange scenes, and the first one exhibits the interior of the medicine-lodge at this moment; with the young men all reclining around its sides, and the conductor or mystery-man lying by the fire, crying to the Great Spirit (Fig. 66). It was just at this juncture that I was ushered into this sacred temple of their worship, with my companions, which was, undoubtedly, the first time that their devotions had ever been trespassed upon by the presence of pale faces; and in this instance had been brought about in the following strange and unexpected manner.

I had, most luckily for myself, painted a full-length portrait of this great magician or high-priest, but a day previous to the commencement of the ceremonies (in which I had represented him in the performance of some of his mysteries), with which he had been so exceedingly pleased, as well as astonished (as "he could see its eyes move"), that I must needs be, in his opinion, deeply skilled in magic and mysteries, and well-entitled to a respectable rank in the craft, to which I had been at once elevated by the unanimous voice of the doctors, and regularly initiated, and styled *Te-ho-pee-nee-wash-ee-waska-pooska,* the *white medicine* (or Spirit) *painter.*

With this very honourable degree which had just been conferred upon me, I was standing in front of the medicine-lodge early in the morning, with my companions by my side, endeavouring to get a peep, if possible, into its sacred interior; when this *master of ceremonies,* guarding and conducting its secrets, as I before described, came out of the door and taking me with a firm *professional* affection by the arm, led me into this *sanctum sanctorum,* which was strictly guarded from even a peep or a gaze from the vulgar, by a vestibule of eight or ten feet in length, guarded with a double screen or door, and two or three dark and frowning sentinels with spears or war-clubs in their hands. I gave the wink to my companions as I was passing in, and the potency of my *medicine* was such as to gain them

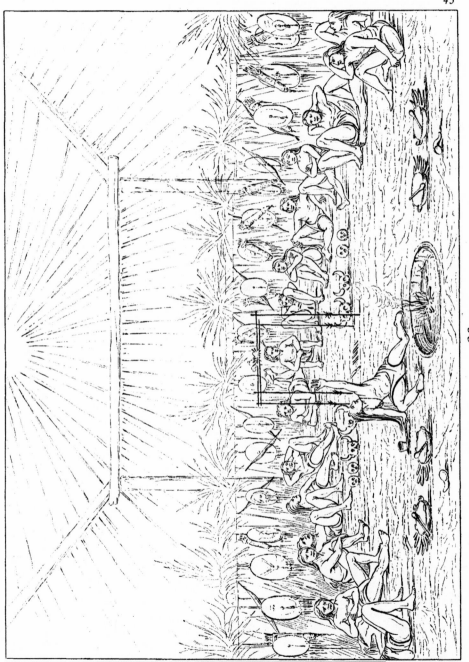

43

G. Carline

a quiet admission, and all of us were comfortably seated on elevated seats, which our conductor soon prepared for us.

We were then in full view of everything that transpired in the lodge, having before us the scene exactly which is represented in the first of the four pictures. To this seat we returned every morning at sunrise, and remained until sundown for four days, the whole time which these strange scenes occupied.

In addition to the preparations and arrangements of the interior of this sanctuary, as above described, there was a curious, though a very strict arrangement of buffalo and human skulls placed on the floor of the lodge, and between them (which were divided into two parcels), and in front of the reclining group of young candidates, was a small and very delicate scaffold, elevated about five feet from the ground, made of four posts or crotches, not larger than a gun-rod, and placed some four or five feet apart, supporting four equally delicate rods, resting in the crotches; thus forming the frame of the scaffold, which was completed by a number of still smaller and more delicate sticks, transversely resting upon them. On the centre of this little frame rested some small object, which I could not exactly understand from the distance of twenty or thirty feet which intervened between it and my eye. I started several times from my seat to approach it, but all eyes were instantly upon me, and every mouth in the assembly sent forth a hush—sh—! which brought me back to my seat again; and I at length quieted my stifled curiosity as well as I could, upon learning the fact, that so sacred was that object, and so important its secrets or mysteries, that not *I* alone, but even the young men who were passing the ordeal, and all the village, save the conductor of the mysteries, were stopped from approaching it, or knowing what it was.

This little mystery-thing, whatever it was, had the appearance from where I sat, of a small tortoise or frog lying on its back, with its head and legs quite extended, and wound and tasselled off with exceedingly delicate red and blue, and yellow ribbons or tassels, and other bright coloured ornaments; and seemed, from the devotions paid to it, to be the very nucleus of their mysteries—the *sanctissimus sanctorum,* from which seemed to emanate all the sanctity of their proceedings, and to which all seemed to be paying the highest devotional respect.

This strange, yet important *essence* of their mysteries, I made every inquiry about; but got no further information of, than what I could learn by my eyes, at the distance at which I saw it, and from the silent respect which I saw paid to it. I tried with the doctors, and all of the *fraternity* answered me, that that was *"great medicine,"* assuring me that it "could not be told." So I quieted my curiosity as well as I could, by the full conviction that I had a *degree* or two yet to take before I could fathom all the arcana of Indian super-stitions; and that this little, seemingly wonderful, relic of antiquity, symbol of some grand event, or "secret too valuable to be told," might have been at last nothing but a silly bunch of strings and toys, to which they pay some great peculiar regard; giving thereby to some favourite Spirit or essence an ideal existence, and which, when called upon to describe, they refuse to do so, calling it *"Great Medicine,"* for the very reason that there is nothing in it to reveal or describe.

Immediately under the little frame or scaffold described, and on the floor of the lodge, was placed a knife, and by the side of it a bundle of splints or skewers, which were kept in readiness for the infliction of the cruelties directly to be explained. There were seen also, in this stage of the affair, a number of cords of rawhide hanging down from the top of the lodge, and passing through its roof, with which the young men were to be suspended by the splints passed through their flesh, and drawn up by men placed on the top of the lodge for the purpose, as will be described in a few moments.

There were also four articles of great veneration and importance lying on the floor of the lodge, which were sacks, containing in each some three or four gallons of water. These also were objects of superstitious regard, and made with great labour and much ingenuity; each one of them being constructed of the skin of the buffalo's neck, and most elaborately sewed together in the form of a large tortoise lying on its back, with a bunch of eagle's quills appended to it as a tail; and each of them having a stick, shaped like a drum-stick, lying on them, with which, in a subsequent stage of these ceremonies, as will be seen, they are beaten upon by several of their mystery-men, as a part of the music for their strange dances and mysteries. By the side of these sacks, which they call *Eeh-teeh-ka,* are two other articles of equal importance, which they call *Eeh-na-dee* (rattles), in the form of a gourd-shell, made also of dried skins, and used at the same time as the others, in the music (or rather *noise* and *din)* for their dances, etc.

These four sacks of water have the appearance of very great antiquity; and by inquiring of my very ingenious friend and patron, the *medicine-man,* after the ceremonies were over, he very gravely told me, that "those four tortoises contained the waters from the four quarters of the world—that these waters had been contained therein ever since the settling down of the waters!" I did not think it best

44

67

G. Catlin.

to advance any argument against so ridiculous a theory, and therefore could not even inquire or learn at what period they had been instituted, or how often, or on what occasions, the water in them had been changed or replenished.

I made several propositions, through my friend Mr Kipp, the trader and interpreter, to purchase one of these strange things by offering them a very liberal price; to which I received an answer that these, and all the very numerous articles used in these ceremonies, being a *society property* were *medicine,* and could not be sold for any consideration; so I abandoned all thoughts of obtaining anything, except what I have done by the *medicine* operation of my pencil, which was applied to everything, and even upon that they looked with decided distrust and apprehension, as a sort of theft or sacrilege.

Such then was the group, and such the appearence of the interior of the medicine-lodge during the three first, and part of the fourth day also, of the Mandan religious ceremonies. The medicine-man, with a group about him of young aspirants who were under his sole control, as was every article and implement to be used, and the sanctity of this solitary and gloomy looking place, which could not be trespassed upon by any man's presence without his most sovereign permission.

During the three first days of this solemn conclave, there were many very curious forms and amusements enacted in the open area in the middle of the village, and in front of the medicine-lodge, by other members of the community, one of which formed a material part or link of these strange ceremonials. This very curious and exceedingly grotesque part of their performance, which they denominated *Bel-lohck-nah-pick* (the bull-dance), of which I have before spoken as one of the avowed objects for which they held this annual fête, and to the strictest observance of which they attribute the coming of buffaloes to supply them with food during the season—is repeated four times during the first day, eight times on the second day, twelve times on the third day, and sixteen times on the fourth day; and always around the curb, or *"big canoe,"* of which I have before spoken.

This subject I have selected for my second picture, and the principal actors in it were eight men, with the entire skins of buffaloes thrown over their backs, with the horns and hoofs and tails remaining on; their bodies in a horizontal position, enabling them to imitate the actions of the buffalo, whilst they were looking out of its eyes as through a mask (Fig. 67).

The bodies of these men were chiefly naked, and all painted in the most extraordinary manner, with the nicest adherence to exact similarity; their limbs, bodies and faces, being in every part covered, either with black, red, or white paint. Each one of these strange characters had also a lock of buffalo's hair tied around his ankles— in his right hand a rattle, and a slender white rod or staff, six feet long, in the other; and carried on his back a bunch of green willow boughs, about the usual size of a bundle of straw. These eight men, being divided into four pairs, took their positions on the four different sides of the curb or big canoe, representing thereby the four cardinal points; and between each group of them, with the back turned to the big canoe, was another figure, engaged in the same dance, keeping step with them, with a similar staff or wand in one hand and a rattle in the other, and (being four in number) answering again to the four cardinal points. The bodies of these four young men were chiefly naked, with no other dress upon them than a beautiful kelt (or quartz-quaw), around the waist, made of eagle's quills and ermine, and very splendid head-dresses made of the same materials. Two of these figures were painted entirely black with pounded charcoal and grease, whom they called the "firmament or night," and the numerous white spots which were dotted all over their bodies, they called "stars." The other two were painted from head to foot as red as vermilion could make them; these they said represented the day, and the white streaks which were painted up and down over their bodies, were "ghosts which the morning rays were chasing away."

These twelve are the only persons actually engaged in this strange dance, which is each time repeated in the same form, without the slightest variation. There are, however, a great number of characters engaged in giving the whole effect and wildness to this strange and laughable scene, each one acting well his part, and whose offices, strange and inexplicable as they are, I will endeavour to point out and explain as well as I can, from what I saw elucidated by their own descriptions.

This most remarkable scene, then, which is witnessed more or less often on each day, takes place in presence of the whole nation, who are generally gathered around, on the tops of the wigwams or otherwise, as spectators, whilst the young men are reclining and fasting in the lodge as above described. On the first day, this *"bull-dance"* is given *once* to each of the cardinal points, and the medicine-man smokes his pipe in those directions. On the second day, *twice* to each; *three times* to each on the third day, and *four times* to each on the fourth. As a signal for the dancers and other characters (as well as the public) to assemble, the old man, master of ceremonies, with the medicine-pipe in hand, dances out of the lodge, singing (or rather crying) forth a most pitiful lament, until he approaches the big canoe, against which he leans, with the pipe in his hand and continues to cry. At this instant, four very aged and patriarchal looking men, whose bodies are painted red, and who have been guarding the four sides of the lodge, enter it and bring out the four sacks of water, which they place near the big canoe, where they seat themselves by the side of them and commence thumping on them with the mallets or drumsticks which have been lying on them; and another brandishes and shakes the *eeh-na-dees* or rattles, and all unite to them their voices, raised to the highest pitch possible, as the music, for the *bull-dance,* which is then commenced and continued for fifteen minutes or more, in perfect time, and without cessation or intermission. When the music and dancing stop, which are always perfectly simultaneous, the whole nation raise the huzza! and deafening shout of approbation; the master of ceremonies dances back to the medicine-lodge, and the old men return to their former place; the sacks of water, and all rest as before, until, by the same method, they are again called into a similar action.

The supernumeraries or other characters who play their parts in this grand spectacle, are numerous, and well worth description. By the side of the big canoe are seen two men with the skins of grizzly bears thrown over them, using the skins as a mask over their heads. These ravenous animals are continually growling and threatening to devour everything before them, and interfering with the forms of their religious ceromony. To appease them, the women are continually bringing and placing before them dishes of meat, which are as often snatched up and carried to the prairie by two men, whose bodies are painted black and their heads white, whom they called bald eagles, who are darting by them and grasping their food from before them as they pass. These are again chased upon the plains by a hundred or more small boys, who are naked, with their bodies painted yellow and their heads white, whom they call *Cabris* or antelopes; who at length get the food away from them, and devour it; thereby inculcating (perhaps) the beautiful moral, that by the dispensations of Providence his bountiful gifts will fall at last to the hands of the innocent.

During the intervals between these dances, all these characters, except those from the medicine-lodge, retire to a wigwam close by, which they use on the occasion also as a sacred place, being occupied exclusively by them while they are at rest, and also for the purpose of painting and ornamenting their bodies for the occasion.

During each and every one of these dances, the old men who

beat upon the sacks and sing, are earnestly chanting forth their supplications to the Great Spirit, for the continuation of his influence in sending them buffaloes to supply them with food during the year; they are administering courage and fortitude to the young men in the lodge, by telling them, that "the Great Spirit has opened his ears in their behalf—that the very atmosphere all about them is peace—that their women and children can hold the mouth of the grizzly bear—that they have invoked from day to day O-kee-hee-de (the Evil Spirit)—that they are still challenging him to come, and yet he has not dared to make his appearance!"

But alas! in the last of these dances, on the fourth day, in the midst of all their mirth and joy, and about noon, and in the height of all these exultations, an instant scream burst forth from the tops of the lodges!—men, women, dogs and all, seemed actually to howl and shudder with alarm, as they fixed their glaring eye-balls upon the prairie bluff, about a mile in the west, down the side of which a man was seen descending at full speed towards the village! This strange character darted about in a zig-zag course in all directions on the prairie, like a boy in pursuit of a butterfly, until he approached the piquets of the village, when it was discovered that his body was entirely naked, and painted as black as a negro, with pounded charcoal and bear's grease; his body was therefore everywhere of a shining black, except occasionally white rings of an inch or more in diameter, which were marked here and there all over him; and frightful indentures of white around his mouth, resembling canine teeth. Added to his hideous appearance, he gave the most frightful shrieks and screams as he dashed through the village and entered the terrified group, which was composed (in that quarter) chiefly of females, who had assembled to witness the amusements which were transpiring around the "big canoe."

This unearthly-looking creature carried in two hands a wand or staff of eight or nine feet in length, with a red ball at the end of it, which he continually slid on the ground ahead of him as he ran. All eyes in the village, save those of the persons engaged in the dance, were centred upon him, and he made a desperate rush towards the women, who screamed for protection as they were endeavouring to retreat; and falling in groups upon each other as they were struggling to get out of his reach. In this moment of general terror and alarm there was an instant check! and all for a few moments were as silent as death.

The old master of ceremonies, who had run from his position at the big canoe, had met this monster of fiends, and having thrust the *medicine-pipe* before him, held him still and immovable under its charm! This check gave the females an opportunity to get out of his reach, and when they were free from their danger, though all hearts beat yet with the instant excitement, their alarm soon cooled down into the most exorbitant laughter and shouts of applause at his sudden defeat, and the awkward and ridiculous posture in which he was stopped and held. The old man was braced stiff by his side, with his eye-balls glaring him in the face, whilst the medicine-pipe held in its mystic chains his *Satanic* Majesty, annulling all the the powers of his magical wand, and also depriving him of the powers of locomotion! Surely no two human beings ever presented a more striking group than these two individuals did for a few moments, with their eye-balls set in direct mutual hatred upon each other; both struggling for the supremacy, relying on the potency of their medicine or mystery. The one held in check, with his body painted black, representing (or rather assuming to be) his sable majesty, O-kee-hee-de (the Evil Spirit), frowning everlasting vengeance on the other, who sternly gazed him back with a look of exultation and contempt, as he held him in check and disarmed under the charm of his sacred mystery-pipe.

When the superior powers of the medicine-pipe (on which hang all these annual mysteries) had been thus fully tested and acknowledged, and the women had had requisite time to withdraw from the reach of this fiendish monster, the pipe was very gradually withdrawn from before him, and he seemed delighted to recover the use of his limbs again, and power of changing his position from the exceedingly unpleasant and really ridiculous one he appeared in, and was compelled to maintain, a few moments before; rendered more superlatively ridiculous and laughable, from the further information, which I am constrained to give, of the plight in which this demon of terror and vulgarity made his *entrée* into the midst of the Mandan village, and to the centre and nucleus of their first and greatest religious ceremony.

Then, to proceed; I said that this strange personage's body was naked—was painted jet black with charcoal and bear's grease, with a wand in his hands of eight feet in length with a red ball at the end of it, which he was rubbing about on the ground in front of him as he ran. In addition to this he *had—ung gee ah waheea notch, toheks tcha, ung gee an ung hutch tow a tow ah ches menny. Ung gee ah to to wun nee, ahkst to wan ee eigh's ta w.*

In this plight, in which I have not dared fully to represent him in the picture, he pursued the groups of females, spreading dismay and alarm wherever he went, and consequently producing the awkward and exceedingly laughable predicament in which he was placed by the sudden check from the medicine-pipe, as I have above stated, when all eyes were intently fixed upon him, and all joined in rounds of applause for the success of the magic spell that was placed upon him; all voices were raised in shouts of satisfaction at his defeat, and all eyes gazed upon him; of chiefs and of warriors —matrons, and even of their tender-aged and timid daughters, whose education had taught them to receive the *moral* of these scenes without the shock of impropriety, that would have startled a more fastidious and consequently sensual-thinking people.

After repeated attempts thus made, and thus defeated in several parts of the crowd, this blackened monster was retreating over the ground where the buffalo-dance was going on, and having (apparently, par accident) swaggered against one of the men placed under the skin of a buffalo and engaged in the "bull-dance," he started back, and placing himself in the attitude of a buffalo—*hi ung ee a wahkstia, chee a nahk s tammee ung s towa; ee ung ee aht gwaht ee o nunghths tcha ho a, tummee oxt no ah, ughstono ah hi en en ah nahxt gwi aht gahtch gun ne. Gwee en on doatcht chee en aht gunne how how en ahxst tehu!*

After this he paid his visits to three others of the eight, in succession, receiving as before the deafening shouts of approbation which pealed from every mouth in the multitude, who were all praying to the Great Spirit to send them buffaloes to supply them with food during the season, and who attribute the coming of buffaloes for this purpose entirely to the strict and critical observance of this ridiculous and disgusting part of the ceremonies.

During the half-hour or so that he had been jostled about amongst man and beasts, to the great amusement and satisfaction of the lookers-on, he seemed to have become exceedingly exhausted, and anxiously looked out for some feasible mode of escape.

In this awkward predicament he became the laughing-stock and butt for the women, who being no longer afraid of him, were gathering in groups around, to tease and tantalise him; and in the midst of this dilemma, which soon became a very sad one—one of the women, who stole up behind him with both hands full of yellow dirt—dashed it into his face and eyes, and all over him, and his body being covered with grease, took instantly a different hue. He seemed heart-broken at this signal disgrace, and commenced crying most vehemently, when, *al'instant,* another caught his *wand* from his hand, and broke it across her knee. It was snatched for by

45

G. Catlin

others who broke it still into bits, and then threw them at him. His power was now gone—his bodily strength was exhausted, and he made a bolt for the prairie—he dashed through the crowd, and made his way through the piquets on the back part of the village, where were placed for the purpose, an hundred or more women and girls, who escorted him as he ran on the prairie for half a mile or more, beating him with sticks, and stones, and dirt, and kicks, and cuffs, until he was at length seen escaping from their clutches, and making the best of his retreat over the prairie bluffs, from whence he first appeared.

At the moment of this signal victory, and when all eyes lost sight of him as he disappeared over the bluffs, the whole village united their voices in shouts of satisfaction. The bull-dance then stopped, and preparations were instantly made for the commencement of the cruelties which were to take place within the lodge, leaving us to draw, from what had just transpired, the following beautiful moral:—

That in the midst of their religious ceremonies, the Evil Spirit (O-kee-hee-de) made his entrée for the purpose of doing mischief, and of disturbing their worship—that he was held in check, and defeated by the superior influence and virtue of the *medicine-pipe,* and at last, driven in disgrace out of the village, by the very part of the community whom he came to abuse.

At the close of this exciting scene, preparations were made, as above stated, by the return of the master of ceremonies and musicians to the medicine-lodge, where also were admitted at the same time a number of men, who were to be instruments of the cruelties to be inflicted; and also the chief and doctors of the tribe, who were to look on, and bear witness to, and decide upon, the comparative degree of fortitude, with which the young men sustain themselves in this most extreme and excruciating ordeal. The chiefs having seated themselves on one side of the lodge, dressed out in their robes and splendid head-dresses—the band of music seated and arranged themselves in another part; and the old master of ceremonies having placed himself in front of a small fire in the centre of the lodge, with his "big pipe" in his hands, and having commenced smoking to the Great Spirit, with all possible vehemence for the success of these aspirants, presented the subject for the third picture, which they call *"pohk-hong,"* the cutting scene (Fig. 68). Around the sides of the lodge are seen, still reclining, as I have before mentioned, a part of the group, whilst others of them have passed the ordeal of self-tortures, and have been removed out of the lodge; and others still are seen in the very act of submitting to them, which were inflicted in the following manner:—After having removed the *sanctum sanctorum,* or little scaffold, of which I before spoke, and having removed also the buffalo and human skulls from the floor, and attached them to the posts of the lodge; and two men having taken their positions near the middle of the lodge, for the purpose of inflicting the tortures— the one with the scalping-knife, and the other with the bunch of splints (which I have before mentioned) in his hand; one at a time of the young fellows, already emaciated with fasting, and thirsting, and waking, for nearly four days and nights, advanced from the side of the lodge, and placed himself on his hands and feet, or otherwise, as best suited for the performance of the operation, where he submitted to the cruelties in the following manner:—An inch or more of the flesh on each shoulder, or each breast was taken up between the thumb and finger by the man who held the knife in his right hand; and the knife, which had been ground sharp on both edges, and then hacked and notched with the blade of another, to make it produce as much pain as possible, was forced through the flesh below the fingers, and being withdrawn, was followed with a splint or skewer from the other, who held a bunch of such in his left hand, and was ready to force them through the wound. There were then two cords lowered down from the top of the lodge (by men who were placed on the lodge outside for the purpose), which were fastened to these splints or skewers, and they instantly began to haul him up; he was thus raised until his body was just suspended from the ground where he rested, until the knife and a splint were passed through the flesh or integuments in a similar manner on each arm below the shoulder (over the *brachialis externus),* below the elbow (over the *extensor carpi radialis),* on the thighs (over the *vastus externus),* and below the knees (over the *peroneus).*

In some instances they remained in a reclining position on the ground until this painful operation was finished, which was performed, in all instances, exactly on the same parts of the body and limbs; and which, in its progress, occupied some five or six minutes.

Each one was then instantly raised with the cords, until the weight of his body was suspended by them, and then, while the blood was streaming down their limbs, the bystanders hung upon the splints each man's appropriate shield, bow and quiver, etc.; and in many instances, the skull of a buffalo with the horns on it, was attached to each lower arm and each lower leg, for the purpose, probably, of preventing by their great weight, the struggling, which might otherwise take place to their disadvantage whilst they were hung up.

When these things were all adjusted, each one was raised higher by the cords, until these weights all swung clear from the ground, leaving his feet, in most cases, some six or eight feet above the ground. In this plight they at once became appalling and frightful to look at —the flesh, to support the weight of their bodies, with the additional weights which were attached to them, was raised six or eight inches by the skewers; and their heads sunk forward on the breasts, or thrown backwards, in a much more frightful condition, according to the way in which they were hung up.

The unflinching fortitude with which every one of them bore this part of the torture surpassed credulity; each one as the knife was passed through his flesh sustained an unchangeable countenance; and several of them, seeing me making sketches, beckoned me to look at their faces, which I watched through all this horrid operation, without being able to detect anything but the pleasantest smiles as they looked me in the eye, while I could hear the knife rip through the flesh, and feel enough of it myself to start involuntary and uncontrollable tears over my cheeks.

When raised to the condition above described, and completely suspended by the cords, the sanguinary hands, through which he had just passed, turned back to perform a similar operation on another who was ready, and each one in his turn passed into the charge of others, who instantly introduced him to a new and improved stage of their refinements in cruelty.

Surrounded by imps and demons as they appear, a dozen or more, who seem to be concerting and devising means for his exquisite agony, gather around him, when one of the number advances towards him in a sneering manner, and commences turning him around with a pole which he brings in his hand for the purpose. This is done in a gentle manner at first; but gradually increased, when the brave fellow, whose proud spirit can control its agony no longer, burst out in the most lamentable and heart-rending cries that the human voice is capable of producing, crying forth a prayer to the Great Spirit to support and protect him in this dreadful trial; and continually repeating his confidence in his protection. In this condition he is continued to be turned, faster and faster—and there is no hope of escape from it, nor chance for the slightest relief, until by fainting, his voice falters, and his struggling ceases, and he hangs, apparently, a still and lifeless corpse! 'When he is, by turning, gradually brought to this condition, which is generally done within ten or fifteen minutes, there is a close scrutiny passed upon him among his tormentors, who are checking and holding each other back as long as the least struggling or tremor can be discovered, lest he should be removed before he is (as they term it) "entirely dead."

When brought to this alarming and most frightful condition, and the turning has gradually ceased, as his voice and his strength have given out, leaving him to hang entirely still, and apparently lifeless; when his tongue is distended from his mouth, and his *medicine-bag,* which he has affectionately and superstitiously clung to with his left hand, has dropped to the ground; the signal is given to the men on top of the lodge, by gently striking the cord with the pole below, when they very gradually and carefully lower him to the ground.

In this helpless condition he lies, like a loathsome corpse to look at, though in the keeping (as they call it) of the Great Spirit, whom he trusts will protect him, and enable him to get up and walk away. As soon as he is lowered to the ground thus, one of the bystanders advances, and pulls out the two splints or pins from the breasts and shoulders, thereby disengaging him from the cords by which he has been hung up; but leaving all the others with their weights, etc., hanging to his flesh.

In this condition he lies for six or eight minutes, until he gets strength to rise and move himself, for no one is allowed to assist or offer him aid, as he is here enjoying the most valued privilege which a Mandan can boast of, that of "trusting his life to the keeping of the Great Spirit," in this time of extreme peril.

As soon as he is seen to get strength enough to rise on his hands and feet, and drag his body around the lodge, he crawls with the weights still hanging to his body, to another part of the lodge, where there is another Indian sitting with a hatchet in his hand, and a dried buffalo skull before him; and here, in the most earnest and humble manner, by holding up the little finger of his left hand to the Great Spirit, he expresses to Him, in a speech of a few words, his willingness to give it as a sacrifice; when he lays it on the dried buffalo skull, where the other chops it off near the hand, with a blow of the hatchet!

Nearly all of the young men whom I saw passing this horrid ordeal, gave in the above manner, the little finger of the left hand; and I saw also several, who immediately afterwards (and apparently with very little concern or emotion), with a similar speech, extended in the same way, the *fore-*finger of the same hand, and that too was struck off; leaving on the left hand only the two middle fingers and the thumb; all which they deem absolutely essential for holding the bow, the only weapon for the left hand.

One would think that this mutilation had thus been carried quite far enough; but I have since examined several of the head chiefs and dignitaries of the tribe, who have also given, in this manner, the little finger of the right hand, which is considered by them to be a much greater sacrifice than both of the others; and I have found also a number of their most famous men, who furnish me incontestible proof, by five or six corresponding scars on each arm, and each breast, and each leg, that they had so many times in their lives submitted to this almost incredible operation, which seems to be optional with them; and the oftener they volunteer to go through it, the more famous they become in the estimation of their tribe.

No bandages are applied to the fingers which have been amputated, nor any arteries taken up; nor is any attention whatever, paid to them or the other wounds; but they are left (as they say) "for the Great Spirit to cure, who will surely take good care of them." It is a remarkable fact (which I learned from a close inspection of their wounds from day to day) that the bleeding is but very slight, and soon ceases, probably from the fact of their extreme exhaustion and debility, caused by want of sustenance and sleep, which checks the natural circulation, and admirably at the same time prepares them to meet the severity of these tortures without the same degree of sensibility and pain, which, under other circumstances, might result in inflammation and death.

During the whole of the time of this cruel part of these most extraordinary inflictions, the chiefs and dignitaries of the tribe are looking on, to decide who are the hardiest and "stoutest hearted"—who can hang the longest by his flesh before he faints, and who will be soonest up, after he has been clown; that they may know whom to appoint to lead a war-party, or place at the most honourable and desperate post. The four old men are incessantly beating upon the sacks of water and singing the whole time, with their voices strained to the highest key, vaunting forth, for the encouragement of the young men, the power and efficacy of the *medicinc-pipe,* which has disarmed the monster O-kee-he-de (or Evil Spirit), and driven him from the village, and will be sure to protect them and watch over them through their present severe trial.

As soon as six or eight had passed the ordeal as above described, they were led out of the lodge, with their weights hanging to their flesh, and dragging on the ground, to undergo another, and a still more appalling mode of suffering in the centre of the village, and in presence of the whole nation, in the manner as follows:—

The signal for the commencement of this part of the cruelties was given by the old master of ceremonies, who again ran out as in the buffalo-dance, and leaning against the big canoe, with his *medicine-pipe* in his hand, began to cry. This was done several times in the afternoon, as often as there were six or eight who had passed the ordeal just described within the lodge, who were then taken out in the open area, in the presence of the whole village, with the buffalo skulls and other weights attached to their flesh, and dragging on the ground! There were then in readiness, and prepared for the purpose, about twenty young men, selected of equal height and equal age; with their bodies chiefly naked, with beautiful (and similar) head-dresses of war-eagle's quills, on their heads, and a wreath made of willow boughs held in the hands between them, connecting them in a chain or circle in which they ran around the *big canoe,* with all possible speed, raising their voices in screams and yelps to the highest pitch that was possible, and keeping the curb or big canoe in the centre, as their nucleus.

Then were led forward the young men who were further to suffer, and being placed at equal distances apart, and outside of the ring just described, each one was taken in charge of two athletic young men, fresh and strong, who stepped up to him, one on each side, and by wrapping a broad leather strap around his wrists, without tying it, grasped it firm underneath the hand, and stood prepared for what they call *Eh-Ke-na-ka-nah-pick* (the last race, Fig. 69). This, the spectator looking on would suppose was most correctly named, for he would think it was the last race they could possibly run in this world.

In this condition they stand, pale and ghastly, from abstinence and loss of blood, until all are prepared, and the word is given, when all start and run around, outside of the other ring; and each poor fellow, with his weights dragging on the ground, and his furious conductors by his side, who hurry him forward by the wrists, struggles in the desperate emulation to run longer without "dying" (as they call it) than his comrades, who are fainting around him and sinking down, like himself, where their bodies are dragged with all possible speed, and often with their faces in the dirt. In the commencement of this dance or race they all start at a moderate pace, and their speed being gradually increased, the pain becomes so excruciating that their languid and exhausted frames give out, and they are dragged by their wrists until they are disengaged from the weights that were attached to their flesh, and this must be done by such violent force as to tear the flesh out with the splint, which (as they say) can never be pulled out endwise, without greatly offending the Great Spirit and defeating the object for which they have thus far suffered.

46

G. Catlin

The splints or skewers which are put through the breast and the shoulders, take up a part of the pectoral or trapegius muscle, which is necessary for the support of the great weight of their bodies, and which, as I have before mentioned, are withdrawn as soon as he is lowered down—but all the others, on the legs and arms, seem to be very ingeniously passed through the flesh and integuments without taking up the muscle, and even these, to be broken out, require so strong and so violent a force that most of the poor fellows fainted under the operation, and when they were freed from the last of the buffalo skulls and other weights, (which was often done by some of the bystanders throwing the weight of their bodies on to them as they were dragging on the ground) they were in every instance dropped by the persons who dragged them, and their bodies were left, appearing like nothing but a mangled and a loathsome corpse! At this strange and frightful juncture, the two men who had dragged them, fled through the crowd and away upon the prairie, as if they were guilty of some enormous crime, and were fleeing from summary vengeance.

Each poor fellow, having thus patiently and manfully endured the privations and tortures devised for him, and (in this last struggle with the most appalling effort) torn himself loose from them and his tormentors, he lies the second time, in the "keeping (as he terms it) of the Great Spirit," to whom he issued his repeated prayers, and entrusted his life: and in whom he reposes the most implicit confidence for his preservation and recovery. As an evidence of this, and of the high value which these youths set upon this privilege, there is no person, not a relation nor a chief of the tribe, who is allowed, or who would dare, to step forward to offer an aiding hand, even to save his life; for not only the rigid customs of the nation, and the pride of the individual who has entrusted his life to the keeping of the Great Spirit, would sternly reject such a tender; but their superstition, which is the strongest of all arguments in an Indian community, would alone, hold all the tribe in fear and dread of interfering, when they consider they have so good a reason to believe that the Great Spirit has undertaken the special care and protection of his devoted worshippers.

In this "last race," which was the struggle that finally closed their sufferings, each one was dragged until he fainted, and was thus left, looking more like the dead than the living: and thus each one lay, until, by the aid of the Great Spirit, he was in a few minutes seen gradually rising, and at last reeling and staggering, like a drunken man, through the crowd (which. made way for him) to his wigwam, where his friends and relatives stood ready to take him into hand and restore him.

In this frightful scene, as in the buffalo-dance, the whole nation was assembled as spectators, and all raised the most piercing and violent yells and screams they could possibly produce, to drown the cries of the suffering ones, that no heart could even be touched with sympathy for them. I have mentioned before, that six or eight of the young men were brought from the medicine-lodge at a time, and when they were thus passed through this shocking ordeal, the medicine-men and the chiefs returned to the interior, where as many more were soon prepared, and underwent a similar treatment; and after that another batch, and another, and so on, until the whole number, some forty-five or fifty had run in this sickening circle, and, by leaving their weights, had opened the flesh for honourable scars. I said *all,* but there was one poor fellow though (and I shudder to tell it), who was dragged around and around the circle, with the skull of an elk hanging to the flesh on one of his legs,—several had jumped upon it, but to no effect, for the splint was under the sinew, which could not be broken. The dragging, became every instant more and more furious, and the apprehensions for the poor fellow's life, apparent by the piteous howl which was set up for him by the multitude around; and at last the medicine-man ran, with his medicine-pipe in his hand, and held them in check, when the body was dropped, and left upon the ground, with the skull yet hanging to it. The boy, who was an extremely interesting and fine-looking youth, soon recovered his senses and his strength, looking deliberately at his torn and bleeding limbs; and also with the most pleasant smile of defiance, upon the misfortune which had now fallen to his peculiar lot, crawled through the crowd (instead of walking, which they are never again at liberty to do until the flesh is torn out, and the article left) to the prairie, and over which, for the distance of half a mile, to a sequestered spot, without any attendant, where he lay three days and three nights, yet longer, without food, and praying to the Great Spirit, until suppuration took place in the wound, and by the decaying of the flesh the weight was dropped, and the splint also, which he dare not extricate in another way. At the end of this, he crawled back to the village on his hands and knees, being too much emaciated to walk, and begged for something to eat, which was at once given him, and he was soon restored to health.

These extreme and difficult cases often occur, and I learn that in such instances the youth has it at his option to get rid of the weight that is thus left upon him, in such way as he may choose, and some of those modes are far more extraordinary than the one which I have just named. Several of the Traders, who have been for a number of years in the habit of seeing this part of the ceremony, have told me that two years since, when they were looking on, there was one whose flesh on the arms was so strong that the weights could not be left, and he dragged them with his body to the river by the side of the village, where he set a stake fast in the ground on the top of the bank, and fastening cords to it, he let himself half-way down a perpendicular wall of rock, of twenty-five or thirty feet, where. the weight of his body was suspended by the two cords attached to the flesh of his arms. In this awful condition he hung for several days, equi-distant from the top of the rock and the deep water below, into which he at last dropped and saved himself by swimming ashore!

I need record no more of these shocking and disgusting instances, of which I have already given enough to convince the world of the correctness of the established fact of the Indian's superior stoicism and power of endurance, although some recent writers have, from motives of envy, from ignorance, or something else, taken great pains to cut the poor Indian short in everything, and in *this,* even as if it were a virtue.

I am ready to accord to them in this particular, the palm; the credit of outdoing anything and everybody, and of enduring more than civilised man ever aspired to or ever thought of. My heart has sickened also with disgust for so abominable and ignorant a custom, and still I stand ready with all my heart, to excuse and forgive them for adhering so strictly to an ancient celebration, founded in superstitions and mysteries, of which they know not the origin, and constituting a material part and. feature in the code and forms of their religion.

Reader, I will return with you a moment to the medicine-lodge, which is just to be closed, and then we will indulge in some general reflections upon what has passed, and in what, and for what purposes this strange batch of mysteries has been instituted and perpetuated.

After these young men, who had for the last four days occupied the medicine-lodge, had been operated on, in the manner above described, and taken out of it, the old medicine-man, master of ceremonies returned (still crying to the Great Spirit), sole tenant of that sacred place, and brought out the "edged-tools," which I before said had been collected at the door of every man's wigwam, to be given as a sacrifice to the water, and leaving the lodge securely fastened, he approached the bank of the river, when all the medicine-men attended him, and all the nation were spectators; and in their presence he threw them from a high bank into very deep water, from which they cannot be recovered, and where they are, correctly speaking, made a sacrifice to the water. This part of the affair takes place just exactly at sundown, and closes the scene, being the end or finale of the *Mandan religious ceremony.*

The reader will forgive me for here inserting the Certificates which I have just received from Mr Kipp, of the city of New York, and two others, who were with me; which I offer for the satisfaction of the world, who read the above account.

"We hereby certify, that we witnessed, in company with Mr Catlin, in the Mandan Village, the ceremonies represented in the four paintings, and described in his Notes, to which this certificate refers; and that he has therein faithfully represented those scenes as we saw them transacted, without any addition or exaggeration.

"J. KIPP, *Agent Amer. Fur Company.*
"Mandan Village,　　　　L. CRAWFORD, *Clerk.*
July 20, 1833.　　　　ABRAHAM BOGARD."

The strange country that I am in—its excitements—its accidents and wild incidents which startle me at almost every moment, prevent me from any very elaborate disquisition upon the above remarkable events at present; and even had I all the time and leisure of a country gentleman, and all the additional information which I am daily procuring, and daily expect to procure hereafter in explanation of these unaccountable mysteries, yet do I fear that there would be that inexplicable difficulty that hangs over most of the customs and traditions of these simple people, who have no history to save facts and systems from falling into the most absurd and disjointed fable and ignorant fiction.

What few plausible inferences I have as yet been able to draw from the above strange and peculiar transactions I will set forth, but with some diffidence, hoping and trusting that by further intimacy and familiarity with these people I may yet arrive at more satisfactory and important results.

That these people should have a tradition of the Flood is by no means surprising; as I have learned from every tribe I have visited, that they all have some high mountain in their vicinity, where they insist upon it the big canoe landed; but that these people should hold an annual celebration of the event, and the season of that decided by such circumstances as the full leaf of the willow, and the medicine-lodge opened by such a man as Nu-mohk-muck-a-nah (who appears to be a white man), and making his appearance "from the high-mountains in the West;" and some other circumstances, is surely a very remarkable thing, and requires some extraordinary attention.

This Nu-mohk-muck-a-nah (first or only man) is undoubtedly some mystery or medicine-man of the tribe, who has gone out on the prairie on the evening previous, and having dressed and painted himself for the occasion, comes into the village in the morning, endeavouring to keep up the semblance of reality; for their tradition says, that at a very ancient period such a man did actually come from the West—that his body was of the white colour, as this man's body is represented—that he wore a robe of four white wolf skins—his head-dress was made of two ravens' skins—and in his left hand was a huge pipe. He said, "he was at one time the only man—he told them of the destruction of every thing on the earth's surface by water—that he stopped in his *big canoe* on a high mountain in the West, where he landed and was saved."

"That the Mandans, and all other people were bound to make yearly sacrifices of some edged-tools to the water, for of such things the big canoe was made. That he instructed the Mandans how to build their medicine-lodge, and taught them also the forms of these annual ceremonies; and told them that as long as they made these sacrifices, and performed their rites to the full letter, they might be assured of the fact, that they would be the favourite people of the Almighty, and would always have enough to eat and drink; and that so soon as they should depart in one tittle from these forms, they might be assured, that their race would decrease, and finally run out; and that they might date their nation's calamity to that omission or neglect."

These people have, no doubt, been long living under the dread of such an injunction, and in the fear of departing from it; and while they are living in total ignorance of its origin, the world must remain equally ignorant of much of its meaning, as they needs must be of all Indian customs resting on ancient traditions, which soon run into fables, having lost all their system, by which they might have been construed.

This strange and unaccountable custom, is undoubtedly peculiar to the Mandans; although, amongst the Minatarees, and some others of the neighbouring tribes, they have seasons of abstinence and self-torture, somewhat similar, but bearing no other resemblance to this than a mere feeble effort or form of imitation.

It would seem from their tradition of the willow branch, and the dove, that these people must have had some proximity to some part of the civilised world; or that missionaries or others have been formerly among them, inculcating the Christian religion and the Mosaic account of the Flood; which is, in this and some other respects, decidedly different from the theory which most natural people have distinctly established of that event.

There are other strong, and almost decisive proofs in my opinion, in support of the assertion, which are to be drawn from the diversity of colour in their hair and complexions, as I have before described, as well as from their tradition just related, of the *"first or only man,"* whose body was white, and who came from the West, telling them of the destruction of the earth by water, and instructing them in the forms of these mysteries; and, in addition to the above, I will add the two following very curious stories, which I had from several of their old and dignified chiefs, and which are, no doubt, standing and credited traditions of the tribe.

"The Mandans (people of the pheasants) were the first people created in the world, and they originally lived inside of the earth; they raised many vines, and one of them had grown up through a hole in the earth, over head, and one of their young men clumb up it until he came out on the top of the ground, on the bank of the river, where the Mandan village stands. He looked around, and admired the beautiful country and prairies about him—saw many buffaloes —killed one with his bow and arrows, and found that its meat was good to eat. He returned and related what he had seen; when a number of others went up the vine with him, and witnessed the same things. Amongst those who went up, were two very pretty young women, who were favourites of the chiefs, because they were virgins; and amongst those who were trying to get up, was a very large and fat woman, who was ordered by the chiefs not to go up, but whose curiosity led her to try it as soon as she got a secret opportunity, when there was no one present. When she got part of the way up, the vine broke under the great weight of her body, and let her down. She was very much hurt by the fall, but did not die. The Mandans were very sorry about this; and she was disgraced for being the cause of a very great calamity, which she had brought upon them, and which could never be averted; for no more could ever ascend, nor could those descend who had got up; but they built the Mandan village, where it formerly stood, a great ways below on the river; and the remainder of the people live under ground to this day."

The above tradition is told with great gravity by their chiefs and doctors or mystery-men; and the latter profess to hear their friends talk through the earth at certain times and places, and even consult them for their opinions and advice on many important occasions.

The next tradition runs thus:—

"At a very ancient period, O-kee-hee-de (the Evil Spirit, the black fellow mentioned in the religious ceremonies) came to the Mandan village with Nu-mohk-muck-a-nah (the first or only man) from the West, and sat down by a woman who had but one eye, and was hoeing corn. Her daughter, who was very pretty, came up to her, and the Evil Spirit desired her to go and bring some water; but wished that before she started, she would come to him and eat some buffalo meat. He told her to take a piece out of his side, which she did and ate it, which proved to be buffalo-fat. She then went for the water, which she brought, and met them in the village where they had walked, and they both drank of it—nothing more was done.

"The friends of the girl soon after endeavoured to disgrace her, by telling her that she was *enciente,* which she did not deny. She declared her innocence at the same time, and boldly defied any man in the village to come forward and accuse her. This raised a great excitement in the village, and as no one could stand forth to accuse her, she was looked upon as *great medicine.* She soon after went off secretly to the upper Mandan village, where the child was born.

"Great search was made for her before she was found; as it was expected that the child would also be great *medicine* or mystery, and of great importance to the existence and welfare of the tribe. They were induced to this belief from the very strange manner of its conception and birth, and were soon confirmed in it from the wonderful things which it did at an early age. They say, that amongst other miracles which he performed, when the Mandans were like to starve, he gave them four buffalo bulls, which filled the whole village—leaving as much meat as there was before they had eaten; saying that these four bulls would supply them for ever. Nu-mohk-muck-a-nah (the first or only man) was bent on the destruction of the child, and after making many fruitless searches for it, found it hidden in a dark place, and put it to death by throwing it into the river.

"When O-kee-hee-de (the Evil Spirit) heard of the death of this child, he sought for Nu-mohk-muck-a-nah with intent to kill him. He traced him a long distance, and at length found him at *Heart River,* about seventy miles below the village, with the big medicine-pipe in his hand, the charm or mystery of which protects him from all of his enemies. They soon agreed, however, to become friends, smoked the big pipe together, and returned to the Mandan village. The Evil Spirit was satisfied; and Nu-mohk-muck-a-nah told the Mandans never to pass Heart River to live, for it was the centre of the world, and to live beyond it would be destruction to them; and he named it *Nat-com-pa-sa-hah* (heart or centre of the world)."

Such are a few of the principal traditions of these people, which I have thought proper to give in this place, and I have given them in their own way, with all the imperfections and absurd inconsistencies which should be expected to characterise the history of all ignorant and superstitious people who live in a state of simple and untaught nature, with no other means of perpetuating historical events, than by oral traditions.

I advance these vague stories then, as I have done, and shall do in other instances, not in support of any theory, but merely as I have heard them related by the Indians; and preserved them, as I have everything else that I could meet in the Indian habits and character, for the information of the world, who may get more time to theorise than I have at present: and who may consider better than I can, how far such traditions should be taken as evidence of the facts, that these people have for a long period preserved and perpetuated an imperfect knowledge of the Deluge—of the appearance and death of a Saviour—and of the transgressions of Mother Eve.

I am not yet able to learn from these people whether they have any distinct theory of the creation; as they seem to date nothing further back than their own existence as a people; saying (as I have before mentioned), that they were the first people created; involving the glaring absurdities that they were the only people on earth before the Flood, and the only one saved was a white man; or that they were created inside of the earth, as their tradition says; and that they did not make their appearance on its outer surface until after the Deluge. When an Indian story is told, it is like all other gifts, "to be taken for what it is worth," and for any seeming inconsistency in their traditions there is no remedy; for as far as I have tried to reconcile them by reasoning with, or questioning them, I have been entirely defeated; and more than that, have generally incurred their distrust and ill-will. One of the Mandan doctors told me very gravely a few days since, that the earth was a large tortoise, that it carried the dirt on its back—that a tribe of people, who are now dead, and whose faces were white, used to dig down very deep in this ground to catch *badgers;* and that one day they stuck a knife through the tortoise-shell, and it sunk down so that the water ran over its back, and drowned all but one man. And on the next day while I was painting his portrait, he told me there were *four tortoises,*—one in the North—one in the East —one in the South, and one in the West; that each one of these rained ten days, and the water covered over the earth.

These ignorant and conflicting accounts, and both from the same man, give as good a demonstration, perhaps, of what I have above-mentioned, as to the inefficiency of Indian traditions as anything I could at present mention. They might, perhaps, have been in this instance however the creeds of different sects, or of different priests amongst them, who often advance diametrically opposite theories and traditions relative to history and mythology.

And however ignorant and ridiculous they may seem, they are yet worthy of a little further consideration, as relating to a number of curious circumstances connected with the unaccountable religious ceremonies which I have just described.

The Mandan chiefs and doctors, in all their feasts, where the pipe is lit and about to be passed around, deliberately propitiate the good-will and favour of the Great Spirit, by extending the stem of the pipe *upwards* before they smoke it themselves; and also as deliberately and as strictly offering the stem to the four *cardinal points* in succession, and then drawing a whiff through it, passing it around amongst the group.

The *annual religious ceremony* invariably lasts *four* days, and the other following circumstances attending these strange forms, and seeming to have some allusion to the *four* cardinal points, or the "four tortoises," seem to me to be worthy of further notice. *Four* men are selected by Nu-mohk-muck-a-nah (as I have before said), to cleanse out and prepare the medicine-lodge for the occasion—one he calls from the *north* part of the village—one from the *east*—one from the *south,* and one from the *west.* The *four* sacks of water, in form of large tortoises, resting on the floor of the lodge and before described, would seem to be typical of' the same thing; and also the *four* buffalo, and the *four* human skulls resting on the floor of the same lodge— the *four* couples of dancers in the "bull-dance," as before described; and also the *four* intervening dancers in the same dance, and also described.

The bull-dance in front of the medicine-lodge, repeated on the *four* days, is danced *four* times on the first day, *eight* times on the second, *twelve* times on the third, and *sixteen* times on the fourth; (adding *four* dances on each of the *four* days,) which added together make *forty,* the exact number of days that it rained upon the earth, according to the Mosaic account, to produce the Deluge. There are *four* sacrifices of black and blue cloths erected over the door of the medicine-lodge—the visits of Oh-kee-hee-de (or Evil Spirit) were paid to *four* of the buffaloes in the buffalo-dance, as above described; and in every instance, the young men who underwent the tortures before explained, had *four* splints or skewers run through the flesh on their legs—*four* through the arms and *four* through the body.

Such is a brief account of these strange scenes which I have just been witnessing, and such my brief history of the Mandans. I might write much more on them, giving yet a volume on their stories and traditions; but it would be a volume of fables, and scarce worth recording. A nation of Indians in their primitive condition, where there are no historians, have but a temporary historical existence, for the reasons above advanced, and their history, what can be certainly learned of it, may be written in a very small compass.

I have dwelt longer on the history and customs of these people than I have or shall on any other tribe, in all probability, and that from the fact that I have found them a very peculiar people, as will have been seen by my notes.

From these very numerous and striking peculiarities in their personal appearance—their customs—traditions and language, I have been led conclusively to believe that they are a people of decidedly a different origin from that of any other tribe in those regions.

From these reasons, as well as from the fact that they are a small and feeble tribe, against whom the powerful tribe of Sioux are waging a deadly war with the prospect of their extermination; and who with their limited numbers, are not likely to hold out long in their struggle for existence, I have taken more pains to pourtray their whole character, than my limited means will allow me to bestow upon other tribes.

From the ignorant and barbarous and disgusting customs just recited, the world would naturally infer, that these people must be the most cruel and inhuman beings in the world—yet, such is not the case, and it becomes my duty to say it; a better, more honest, hospitable and kind people, as a community, are not to be found in the world. No set of men that ever I associated with have better hearts than the Mandans, and none are quicker to embrace and welcome a white man than they are—none will press him closer to his bosom, that the pulsation of his heart may be felt, than a Mandan; and no man in any country will keep his word and guard his honour more closely.

The shocking and disgusting custom that I have just described, sickens the heart and even the stomach of a traveller in the country, and he weeps for their ignorance—he pities them with all his heart for their blindness, and laments that the light of civilisation, of agriculture and religion, cannot be extended to them, and that their hearts which are good enough, could not be turned to embrace something more rational and conducive to their true happiness.

Many would doubtless ask, whether such a barbarous custom could be eradicated from these people? and whether their thoughts and tastes, being turned to agriculture and religion, could be made to abandon the dark and random channel in which they are drudging, and made to flow in the light and life of civilisation?

To this query I answer *yes*. Although this is a custom of long standing, being a part of their religion; and probably valued as one of their dearest rights; and notwithstanding the difficulty of making inroads upon the religion of a people in whose country there is no severance of opinions, and consequently no division into different sects, with different creeds to shake their faith; I still believe, and I *know,* that by a judicious and persevering effort, this abominable custom, and others, might be extinguished, and the beautiful green fields about the Mandan village might be turned into productive gardens, and the waving green bluffs that are spread in the surrounding distance, might be spotted with lowing kine, instead of the sneaking wolves and the hobbled war-horses that are now stalking about them.

All ignorant and superstitious people, it is a well-known fact, are the most fixed and stubborn in their religious opinions, and perhaps the most difficult to divert from their established belief, from the very fact that they are the most difficult to reason with. Here is an ignorant race of human beings, who have from time immemorial been in the habit of worshipping in their own way, and of enjoying their religious opinions without ever having heard any one to question their correctness; and in those opinions they are quiet and satisfied, and it requires a patient, gradual, and untiring effort to convince such a people that they are wrong, and to work the desired change in their belief, and consequently in their actions.

It is decidedly my opinion, however, that such a thing *can* b e done, and I do not believe there is a race of wild people on earth where the experiment could be more successfully made than amongst the kind and hospitable Mandans, nor any place where the Missionary labours of pious and industrious men would be more sure to succeed, or more certain to be rewarded in the world to come.

I deem such a trial of patience and perseverance with these people of great importance, and well worth the experiment. One which I shall hope soon to see accomplished, and which, if properly conducted, I am sure will result in success. Severed as they are from the contaminating and contracting vices which oppose and thwart most of the best efforts of the Missionaries along the frontier, and free from the almost fatal prejudices which they have there to contend with; they present a better field for the labours of such benevolent teachers than they have yet worked in, and a far better chance than they have yet had of proving to the world that the poor Indian is not a brute—that he is a human and humane being, that he is capable of improvement—and that his mind is a beautiful blank on which anything can be written if the proper means be taken.

The Mandans being but a small tribe, of two thousand only, and living all in two villages, in sight of each other, and occupying these permanently, without roaming about like other neighbouring tribes, offer undoubtedly, the best opportunity for such an experiment of any tribe in the country. The land about their villages is of the best quality for ploughing and grazing, and the water just such as would be desired. Their villages are fortified with piquets or stockades, which protect them from the assaults of their enemies at home; and the introduction of agriculture (which would supply them with the necessaries and luxuries of life, without the necessity of continually exposing their lives to their more numerous enemies on the plains, when they are seeking in the chase the means of their subsistence) would save them from the continual wastes of life, to which, in their wars and the chase they are continually exposed, and which are calculated soon to result in their extinction.

I deem it not folly nor idle to say that these people *can be saved,* nor officious to suggest to some of the very many excellent and pious men, who are almost throwing away the best energies of their lives along the debased frontier, that if they would introduce the ploughshare and their prayers amongst these people, who are so far separated from the taints and contaminating vices of the frontier, they would soon see their most ardent desires accomplished, and be able to solve to the world the perplexing enigma, by presenting a nation of savages, civilised and christianised (and consequently *saved*), in the heart of the American wilderness.

LETTER—No. 23

MINATAREE VILLAGE, *UPPER MISSOURI*

SOON after witnessing the curious scenes described in the former Letters, I changed my position to the place from whence I am now writing—to the village of the Minatarees, which is also located on the west bank of the Missouri river, and only eight miles above the Mandans. On my way down the river in my canoe, I passed this village without attending to their earnest and clamorous invitations for me to come ashore, and it will thus be seen that I am retrograding a little, to see all that is to be seen in this singular country.

I have been residing here some weeks, and am able already to say of these people as follows:—

The Minatarees (people of the willows) are a small tribe of about 1500 souls, residing in three villages of earth-covered lodges, on the banks of Knife river; a small stream, so called, meandering through a beautiful and extensive prairie, and uniting its waters with the Missouri.

This small community is undoubtedly a part of the tribe of Crows, of whom I have already spoken, living at the base of the Rocky Mountains, who have at some remote period, either in their war or hunting excursions, been run off by their enemy, and their retreat having been prevented, have thrown themselves upon the hospitality of the Mandans, to whom they have looked for protection, and under whose wing they are now living in a sort of confederacy, ready to intermarry and also to join, as they often have done, in the common defence of their country.

In language and personal appearance, as well as in many of their customs, they are types of the Crows; yet having adopted and so long lived under its influence, the system of the Mandans, they are much like them in many respects, and continually assimilating to the modes of their patrons and protectors. Amongst their vague and various traditions they have evidently some disjointed authority for the manner in which they came here; but no account of the time. They say, that they came poor—without wigwams or horses —were nearly all women, as their warriors had been killed off in their flight; that the Mandans would not take them into their village, nor let them come nearer than where they are now living, and there assisted them to build their villages. From these circumstances their wigwams have been constructed exactly in the same manner as those of the Mandans, which I have already described, and entirely distinct from any custom to be seen in the Crow tribe.

Notwithstanding the long familiarity in which they have lived with the Mandans, and the complete adoption of most of their customs, yet it is almost an unaccountable fact, that there is scarcely a man in the tribe who can speak half a dozen words of the Mandan language; although on the other hand, the Mandans are most of them able to converse in the Minataree tongue; leaving us to conclude, either that the Minatarees are a very inert and stupid people, or that the Mandan language (which is most probably the case) being different from any other language in the country, is an exceedingly difficult one to learn.

The principal village of the Minatarees which is built upon the bank of the Knife river (Fig. 70), contains forty or fifty earth-covered wigwams, from forty to fifty feet in diameter, and being elevated, overlooks the other two, which are on lower ground and almost lost amidst their numerous corn fields and other profuse vegetation which cover the earth with their luxuriant growth.

The scenery along the banks of this little river, from village to village, is quite peculiar and curious; rendered extremely so by the continual wild and garrulous groups of men, women, and children, who are wending their way along its winding shores, or dashing and plunging through its blue waves, enjoying the luxury of swimming, of which both sexes seem to be passionately fond. Others are paddling about in their tublike canoes, made of the skins of buffaloes; and every now and then, are to be seen their sudatories, or vapour-baths (Fig. 71), where steam is raised by throwing water on to heated stones; and the patient jumps from his sweating-house and leaps into the river in the highest state of perspiration, as I have more fully described whilst speaking of the bathing of the Mandans.

The chief sachem of this tribe is a very ancient and patriarchal looking man, by the name of Eeh-tohk-pah-shee-pee-shah (the black moccasin), and counts, undoubtedly, more than an hundred *snows*. I have been for some days an inmate of his hospitable lodge, where he sits tottering with age, and silently reigns sole monarch of his little community around him, who are continually dropping in to cheer his sinking energies, and render him their homage. His voice and his sight are nearly gone; but the gestures of his hands are yet energetic and youthful, and freely speak the language of his kind heart.

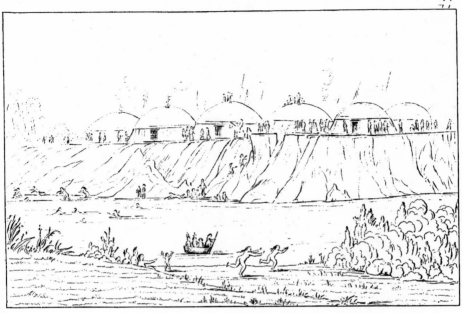

70

71

48

G Catlin.

I have been treated in the kindest manner by this old chief; and have painted his portrait (Fig. 72) as he was seated on the floor of his wigwam, smoking his pipe, whilst he was recounting over to me some of the extraordinary feats of his life, with a beautiful Crow robe wrapped around him, and his hair wound up in a conical form upon his head, and fastened with a small wooden pin, to keep it in its place.

This man has many distinct recollections of Lewis and Clarke, who were the first explorers of this country, and who crossed the Rocky Mountains thirty years ago. It will be seen by reference to their very interesting history of their tour, that they were treated with great kindness by this man; and that they in consequence constituted him chief of the tribe, with the consent of his people; and he has remained their chief ever since. He inquired very earnestly for "Red Hair" and "Long Knife" (as he had ever since termed Lewis and Clarke), from the fact, that one had red hair (an unexampled thing in his country), and the other wore a broad sword, which gained for him the appellation of "Long Knife."

I have told him that "Long Knife" has been many years dead; and that "Red Hair" is yet living in St Louis, and no doubt, would be glad to hear of him; at which he seemed much pleased, and has signified to me that he will make me bearer of some peculiar dispatches to him.*

The name by which these people are generally called (Grosventres) is one given them by the French Traders, and has probably been applied to them with some degree of propriety or fitness, as contradistinguished from the Mandans, amongst whom these Traders were living; and who are a small race of Indians, being generally at or below the average stature of man; whilst the Minatarees are generally tall and heavily built. There is no tribe in the western wilds, perhaps, who are better entitled to the style of warlike, than the Minatarees; for they, unlike the Mandans, are continually carrying war into their enemies' country; oftentimes drawing the poor Mandans into unnecessary broils, and suffering so much themselves in their desperate war-excursions, that I find the proportion of women to the number of men as two or three to one, through the tribe.

* About a year after writing the above, and whilst I was in St Louis, I had the pleasure of presenting the compliments of this old veteran to General Clarke, and also of showing to him the portrait, which he instantly recognised amongst hundreds of others; saying that, "they had considered the Black Moccasin quite an old man when they appointed him chief thirty-two years ago."

The son of Black Moccasin, whose name is Ee-a-chin-che-a (the red thunder), and who is reputed one of the most desperate warriors of his tribe, I have also painted at full length, in his war-dress (Fig. 73), with his bow in his hand, his quiver slung, and his shield upon his arm. In this plight, *sans* head-dress, *sans* robe, and *sans* everything that might be an useless incumbrance—with the body chiefly naked, and profusely bedaubed with red and black paint, so as to form an almost perfect disguise, the Indian warriors invariably sally forth to war; save the chief, who always plumes himself, and leads on his little band, tendering himself to his enemies a conspicuous mark, with all his ornaments and trophies upon him; that his enemies, if they get him, may get a prize worth the fighting for.

Besides chiefs and warriors to be admired in this little tribe, there are many beautiful and voluptuous looking women, who are continually crowding in throngs, and gazing upon a stranger; and possibly shedding more bewitching smiles from a sort of necessity, growing out of the great disparity in numbers between them and the rougher sex, to which I have before alluded.

From the very numerous groups of these that have from day to day constantly pressed upon me, overlooking the operations of my brush; I have been unable to get more than one who would consent to have her portrait painted, owing to some fear or dread of harm that might eventually ensue in consequence; or from a natural coyness or timidity, which is surpassing all description amongst these wild tribes, when in presence of strangers.

The one whom I have painted (Fig. 74) is a descendant from the old chief; and though not the most beautiful, is yet a fair sample of them, and dressed in a beautiful costume of the mountain-sheep skin, handsomely garnished with porcupine quills and beads. This girl was almost *compelled* to stand for her picture by her relatives who urged her on, whilst she modestly declined, offering as her excuse that "she was not pretty enough, and that her picture would be laughed at." This was either ignorance or excessive art on her part; for she was certainly more than comely, and the beauty of her name, Seet-se-be-a (the midday sun) is quite enough to make up for a deficiency, if there were any, in the beauty of her face.

I mentioned that I found these people raising abundance of corn or maize; and I have happened to visit them in the season of their festivities, which annually take place when the ears of corn are of the proper size for eating. The green corn is considered a great luxury by all those tribes who cultivate it; and is ready for eating as soon as the ear is of full size, and the kernels are expanded to

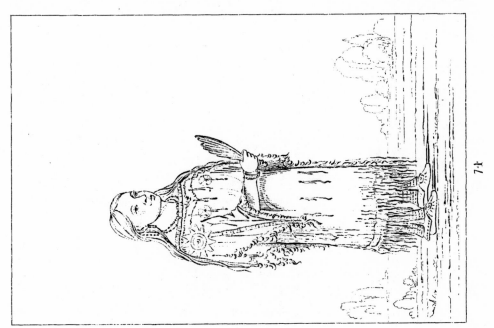

49

74

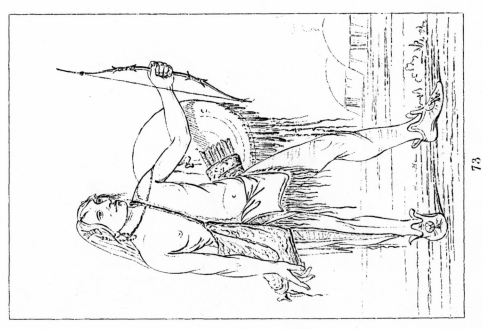

73

G. Catlin.

their full growth, but are yet soft and pulpy. In this green state of the corn, it is boiled and dealt out in great profusion to the whole tribe, who feast and surfeit upon it whilst it lasts; rendering thanks to the *Great Spirit,* for the return of this joyful season, which they do by making sacrifices, by dancing, and singing songs of thanksgiving. This joyful occasion is one valued alike, and conducted in a similar manner, by most of the tribes who raise the corn, however remote they may be from each other. It lasts but for a week or ten days; being limited to the longest term that the corn remains in this tender and palatable state; during which time all hunting, and all war-excursions, and all other avocations, are positively dispensed with; and all join in the most excessive indulgence of gluttony and conviviality that can possibly be conceived. The fields of corn are generally pretty well stripped during this excess; and the poor improvident Indian thanks the Great Spirit for the indulgence he has had, and is satisfied to ripen merely the few ears that are necessary for his next year's planting, without reproaching himself for his wanton lavishness, which has laid waste his fine fields, and robbed him of the golden harvest, which might have gladdened his heart, with those of his wife and little children, through the cold and dreariness of winter.

The most remarkable feature of these joyous occasions is the *green corn-dance,* which is always given as preparatory to the feast, and by most of the tribes in the following manner:—

At the usual season, and the time when from outward appearance of the stalks and ears of the corn, it is supposed to be nearly ready for use, several of the old women who are the owners of fields or patches of corn (for such are the proprietors and cultivators of all crops in Indian countries, the men never turning their hands to such degrading occupations) are delegated by the medicine-men to look at the corn fields every morning at sun-rise, and bring into the council-house, where the kettle is ready, several ears of corn, the husks of which the women are not allowed to break open or even to peep through. The women then are from day to day discharged and the doctors left to decide, until from repeated examinations they come to the decision that it will do; when they. dispatch *runners* or *criers,* announcing to every part of the village or tribe that the Great Spirit has been kind to them, and they must all meet on the next day to return thanks for his goodness. That all must empty their stomachs, and prepare for the feast that is approaching.

On the day appointed by the doctors, the villagers are all assembled, and in the midst of the group a kettle is hung over a fire and filled with the green corn, which is well boiled, to be given to the Great

Spirit, as a sacrifice necessary to be made before any one can indulge the cravings of his appetite. Whilst this first kettleful is boiling, four medicine-men, with a stalk of the corn in one hand and a rattle (she-she-quoi) in the other, with their bodies painted with white clay, dance around the kettle, chanting a song of thanksgiving to the Great Spirit to whom the offering is to be made (Fig. 75). At the same time a number of warriors are dancing around in a more extended circle, with stalks of the corn in their hands, and joining also in the song of thanksgiving, whilst the villagers are all assembled and looking on. During this scene there is an arrangement of wooden bowls laid upon the ground, in which the feast is to be dealt out, each one having in it a spoon made of the buffalo or mountain-sheep's horn.

In this wise the dance continues until the doctors decide that the corn is sufficiently boiled; it then stops for a few moments, and again assumes a different form and a different song, whilst the doctors are placing the ears on a little scaffold of sticks, which they erect immediately over the fire where it is entirely consumed, as they join again in the dance around it.

The fire is then removed, and with it the ashes, which together are buried in the ground, and *new fire* is originated on the same spot where the old one was, by friction, which is done by a desperate and painful exertion by three men seated on the ground, facing each other and violently drilling the end of a stick into a hard block of wood by rolling it between the hands, each one catching it in turn from the others without allowing the motion to stop until smoke, and at last a spark of fire is seen and caught in a piece of spunk, when there is great rejoicing in the crowd. With this a fire is kindled, and the kettleful of corn again boiled for the feast, at which the chiefs, doctors, and warriors are seated; and after this an unlimited licence is given to the whole tribe, who surfeit upon it and indulge in all their favourite amusements and excesses, until the fields of corn are exhausted, or its ears have become too hard for their comfortable mastication.

Such are the general features of the green corn festivity and dance amongst most of the tribes; and amongst some there are many additional forms and ceremonies gone through, preparatory to the indulgence in the feast.

Some of the southern tribes concoct a most bitter and nauseating draught, which they call *asceola* (the black drink), which they drink to excess for several days previous to the feast; ejecting everything from their stomachs and intestines, enabling them after this excessive and painful purgation, to commence with the green corn upon an empty and keen stomach.

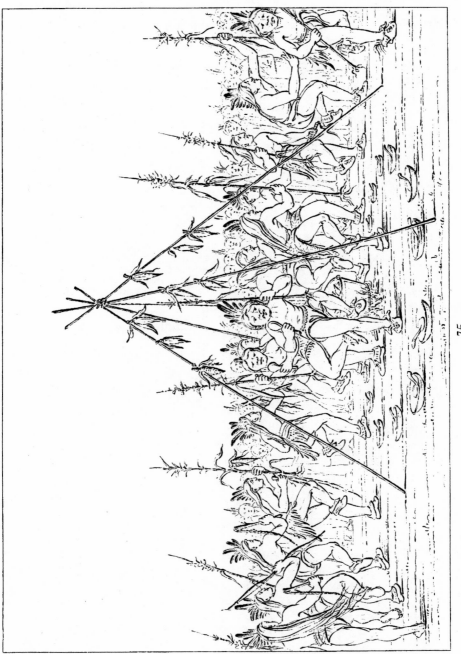

50

G.Catlin.

EPISTLES from such a strange place as this, where I have no desk to write from, or mail to send them by, are hastily scribbled off in my note-book, as I can steal a little time from the gaze of the wild group that is continually about me; and instead of *sending* them, *keeping* them to bring with me when I make my retreat from the country.

The only place where I can satisfactorily make these entries is in the shade of some sequestered tree, to which I occasionally resort, or more often from my bed (from which I am now writing), enclosed by a sort of curtains made of the skins of elks or buffaloes, completely encompassing me, where I am reclining on a sacking-bottom, made of the buffalo's hide; making my entries and notes of the incidents of the past day, amidst the roar and unintelligible din of savage conviviality that is going on under the same roof, and under my own eye, whenever I feel disposed to apply it to a small aperture which brings at once the whole interior and all its inmates within my view.

There are at this time some distinguished guests, besides *myself,* in the lodge of the Black Moccasin; two chiefs or leaders of a party of Crows, who arrived here a few days since, on a visit to their ancient friends and relatives. The consequence has been, that feasting and carousing have been the "order of the day" here for some time; and I have luckily been a welcome participator in their entertainments. A distinguished chief of the Minatarees, with several others in company, has been for some months past on a visit to the Crows and returned, attended by some remarkably fine-looking fellows, all mounted on fine horses. I have said something of these fine specimens of the human race heretofore; and as I have been fastening more of them to the canvas within the few days past, I must use this occasion to add what follows:—

I think I have said that no part of the human race could present a more picturesque and thrilling appearance on horseback than a party of Crows, rigged out in all their plumes and trappings—galloping about and yelping, in what they call a war-parade, *i.e.* in a sort of tournament or sham-fight, passing rapidly through the evolutions of battle, and vaunting forth the wonderful character of their military exploits. This is an amusement, of which they are excessively fond; and great preparations are invariably made for these occasional shows.

No tribe of Indians on the Continent are better able to produce a pleasing and thrilling effect in these scenes, nor any more vain, and consequently better prepared to draw pleasure and satisfaction from them, than the Crows. They may be justly said to be the most beautifully clad of all the Indians in these regions, and bringing from the base of the Rocky Mountains a fine and spirited breed of the wild horses, have been able to create a great sensation amongst the Minatarees, who have been paying them all attention and all honours for some days past.

From amongst these showy fellows who have been entertaining us and pleasing themselves with their extraordinary feats of horsemanship, I have selected one of the most conspicuous, and transferred him and his horse, with arms and trappings, as faithfully as I could to the canvas, for the information of the world, who will learn vastly more from lines and colours than they could from oral or written delineations.

I have painted him as he sat for me, balanced on his leaping wild horse (Fig. 76) with his shield and quiver slung on his back, and his long lance decorated with the eagle's quills, trailed in his right hand. His shirt and his leggings, and moccasins, were of the mountain-goat skins, beautifully dressed; and their seams everywhere fringed with a profusion of scalp-locks taken from the heads of his enemies slain in battle. His long hair, which reached almost to the ground whilst he was standing on his feet, was now lifted in the air, and floating in black waves over the hips of his leaping charger. On his head, and over his shining black locks, he wore a magnificent crest or head-dress, made of the quills of the war-eagle and ermine skins; and on his horse's head also was another of equal beauty and precisely the same in pattern and material. Added to these ornaments there were yet many others which contributed to his picturesque appearance, and amongst them a beautiful netting of various colours, that completely covered and almost obscured the horse's head and neck, and extended over its back and its hips, terminating in a most extravagant and magnificent crupper, embossed and fringed with rows of beautiful shells and porcupine quills of various colours.

With all these picturesque ornaments and trappings upon and about him, with a noble figure, and the bold stamp of a wild *gentleman* on his face, added to the rage and spirit of his wild horse, in time with whose leaps he issued his startling (though smothered) yelps, as

76

G. Catlin

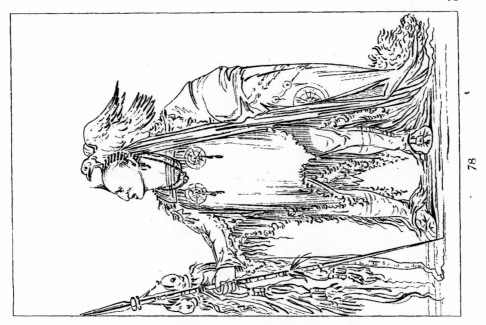

78

77

G. Catlin

he gracefully leaned to and fro, leaving his plumes and his plumage, his long locks and his fringes, to float in the wind, he galloped about; and felt exceeding pleasure in displaying the extraordinary skill which a lifetime of practice and experiment had furnished him in the beautiful art of riding and managing his horse, as well as in displaying to advantage his weapons and ornaments of dress, by giving them the grace of motion, as they were brandished in the air and floating in the wind.

I have also secured the portraits of Ee-he-a-duck-chee-a (he who ties his hair before, Fig. 78), and Pa-ris-ka-roo-pa (the two Crows, Fig. 77); fine and fair specimens of this tribe, in both of which are exhibited the extraordinary instances of the natural hair reaching to the ground, peculiarities belonging almost exclusively to this tribe, and of which I have in a former Letter given some account. In presenting such instances as these, I offer them (and the reader will take them of course) as extraordinary and rare occurrences amongst the tribe, who generally fall short of these in this peculiarity, and also in elegance of dress and ornament; although many others from their numbers might be selected of equal extravagance. The Crows are generally handsome, and comfortably clad; every man in the nation oils his hair with a profusion of bear's grease, and promotes its growth to the utmost of his ability; and the greater part of them cultivate it down on to the calf of the leg, whilst a few are able to make it sweep the ground.

In a former Letter I gave some account of the form of the head peculiar to this tribe which may well be recorded as a national characteristic, and worthy of further attention, which I shall give it on a future occasion. This striking peculiarity is quite conspicuous in the two portraits of which I have just spoken, exhibiting fairly, as they are both in profile, the *semi-lunar* outline of the face of which I have before spoken, and which strongly characterises them as distinct from any relationship or resemblance to, the Blackfeet, Shiennies, Knisteneaux, Mandans, or other tribes now existing in these regions. The peculiar character of which I am speaking, like all other national characteristics, is of course met by many exceptions in the tribe, though the greater part of the men are thus strongly marked with a bold and prominent anti-angular nose, with a clear and rounded arch, and a low and receding forehead; the frontal bone oftentimes appearing to have been compressed by some effort of art, in a certain degree approaching to the horrid distortion thus produced amongst the Flatheads beyond the Rocky Mountains. I learned however from repeated inquiries, that no such custom is practised amongst them, but their heads, such as they are, are the results of a natural growth, and therefore may well be offered as the basis of a national or tribal *character.*

I recollect to have seen in several publications on the antiquities of Mexico, many rude drawings made by the ancient Mexicans, of which the singular profiles of these people forcibly remind me, almost bringing me to the conclusion that these people may be the descendants of the race who have bequeathed those curious and inexplicable remains to the world, and whose scattered remnants, from dire and unknown necessities of those dark and veiled ages that have gone by, have been jostled and thrown along through the hideous and almost impenetrable labyrinths of the Rocky Mountains to the place of their destination where they now live. I am stopped, however, from advancing such as a *theory,* and much prefer to leave it to other hands, who may more easily get over difficulties which I should be afraid to encounter in the very outset, from the very important questions raised in my mind, as to the correctness of those rude and ignorant outlines, in truly establishing the looks and character of a people. Amongst a people so ignorant and so little advanced in the arts as the ancient Mexicans were, from whose tracings those very numerous drawings are copied, I think it would be assuming a great deal too much for satisfactory argument, to claim that such records were to set up to the world the looks and character of a people who have sunk into oblivion, when the heads of horses and other animals, drawn by the same hands, are so rude and so much out of drawing as scarcely to be distinguished, one from the other. I feel as if such rude outlines should be received with great caution and distrust, in establishing the character of a people; and for a fair illustration of the objection I am raising, I would refer the reader to a number of *facsimile* drawings which I have copied from some of the paintings of the Mandans (on the three Figs. following Fig. 65), where most of the figures have the forehead and nose answering exactly to these Mexican outlines, and strikingly resembling the *living Crows,* also, when they have certainly borrowed nothing from either, nor have they any living outlines like them in their own tribe to have copied from.

Since writing the above I have passed through many vicissitudes, and witnessed many curious scenes worthy of relating, some of which I will scribble now, and leave the rest for a more leisure occasion. I have witnessed many of the valued games and amusements of this tribe, and made sketches of them; and also have painted a number of portraits of distinguished warriors and braves which will be found in my collection.

I have just been exceedingly amused with a formal and grave meeting which was called around me, formed by a number of young men, and even chiefs and doctors of the tribe, who, having heard that I was *great medicine,* and a great chief, took it upon themselves to suppose that I might (or perhaps must) be, a man of influence amongst the "pale faces," and capable of rendering them some relief in a case of very great grievance, under which they represented that they were suffering. Several most profound speeches were made to me, setting forth these grievances, somewhat in the following manner: – They represented, that about five or six years ago, an unknown, small animal – not far differing in size from a ground squirrel, but with a long, round tail, showed himself slily about one of the chief's wigwams, peeping out from under the pots and kettles, and other such things; which they looked upon as great *medicine–* and no one dared to kill it; but hundreds came to watch and look at it. On one of these occasions, one of the spectators saw this strange animal catching and devouring a small "deer mouse," of which little and very destructive animals their lodges contained many. It was then at once determined that this had been an act of the Great Spirit, as a means of putting a stop to the spoliations committed by these little sappers, who were cutting their clothing, and other manufactures to pieces in a lamentable manner. Councils had been called and solemn decrees issued for the countenance and protection of this welcome visitor and its progeny, which were soon ascertained to be rapidly increasing, and calculated soon to rid them of these thousands of little depredators. It was soon, however, learned from one of the Fur Traders, that this distinguished object of their superstition (which my man Ba'tiste familiarly calls *"Monsr. Ratapon")* had, a short time before, landed himself from one of their keel boats, which had ascended the Missouri river for the distance of 1800 miles; and had taken up its residence, without introduction or invitation, in one of their earth-covered wigwams.

This information, for a while, curtailed the extraordinary respect they had for some time been paying to it; but its continual war upon these little mice, which it was using for its food, in the absence of all other nutriment, continued to command their respect, in spite of the manner in which it had been introduced; being unwilling to believe that it had come from that source, even, without the agency in some way of the Great Spirit.

Having been thus introduced and nurtured, and their numbers having been so wonderfully increased in the few last years, that every wigwam was infested with them-that their caches, where they bury their corn and other provisions, were robbed and sacked; and the very pavements under their wigwams were so vaulted and sapped, that they were actually falling to the ground; they were now looked upon as a most disastrous nuisance, and a public calamity, to which it was the object of this meeting to call my attention, evidently in hopes that I might be able to designate some successful mode of relieving them from this real misfortune. I got rid of them at last, by assuring them of my deep regret for their situation, which was, to be sure, a very unpleasant one; and told them, that there was really a great deal of *medicine* in the thing, and that I should therefore be quite unwilling to have anything to do with it. Ba'tiste and Bogard, who are yet my daily and almost hourly companions, took to themselves a great deal of fun and amusement at the end of this interview, by suggesting many remedies for the evil, and enjoying many hearty laughs; after which, Ba'tiste, Bogard and I, took our hats; and I took my sketch-book in hand, and we started on a visit to the upper town of the Minatarees, which is half a mile or more distant, and on the other bank of the Knife river, which we crossed in the following manner: – The old chief, having learned that we were to cross the river, gave direction to one of the women of his numerous household, who took upon her head a skin-canoe (more familiarly called in this country, a bull-boat), made in the form of a large tub, of a buffalo's skin, stretched on a frame of willow boughs, which she carried to the water's edge; and placing it in the water, made signs for us three to get into it. When we were in, and seated flat on its bottom, with scarce room in any way to adjust our legs and our feet (as we sat necessarily facing each other), she stepped before the boat, and pulling it along, waded towards the deeper water, with her back towards us, carefully with the other hand attending to her dress, which seemed to be but a light slip, and floating upon the surface until the water was above her waist, when it was instantly turned off, over her head, and thrown ashore; and she boldly plunged forward, swimming and drawing the boat with one hand, which she did with apparent ease. In this manner we were conveyed to the middle of the stream, where we were soon surrounded by a dozen or more beautiful girls, from twelve to fifteen and eighteen years of age, who were at that time bathing on the opposite shore.

They all swam in a bold and graceful manner, and as confidently as so many otters or beavers; and gathering around us, with their long black hair floating about on the water, whilst their faces were glowing with jokes and fun, which they were cracking about us, and which we could not understand.

In the midst of this delightful little aquatic group, we three sat in our little skin-bound tub (like the "three wise men of Gotham, who went to sea in a bowl," etc.), floating along down the current, losing sight, and all thoughts, of the shore, which was equi-distant from us on either side; whilst we were amusing ourselves with the playfulness of these dear little creatures who were floating about under the clear blue water, catching their hands on to the sides of our boat; occasionally raising one-half of their bodies out of the water, and sinking again, like so many mermaids.

In the midst of this bewildering and tantalising entertainment, in which poor Ba'tiste and Bogard, as well as myself, were all taking infinite pleasure, and which we supposed was all intended for our especial amusement; we found ourselves suddenly in the delightful dilemma of floating down the current in the middle of the river; and of being turned round and round to the excessive amusement of the villagers, who were laughing at us from the shore, as well as these little tyros, whose delicate hands were besetting our tub on all sides; and for an escape from whom, or for fending off, we had neither an oar, or anything else, that we could wield in self-defence, or for self-preservation. In this awkward predicament, our feelings of excessive admiration were immediately changed, to those of exceeding vexation, as we now learned that they had peremptorily discharged from her occupation our fair conductress, who had under-taken to ferry us safely across the river; and had also very ingeniously laid their plans, of which we had been ignorant until the present moment, to extort from us in this way, some little evidences of our liberality, which, in fact, it was impossible to refuse them, after so liberal and bewitching an exhibition on their part, as well as from the imperative obligation which the awkwardness of our situation had laid us under. I had some awls in my pockets, which I presented to them, and also a few strings of beautiful beads, which I placed over their delicate necks as they raised them out of the water by the side of our boat; after which they all joined in conducting our craft to the shore, by swimming by the sides of, and behind it, pushing it along in the direction where they designed to land it, until the water became so shallow, that their feet were upon the bottom, when they waded along with great coyness, dragging us towards the shore, as long as their bodies, in a crouching position, could possibly be half concealed under the water, when they gave our boat the last push for the shore, and raising a loud and exulting laugh, plunged back again into the river; leaving us the only alter-native of sitting still where we were, or of stepping out into the water at half leg deep, and of wading to the shore, which we at once did, and soon escaped from the view of our little tormentors, and the numerous lookers-on, on our way to the upper village, which I have before mentioned.

Here I was very politely treated by the *Yellow Moccasin,* quite an old man, and who seemed to be chief of this band or family, constituting their little community of thirty or forty lodges, averaging, perhaps, twenty persons to each. I was feasted in this man's lodge —and afterwards invited to accompany him and several others to a beautiful prairie, a mile or so above the village, where the young men and young women of this town, and many from the village below, had assembled for their amusements; the chief of which seemed to be that of racing their horses. In the midst of these scenes, after I had been for some time a looker-on, and had felt some considerable degree of sympathy for a fine-looking young fellow, whose horse had been twice beaten on the course, and whose losses had been considerable; for which, his sister, a very modest and pretty girl, was most piteously howling and crying. I selected and brought forward an ordinary-looking pony, that was evidently too fat and too sleek to run against his fine-limbed little horse that had disappointed his high hopes; and I began to comment extravagantly upon its muscle, etc., when I discovered him evidently cheering up with the hope of getting me and my pony on to the turf with him; for which he soon made me a proposition; and I, having lauded the limbs of my little nag too much to "back out," agreed to run a short race with him of half a mile, for three yards of scarlet cloth, a knife, and half a dozen strings of beads, which I was willing to stake against a handsome pair of leggings, which he was wearing at the time. The greatest imaginable excitement was now raised amongst the crowd by this arrangement; to see a white man preparing to run with an Indian jockey, and that with a scrub of a pony, in whose powers of running no Indian had the least confidence. Yet, there was no one in the crowd, who dared to take up the several other little bets I was willing to tender (merely for their amusement, and for their final exultation); owing, undoubtedly, to the bold and confident manner in which I had ventured on the merits of this little horse, which the tribe had all overlooked; and needs must have some *medicine* about it.

So far was this panic carried, that even my champion was ready to withdraw; but his friends encouraged him at length, and we galloped our horses off to the other end of the course, where we were to start; and where we were accompanied by a number of horsemen, who were to witness the "set off." Some considerable delay here took place, from a *condition,* which was then named to me, and which I had not observed before, that in all the races of this day, every rider was to run entirely denuded, and ride a naked horse! Here I was completely balked, and having no one by me to interpret a word, I was quite at a loss to decide what was best to do. I found however, that remonstrance was of little avail; and as I had volunteered in this thing to gratify and flatter them, I thought it best not positively to displease them in this; so I laid off my clothes, and straddled the naked back of my round and glossy little pony, by the side of my competitor, who was also mounted and stripped to the skin, and panting with a restless anxiety for the start.

Reader! did you ever imagine that in the *middle of a man's life* there could be a thought or a feeling so *new* to him, as to throw him instantly back to infancy; with a new world and a new genius before him—started afresh, to navigate and breathe the elements of naked and untasted liberty, which clothe him in their cool and silken robes that float about him; and wafting their life-inspiring folds to his inmost lungs? If you never have been inspired with such a feeling, and have been in the habit of believing that you have thought of, and imagined a little of every thing, try for a moment, to disrobe your mind and your body, and help me through feelings to which I cannot give utterance. Imagine yourselves as I was, with my trembling little horse underneath me, and the cool atmosphere that was floating about, and ready, more closely and familiarly to embrace me, as it did, at the next moment, when we "were off," and struggling for the goal and the prize.

Though my little Pegasus seemed to dart through the clouds, and I to be wafted on the wings of Mercury, yet my red adversary was leaving me too far behind for further competition; and I wheeled to the left, making a circuit on the prairie, and came in at the starting point, much to the satisfaction and exultation of the jockeys; but greatly to the murmuring disappointment of the women and children, who had assembled in a dense throng to witness the "coming out" of the "white medicine-man." I clothed myself instantly, and came back, acknowledging my defeat, and the superior skill of my competitor, as well as the wonderful muscle of his little charger, which pleased him much; and his sister's lamentations were soon turned to joy, by the receipt of a beautiful scarlet robe, and a profusion of vari-coloured beads, which were speedily paraded on her copper-coloured neck.

After I had seen enough of these amusements, I succeeded with some difficulty, in pulling Ba'tiste and Bogard from amongst the groups of women and girls, where they seemed to be successfully ingratiating themselves; and we trudged back to the little village of earth-covered lodges, which were hemmed in, and almost obscured from the eye, by the fields of corn and luxuriant growth of wild sun-flowers, and other vegetable productions of the soil, whose spontaneous growth had reared their heads in such profusion, as to appear all but like a dense and formidable forest.

We loitered about this little village awhile, looking into most of its lodges, and tracing its winding avenues, after which we re-crossed the river and wended our way back again to head-quarters, from whence we started in the morning, and where I am now writing. This day's ramble showed to us all the inhabitants of this little tribe, except a portion of their warriors who are out on a war-excursion against the Riccarees; and I have been exceedingly pleased with their general behaviour and looks, as well as with their numerous games and amusements, in many of which I have given them great pleasure by taking a part.

The Minatarees, as I have before said, are a bold, daring, and warlike tribe; quite different in these respects from their neighbours the Mandans, carrying war continually in their enemies' country, thereby exposing their lives and diminishing the number of their warriors to that degree that I find two or three women to a man, through the tribe. They are bold and fearless in the chase also, and in their eager pursuits of the bison, or buffaloes, their feats are such as to excite the astonishment and admiration of all who behold them. Of these scenes I have witnessed many since I came into this country, and amongst them all, nothing have I seen to compare with one to which I was an eye-witness a few mornings since, and well worthy of being described.

The Minatarees, as well as the Mandans, had suffered for some months past for want of meat, and had indulged in the most alarming fears, that the herds of buffaloes were emigrating so far off from them, that there was great danger of their actual starvation, when it was suddenly announced through the village one morning at an early hour, that a herd of buffaloes was in sight, when an hundred or more young men mounted their horses with weapons in hand and steered their course to the prairies. The chief informed me that one of his horses was in readiness for me at the door of his wigwam, and that I had better go and see the curious affair. I accepted his polite offer, and mounting the steed, galloped off with the hunters to the prairies, where we soon descried at a distance, a fine herd of buffaloes grazing, when a halt and a council were ordered, and the mode of attack was agreed upon. I had armed myself with my

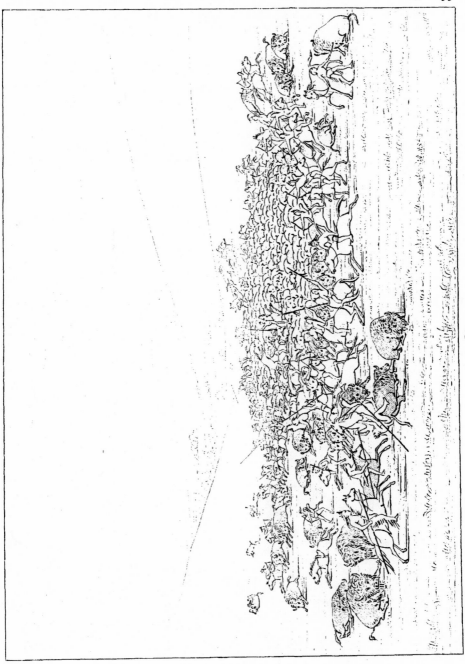

pencil and my sketch-book only, and consequently took my position generally in the rear, where I could see and appreciate every manœuvre.

The plan of attack, which in this country is familiarly called a *"surround,"* was explicitly agreed upon, and the hunters who were all mounted on their "buffalo horses" and armed with bows and arrows or long lances, divided into two columns, taking opposite directions, and drew themselves gradually around the herd at a mile or more distance from them; thus forming a circle of horsemen at equal distances apart, who gradually closed in upon them with a moderate pace, at a signal given. The unsuspecting herd at length "got the wind" of the approaching enemy and fled in a mass in the greatest confusion. To the point where they were aiming to cross the line, the horsemen were seen at full speed, gathering and forming in a column, brandishing their weapons and yelling in the most frightful manner, by which means they turned the black and rushing mass which moved off in an opposite direction where they were again met and foiled in a similar manner, and wheeled back in utter confusion; by which time the horsemen had closed in from all directions, forming a continuous line around them, whilst the poor affrighted animals were eddying about in a crowded and confused mass, hooking and climbing upon each other; when the work of death commenced. I had rode up in the rear and occupied an elevated position at a few rods distance, from which I could (like the general of a battle-field) survey from my horse's back, the nature and the progress of the grand mêlée; but (unlike him) without the power of issuing a command or in any way directing its issue.

In this grand turmoil (Fig. 79), a cloud of dust was soon raised, which in parts obscured the throng where the hunters were galloping their horses around and driving the whizzing arrows or their long lances to the hearts of these noble animals; which in many instances, becoming infuriated with deadly wounds in their sides, erected their shaggy manes over their blood-shot eyes and furiously plunged forward at the sides of their assailants' horses, sometimes goring them to death at a lunge, and putting their dismounted riders to flight for their lives; sometimes their dense crowd was opened, and the blinded horsemen, too intent on their prey amidst the cloud of dust, were hemmed and wedged in amidst the crowding beasts, over whose backs they were obliged to leap for security, leaving their horses to the fate that might await them in the results of this wild and desperate war. Many were the bulls that turned upon their assailants and met them with desperate resistance; and many were the warriors who were dismounted, and saved themselves by the superior muscles of their legs; some who were closely pursued by the bulls, wheeled suddenly around and snatching the part of a buffalo robe from around their waists, threw it over the horns and the eyes of the infuriated beast, and darting by its side drove the arrow or the lance to its heart. Others suddenly dashed off upon the prairies by the side of the affrighted animals which had escaped from the throng, and closely escorting them for a few rods, brought down their hearts' blood in streams, and their huge carcasses upon the green and enamelled turf.

In this, way this grand hunt soon resolved itself into a desperate battle: and in the space of fifteen minutes, resulted in the total destruction of the whole herd, which in all their strength and fury were doomed, like every beast and living thing else, to fall before the destroying hands of mighty man.

I had sat in trembling silence upon my horse, and witnessed this extraordinary scene, which allowed not one of these animals to escape out of my sight. Many plunged off upon the prairie for a distance, but were overtaken and killed; and although I could not distinctly estimate the number that were slain, yet I am sure that some hundreds of these noble animals fell in this grand mêlée.

The scene after the battle was over was novel and curious in the extreme; the hunters were moving about amongst the dead and dying animals, leading their horses by their halters, and claiming their victims by their private marks upon their arrows, which they were drawing from the wounds in the animals' sides.

Amongst the poor affrighted creatures that had occasionally dashed through the ranks of their enemy, and sought safety in flight upon the prairie (and in some instances, had undoubtedly gained it), I saw them stand awhile, looking back, when they turned, and, as if bent on their own destruction, retraced their steps, and mingled themselves and their deaths with those of the dying throng. Others had fled to a distance on the prairies, and for want of company, of friends or of foes, had stood and gazed on till the battle-scene was over; seemingly taking pains to stay, and hold their lives in readiness for their destroyers, until the general destruction was over, when they fell easy victims to their weapons—making the slaughter complete.

After this scene, and after arrows had been claimed and recovered, a general council was held, when all hands were seated on the ground, and a few pipes smoked; after which, all mounted their horses and rode back to the village.

A deputation of several of the warriors was sent to the chief, who explained to him what had been their success; and the same intelligence was soon communicated by little squads to every family in the village; and preparations were at once made for securing the meat. For this purpose, some hundreds of women and children, to whose lots fall all the drudgeries of Indian life, started out upon the trail, which led them to the battle-field, where they spent the day in skinning the animals, and cutting up the meat, which was mostly brought into the villages on their backs, as they tugged and sweated under their enormous and cruel loads.

I rode out to see this curious scene; and I regret exceedingly that I kept no memorandum of it in my sketch-book. Amidst the throng of women and children, that had been assembled, and all of whom seemed busily at work, were many superannuated and disabled nags, which they had brought out to assist in carrying in the meat; and at least, one thousand semi-loup dogs, and whelps, whose keen appetites and sagacity had brought them out, to claim their shares of this abundant and sumptuous supply.

I stayed and inspected this curious group for an hour or more, during which time, I was almost continually amused by the clamorous contentions that arose, and generally ended, in desperate combats; both amongst the dogs and women, who seemed alike tenacious of their local and recently acquired rights; and disposed to settle their claims by "tooth and nail"—by manual and brute force.

When I had seen enough of this I rode to the top of a beautiful prairie bluff, a mile or two from the scene, where I was exceedingly amused by overlooking the route that lay between this and the village, which was over the undulating green fields for several miles, that lay beneath me; over which there seemed a continual string of women, dogs and horses, for the rest of the day, passing and repassing as they were busily bearing home their heavy burthens to their village, and in their miniature appearance, which the distance gave them, not unlike to a busy community of ants as they are sometimes seen, sacking and transporting the treasures of a cupboard, or the sweets of a sugar bowl.

LITTLE MANDAN VILLAGE, *UPPER MISSOURI*

IN speaking of the Mandans, in a former Letter, I mentioned that they were living in two villages, which are about two miles apart. Of their principal village I have given a minute account, which precludes the necessity of my saying much of their smaller town, to which I descended a few days since, from the Minatarees; and where I find their modes and customs, precisely the same as I have heretofore described. This village contains sixty or eighty lodges, built in the same manner as those which I have already mentioned, and I have just learned that they have been keeping the annual ceremony here, precisely in the same manner as that which I witnessed in the lower or larger town, and have explained.

I have been treated with the same hospitality here that was extended to me in the other village; and have painted the portraits of several distinguished persons, which has astonished and pleased them very much. The operation of my brush always gains me many enthusiastic friends wherever I go amongst these wild folks; and in this village I have been unusually honoured and even *afflicted,* by the friendly importunities of one of these reverencing parasites, who (amongst various other offices of hospitality and kindness which he has been bent upon extending to me), has insisted on, and for several nights been indulged in, the honour as he would term it, of offering his body for my pillow, which *I* have not had the heart to reject, and of course *he* has not lacked the vanity to boast of, as an act of signal kindness and hospitality on his part, towards a *great* and *a distinguished stranger!*

I have been for several days suffering somewhat with an influenza, which has induced me to leave my bed, on the side of the lodge, and sleep on the floor, wrapped in a buffalo robe, with my feet to the fire in the centre of the room, to which place the genuine politeness of my constant and watchful friend has as regularly drawn him, where his irresistible importunities have brought me, night after night, to the only alternative of using his bedaubed and bear-greased body for a pillow.

Being unwilling to deny the poor fellow the satisfaction he seemed

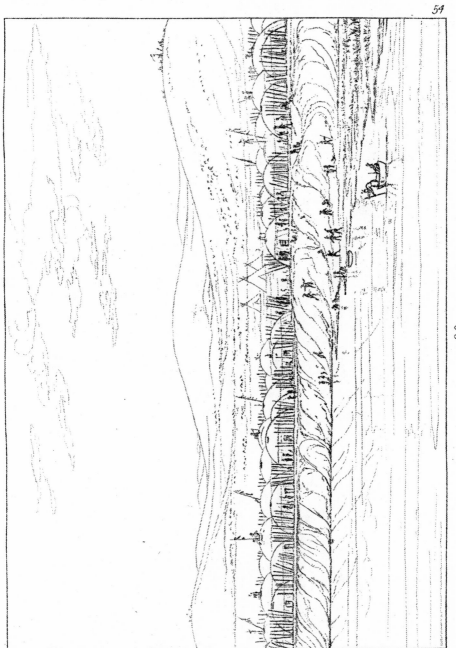

G. Catlin.

80

82

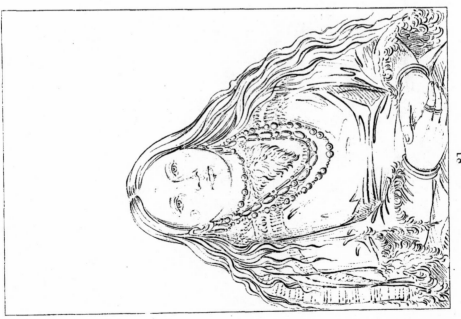

81

G. Catlin.

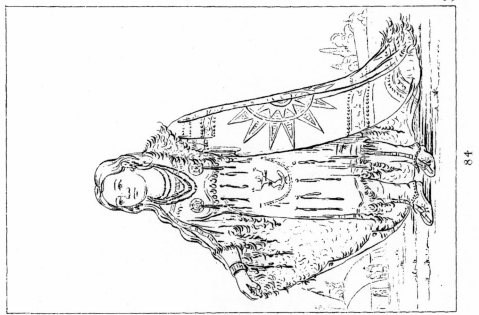

56

84

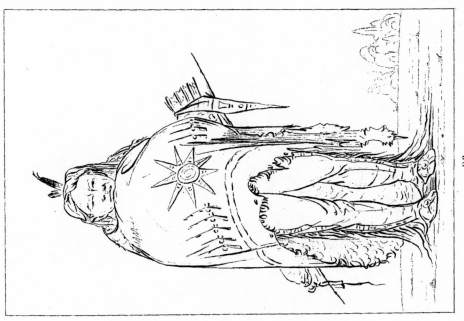

83

G. Catlin

to be drawing from this singular freak, I took some pains to inquire into his character; and learned that he was a Riccaree brave, by the name of Pah-too-ca-ra (he who strikes), who is here with several others of his tribe, on a friendly visit (though in a hostile village), and living as they are, unprotected, except by the mercy of their enemies. I think it probable, therefore, that he is ingeniously endeavouring thus to ingratiate himself in my affections, and consequently to insure my guardianship and influence for his protection. Be this as it may, he is rendering me many kind services, and I have in return traced him on my canvas for immortality (Fig. 83).

By the side of him (Fig. 84), I have painted a beautiful little girl of the same tribe, whose name is Pshan-shaw (the sweet-scented grass), giving a very pretty specimen of the dress and fashion of the women in this tribe. The inner garment, which is like a slip or a frock, is entire in one piece, and beautifully ornamented with embroidery and beads, with a row of elks' teeth passing across the breast, and a robe of the young buffalo's skin, tastefully and elaborately embroidered, gracefully thrown over her shoulders, and hanging down to the ground behind her.

Fig. 82 gives a portrait of one of the chiefs of this tribe by the name of Stan-au-pat (the bloody hand), and (Fig. 81) of Kah-beck-a (the twin), a good-looking matron, who was painted a few weeks since in the principal Mandan village.

The dresses in both of these portraits are very beautiful, and I have procured them, as well as the one before spoken of, for my collection.

Fig. 80 gives a view of the Riccaree village, which is beautifully situated on the west bank of the river, 200 miles below the Mandans; and built very much in the same manner; being constituted of 150 earth-covered lodges, which are in part surrounded by an imperfect and open barrier of piquets set firmly in the ground, and of ten or twelve feet in height.

This village is built upon an open prairie, and the gracefully undulating hills that rise in distance behind it are everywhere covered with a verdant green turf, without a tree or a bush anywhere to be seen. This view was taken from the deck of the steamer when I was on my way up the river; and probably it was well that I took it then, for so hostile and deadly are the feelings of these people towards the *pale faces,* at this time, that it may be deemed most prudent for me to pass them on my way down the river, without stopping to make them a visit. They certainly are harbouring the most resentful feelings at this time towards the Traders, and others passing on the river;

and no doubt, that there is great danger of the lives of any white men, who unluckily fall into their hands. They have recently sworn death and destruction to every white man, who comes in their way; and there is no doubt, that they are ready to execute their threats.

When Lewis and Clarke first visited these people thirty years since, it will be found by a reference to their history, that the Riccarees received and treated them with great kindness and hospitality; but owing to the system of trade, and the manner in which it has been conducted in this country, they have been inflicted with real or imaginary abuses, of which they are themselves, and the Fur Traders, the best judges; and for which they are now harbouring the most inveterate feelings towards the whole civilised race.

The Riccarees are unquestionably a part of the tribe of Pawnees, living on the Platte River, some hundreds of miles below this, inasmuch as their language is nearly or quite the same; and their personal appearance and customs as similar as could be reasonably expected amongst a people so long since separated from their parent tribe, and continually subjected to innovations from the neighbouring tribes around them; amongst whom, in their erratic wanderings in search of a location, they have been jostled about in the character, alternately, of friends and of foes.

I shall resume my voyage down the river in a few days in my canoe; and I may, perhaps, stop and pay these people a visit, and consequently, be able to say more of them; or, I may be *hauled in,* to the shore, and my boat plundered, and my *"scalp danced,"* as they have dealt quite recently with the *last trader,* who has dared for several years past, to continue his residence with them, after they had laid fatal hands on each one of his comrades before him, and divided and shared their goods.

Of the Mandans, who are about me in this little village, I need say nothing, except that they are in every respect, the same as those I have described in the lower village—and in fact, I believe this little town is rather a *summer residence* for a few of the noted families, than anything else; as I am told that none of their wigwams are tenanted through the winter. I shall leave them in the morning, and take up my residence a few days longer with my hospitable friends Mr Kipp, Mah-to-toh-pa, etc., in the large village; and then with my canvas and easel, and paint-pots in my canoe; with Ba'tiste and Bogard to paddle, and my own oar to steer, wend my way again on the mighty Missouri towards my native land, bidding everlasting farewell to the kind and hospitable Mandans.

In taking this final leave of them, which will be done with some decided feelings of regret, and in receding from their country, I shall look back and reflect upon them and their curious and peculiar modes with no small degree of pleasure, as well as surprise; inasmuch as their hospitality and friendly treatment have fully corroborated my fixed belief that the North American Indian in his primitive state is a high-minded, hospitable and honourable being—and their singular and peculiar customs have raised an irresistible belief in my mind that they have had a different origin, or are of a different compound of character from any other tribe that I have yet seen, or that can be probably seen in North America.

In coming to such a conclusion as this, the mind is at once filled with a flood of inquiries as to the source from which they have sprung, and eagerly seeking for the evidence which is to lead it to the most probable and correct conclusion. Amongst these evidences of which there are many, and forcible ones to be met with amongst these people, and many of which I have named in my former epistles, the most striking ones are those which go, I think, decidedly to suggest the existence of looks and of customs amongst them, bearing incontestible proofs of an amalgam of civilised and savage; and that in the absence of all proof of any recent proximity of a civilised stock that could in any way have been engrafted upon them.

These facts then, with the host of their peculiarities which stare a traveller in the face, lead the mind back in search of some more remote and national cause for such striking singularities; and in this dilemma, I have been almost disposed (not to advance it as a *theory,* but) to inquire whether here may not be found, yet existing, the remains of the *Welsh* colony—the followers of Madoc; who history tells us, if I recollect right, started with ten ships, to colonise a country which he had discovered in the Western Ocean; whose expedition I think has been pretty clearly traced to the mouth of the Mississippi, or the coast of Florida, and whose fate further than this seems sealed in unsearchable mystery.

I am travelling in this country, as I have before said, not to advance or to prove *theories,* but to see all that I am able to see, and to tell it in the simplest and most intelligible manner I can to the world, for their own conclusions, or for theories I may feel disposed to advance, and be better able to defend after I get out of this singular country; where all the powers of one's faculties are required, and much better employed I consider, in helping him along and in gathering materials, than in stopping to draw too nice and delicate conclusions by the way.

If my indefinite recollections of the fate of that colony, however, as recorded in history be correct, I see no harm in suggesting the inquiry, whether they did not sail up the Mississippi river in their ten ships, or such number of them as might have arrived safe in its mouth; and having advanced up the Ohio from its junction, (as they naturally would, it being the widest and most gentle current) to a rich and fertile country, planted themselves as agriculturists on its rich banks, where they lived and flourished, and increased in numbers, until they were attacked, and at last besieged by the numerous hordes of savages who were jealous of their growing condition; and as a protection against their assaults, built those numerous *civilised* fortifications, the ruins of which are now to be seen on the Ohio and the Muskingum, in which they were at last all destroyed, except some few families who had intermarried with the Indians, and whose offspring, being half-breeds, were in such a manner allied to them that their lives were spared; and forming themselves into a small and separate community, took up their residence on the banks of the Missouri; on which, for the want of a permanent location, being on the lands of their more powerful enemies, were obliged repeatedly to remove; and continuing their course up the river, have in time migrated to the place where they are now living, and consequently found with the numerous and almost unaccountable peculiarities of which I have before spoken, so inconsonant with the general character of the North American Indians; with complexions of every shade; with hair of all the colours in civilised society, and many with hazel, with grey, and with blue eyes.

The above is a suggestion of a *moment;* and I wish the reader to bear it in mind, that if I ever advance such as a *theory,* it will be after I have collected other proofs, which I shall take great pains to do; after I have taken a vocabulary of their language, and also in my transit down the river in my canoe, I may be able from my own examinations of the ground, to ascertain whether the shores of the Missouri bear evidences of their former locations; or whether amongst the tribes who inhabit the country below, there remain any satisfactory traditions of their residences in, and transit through their countries.

I close here my book (and probably for some time, my remarks), on the friendly and hospitable Mandans.

NOTE—Several years having elapsed since the above account of the Mandans was written, I open the book to convey to the reader the melancholy intelligence of the *destruction* of this interesting tribe, which happened a short time after I left their country; and the manner and causes of their misfortune I have explained in the Appendix to the Second Volume of this Work; as well as some further considerations of the subject just above-named, relative to their early history, and the probable fate of the followers of *Madoc,* to which I respectfully refer the reader before he goes further in the body of the Work. See Appendix A.

MOUTH OF TETON RIVER, *UPPER MISSOURI*

SINCE writing the above Letter I have descended the Missouri, a distance of six or seven hundred miles, in my little bark, with Ba'tiste and Bogard, my old *"compagnons du voyage,"* and have much to say of what we three did and what we saw on our way, which will be given anon.

I am now in the heart of the country belonging to the numerous tribe of Sioux or Dahcotas, and have Indian faces and Indian customs in abundance around me. This tribe is one of the most numerous in North America, and also one of the most vigorous and warlike tribes to be found, numbering some forty or fifty thousand, and able undoubtedly to muster, if the tribe could be moved simultaneously, at least eight or ten thousand warriors, well mounted and well armed. This tribe take vast numbers of the wild horses on the plains towards the Rocky Mountains, and many of them have been supplied with guns; but the greater part of them hunt with their bows and arrows and long lances, killing their game from their horses' backs while at full speed.

The name Sioux (pronounced *see-00)* by which they are familiarly called, is one that has been given to them by the French traders, the meaning of which I never have learned; their own name being, in their language, Dah-co-ta. The personal appearance of these people is very fine and prepossessing, their persons tall and straight, and their movements elastic and graceful. Their stature is considerably above that of the Mandans and Riccarees, or Blackfeet; but about equal to that of the Crows, Assinneboins and Minatarees, furnishing at least one half of their warriors of six feet or more in height.

I am here living with, and enjoying the hospitality of a gentleman by the name of *Laidlaw,* a Scotchman, who is attached to the American Fur Company, and who, in company with Mr M'Kenzie (of whom I have before spoken) and Lamont, has the whole agency of the Fur Company's transactions in the regions of the Upper Missouri and the Rocky Mountains.

This gentleman has a finely-built Fort here, of two or three hundred feet square, enclosing eight or ten of their factories, houses and stores, in the midst of which he occupies spacious and comfortable apartments, which are well supplied with the comforts and luxuries of life and neatly and respectably conducted by a fine looking, modest, and dignified Sioux woman, the kind and affectionate mother of his little flock of pretty and interesting children.

This Fort is undoubtedly one of the most important and productive of the American Fur Company's posts, being in the centre of the great Sioux country, drawing from all quarters an immense and almost incredible number of buffalo robes, which are carried to the New York and other Eastern markets, and sold at a great profit. This post is thirteen hundred miles above St Louis, on the west bank of the Missouri, on a beautiful plain near the mouth of the Teton River which empties into the Missouri from the West, and the Fort has received the name of Fort Pierre, in compliment to Monsr. Pierre Chouteau, who is one of the partners in the Fur Company, residing in St Louis; and to whose politeness I am indebted, as I have before mentioned, for my passage in the Company's steamer, on her first voyage to the Yellow Stone; and whose urbane and gentlemanly society, I have before said, I had during my passage.

The country about this Fort is almost entirely prairie, producing along the banks of the river and streams only, slight skirtings of timber. No site could have been selected more pleasing or more advantageous than this; the Fort is in the centre of one of the Missouri's most beautiful plains, and hemmed in by a series of gracefully undulating grass-covered hills, on all sides; rising like a series of terraces, to the summit level of the prairies, some three or four hundred feet in elevation, which then stretches off in an apparently boundless ocean of gracefully swelling waves and fields of green. On my way up the river I made a painting of this lovely spot, taken from the summit of the bluffs, a mile or two distant (Fig. 85), showing an encampment of Sioux, of six hundred tents or skin lodges, around the Fort, where they had concentrated to make their spring trade; exchanging their furs and peltries for articles and luxuries of civilised manufactures.

The great family of Sioux who occupy so vast a tract of country, extending from the banks of the Mississippi river to the base of the Rocky Mountains, are everywhere a migratory or roaming tribe, divided into forty-two bands or families, each having a chief who all acknowledge a superior or head chief, to whom they all are held subordinate. This subordination, however, I should rather record

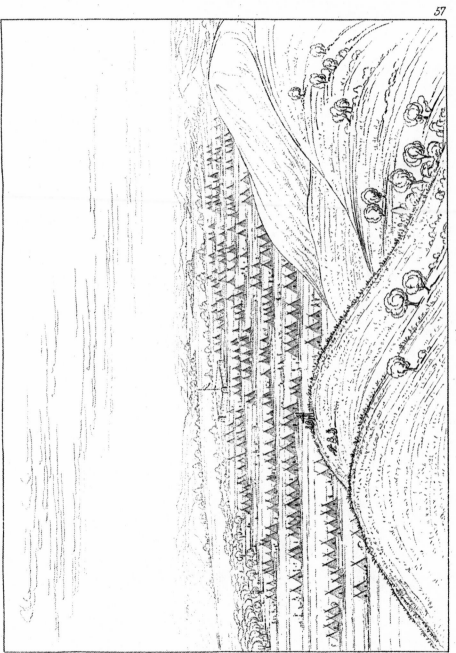

G. Catlin

as their *former* and *native* regulation, of which there exists no doubt, than an *existing* one, since the numerous innovations made amongst these people by the Fur Traders, as well as by the proximity of civilisation along a great deal of their frontier, which soon upset and change many native regulations, and particularly those relating to their government and religion.

There is one principal and familiar division of this tribe into what are called the *Mississippi* and *Missouri* Sioux. Those bordering on the banks of the Mississippi, concentrating at Prairie du Chien and Fort Snelling, for the purposes of trade, etc., are called the Mississippi Sioux. These are somewhat advanced towards civilisation, and familiar with white people, with whom they have held intercourse for many years, and are consequently excessive whiskey drinkers, though constituting but a meagre proportion, and at the same time, but a very unfair and imperfect sample of the great mass of this tribe who inhabit the shores of the Missouri, and fearlessly roam on the vast plains intervening between it and the Rocky Mountains, and are still living entirely in their primitive condition.

There is no tribe on the Continent, perhaps, of finer looking men than the Sioux; and few tribes who are better and more comfortably clad, and supplied with the necessaries of life. There are no parts of the great plains of America which are more abundantly stocked with buffaloes and wild horses, nor any people more bold in destroying the one for food, and appropriating the other to their use. There has gone abroad, from the many histories which have been written of these people, an opinion which is too current in the world, that the Indian is necessarily a poor, drunken, murderous wretch; which account is certainly unjust as regards the savage, and doing less than justice to the world for whom such histories have been prepared. I have travelled several years already amongst these people and I have not had my scalp taken, nor a blow struck me; nor had occasion to raise my hand against an Indian; nor has my property been stolen, as yet to my knowledge, to the value of a shilling; and that in a country where no man is punishable by law for the crime of stealing; still some of them steal, and murder too; and if white men did not do the same, and that in defiance of the laws of God and man, I might take satisfaction in stigmatising the Indian character as thievish and murderous. That the Indians in their *native state* are *"drunken,"* is false; for they are the only temperance people, literally speaking, that ever I saw in my travels, or ever expect to see. If the civilised world are startled at this, it is the *fact* that they must battle with, not with me; for these people manufacture no spirituous liquor themselves, and know nothing of it until it is brought into their country and tendered to them by Christians. That these people are *"naked"* is equally untrue, and as easily disproved; for I am sure that with the paintings I have made amongst the Mandans and Crows, and other tribes; and with their beautiful costumes which I have procured and shall bring home, I shall be able to establish the fact that many of these people dress, not only with clothes comfortable for any latitude, but that they also dress with some considerable taste and elegance. Nor am I quite sure that they are entitled to the name of *"poor,"* who live in a boundless country of green fields, with good horses to ride; where they are all joint tenants of the soil, together; where the Great Spirit has supplied them with an abundance of food to eat—where they are all indulging in the pleasures and amusements of a lifetime of idleness and ease, with no business hours to attend to, nor professions to learn—where they have no notes in bank or other debts to pay—no taxes, no tithes, no rents, nor beggars to touch and tax the sympathy of their souls at every step they go. Such might be poverty in the Christian world, but is sure to be a blessing where the pride and insolence of comparative wealth are unknown.

I mentioned that this is the nucleus or place of concentration of the numerous tribe of the Sioux, who often congregate here in great masses to make their trades with the American Fur Company; and that on my way up the river, some months since, I found here encamped, six hundred families of Sioux, living in tents covered with buffalo hides. Amongst these there were twenty or more of the different bands, each one with their chief at their head, over whom was a *superior chief* and leader, a middle-aged man, of middling stature, with a noble countenance, and a figure almost equalling the Apollo, and I painted his portrait (Fig. 86). The name of this chief is Ha-wan-je-tah (the one horn) of the Mee-ne-cow-e-gee band, who has risen rapidly to the highest honours in the tribe, from his own extraordinary merits, even at so early an age. He told me that he took the name of "One Horn" (or shell) from a simple small shell that was hanging on his neck, which descended to him from his father, and which, he said, he valued more than anything he possessed; affording a striking instance of the living affection which these people often cherish for the dead, inasmuch as he chose to carry this name through life, in preference to many others and more honourable ones he had a right to have taken, from different battles

58

G. Catlin.

86

and exploits of his extraordinary life. He treated me with great kindness and attention, considering himself highly complimented by the signal and unprecedented honour I had conferred upon him by painting his portrait, and that before I had invited any other. His costume was a very handsome one, and will have a place in my INDIAN GALLERY by the side of his picture. It is made of elk skins beautifully dressed, and fringed with a profusion of porcupine quills and scalp-locks; and his hair, which is very long and profuse, divided into two parts, and lifted up and crossed, over the top of his head, with a simple tie, giving it somewhat the appearance of a Turkish turban.

This extraordinary man, before he was raised to the dignity of chief, was the renowned of his tribe for his athletic achievements. In the chase he was foremost; he could run down a buffalo, which he often had done, on his own legs, and drive his arrow to the heart. He was the fleetest in the tribe; and in the races he had run, he had always taken the prize.

It was proverbial in his tribe, that Ha-wan-je-tah's bow never was drawn in vain, and his wigwam was abundantly furnished with scalps that he had taken from his enemies' heads in battle.

Having descended the river thus far, then, and having hauled out my canoe, and taken up my quarters for awhile with mine hospitable host, Mr Laidlaw, as I have before said; and having introduced my readers to the country and the people, and more particularly to the chief dignitary of the Sioux; and having promised in the beginning of this Letter also, that I should give them some amusing and curious information that we picked up, and incidents that we met with, on our voyage from the Mandans to this place; I have again to beg that they will pardon me for withholding from them yet awhile longer, the incidents of that curious and most important part of my Tour, the absence of which, at this time, seems to make a "hole in the ballad," though I promise my readers they are written, and will appear in the book in a proper and appropriate place.

Taking it for granted then, that I will be indulged in this freak, I am taking the liberty of presuming on my readers' patience in proposing another, which is to offer them here an extract from my Notes, which were made on my journey of 1300 miles from St Louis to this place, where I stopped, as I have said, amongst several thousands of Sioux; where I remained for some time, and painted my numerous portraits of their chiefs, etc.; one of whom was the head and leader of the Sioux, whom I have already introduced.

On the long and tedious route that lies between St Louis and this place, I passed the Sacs and Ioways—the Konzas—the Omahaws, and the Ottoes (making notes on them all, which are reserved for another place), and landed at the Puncahs, a small tribe residing in one village, on the west bank of the river, 300 miles below this, and 1000 from St Louis.

The Puncahs are all contained in seventy-five or eighty lodges, made of buffalo skins, in the form of tents; the frames for which are poles of fifteen or twenty feet in length, with the butt ends standing on the ground, and the small ends meeting at the top, forming a cone, which sheds off the rain and wind with perfect success. This small remnant of a tribe are not more than four or five hundred in numbers; and I should think, at least, two-thirds of those are women. This disparity in numbers having been produced by the continual losses which their men suffer, who are penetrating the buffalo country for meat, for which they are now obliged to travel a great way (as the buffaloes have recently left their country), exposing their lives to their more numerous enemies about them.

The chief of this tribe, whose name is Shoo-de-ga-cha (smoke), I painted at full length (Fig. 87), and his wife also, a young and very pretty woman (Fig. 88), whose name is Hee-la'h-dee (the pure fountain); her neck and arms were curiously tattooed, which is a very frequent mode of ornamenting the body amongst this and some other tribes, which is done by pricking into the skin, gunpowder and vermilion.

The chief, who was wrapped in a buffalo robe, is a noble specimen of native dignity and philosophy. I conversed much with him; and from his dignified manners, as well as from the soundness of his reasoning, I became fully convinced that he deserved to be the sachem of a more numerous and prosperous tribe. He related to me with great coolness and frankness, the poverty and distress of his nation; and with the method of a philosopher, predicted the certain and rapid extinction of his tribe, which he had not the power to avert. Poor, noble chief; who was equal to, and worthy of a greater empire! He sat upon the deck of the steamer, overlooking the little cluster of his wigwams mingled amongst the trees; and, like Caius Marius, weeping over the ruins of Carthage, shed tears as he was descanting on the poverty of his ill-fated little community, which he told me "had once been powerful and happy; that the buffaloes which the Great Spirit had given them for food, and which formerly spread all over their green prairies, had all been killed or driven out by the approach of white men, who wanted their skins; that their

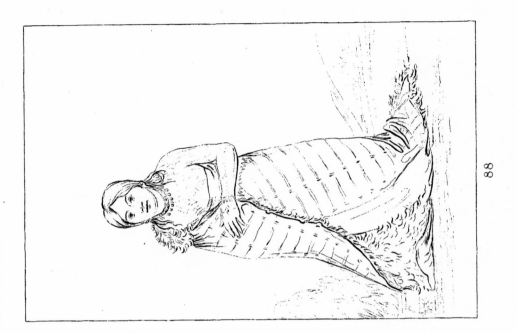

59

88

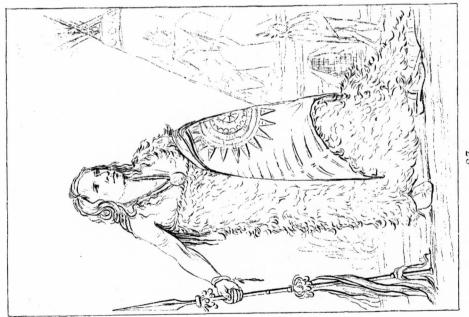

87

G. Catlin.

country was now entirely destitute of game, and even of roots for their food, as it was one continued prairie; and that his young men penetrating the countries of their enemies for buffaloes, which they were obliged to do, were cut to pieces and destroyed in great numbers. That his people had foolishly become fond of *fire-water* (whiskey), and had given away everything in their country for it—that it had destroyed many of his warriors, and soon would destroy the rest— that his tribe was too small, and his warriors too few to go to war with the tribes around them; that they were met and killed by the Sioux on the North, by the Pawnees on the West; and by the Osages and Konzas on the South; and still more alarmed from the constant advance of the pale faces—their enemies from the East; with whiskey and small-pox, which already had destroyed four-fifths of his tribe, and soon would impoverish, and at last destroy the remainder of them."

In this way did this shrewd philosopher lament over the unlucky destiny of his tribe; and I pitied him with all my heart. I have no doubt of the correctness of his representations; and I believe there is no tribe on the frontier more in want, nor any more deserving of the sympathy and charity of the government and Christian societies of the civilised world.

The son of this chief, a youth of eighteen years, and whose portrait I painted (Fig. 90), distinguished himself in a singular manner the day before our steamer reached their village, by taking to him *four wives in one day!* This extraordinary and unprecedented freak of his, was just the thing to make him the greatest sort of *medicine* in the eyes of his people; and probably he may date much of his success and greatness through life, to this bold and original step, which suddenly raised him into notice and importance.

The old chief Shoo-de-ga,-cha, of whom I have spoken above, considering his son to have arrived to the age of maturity, fitted him out for house-keeping, by giving him a handsome wigwam to live in, and nine horses, with many other valuable presents; when the boy, whose name is Hongs-kay-de (the great chief), soon laid his plans for the proud and pleasant epoch in his life, and consummated them in the following ingenious and amusing manner.

Wishing to connect himself with, and consequently to secure the countenance of some of the most influential men in the tribe, he had held an interview with one of the most distinguished; and easily (being the son of a chief) made an arrangement for the hand of his daughter, which he was to receive on a certain day, and at a certain hour, for which he was to give two horses, a gun, and several pounds of tobacco. This was enjoined on the father as a profound secret, and as a condition of the espousal. In like manner he soon made similar arrangements with three other leading men of the tribe, each of whom had a young and beautiful daughter of marriageable age. To each of the fathers he had promised two horses, and other presents similar to those stipulated for in the first instance, and all under the same injunctions of secrecy, until the hour approached, when he had announced to the whole tribe that he was to be married. At the time appointed, they all assembled, and all were in ignorance of the fair hand that was to be placed in his on this occasion. He had got some of his young friends who were prepared to assist him, to lead up the eight horses. He took two of them by the halters, and the other presents agreed upon in his other hand, and advancing to the first of the parents, whose daughter was standing by the side of him, saying to him, "you promised me the hand of your daughter on this day, for which I was to give you two horses." The father assented with a "ugh!" receiving the presents, and giving his child; when some confusion ensued from the simultaneous remonstrances, which were suddenly made by the other three parents, who had brought their daughters forward and were shocked at this sudden disappointment, as well as by the mutual declarations they were making, of similar contracts that each one had entered into with him! As soon as they could be pacified, and silence was restored, he exultingly replied, "You have all acknowledged in public your promises with me, which I shall expect you to fulfil. I am here to perform all the engagements which I have made, and I expect you all to do the same"—No more was said. He led up the two horses for each, and delivered the other presenes; leading off to his wigwam his four brides—taking two in each hand, and commenced at once upon his new mode of life; reserving only one of his horses for his own daily use.

I visited the wigwam of this young installed *medicine-man* several times, and saw his four modest little wives seated around the fire, where all seemed to harmonise very well; and for aught I could discover, were entering very happily on the duties and pleasures of married life. I selected one of them for her portrait, and painted it (Fig. 89), Mong-shong-shaw (the bending willow), in a very pretty dress of deer skins, and covered with a young buffalo's robe, which was handsomely ornamented, and worn with much grace and pleasing effect.

Mr Chouteau of the Fur Company, and Major Sanford, the agent for the Upper Missouri Indians, were with me at this time; and

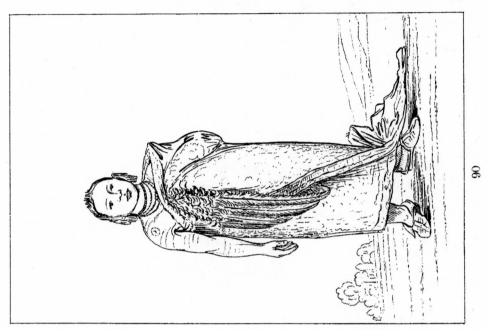

60

90

89

both of these gentlemen, highly pleased with so ingenious and *innocent* a freak, felt disposed to be liberal, and sent them many presents from the steamer.

The ages of these young brides were probably all between twelve and fifteen years, the season of life in which most of the girls in this wild country contract marriage.

It is a surprising fact, that women mature in these regions at that early age, and there have been some instances where marriage has taken place, even at eleven; and the juvenile mother has been blest with her first offspring at the age of twelve!

These facts are calculated to create surprise and almost incredulity in the mind of the reader, but there are circumstances for his consideration yet to be known, which will in a manner account for these extraordinary facts.

There is not a doubt but there is a more early approach to maturity amongst the females of this country than in civilised communities, owing either to a natural and constitutional difference, or to the exposed and active life they lead. Yet there is another and more general cause of early marriages (and consequently apparent maturity), which arises out of the modes and forms of the country, where most of the marriages are contracted with the parents, hurried on by the impatience of the applicant, and prematurely accepted and consummated on the part of the parents, who are often impatient to be in receipt of the presents they are to receive as the price of their daughters. There is also the facility of dissolving the marriage contract in this country, which does away with one of the most serious difficulties which lies in the way in the civilised world, and calculated greatly to retard its consummation, which is not an equal objection in Indian communities. Education and accomplishments, again, in the fashionable world, and also a time and a season to flourish and show them off, necessarily engross that part of a young lady's life, when the poor Indian girl, who finds herself weaned from the familiar embrace of her parents, with her mind and her body maturing, and her thoughts and her passions straying away in the world for some theme or some pleasure to cling to, easily follows their juvenile and ardent dictates, prematurely entering on that system of life, consisting in reciprocal dependence and protection.

In the instance above described, the young man was in no way censured by his people, but most loudly applauded; for in this country polygamy is allowed; and in this tribe, where there are two or three times the number of women that there are of men, such an arrangement answers a good purpose, whereby so many of the females are provided for and taken care of; and particularly so, and to the great satisfaction of the tribe, as well as of the parties and families concerned, when so many fall to the lot of a chief, or the son of a chief, into whose wigwam it is considered an honour to be adopted, and where they are the most sure of protection.

LETTER—No. 27

MOUTH OF TETON RIVER, *UPPER MISSOURI*

WHEN we were about to start on our way up the river from the village of the Puncahs, we found that they were packing up all their goods and preparing to start for the prairies, farther to the West, in pursuit of buffaloes, to dry meat for their winter's supplies. They took down their wigwams of skins to carry with them, and all were flat to the ground and everything packing up ready for the start. My attention was directed by Major Sanford, the Indian Agent, to one of the most miserable and helpless looking objects that I ever had seen in my life, a very aged and emaciated man of the tribe, who he told me was to be *exposed*.

The tribe were going where hunger and dire necessity compelled them to go, and this pitiable object, who had once been a chief, and a man of distinction in his tribe, who was now too old to travel, being reduced to mere skin and bones, was to be left to starve, or meet with such death as might fall to his lot, and his bones to be picked by the wolves! I lingered around this poor old forsaken patriarch for hours before we started, to indulge the tears of sympathy which were flowing for the sake of this poor benighted and decrepit old man, whose worn-out limbs were no longer able to support him; their kind and faithful offices having long since been performed, and his body and his mind doomed to linger into the withering agony of decay, and gradual solitary death. I wept, and it was a pleasure to weep, for the painful looks, and the dreary prospects of this old veteran, whose eyes were dimmed, whose venerable locks were whitened by an hundred years, whose limbs were almost naked, and trembling as he sat by a small fire which his friends had left him, with a few sticks of wood within his reach, and a buffalo's skin stretched upon some crotches over his head. Such was to be his only dwelling, and such the chances for his life, with only a few half-picked bones that were laid within his reach, and a dish of water, without weapons or means of any kind to replenish them, or strength to move his body from its fatal locality. In this sad plight I mournfully contemplated this miserable remnant of existence, who had unluckily outlived the fates and accidents of wars to die alone, at death's leisure. His friends and his children had all left him, and were preparing in a little time to be on the march. He had told them to leave him, "he was old," he said "and too feeble to march." "My children," said he, "our nation is poor, and it is necessary that you should all go to the country where you can get meat—my eyes are dimmed and my strength is no more; my days are nearly all numbered, and I am a burthen to my children —I cannot go, and I wish to die. Keep your hearts stout, and think not of me; I am no longer good for anything." In this way they had finished the ceremony of *exposing* him, and taken their final leave of him. I advanced to the old man, and was undoubtedly the last human being who held converse with him. I sat by the side of him, and though he could not distinctly see me, he shook me heartily by the hand and smiled, evidently aware that I was a white man, and that I sympathised with his inevitable misfortune. I shook hands again with him, and left him, steering my course towards the steamer which was a mile or more from me, and ready to resume her voyage up the Missouri.*

This cruel custom of exposing their aged people, belongs, I think, to all the tribes who roam about the prairies, making severe marches, when such decrepit persons are totally unable to go, unable to ride or to walk—when they have no means of carrying them. It often becomes absolutely necessary in such cases that they should be left; and they uniformly insist upon it, saying as this old man did, that they are old and of no further use—that they left their fathers in the same manner—that they wish to die, and their children must not mourn for them.

From the Puncah village, our steamer made regular progress from day to day towards the mouth of the Teton, from where I am now writing; passing the whole way a country of green fields, that come sloping down to the river on either side, forming the loveliest scenes in the world.

From day to day we advanced, opening our eyes to something new and more beautiful every hour that we progressed, until at last our boat was aground; and a day's work of sounding told us at last, that there was no possibility of advancing further, until there should be a rise in the river, to enable the boat to get over the bar. After lying in the middle of the river about a week, in

* When passing by the site of the Puncah village a few months after this, in my canoe, I went ashore with my men, and found the poles and the buffalo skin, standing as they were left, over the old man's head. The firebrands were lying nearly as I had left them, and I found at a few yards distant the skull, and others of his bones, which had been picked and cleaned by the wolves; which is probably all that any human being can ever know of his final and melancholy fate.

this unpromising dilemma, Mr Chouteau started off twenty men on foot, to cross the plains for a distance of 200 miles to Laidlaw's Fort, at the mouth of Teton river. To this expedition, I immediately attached myself; and having heard that a numerous party of Sioux were there encamped, and waiting to see the steamer, I packed on the backs, and in the hands of several of the men, such articles for painting, as I might want; canvas, paints, and brushes, with my sketch-book slung on my back, and my rifle in my hand, and I started off with them.

We took leave of our friends on the boat, and mounting the green bluffs, steered our course from day to day over a level prairie, without a tree or a bush in sight, to relieve the painful monotony, filling our canteens at the occasional little streams that we passed, kindling our fires with dried buffalo dung, which we collected on the prairie, and stretching our tired limbs on the level turf whenever we were overtaken by night.

We were six or seven days in performing this march; and it gave me a good opportunity of testing the muscles of my legs, with a number of half-breeds and Frenchmen, whose lives are mostly spent in this way, leading a novice, a cruel, and almost killing journey. Every rod of our way was over a continuous prairie, with a verdant green turf of wild grass of six or eight inches in height; and most of the way enamelled with wild flowers, and filled with a profusion of strawberries.

For two or three of the first days, the scenery was monotonous, and became exceedingly painful from the fact, that we were (to use a phrase of the country) "out of sight of land," *i.e.,* out of sight of anything rising above the horizon, which was a perfect straight line around us, like that of the blue and boundless ocean. The pedestrian over such a discouraging sea of green, without a landmark before or behind him; without a beacon to lead him on, or define his progress, feels weak and overcome when night falls; and he stretches his exhausted limbs, apparently on the same spot where he has slept the night before, with the same prospect before and behind him; the same grass, and the same wild flowers beneath and about him; the same canopy over his head, and the same cheerless sea of green to start upon in the morning. It is difficult to describe the simple beauty and serenity of these scenes of solitude, or the feelings of feeble man, whose limbs are toiling to carry him through them— without a hill or tree to mark his progress, and convince him that he is not, like a squirrel in his cage, after all his toil, standing still. One commences on peregrinations like these, with a light heart, and a nimble foot, and spirits as buoyant as the very air that floats along by the side of him; but his spirit soon tires, and he lags on the way that is rendered more tedious and intolerable by the tantalising *mirage* that opens before him beautiful lakes, and lawns, and copses; or by the *looming* of the prairie ahead of him, that seems to rise in a parapet, and decked with its varied flowers, phantom-like, flies and moves along before him.

I got on for a couple of days in tolerable condition, and with some considerable applause; but my half-breed companions took the lead at length, and left me with several other novices far behind, which gave me additional pangs; and I at length felt like giving up the journey, and throwing myself upon the ground in hopeless despair. I was not alone in my misery, however, but was cheered and encouraged by looking back and beholding several of our party half a mile or more in the rear of me, jogging along, and suffering more agony in their new experiment than I was suffering myself. Their loitering and my murmurs, at length, brought our leaders to a halt, and we held a sort of council, in which I explained that the pain in my feet was so intolerable, that I felt as if I could go no further; when one of our half-breed leaders stepped up to me, and addressing me in French, told me that I must *"turn my toes in"* as the Indians do, and that I could then go on very well. We halted a half-hour, and took a little refreshment, whilst the little Frenchman was teaching his lesson to the rest of my fellow-novices, when we took up our march again; and I soon found upon trial, that by turning my toes in, my feet went more easily through the grass; and by turning the weight of my body more equally on the toes (enabling each one to support its proportionable part of the load, instead of throwing it all on to the joints of the big toes, which is done when the toes are turned out); I soon got relief, and made my onward progress very well. I rigidly adhered to this mode, and found no difficulty on the third and fourth days, of taking the lead of the whole party, which I constantly led until our journey was completed.*

* On this march we were all travelling in moccasins, which being made without any soles, according to the Indian custom, had but little support for the foot underneath; and consequently, soon subjected us to excruciating pain, whilst walking according to the civilised mode, with the toes turned out. From this very painful experience I learned to my complete satisfaction, that man in a state of nature who walks on his naked feet, *must* walk with his toes turned in, that each may perform the duties assigned to it in proportion to its size and strength; and that civilised man *can* walk with his toes turned out if he chooses, if he will use a stiff sole under his feet, and will be content at last to put up with an acquired deformity of the big toe joint, which too many know to be a frequent and painful occurrence.

On this journey we saw immense herds of buffaloes; and although we had no horses to *run* them, we successfully *approached* them on foot, and supplied ourselves abundantly with fresh meat. After travelling for several days, we came in sight of a high range of blue hills in distance on our left, which rose to the height of several hundred feet above the level of the prairies. These hills were a conspicuous landmark at last, and some relief to us. I was told by our guide, that they were called the Bijou Hills, from a Fur Trader of that name, who had had his trading-house at the foot of them on the banks of the Missouri river, where he was at last destroyed by the Sioux Indians.

Not many miles back of this range of hills, we came in contact with an immense saline, or "salt meadow," as they are termed in this country, which turned us out of our path, and compelled us to travel several miles out of our way, to get by it; we came suddenly upon a great depression of the prairie, which extended for several miles, and as we stood upon its green banks, which were gracefully sloping down, we could overlook some hundreds of acres of the prairie which were covered with an incrustation of salt, that appeared the same as if the ground was everywhere covered with snow.

These scenes, I am told are frequently to be met with in these regions, and certainly present the most singular and startling effect, by the sudden and unexpected contrast between their snow-white appearance, and the green fields that hem them in on all sides. Through each of these meadows there is a meandering small stream which arises from salt springs, throwing out in the spring of the year great quantities of water, which flood over these meadows to the depth of three or four feet; and during the heat of summer, being exposed to the rays of the sun, entirely evaporates, leaving the incrustation of *muriate* on the surface, to the depth of one or two inches. These places are the constant resort of buffaloes, which congregate in thousands about them, to lick up the salt; and on approaching the banks of this place we stood amazed at the almost incredible numbers of these animals, which were in sight on the opposite banks, at the distance of a mile or two from us, where they were lying in countless numbers, on the level prairie above, and stretching down by hundreds, to lick at the salt, forming in distance, large masses of black, most pleasingly to contrast with the snow white, and the vivid green, which I have before mentioned.

After several days toil in the manner above-mentioned, all the way over soft and green fields, and amused with many pleasing incidents and accidents of the chase, we arrived, pretty well jaded, at Fort Pierre, mouth of Teton river, from whence I am now writing; where for the first time I was introduced to Mr M'Kenzie (of whom I have before spoken), to Mr Laidlaw, mine host, and Mr Halsey, a chief clerk in the establishment; and after, to the head chief and dignitaries of the great Sioux nation, who were here encamped about the Fort, in six or seven hundred skin lodges, and waiting for the arrival of the steamer, which they had heard, was on its way up the river, and which they had great curiosity to see.

After resting a few days, and recovering from the fatigues of my journey, having taken a fair survey of the Sioux village, and explained my views to the Indians, as well as to the gentlemen whom I have above named; I commenced my operations with the brush, and first of all painted the portrait of the head-chief of the Sioux (the one horn), whom I have before spoken of. This truly noble fellow sat for his portrait, and it was finished before any one of the tribe knew anything of it; several of the chiefs and doctors were allowed to see it, and at last it was talked of through the village; and of course, the greater part of their numbers were at once gathered around me. Nothing short of hanging it out of doors on the side of my wigwam, would in any way answer them; and here I had the peculiar satisfaction of beholding, through a small hole I had made in my wigwam, the high admiration and respect they all felt for their chief, as well as the very great estimation in which they held me as a painter and a magician, conferring upon me at once the very distinguished appellation of Ee-cha-zoo-kah-ga-wa-kon (the medicine painter).

After the exhibition of this chief's picture, there was much excitement in the village about it; the doctors generally took a decided and noisy stand against the operations of my brush; haranguing the populace, and predicting bad luck, and premature death, to all who submitted to so strange and unaccountable an operation! My business for some days was entirely at a stand for want of sitters; for the doctors were opposing me with all their force; and the women and children were crying, with their hands over their mouths, making the most pitiful and doleful laments, which I never can explain to my readers; but for some just account of which, I must refer them to my friends M'Kenzie and Halsey, who overlooked with infinite amusement, these curious scenes, and are able, no doubt, to give them with truth and effect to the world.

In this sad and perplexing dilemma, this noble chief stepped forward, and addressing himself to the chiefs and the doctors, to the braves and to the women and children, he told them to be quiet, and to treat me with friendship; that I had been travelling a great way to see them, and smoke with them; that I was great *medicine,* to be sure; that I was a great chief, and that I was the friend of Mr Laidlaw and Mr M'Kenzie, who had prevailed upon him to sit for his picture, and fully assured him that there was no harm in it. His speech had the desired effect, and I was shaken hands with by hundreds of their worthies, many of whom were soon dressed and ornamented, prepared to sit for their portraits.*

The first who then stepped forward for his portrait was Ee-ah-sa-pa

* Several years after I painted the portrait of this extraordinary man, and whilst I was delivering my Lectures in the City of New York, I first received intelligence of his death, in the following singular manner:—I was on the platform in my Lecture-room, in the Stuyvesant Institute, with an audience of twelve or fourteen hundred persons, in the midst of whom were seated a delegation of thirty or forty Sioux Indians under the charge of Major Pilcher, their agent; and I was successfully passing before their eyes the portraits of a number of Sioux chiefs, and making my remarks upon them. The Sioux instantly recognised each one as it was exhibited, which they instantly hailed by a sharp and startling yelp. But when the portrait of this chief was placed before them, instead of the usual recognition, each one placed his hand over his mouth, and gave a "hush—sh—" and hung down their heads, their usual expressions of grief in case of a death. From this sudden emotion, I knew instantly, that the chief must be dead, and so expressed my belief to the audience. I stopped my Lecture a few moments to converse with Major Pilcher who was by my side, and who gave me the following extraordinary account of his death, which I immediately related to the audience; and which being translated to the Sioux Indians, their chief arose and addressed himself to the audience, saying that the account was true, and that Ha-wan-je-tah was killed but a few days before they left home.

The account which Major Pilcher gave was nearly as follows:—

"But a few weeks before I left the Sioux country with the delegation, Ha-wan-je-tah (the one horn) had in some way been the accidental cause of the death of his only son, a very fine youth; and so great was the anguish of his mind at times, that he became frantic and insane. In one of these moods he mounted his favourite war-horse with his bow and his arrows in his hand, and dashed off at full speed upon the prairies, repeating the most solemn oath, 'that he would slay the first living thing that fell in his way, be it man or beast, or friend or foe.'

"No one dared to follow him, and after he had been absent an hour or two, his horse came back to the village with two arrows in its body, and covered with blood! Fears of the most serious kind were now entertained for the fate of the chief, and a party of warriors immediately mounted their horses, and retraced the animal's tracks to the place of the tragedy, where they found the body of their chief horribly mangled and gored by a buffalo bull, whose carcass was stretched by the side of him.

"A close examination of the ground was then made by the Indians, who ascertained by the tracks, that their unfortunate chief, under his unlucky resolve, had met a buffalo bull in the season when they are very stubborn, and unwilling to run from any one; and had incensed the animal by shooting a number of arrows into him, which had brought him into furious combat. The chief had then dismounted, and turned his horse loose, having given it a couple of arrows from his bow, which sent it home at full speed, and then had thrown away his bow and quiver, encountering the infuriated animal with his knife alone, and the desperate battle resulted as I have before-mentioned, in the death of both. Many of the bones of the chief were broken, as he was gored and stamped to death, and his huge antagonist had laid (the Black Rock) chief of the Nee-caw-wee-gee band (Fig. 91), a tall and fine-looking man, of six feet or more in stature; in a splendid dress, with his lance in his hand; with his pictured robe thrown gracefully over his shoulders, and his head-dress made of war-eagle's quills and ermine skins, falling in a beautiful crest over his back, quite down to his feet, and surmounted on the top with a pair of horns denoting him (as I have explained in former instances) head leader or war-chief of his band.

This man has been a constant and faithful friend of Mr M'Kenzie and others of the Fur Traders, who held him in high estimation, both as an honourable and valiant man, and an estimable companion.

The next who sat to me was Tchan-dee, tobacco (Fig. 92), a desperate warrior, and represented to me by the traders, as one of the most respectable and famous chiefs of the tribe. After him sat Toh-ki-ee-to, the stone with horns (Fig. 93), chief of the Yanc-ton band, and reputed the principal and most eloquent *orator* of the nation. The neck, and breast, and shoulders of this man, were curiously tattooed, by pricking in gunpowder and vermilion, which in this extraordinary instance, was put on in such elaborate profusion as to appear at a little distance like a beautiful embroidered dress. In his hand he held a handsome pipe, the stem of which was several feet long, and all the way wound with ornamented braids of the porcupine quills. Around his body was wrapped a valued robe, made of the skin of the grizzly bear, and on his neck several strings of *wampum,* an ornament seldom seen amongst the Indians in the Far West and the North.* I was much

his body by the side of him, weltering in blood from an hundred wounds made by the chief's long and two-edged knife."

So died this elegant and high-minded nobleman of the wilderness, whom I confidently had hoped to meet and admire again at some future period of my life. (*Vide* Fig. 86.)

* *Wampum* is the Indian name of ornaments manufactured by the Indians from vari-coloured shells, which they get on the shores of the fresh water streams, and file or cut into bits of half an inch, or an inch in length, and perforate (giving to them the shape of pieces of broken pipe stems), which they string on deer's sinews, and wear on their necks in profusion; or weave them ingeniously into war-belts for the waist.

Amongst the numerous tribes who have formerly inhabited the Atlantic Coast, and that part of the country which now constitutes the principal part of the United States, wampum has been invariably manufactured, and highly valued as a circulating medium (instead of coins, of which the Indians have no knowledge); so many strings, or so many hands-breadth, being the fixed value of a horse, a gun, a robe, etc.

In treaties, the wampum belt has been passed as the pledge of friendship, and from time immemorial sent to hostile tribes, as the messenger of peace; or paid by so many fathoms length, as tribute to conquering enemies, and Indian kings.

It is a remarkable fact, and worthy of observation in this place, that after I passed

91

G Catlin.

92   93

94   95

G. Catlion.

amused with the excessive vanity and egotism of this notorious man, who, whilst sitting for his picture, took occasion to have the interpreter constantly explaining to me the wonderful effects which his oratory had at different times produced on the minds of the chiefs and people of his tribe.

He told me, that it was a very easy thing for him to set all the women of the tribe to crying: and that all the chiefs listened profoundly to his voice before they went to war; and at last, summed up by saying, that he was "the greatest orator in the Sioux nation," by which he undoubtedly meant the greatest in the *world*.

Besides these *distingués* of this great and powerful tribe, I painted in regular succession, according to their rank and standing, Wan-ee-ton, chief of the *Susseton band;* Tah-zee-kah-da-cha (the torn belly), a brave of the *Yancton band;* Ka-pes-ka-day (the shell), a brave of the *O-gla-la band;* Wuk-mi-ser (corn), a warrior of the *Nee-cow-ee-gee band;* Cha-tee-wah-nee-chee (no heart), chief of the *Wah-nee-watch-to-nee-nah band;* Mah-to-ra-rish-nee-eeh-ee-rah (the grizzly bear that runs without regard), a brave of the *Onc-pa-pa band;* Mah-to-chee-ga (the little bear), a distinguished brave; Shon-ka (the dog), chief of the *Ca-za-zhee-ta* (bad arrow points) *band;* Tah-teck-a-da-hair (the steep wind), a brave of the same band; Hah-ha-ra-pah (the elk's head), chief *of* the *Ee-ta-sip-shov band;* Mah-to-een-nah-pa (the white bear that goes out), chief of the *Blackfoot Sioux band;* Shon-ga-ton-ga-chesh-en-day (the horse dung), chief of a band, a great conjuror and magician.

The portraits of all the above dignitaries can be always seen, as large as life, in my very numerous Collection, provided I get them safe home; and also the portraits of two very pretty Sioux women (Fig. 94), Wi-looh-tah-eeh-tchah-ta-mah-nee (the red thing that touches in marching), and (Fig. 95), Tchon-su-mons-ka (the sand bar). The first of these women (Fig. 94) is the daughter of the

the Mississippi, I saw but very little wampum used; and on ascending the Missouri, I do not recollect to have seen it worn at all by the Upper Missouri Indians, although the same materials for its manufacture are found in abundance through those regions. I met with but very few strings of it amongst the Missouri Sioux, and nothing of it amongst the tribes north and west of them. Below the Sioux, and along the whole of our Western frontier, the different tribes are found loaded and beautifully ornamented with it, which they can now afford to do, for they consider it of little value, as the Fur Traders have ingeniously introduced a spurious imitation of it, manufactured by steam or otherwise, of porcelain or some composition closely resembling it, with which they have flooded the whole Indian country, and sold at so reduced a price, as to cheapen, and consequently destroy, the value and meaning of the original wampum, a string of which can now but very rarely be found in any part of the country.

famous chief called Black Rock, of whom I have spoken, and whose portrait has been given (Fig. 91). She is an unmarried girl, and much esteemed by the whole tribe, for her modesty, as well as beauty. She was beautifully dressed in skins, ornamented profusely with brass buttons and beads. Her hair was plaited, her ears supported a great profusion of curious beads—and over her other dress she wore a handsomely garnished buffalo robe.

So highly was the Black Rock esteemed (as I have before mentioned), and his beautiful daughter admired and respected by the Traders, that Mr M'Kenzie employed me to make him copies of their two portraits, which he has hung up in Mr Laidlaw's trading-house, as valued ornaments and keepsakes.*

The second of these women (Fig. 95) was very richly dressed, the upper part of her garment being almost literally covered with brass buttons; and her hair, which was inimitably beautiful and soft, and glossy as silk, fell over her shoulders in great profusion, and in beautiful waves, produced by the condition in which it is generally kept in braids, giving to it, when combed out, a waving form, adding much to its native appearance, which is invariably straight and graceless.

This woman is at present the wife of a white man by the name of Chardon, a Frenchman, who has been many years in the employment of the American Fur Company, in the character of a Trader and Interpreter; and who by his bold and daring nature, has not only carried dread and consternation amongst the Indian tribes wherever he has gone; but has commanded much respect, and rendered essential service to the Company in the prosecution of

* Several years after I left the Sioux country, I saw Messrs Chardon and Piquot, two of the Traders from that country, who recently had left it, and told me in St Louis, whilst looking at the portrait of this girl, that while staying in Mr Laidlaw's Fort, the chief, Black Rock, entered the room suddenly where the portrait of his daughter was hanging on the wall, and pointing to it with a heavy heart, told Mr Laidlaw that whilst his band was out on the prairies, where they had been for several months "making meat," his daughter had died, and was there buried. "My heart is glad again," said he, "when I see her here alive; and I want the one the medicine-man made of her, which is now before me, that I can see her, and talk to her. My band are all in mourning for her, and at the gate of your Fort, which I have just passed, are ten horses for you, and Ee-ah-sa-pa's wigwam, which you know is the best one in the Sioux nation. I wish you to take down my daughter and give her to me." Mr Laidlaw, seeing the *unusually* liberal price that this nobleman was willing to pay for a portrait, and the true grief that he expressed for the loss of his child, had not the heart to abuse such noble feeling; and taking the painting from the wall, placed it into his hands; telling him that it of right belonged to him, and that his horses and wigwam he must take back and keep them, to mend, as far as possible, his liberal heart, which was broken by the loss of his only daughter.

their dangerous and critical dealings with the Indian tribes. I have said something of this extraordinary man heretofore, and shall take future occasion to say more of him. For the present, suffice it to say, that although from his continual intercourse with the different tribes for twenty-five or thirty years, where he had always been put forward in the front of danger—sent as a sacrifice, or *forlorn hope;* still his cut and hacked limbs have withstood all the blows that have been aimed at them; and his unfaltering courage leads him to "beard the lion in his den," whilst his liberal heart, as it always has, deals out to his friends (and even to strangers, if friends are not by) all the dear earnings which are continually bought with severest toil, and at the hazard of his life.

I acknowledge myself a debtor to this good-hearted fellow for much kindness and attention to me whilst in the Indian country, and also for a superb dress and robe, which had been manufactured and worn by his wife, and which he insisted on adding to my INDIAN GALLERY since her death, where it will long remain to be examined.*

* Several years since writing the above, I made a visit with my wife, to the venerable parent of Mr Chardon, who lives in her snug and neat mansion, near the City of Philadelphia, where we were treated with genuine politeness and hospitality. His mother and two sisters, who are highly respectable, had many anxious questions to ask about him; and had at the same time, living with them, a fine-looking half-breed boy, about ten years old, the son of Monsr. Chardon and his Indian wife, whom I have above spoken of. This fine boy who had received the name of Bolivar, had been brought from the Indian country by the father, and left here for his education, with which they were taking great pains.

W HILST painting the portraits of the chiefs and braves of the Sioux, as described in my last epistle, my painting-room was the continual rendezvous of the worthies of the tribe; and I, the "lion of the day," and my art, the *summum* and *ne plus ultra* of mysteries, which engaged the whole conversation of chiefs and sachems, as well as of women and children. I mentioned that I have been obliged to paint them according to rank, as they looked upon the operation as a very great honour, which I, as "a great chief and medicine-man," was conferring on all who sat to me. Fortunate it was for me, however, that the honour was not a sufficient inducement for all to overcome their fears, which often stood in the way of their consenting to be painted; for if all had been willing to undergo the operation, I should have progressed but a very little way in the *"rank and file"* of their worthies; and should have had to leave many discontented, and (as they would think) neglected. About one in five or eight was willing to be painted, and the rest thought they would be much more sure of "sleeping quiet in their graves" after they were dead, if their pictures were not made. By this lucky difficulty I got great relief, and easily got through with those who were willing, and at the same time decided by the chiefs to be worthy, of so signal an honour.

After I had done with the chiefs and braves, and proposed to paint a few of the women, I at once got myself into a serious perplexity, being heartily laughed at by the whole tribe, both by men and by women, for my exceeding and (to them) unaccountable condescension in seriously proposing to paint a woman; conferring on her the same honour that I had done the chiefs and braves. Those whom I had honoured, were laughed at by hundreds of the jealous, who had been decided unworthy the distinction, and were now amusing themselves with the *very enviable honour* which the *great white medicine-man* had conferred, *especially* on *them,* and was now to confer equally upon the *squaws!*

The first reply that I received from those whom I had painted, was, that if I was to paint women and children, the sooner I destroyed *their* pictures, the better; for I had represented to them that I wanted their pictures to exhibit to white chiefs, to show who were the most distinguished and worthy of the Sioux; and their women had never taken scalps, nor did anything better than make fires and dress skins. I was quite awkward in this dilemma, in explaining to them that I wanted the portraits of the women to hang *under* those of their husbands, merely to show how their women *looked,* and how they *dressed,* without saying any more of them. After some considerable delay of my operations, and much deliberation on the subject, through the village, I succeeded in getting a number of women's portraits, of which the two above introduced are a couple.

The vanity of these men, after they had agreed to be painted was beyond all description, and far surpassing that which is oftentimes immodest enough in civilised society, where the sitter generally leaves the picture, when it is done to speak for, and to take care of, itself; while an Indian often lays down, from morning till night, in front of his portrait, admiring his own beautiful face, and faithfully guarding it from day to day, to save it from accident or harm.

This watching or guarding their portraits, I have observed during all of my travels amongst them as a very curious thing; and in many instances, where my colours were not dry, and subjected to so many accidents, from the crowds who were gathering about them, I have found this peculiar guardianship of essential service to me—relieving my mind oftentimes from a great deal of anxiety.

I was for a long time at a loss for the true cause of so singular a peculiarity, but at last learned that it was owing to their superstitious notion, that there may be life to a certain extent in the picture; and that if harm or violence be done to it, it may in some mysterious way, affect their health or do them other injury.

After I had been several weeks busily at work with my brush in this village, and pretty well used to the modes of life in these regions —and also familiarly acquainted with all the officers and clerks of the Establishment, it was announced one day, that the steamer which we had left, was coming in the river below, where all eyes were anxiously turned, and all ears were listening; when, at length, we discovered the puffing of her steam; and, at last, heard the thundering of her cannon, which were firing from her deck.

The excitement and dismay caused amongst 6000 of these wild people, when the steamer came up in front of their village, was amusing in the extreme. The steamer was moored at the shore, however; and when Mr Chouteau and Major Sanford, their old friend and agent, walked ashore, it seemed to restore their confidence and courage; and the whole village gathered in front of the boat, without showing much further amazement, or even curiosity about it.

The steamer rested a week or two at this place before she started on her voyage for the head-waters of the Missouri; during which time, there was much hilarity and mirth indulged in amongst the Indians, as well as with the hands employed in the service of the Fur Company. The appearance of a steamer in this wild country was deemed a wonderful occurrence, and the time of her presence here, looked upon, and used as a holiday. Some sharp encounters amongst the trappers, who come in here from the mountains, loaded with packs of furs, with sinews hardened by long exposure, and seemingly impatient for a *fight,* which is soon given them by some bullying fisticuff-fellow, who steps forward and settles the matter in a ring, which is made and strictly preserved for *fair play,* until hard raps, and bloody noses, and blind eyes *"settle the hash,"* and satisfy his trappership to lie in bed a week or two, and then graduate a sober and a civil man.

Amongst the Indians we have had numerous sights and amusements to entertain, and some to shock us. Shows of dances—ball-plays—horse-racing—foot-racing, and wrestling in abundance. Feasting—fasting, and prayers we have also had; and penance and tortures, and almost every thing short of self-immolation.

Some few days after the steamer had arrived, it was announced that a grand feast was to be given to the *great white chiefs,* who were visitors amongst them; and preparations were made accordingly for it. The two chiefs, Ha-wan-je-tah and Tchan-dee, of whom I have before spoken, brought their two tents together, forming the two into a semi-circle (Fig. 96), enclosing a space sufficiently large to accommodate 150 men; and sat down with that number of the principal chiefs and warriors of the Sioux nation; with Mr Chouteau, Major Sanford, the Indian agent, Mr M'Kenzie, and myself, whom they had invited in due time, and placed on elevated seats in the centre of the crescent; while the rest of the company all sat upon the ground, and mostly cross-legged, preparatory to the feast being dealt out.

In the centre of the semi-circle was erected a flag-staff, on which was waving a white flag, and to which also was tied the calumet, both expressive of their friendly feelings towards us. Near the foot of the flag-staff were placed in a row on the ground, six or eight kettles, with iron covers on them, shutting them tight, in which were prepared the viands for our *voluptuous* feast. Near the kettles, and on the ground also, bottomside upwards, were a number of wooden bowls, in which the meat was to be served out. And in front, two or three men, who

63

96

97

G. Catlin.

were there placed as waiters, to light the pipes for smoking, and also to deal out the food.

In these positions things stood, and all sat, with thousands climbing and crowding around, for a peep at the grand pageant; when at length, Ha-wan-je-tah (the one horn), head chief of the nation, rose in front of the Indian agent, in a very handsome costume, and addressed him thus:—"My father, I am glad to see you here to-day —my heart is always glad to see my father when he comes—our Great Father, who sends him here is very rich, and we are poor. Our friend Mr M'Kenzie, who is here, we are also glad to see; we know him well, and we shall be sorry when he is gone. Our friend who is on your right-hand we all know is very rich; and we have heard that he owns the great *medicine-canoe;* he is a good man, and a friend to the red men. Our friend the *White Medicine,* who sits with you, we did not know—he came amongst us a stranger, and he has made me very well—all the women know it, and think it very good; he has done many curious things, and we have all been pleased with him—he has made us much amusement—and we know he is great medicine.

"My father, I hope you will have pity on us, we are very poor— we offer you to-day, not the best that we have got; for we have a plenty of good buffalo hump and marrow—but we give you our hearts in this feast—we have killed our faithful dogs to feed you—and the Great Spirit will seal our friendship. I have no more to say."

After these words he took off his beautiful war-eagle head-dress— his shirt and leggings—his necklace of grizzly bears' claws and his moccasins; and tying them together, laid them gracefully down at the feet of the agent as a present; and laying a handsome pipe on top of them, he walked around into an adjoining lodge, where he got a buffalo robe to cover his shoulders, and returned to the feast, taking his seat which he had before occupied.

Major Sanford then rose and made a short speech in reply, thanking him for the valuable present which he had made him, and for the very polite and impressive manner in which it had been done; and sent to the steamer for a quantity of tobacco and other presents, which were given to him in return. After this, and after several others of the chiefs had addressed him in a similar manner; and, like the first, disrobed themselves, and thrown their beautiful costumes at his feet; one of the three men in front deliberately lit a handsome pipe, and brought it to Ha-wan-je-tah to smoke. He took it, and after presenting the stem to the North—to the South—to the East, and the West —and then to the Sun that was over his head, and pronounced the words "How—how—how!" drew a whiff or two of smoke through it, and holding the bowl of it in one hand, and its stem in the other, he then held it to each of our mouths, as we successively smoked it; after which it was passed around through the whole group, who all smoked through it, or as far as its contents lasted, when another of the three waiters was ready with a second, and at length a third one, in the same way, which lasted through the hands of the whole number of guests. This smoking was conducted with the strictest adherence to exact and established form, and the feast the whole way, to the most positive silence. After the pipe is charged, and is being lit, until the time that the chief has drawn the smoke through it, it is considered an evil omen for any one to speak; and if any one break silence in that time, even in a whisper, the pipe is instantly dropped by the chief, and their superstition is such, that they would not dare to use it on this occasion; but another one is called for and used in its stead. If there is no accident of the kind during the smoking, the waiters then proceed to distribute the meat, which is soon devoured in the feast.

In this case the lids were raised from the kettles, which were all filled with dogs' meat alone. It being well-cooked, and made into a sort of a stew, sent forth a very savoury and pleasing smell, promising to be an acceptable and palatable food. Each of us civilised guests had a large wooden bowl placed before us, with a huge quantity of dogs' flesh floating in a profusion of soup, or rich gravy, with a large spoon resting in the dish, made of the buffalo's horn. In this most difficult and painful dilemma we sat; all of us knowing the solemnity and good feeling in which it was given, and the absolute necessity of falling to, and devouring a little of it. We all tasted it a few times, and resigned our dishes, which were quite willingly taken, and passed around with others, to every part of the group, who all ate heartily of the *delicious viands,* which were soon dipped out of the kettles, and entirely devoured; after which each one arose as he felt disposed, and walked off without uttering a word. In this way the feast ended, and all retired silently, and gradually, until the ground was left vacant to the charge of the waiters or officers, who seemed to have charge of it during the whole occasion.

This feast was unquestionably given to us, as the most undoubted evidence they could give us of their friendship; and we, who knew the spirit and feeling in which it was given, could not but treat it respectfully, and receive it as a very high and marked compliment.

Since I witnessed it on this occasion, I have been honoured with numerous entertainments of the kind amongst the other tribes, which

I have visited towards the sources of the Missouri, and all conducted in the same solemn and impressive manner; from which I feel author-ised to pronounce the *dog-feast* a truly religious ceremony, wherein the poor Indian sees fit to sacrifice his faithful companion to bear testimony to the sacredness of his vows of friendship, and invite his friend to partake of its flesh, to remind him forcibly of the reality of the sacri-fice, and the solemnity of his professions.

The dog, amongst all Indian tribes, is more esteemed and more valued than amongst any part of the civilised world; the Indian who has more time to devote to his company, and whose untutored mind more nearly assimilates to that of his faithful servant, keeps him closer company, and draws him nearer to his heart; they hunt to-gether, and are equal sharers in the chase—their bed is one; and on the rocks, and on their coats of arms they carve his image as the symbol of fidelity. Yet, with all of these he will end his affection with this faithful follower, and with tears in his eyes, offer him as a sacrifice to seal the pledge he has made to man; because a feast of venison, or of buffalo meat, is what is due to every one who enters an Indian's wigwam; and of course, conveys but a passive or neutral evidence, that generally goes for nothing.

I have sat at many of these feasts, and never could but appreciate the moral and solemnity of them. I have seen the master take from the bowl the head of his victim, and descant on its former affection and fidelity with tears in his eyes. And I have seen guests at the same time by the side of me, jesting and sneering at the poor Indian's folly and stupidity; and I have said in my heart, that they never deserved a name so good or so honourable as that of the poor animal whose bones they were picking.

At the feast which I have been above describing, each of us tasted a little of the meat, and passed the dishes on to the Indians, who soon demolished everything they contained. We all agreed that the meat was well cooked, and seemed to be a well-flavoured and palatable food; and no doubt, could have been eaten with a good relish, if we had been hungry, and ignorant of the nature of the food we were eating.

The flesh of these dogs, though apparently relished by the Indians, is, undoubtedly, inferior to the venison and buffalo's meat, of which feasts are constantly made where friends are invited, as they are in civilised society, to a pleasant and convivial party; from which fact alone, it would seem clear, that they have some extra-ordinary motive, at all events, for feasting on the flesh of that useful and faithful animal; even when, as in the instance I have been describing, their village is well supplied with fresh and dried meat of the buffalo. The dog-feast is given, I believe, by all tribes in North America; and by them all, I think, this faithful animal, as well as the horse, is sacrificed in several different ways, to appease offended Spirits or Deities; whom it is considered necessary that they should conciliate in this way; and when done, is invariably done by giving the best in the herd or the kennel.

LETTER—No. 29

ANOTHER curious and disgusting scene I witnessed in the after part of the day on which we were honoured with the dog feast. In this I took no part, but was sufficiently near to it, when standing some rods off, and witnessing the cruel operation. I was called upon by one of the clerks in the Establishment to ride up a mile or so, near the banks of the Teton River, in a little plain at the base of the bluffs, where were grouped some fifteen or twenty lodges of the Ting-ta-to-ah band, to see a man (as they said) *"looking at the sun!"* We found him naked, except his breech-cloth, with splints or skewers run through the flesh on both breasts, leaning back and hanging with the weight of his body to the top of a pole which was fastened in the ground, and to the upper end of which he was fastened by a cord which was tied to the splints. In this position he was leaning back, with nearly the whole weight of his body hanging to the pole, the top of which was bent forward, allowing his body to sink about half-way to the ground. His feet were still upon the ground, supporting a small part of his weight; and he held in his left hand his favourite bow, and in his right, with a desperate grip, his medicine-bag. In this condition, with the blood trickling down over his body, which was covered with white and yellow clay, and amidst a great crowd who were looking on, sympathising with and encouraging him, he was hanging and "looking at the sun," without paying the least attention to any one about him. In the group that was reclining around him, were several mystery-men beating their drums and shaking their rattles, and singing as loud as they could yell, to encourage him and strengthen his heart to stand and look at the sun, from its rising in the morning till its setting at night; at which time, if his heart and his strength have not failed him, he is "cut down," receives the liberal donation of presents (which have been thrown into a pile before him during the day), and also the name and the style of a doctor or *medicine-man,* which lasts him, and ensures him respect, through life.

This most extraordinary and cruel custom I never heard of amongst any other tribe, and never saw an instance of it before or after the one I have just named. It is a sort of worship, or penance, of great cruelty; disgusting and painful to behold, with only one palliating circumstance about it, which is, that it is a voluntary torture and of very rare occurrence. The poor and ignorant, misguided and superstitious man who undertakes it, puts his everlasting reputation at stake upon the issue; for when he takes his stand, he expects to face the sun and gradually turn his body in listless silence, till he sees it go down at night; and if he faints and falls, of which there is imminent danger, he loses his reputation as a brave or mystery-man, and suffers a signal disgrace in the estimation of the tribe, like all men who have the presumption to set themselves up for braves or mystery-men, and fail justly to sustain the character.

The Sioux seem to have many modes of worshipping the Great or Good Spirit, and also of conciliating the Evil Spirit; they have numerous fasts and feasts, and many modes of sacrificing, but yet they seem to pay less strict attention to them than the Mandans do, which may perhaps be owing in a great measure to the wandering and predatory modes of life which they pursue, rendering it difficult to adhere so rigidly to the strict form and letter of their customs.

There had been, a few days before I arrived at this place, a great medicine operation held on the prairie, a mile or so back of the Fort, and which, of course, I was not lucky enough to see. The poles were still standing, and the whole transaction was described to me by my friend Mr Halsey, one of the clerks in the Establishment. From the account given of it, it seems to bear some slight resemblance to that of the *Mandan religious ceremony,* but no nearer to it than a feeble effort by so ignorant and superstitious a people, to copy a custom which they most probably have had no opportunity to see themselves, but have endeavoured to imitate from hearsay. They had an awning of immense size erected on the prairie which is yet standing, made of willow bushes supported by posts, with poles and willow boughs laid over; under the centre of which there was a pole set firmly in the ground, from which many of the young men had suspended their bodies by splints run through the flesh in different parts, the numerous scars of which were yet seen bleeding afresh from day to day, amongst the crowds that were about me.

During my stay amongst the Sioux, as I was considered by them to be great *medicine,* I received many pipes and other little things from them as presents, given to me in token of respect for me, and as assurances of their friendship; and I, being desirous to collect and bring from their country every variety of their manufactures, of their

costumes, their weapons, their pipes, and their mystery-things, purchased a great many others, for which, as I was "medicine" and a
"great white chief!" I was necessarily obliged to pay very *liberal*
prices.

Of the various costumes (of this, as well as of other tribes), that
I have collected, there will be seen fair and faithful representations
in the numerous portraits; and of their war-clubs, pipes, etc. I have
set forth in the following illustrations, a few of the most interesting
of the very great numbers of those things which I have collected in
this and other tribes which I have visited.

The luxury of smoking is known to all the North American Indians,
in their primitive state, and that before they have any knowledge of
tobacco; which is only introduced amongst them by civilised adven-
turers, who teach them the use and luxury of whiskey at the same time.

In their native state they are excessive smokers, and many of
them (I would almost venture the assertion), would seem to be
smoking one-half of their lives. There may be two good reasons for
this, the first of which is, that the idle and leisure life that the
Indian leads (who has no trade or business to follow—no office hours
to attend to, or profession to learn), induces him to look for occupation and amusement in so innocent a luxury, which again further
tempts him to its excessive use, from its feeble and harmless effects
on the system. There are many weeds and leaves, and barks of trees,
which are narcotics, and of spontaneous growth in their countries,
which the Indians dry and pulverise, and carry in pouches and smoke
to great excess—and which in several of the languages, when thus
prepared, is called *k'nick-k'neck.*

As smoking is a luxury so highly valued by the Indians, they
have bestowed much pains, and not a little ingenuity, to the construction of their pipes. Of these I have procured a collection of several
hundreds, and in Fig. 98, have given facsimile outlines of a number
of the most curious. The bowls of these are generally made of the red
steatite, or "pipe-stone" (as it is more familiarly called in this country),
and many of them designed and carved with much taste and skill,
with figures and groups in *alto relievo,* standing or reclining upon them.

The red stone of which these pipe bowls are made, is, in my estimation, a great curiosity; inasmuch as I am sure it is a variety of
steatite (if it be steatite), differing from that of any known European
locality, and also from any locality known in America, other than
the one from which all these pipes come; and which are all traceable
I have found to one source; and that source as yet unvisited except
by the red man who describes it, everywhere, as a place of vast im-

portance to the Indians—as given to them by the Great Spirit, for their pipes, and strictly forbidden to be used for anything else.

The source from whence all these pipes come, is, undoubtedly, somewhere between this place and the Mississippi River; and as the Indians all speak of it as a great *medicine*-place, I shall certainly lay my course to it, ere long, and be able to give the world some account of it and its mysteries.

The Indians shape out the bowls of these pipes from the solid stone, which is not quite as hard as marble, with nothing but a knife. The stone, which is of a cherry red, admits of a beautiful polish, and the Indian makes the hole in the bowl of the pipe, by drilling into it a hard stick, shaped to the desired size, with a quantity of sharp sand and water kept constantly in the hole, subjecting him therefore to a very great labour and the necessity of much patience.

The shafts or stems of these pipes, as will be seen in Fig. 98, are from two to four feet long, sometimes round, but most generally flat; of an inch or two in breadth, and wound half their length or more with braids of porcupine's quills; and often ornamented with the beaks and tufts from the wood-pecker's head, with ermine skins and long red hair, dyed from white horse hair or the white buffalo's tail.

The stems of these pipes will be found to be carved in many ingenious forms, and in all cases they are perforated through the centre, quite staggering the wits of the enlightened world to *guess how* the holes have been *bored* through them; until it is simply and briefly explained, that the stems are uniformly made of the stalk of the young ash, which generally grows straight, and has a small pith through the centre, which is easily burned out with a hot wire or a piece of hard wood, by a much slower process.

In Fig. 98, the pipes marked b are ordinary pipes, made and used for the *luxury* only of smoking; and for this purpose, every Indian designs and constructs his own pipe. The *calumet,* or pipe of peace (Fig. 98 *a*), ornamented with the war-eagle's quills, is a sacred pipe, and never allowed to be used on any other occasion than that of *peace-making;* when the chief brings it into treaty, and unfolding the many bandages which are carefully kept around it— has it ready to be mutually smoked by the chiefs, after the terms of the treaty are agreed upon, as the means of *solemnising* or *signing,* by an illiterate people, who cannot draw up an instrument, and sign their names to it, as it is done in the civilised world.

The mode of solemnising is by passing the sacred stem to each chief, who draws one breath of smoke only through it, thereby passing the most inviolable pledge that they can possibly give, for

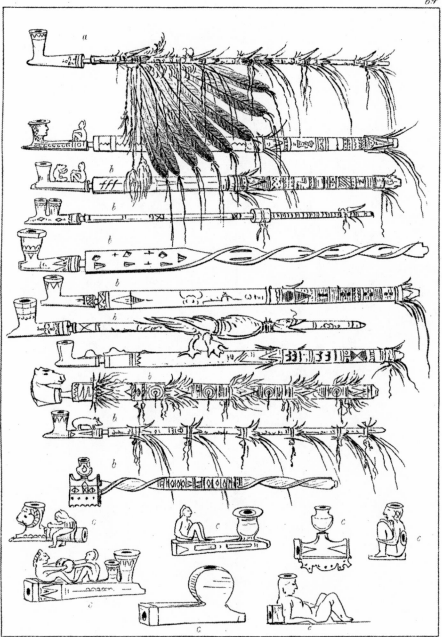

64

G Catlin

the keeping of the peace. This sacred pipe is then carefully folded up, and stowed away in the chief's lodge, until a similar occasion calls it out to be used in a similar manner.

There is no custom more uniformly in constant use amongst the poor Indians than that of smoking, nor any other more highly valued. His pipe is his constant companion through life—his messenger of peace; he pledges his friends through its stem and its bowl—and when its care-drowning fumes cease to flow, it takes a place with him in his solitary grave, with his tomahawk and war-club, companions to his long fancied, "mild and beautiful hunting-grounds."

The weapons of these people, like their pipes, are numerous, and mostly manufactured by themselves. In a former place (Fig. 18) I have described a part of these, such as the bows and arrows, lances, etc., and they have yet many others, specimens of which I have collected from every tribe; and a number of which I have grouped together in Fig. 99; consisting of knives, war-clubs, and tomahawks. I have here introduced the most general and established forms that are in use amongst the different tribes, which are all strictly copied from amongst the great variety of these articles to be found in my Collection.

The scalping-knives a and b, and tomahawks e e e e are of civilised manufacture, made expressly for Indian use, and carried into the Indian country by thousands and tens of thousands, and sold at an enormous price. The scabbards of the knives and handles for the tomahawks, the Indians construct themselves, according to their own taste, and oftentimes ornament them very handsomely. In his rude and unapproached condition, the Indian is a stranger to such weapons as these—he works not in the metals; and his untutored mind has not been ingenious enough to design or execute anything so *savage* or destructive as these civilised *refinements on Indian barbarity*. In his native simplicity he shapes out his rude hatchet from a piece of stone, as in letter *f,* heads his arrows and spears with flints; and his knife is a sharpened bone, or the edge of a broken silex. The war-club c is also another civilised refinement, with a blade of steel, of eight or ten inches in length, and set in a club, studded around and ornamented with some hundreds of brass nails.

Their primitive clubs d are curiously carved in wood, and fashioned out with some considerable picturesque form and grace; are admirably fitted to the hand, and calculated to deal a deadly blow with the spike of iron or bone which is imbedded in the ball or bulb at the end.

Two of the tomahawks that I have named, marked *e,* are what are denominated "pipe-tomahawks," as the heads of them are formed into bowls like a pipe, in which their tobacco is put, and they smoke through the handle. These are the most valued of an Indian's weapons, inasmuch as they are a matter of luxury, and useful for cutting his fire-wood, etc., in time of peace; and deadly weapons in time of war, which they use in the hand, or throw with unerring and deadly aim.

The scalping-knife *b* in a beautiful scabbard, which is carried under the belt, is the form of knife most generally used in all parts of the Indian country, where knives have been introduced. It is a common and cheap butcher knife with one edge, manufactured at Sheffield, in England, perhaps, for sixpence; and sold to the poor Indian in these wild regions for a horse. If I should live to get home, and should ever cross the Atlantic with my Collection, a curious enigma would be solved for the English people, who may inquire for a scalping-knife, when they find that every one in my Collection (and hear also, that nearly every one that is to be seen in the Indian country, to the Rocky Mountains and the Pacific Ocean) bears on its blade the impress of G.R., which they will doubtless understand.

The huge two-edged knife, with its scabbard of a part of the skin of a grizzly bear's head, letter *a,* is one belonging to the famous chief of the Mandans, of whom I have before said much. The manufacture of this knife is undoubtedly American; and its shape differs altogether from those which are in general use.*

The above weapons, as well as the bow and lance, of which I have before spoken, are all carried and used on horseback with great effect. The Indians in this country of green fields, all *ride* for their enemies, and also for their game, which is almost invariably killed whilst their horses are at full speed. They are all cruel masters for their horses; and in war or the chase goad them on with a heavy and cruel whip (Fig. 99 *g*), the handle of which is generally made of a large prong of

---

* This celebrated knife is now in my INDIAN MUSEUM, and there is no doubt, from its authentic history, that it has been several times plunged to the hearts of his enemies by the hand of Mah-to-toh-pa, who wielded it. Several years after I left that country, and one year after the destruction of the Mandans, I received the following letter from Mr M'Kenzie, accompanying the knife and other things sent to me by him from that country: EXTRACT—" The poor Mandans are gone, and amongst them your old friend, Mah-to-toh-pa. I have been able to send you but a very few things, as the Riccarees immediately took possession of everything they had. Amongst the articles I have been able to procure, I send you the war-knife of Mah-to-toh-pa, which is now looked upon as the greatest *medicine* in this country: and as you will recollect it, it will be highly appreciated by you."

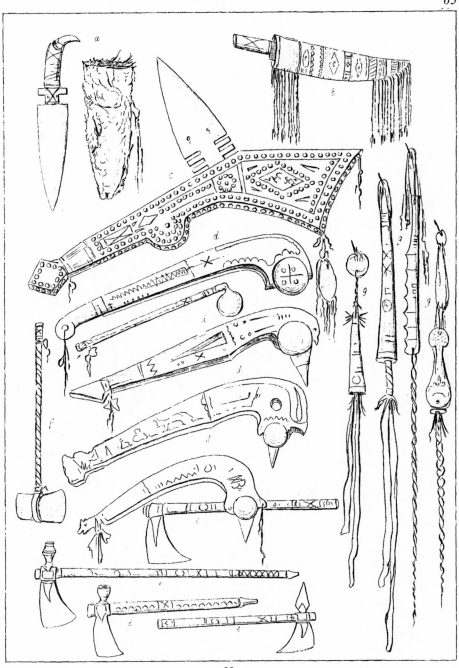

G. Catlin.

the elk's horn or of wood, and the lashes of rawhide are very heavy; being braided, or twisted, or cut into wide straps. These are invariably attached to the wrist of the right arm by a tough thong, so that they can be taken up and used at any moment, and dropped the next, without being lost.

During the time that I was engaged in painting my portraits, I was occasionally inducing the young men to give me their dances, a great variety of which they gave me by being slightly paid; which I was glad to do, in order to enable me to study their character and expression thoroughly, which I am sure I have done; and I shall take pleasure in showing them to the world when I get back. The dancing is generally done by the young men, and considered undignified for the chiefs or doctors to join in. Yet so great was my *medicine,* that chiefs and medicine-men turned out and agreed to compliment me with a dance (Fig. 100). I looked on with great satisfaction; having been assured by the Interpreters and Traders, that this was the highest honour they had ever known them to pay to any stranger amongst them.

In this dance, which I have called "the dance of the chiefs," for want of a more significant title, was given by fifteen or twenty chiefs and doctors; many of whom were very old and venerable men. All of them came out in their head-dresses of war-eagle quills, with a spear or staff in the left hand, and a rattle in the right. It was given in the midst of the Sioux village, in front of the head chief's-lodge; and beside the medicine-man who beat on the drum, and sang for the dance, there were four young women standing in a row, and chanting a sort of chorus for the dancers; forming one of the very few instances that I ever have met, where the women are allowed to take any part in the dancing, or other game or amusement, with the men.

This dance was a very spirited thing, and pleased me much, as well as all the village, who were assembled around to witness what most of them never before had seen, their aged and venerable chiefs united in giving a dance.

As I have introduced the *scalping-knife* above, it may be well for me to give some further account in this place of the custom and the mode of taking the scalp; a custom practised by all the North American Indians, which is done when an enemy is killed in battle, by grasping the left hand into the hair on the crown of the head, and passing the knife around it through the skin, tearing off a piece of the skin with the hair, as large as the palm of the hand, or larger, which is dried, and often curiously ornamented and preserved, and highly valued as a trophy. The scalping is an operation not calculated of itself to take life, as it only removes the skin, without injuring the bone of the head; and necessarily, to be a genuine scalp, must contain and show the crown or centre of the head; that part of the skin which lies directly over what the phrenologists call "self-esteem," where the hair divides and radiates from the centre; of which they all profess to be strict judges, and able to decide whether an effort has been made to produce two or more scalps from one head. Besides taking the scalp, the victor generally if he has time to do it without endangering his own scalp, cuts off and brings home the rest of the hair, which his wife will divide into a great many small locks, and with them fringe off the seams of his shirt and his leggings, as will have been seen in many of the illustrations; which also are worn as trophies and ornaments to the dress, and then are familiarly called *"scalp-locks."* Of these there are many dresses in my Collection, which exhibit a continuous row from the top of each shoulder, down the arms to the wrists, and down the seams of the leggings, from the hips to the feet, rendering them a very costly article to buy from the Indian, who is not sure that his success in his military exploits will ever enable him to replace them.

The scalp, then, is a patch of the skin taken from the head of an enemy killed in battle, and preserved and highly appreciated as the record of a death produced by the hand of the individual who possesses it; and may oftentimes during his life, be of great service to a man living in a community where there is no historian to enrol the names of the famous—to record the heroic deeds of the brave, who have gained their laurels in mortal combat with their enemies; where it is as lawful and as glorious to slay an enemy in battle, as it is in Christian communities; and where the poor Indian is bound to keep the record himself, or be liable to lose it and the honour, for no one in the tribe will keep it for him. As the scalp is taken then as the evidence of a death, it will easily be seen, that the Indian has no business or inclination to take it from the head of the living; which I venture to say is never done in North America, unless it be, as it sometimes has happened, where a man falls in the heat of battle, stunned with the blow of a weapon or a gunshot, and the Indian, rushing over his body, snatches off his scalp, supposing him dead, who afterwards rises from the field of battle, and easily recovers from this superficial wound of the knife, wearing a bald spot on his head during the remainder of his life, of which we have frequent occurrences on our Western frontiers. The scalp must be from the head of *an enemy* also, or it subjects its possessor to disgrace and infamy who carries it. There may be many instances where an Indian is justified in the estimation of his tribe in taking the life of one of his own people; and their laws are such, as oftentimes make it his imperative duty; and yet no circumstances, however aggravating, will justify him or release him from the disgrace of taking the scalp.

There is no custom practised by the Indians, for which they are more universally condemned, than that of taking the scalp; and, at the same time, I think there is some excuse for them, inasmuch as it is a general custom of the country, and founded, like many other apparently absurd and ridiculous customs of these people, in one of the necessities of Indian life, which necessities we are free from in the civilised world, and which customs, of course, we need not and do not practise. From an ancient custom "time out of mind," the warriors of these tribes have been in the habit of going to war, ex- pecting to take the scalps of their enemies whom they may slay in battle, and all eyes of the tribe are upon them, making it their duty to do it; so from custom it is every man's right, and his duty also, to continue and keep up a regulation of his society, which it is not in his power as an individual, to abolish or correct, if he saw fit to do it.

One of the principal denunciations against the custom of taking the scalp, is on account of its alleged *cruelty,* which it certainly has not; as the cruelty would be in the *killing,* and not in the act of cutting the skin from a man's head after he is dead. To say the most of it, it is a disgusting custom, and I wish I could be quite sure that the civilised and Christian world (who kill hundreds, to where the poor Indians kill one), do not often treat their *enemies' dead,* in equally as indecent and disgusting a manner, as the Indian does by taking the scalp.

If the reader thinks that I am taking too much pains to defend the Indians for this, and others of their seemingly abominable customs, he will bear it in mind, that I have lived with these people, until I have learned the necessities of Indian life in which these customs are founded; and also, that I have met with so many acts of kindness and hospitality at the hands of the poor Indian, that I feel bound, when I can do it, to render what excuse I can for a people, who are dying with broken hearts, and never can speak in the civilised world in their own defence.

And even yet, reader, if your education, and your reading of Indian cruelties and Indian barbarities—of scalps and scalping-knives, and scalping, should have ossified a corner of your heart against these un- fortunate people, and would shut out their advocate, I will annoy you no longer on this subject, but withdraw, and leave you to cherish the very beautiful, humane, and parental moral that was carried out by the United States and British Governments during the last, and the revolutionary wars, when they mutually employed thousands of their *"Red children,"* to aid and to bleed, in fighting their battles, and paid them, according to contract, so many pounds, shillings, and pence or so many dollars and cents for every *"scalp"* of a "red" or a "blue coat" they could bring in!

In Fig. 101, there will be seen the principal modes in which the scalps are prepared, and several of the uses to which they are put. The most usual way of preparing and dressing the scalp is that of stretching it on a little hoop at the end of a stick two or three feet long (letter *a*), for the purpose of "dancing it," as they term it; which will be described in the *scalp-dance,* in a few moments. There are many again, which are small, and not "dressed;" sometimes not larger than a crown piece (letter *c*), and hung to different parts of the dress. In public shows and parades, they are often suspended from the bridle bits or halter when they are paraded and carried as trophies (letter *b*). Sometimes they are cut out, as it were into a string, the hair forming a beautiful fringe to line the handle of a war-club (letter *e*). Sometimes they are hung at the *end* of a club (letter *d*), and at other times, by the order of the chief, are hung out, over the wigwams, suspended from a pole, which is called the *"scalp-pole."* This is often done by the chief of a village, in a pleasant day, by his erecting over his wigwam a pole with all the scalps that he had taken, arranged upon it (letter *f*); at the sight of which all the chiefs and warriors of the tribe, who had taken scalps "follow suit;" enabling every member of the community to stroll about the village on that day and "count scalps," learning thereby the standing of every warrior, which is decided in a great degree by the number of scalps they have taken in battles with their enemies. Letters *g, g,* show the usual manner of taking the scalp, and (letter *h*), exhibits the head of a man who had been scalped and recovered from the wound.

So much for scalps and scalping, of which I shall yet say more, unless I should unluckily *lose one* before I get out of the country.

101

IN the last letter I gave an account of many of the weapons
and other manufactures of these wild folks; and as this has been
a day of *packing* and *casing* a great many of these things, which I
have obtained of the Indians, to add to my *Musée Indienne,* I will
name a few more, which I have just been handling over; some description of which may be necessary for the reader in endeavouring
to appreciate some of their strange customs and amusements, which
I am soon to unfold. In Fig. 101½, letters *a* and *b,* will be seen
the *quiver* made of the fawn's skin, and the Sioux *shield* made of
the skin of the buffalo's neck, hardened with the glue extracted
from the hoofs and joints of the same animal. The process of
"smoking the shield" is a very curious, as well as an important
one, in their estimation. For this purpose a young man about to
construct him a shield, digs a hole of two feet in depth, in the
ground, and as large in diameter as he designs to make his shield.
In this he builds a fire, and over it, a few inches higher than the
ground, he stretches the rawhide horizontally over the fire, with
little pegs driven through holes made near the edges of the skin.
This skin is at first, twice as large as the size of the required
shield; but having got his particular and best friends (who are
invited on the occasion), into a ring, to dance and sing around it,
and solicit the Great Spirit to instil into it the power to protect
him harmless against his enemies, he spreads over it the glue,
which is rubbed and dried in, as the skin is heated; and a second
busily drives other and other pegs, inside of those in the ground, as
they are gradually giving way and being pulled up by the contrac-
tion of the skin. By this curious process, which is most dexterously
done, the skin is kept tight whilst it contracts to one-half of its
size, taking up the glue and increasing in thickness until it is
rendered as thick and hard as required (and his friends have
pleaded long enough to make it arrow, and almost ball proof),
when the dance ceases, and the fire is put out. When it is cooled
and cut into the shape that he desires, it is often painted with his
medicine or *totem* upon it, the figure of an eagle, an owl, a buffalo,

or other animal, as the case may be, which he trusts will guard and protect him from harm; it is then fringed with eagle's quills, or other ornaments he may have chosen, and *slung* with a broad leather strap that crosses his breast. These shields are carried by all the warriors in these regions, for their protection in battles, which are almost invariably fought from their horses' backs.

Of *pipes,* and the custom of smoking, I have already spoken; and I then said, that the Indians used several substitutes for tobacco, which they called *K'nick-K'neck.* For the carrying of this delicious weed or bark, and preserving its flavour, the women construct very curious pouches of otter, or beaver, or other skins (letters *c, c, c*), which are ingeniously ornamented with porcupine quills and beads, and generally carried hanging across the left arm, containing a quantity of the precious *narcotic,* with flint and steel, and spunk, for lighting the pipe.

The *musical instruments* used amongst these people are few, and exceedingly rude and imperfect, consisting chiefly of rattles, drums, whistles, and lutes, all of which are used in the different tribes.

In Fig. 101½ (letters *d, d*) will be seen the *rattles* (or She-she-quois) most generally used, made of rawhide, which becomes very hard when dry, and charged with pebbles or something of the kind, which produce a shrill noise to mark the time in their dances and songs. Their *drums* (letters *e, e*) are made in a very rude manner, oftentimes with a mere piece of rawhide stretched over a hoop, very much in the shape of a tambourin; and at other times are made in the form of a keg, with a head of rawhide at each end; on these they beat with a drum-stick, which oftentimes itself is a rattle, the bulb or head of it being made of rawhide and filled with pebbles. In other instances the stick has, at its end, a little hoop wound and covered with buckskin, to soften the sound; with which they beat on the drum with great violence, as the chief and *heel-inspiring* sound for all their dances, and also as an accompaniment for their numerous and never-ending songs of amusement, of thanks-giving, and *medicine* or *metai.* The *mystery whistle* (letter *f*) is another instrument of their invention, and very ingeniously made, the sound being produced on a principle entirely different from that of any wind instrument known in civilised inventions; and the notes produced on it, by the sleight or trick of an Indian boy, in so simple and successful a ma?er, as to baffle entirely all civilised ingenuity, even when it is seen to be played. An Indian boy would stand and blow his notes on this repeatedly, for hundreds of white men who might be lookers-on, not one of whom could

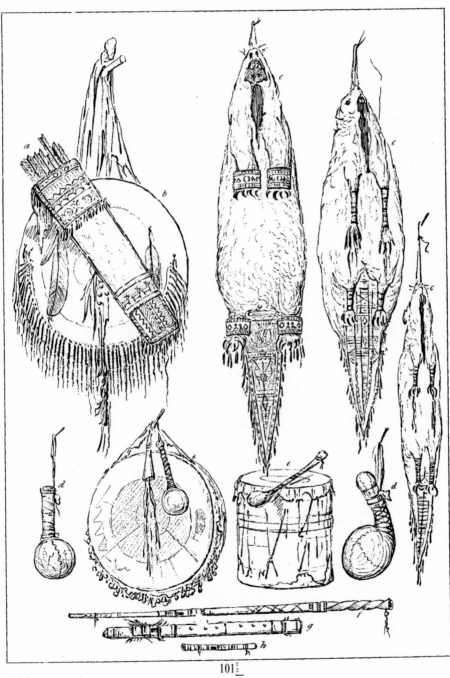

68

101½

G. Catlin.

make the least noise on it, even by practising with it for hours. When I first saw this curious exhibition, I was charmed with the peculiar sweetness of its harmonic sounds, and completely perplexed (as hundreds of white men have no doubt been before me, to the great amusement and satisfaction of the women and children) as to the mode in which the sound was produced, even though it was repeatedly played immediately before my eyes, and handed to me for my vain and amusing endeavours. The sounds of this little simple toy are liquid and sweet beyond description; and, though here only given in harmonics, I am inclined to think, might, by some ingenious musician or musical instrument-maker, be modulated and converted into something very pleasing.

The *War-whistle* (letter *h*) is a well known and valued little instrument, of six or nine inches in length, invariably made of the bone of the deer or turkey's leg, and generally ornamented with porcupine quills of different colours which are wound around it. A chief or leader carries this to battle with him, suspended generally from his neck, and worn under his dress. This little instrument has but two notes, which are produced by blowing in the ends of it. The note produced in one end, being much more shrill than the other, gives the signal for battle, whilst the other sounds a retreat; a thing that is distinctly heard and understood by every man, even in the heat and noise of battle, where all are barking and yelling as loud as possible, and of course unable to hear the commands of their leader.

There is yet another wind instrument which I have added to my Collection, and from its appearance would seem to have been borrowed, in part, from the civilised world (letter *g*). This is what is often on the frontier called a *"deer-skin flute,"* a "Winnebago courting flute," a "tsal-eet-quash-to," etc.; it is perforated with holes for the fingers, sometimes for six, at others for four, and in some instances for three only, having only so many notes with their octaves. These notes are very irregularly graduated, showing clearly that they have very little taste or ear for melody. These instruments are blown in the end, and the sound produced much on the principle of a whistle.

In the vicinity of the Upper Mississippi, I often and familiarly heard this instrument, called the Winnebago courting flute; and was credibly informed by traders and others in those regions, that the young men of that tribe meet with signal success, oftentimes, in wooing their sweethearts with its simple notes, which they blow for hours together, and from day to day, from the bank of some stream—some favourite rock or log on which they are seated, near to the wigwam which contains the object of their tender passion; until her soul is touched, and she responds by some welcome signal, that she is ready to repay the young *Orpheus* for his pains, with the gift of her hand and her heart. How true these representations may have been made, I cannot say, but there certainly must have been some ground for the present cognomen by which it is known in that country.

From these rude and exceedingly defective instruments, it will at once be seen, that music has made but little progress with these people; and the same fact will be still more clearly proved, to those who have an opportunity to hear their vocal exhibitions, which are daily and almost hourly serenading the ears of the traveller through their country.

Dancing is one of the principal and most frequent amusements of all the tribes of Indians in America; and, in all of these, both vocal and instrumental music are introduced. These dances consist in about four different steps, which constitute all the different varieties: but the figures and forms of these scenes are very numerous, and produced by the most violent jumps and contortions, accompanied with the song and beats of the drum, which are given in exact time with their motions. It has been said by some travellers, that the Indian has neither harmony or melody in his music, but I am unwilling to subscribe to such an assertion; although I grant, that for the most part of their vocal exercises, there is a total absence of what the musical world would call melody; their songs being made up chiefly of a sort of violent chant of harsh and jarring gutturals, of yelps and barks, and screams, which are given out in perfect time, not only with "method (but with harmony) in their madness." There are times, too, as every traveller of the Indian country will attest, if he will recall them to his recollection, when the Indian lies down by his fire-side with his drum in his hand, which he lightly and almost imperceptibly touches over, as he accompanies it with his stifled voice of dulcet sounds that might come from the most tender and delicate female.

These quiet and tender songs are very different from those which are sung at their dances, in full chorus and violent gesticulation; and many of them seem to be quite rich in plaintive expression and melody, though barren of change and variety.

Dancing, I have before said, is one of the principal and most valued amusements of the Indians, and much more frequently practised by them than by any civilised society; inasmuch as it

enters into their forms of worship, and is often their mode of appealing to the Great Spirit—of paying their usual devotions to their *medicine*—and of honouring and entertaining strangers of distinction in their country.

Instead of the "giddy maze" of the quadrille or the country dance, enlivened by the cheering smiles and graces of silkened beauty, the Indian performs his rounds with jumps, and starts, and yells much to the satisfaction of his own exclusive self, and infinite amusement of the gentler sex, who are always lookers on, but seldom allowed so great a pleasure, or so signal an honour, as that of joining with their lords in this or any other entertainment. Whilst staying with these people on my way up the river, I was repeatedly honoured with the dance, and I as often hired them to give them, or went to overlook where they were performing them at their own pleasure, in pursuance of their peculiar customs, or for their own amusement, that I might study and correctly herald them to future ages. I saw so many of their different varieties of dances amongst the Sioux, that I should almost be disposed to denominate them the *"dancing Indians."* It would actually seem as if they had dances for every thing. And in so large a village, there was scarcely an hour in any day or night, but what the beat of the drum could somewhere be heard. These dances are almost as various and different in their character as they are numerous—some of them so exceedingly grotesque and laughable, as to keep the bystanders in an irresistible roar of laughter—others are calculated to excite his pity, and forcibly appeal to his sympathies, whilst others disgust, and yet others terrify and alarm him with their frightful threats and contortions.

All the world have heard of the *"bear-dance,"* though I doubt whether more than a very small proportion have ever seen it; here it is (Fig. 102). The Sioux, like all the others of these western tribes, are fond of bear's meat, and must have good stores of the "bear's-grease" laid in, to oil their long and glossy locks, as well as the surface of their bodies. And they all like the fine pleasure of a bear hunt, and also a participation in the bear dance, which is given several days in succession, previous to their starting out, and in which they all join in a song to the *Bear Spirit;* which they think holds somewhere an invisible existence, and must be consulted and conciliated before they can enter upon their excursion with any prospect of success. For this grotesque and amusing scene, one of the chief medicine-men, placed over his body the entire skin of a bear, with a war-eagle's quill on his head, taking the lead in the dance, and looking through the skin which formed a mask that hung over his face. Many others in the dance wore masks on their faces, made of the skin from the bear's head; and all, with the motions of their hands, closely imitated the movements of that animal; some representing its motion in running, and others the peculiar attitude and hanging of the paws, when it is sitting up on its hind feet, and looking out for the approach of an enemy. This grotesque and amusing masquerade oftentimes is continued at intervals, for several days previous to the starting of a party on the bear hunt, who would scarcely count upon a tolerable prospect of success, without a strict adherence to this most important and indispensable form!

Dancing is done here too, as it is oftentimes done in the enlightened world, to get favours—to buy the world's goods; and in both countries danced with about equal merit, except that the Indian has surpassed us in honesty by christening it in his own country, the *"beggar's dance."* This spirited dance (Fig. 103) was given, not by a set of *beggars* though, literally speaking, but by the first and most independent young men in the tribe, beautifully dressed (*i.e.* n o t dressed at all, except with their breech clouts or *kelts,* made of eagle's and raven's quills), with their lances, and pipes, and rattles in their hands, and a medicine-man beating the drum, and joining in the song at the highest key of his voice. In this dance every one sings as loud as he can halloo; uniting his voice with the others, in an appeal to the Great Spirit, to open the hearts of the bystanders to give to the poor, and not to themselves; assuring them that the Great Spirit will be kind to those who are kind to the helpless and poor.

Of *scalps,* and of the modes and objects of scalping, I have before spoken; and I therein stated, "that most of the scalps were stretched on little hoops for the purpose of being used in the scalp-dance, of which I shall say more at a future time."

The *Scalp-dance* (Fig. 104) is given as a celebration of a victory; and amongst this tribe, as I learned whilst residing with them, danced in the night, by the light of their torches, and just before retiring to bed. When a war party returns from a war excursion, bringing home with them the scalps of their enemies, they generally "dance them" for fifteen nights in succession, vaunting forth the most extravagant boasts of their wonderful prowess in war, whilst they brandish their war weapons in their hands. A number of young women are selected to aid (though they do not actually join in the dance), by stepping into the centre of the ring, and holding up the scalps that have been recently taken, whilst the warriors dance (or rather *jump*), around in a circle, brandishing their weapons, and barking and yelping in the most frightful manner, all jumping on both feet at a time, with a

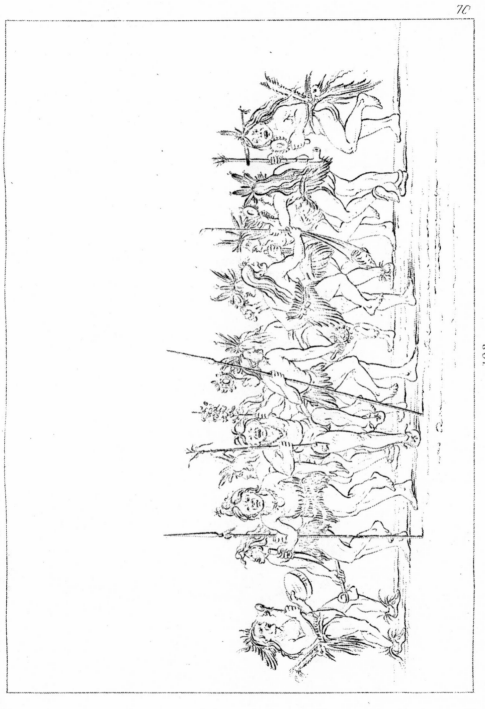

simultaneous stamp, and blow, and thrust of their weapons; with which it would seem as if they were actually cutting and carving each other to pieces. During these frantic leaps and yelps, and thrusts, every man distorts his face to the utmost of his muscles, darting about his glaring eye-balls and snapping his teeth, as if he were in the heat (and actually breathing through his inflated nostrils the very hissing death) of battle! No description that can be written, could ever convey more than a feeble outline of the frightful effects of these scenes enacted in the dead and darkness of night, under the glaring light of their blazing flambeaux; nor could all the years allotted to mortal man, in the least obliterate or deface the vivid impress that one scene of this kind would leave upon his memory.

The precise object for which the scalp is taken, is one which is definitely understood, and has already been explained; but the motive (or motives) for which this strict ceremony is so scrupulously held by all the American tribes, over the scalp of an enemy, is a subject, as yet not satisfactorily settled in my mind. There is no doubt, but one great object in these exhibitions is public exultation; yet there are several conclusive evidences, that there are other and essential motives for thus formally and strictly displaying the scalp. Amongst some of the tribes, it is the custom to bury the scalps after they have gone through this series of public exhibitions; which may in a measure have been held for the purpose of giving them notoriety, and of awarding public credit to the persons who obtained them, and now, from a custom of the tribe, are obliged to part with them. The great respect which seems to be paid to them whilst they use them, as well as the pitying and mournful song which they howl to the *manes* of their unfortunate victims; as well as the precise care and solemnity with which they afterwards bury the scalps, sufficiently convince me that they have a superstitious dread of the spirits of their slain enemies, and many conciliatory offices to perform, to ensure their own peace; one of which is the ceremony above described.

IN former Letters I have given some account of the *Bisons, or* (as they are more familiarly denominated in this country) *Buffaloes,* which inhabit these regions in numerous herds; and of which I must say yet a little more.

These noble animals of the ox species, and which have been so well described in our books on Natural History, are a subject of curious interest and great importance in this vast wilderness; rendered peculiarly so at this time, like the history of the poor savage; and from the same consideration, that they are rapidly wasting away at the approach of civilised man—and like him and his character, in a very few years, to live only in books or on canvas.

The word buffalo is undoubtedly most incorrectly applied to these animals, and I can scarcely tell why they have been so called; for they bear just about as much resemblance to the Eastern buffalo, as they do to a zebra or to a common ox. How nearly they may approach to the bison of Europe, which I never have had an opportunity to see, and which, I am inclined to think, is now nearly extinct, I am unable to say; yet if I were to judge from the numerous engravings I have seen of those animals, and descriptions I have read of them, I should be inclined to think, there was yet a wide difference between the bison of the American prairies, and those in the North of Europe and Asia. The American bison, or (as I shall hereafter call it) buffalo, is the largest of the ruminating animals that is now living in America; and seems to have been spread over the plains of this vast country, by the Great Spirit, for the use and subsistence of the red men, who live almost exclusively on their flesh, and clothe themselves with their skins. The reader, by referring back to Figs. 7 and 8, in the beginning of this Work, will see faithful traces of the male and female of this huge animal, in their proud and free state of nature, grazing on the plains of the country to which they appropriately belong. Their colour is a dark brown, but changing very much as the season varies from warm to cold; their hair or fur, from its great length in the winter and spring, and exposure to the weather, turning quite light, and almost to a jet black, when the winter coat is shed off, and a new growth is shooting out.

The buffalo bull often grows to the enormous weight of 2000 pounds, and shakes a long and shaggy black mane, that falls in great profusion and *confusion,* over his head and shoulders; and oftentimes falling down quite to the ground. The horns are short, but very large, and have but one turn, *i.e.* they are a simple arch, without the least approach to a spiral form, like those of the common ox, or of the goat species.

The female is much smaller than the male, and always distinguishable by the peculiar shape of the horns, which are much smaller and more crooked, turning their points more in towards the centre of the forehead.

One of the most remarkable characteristics of the buffalo, is the peculiar formation and expression of the eye, the ball of which is very large and white, and the iris jet black. The lids of the eye seem always to be strained quite open, and the ball rolling forward and down; so that a considerable part of the iris is hidden behind the lower lid, while the pure white of the eyeball glares out over it in an arch, in the shape of a moon at the end of its first quarter.

These animals are, truly speaking, gregarious, but not migratory— they graze in immense and almost incredible numbers at times, and roam about and over vast tracts of country, from East to West, and from West to East, as often as from North to South; which has often been supposed they naturally and habitually did to accommodate themselves to the temperature of the climate in the different latitudes. The limits within which they are found in America, are from the 30th to the 55th degrees of North latitude; and their extent from East to West, which is from the border of our extreme Western frontier limits, to the Western verge of the Rocky Mountains, is defined by quite different causes, than those which the degrees of temperature have prescribed to them on the North and the South. Within these 25 degrees of latitude, the buffaloes seem to flourish, and get their living without the necessity of evading the rigour of the climate, for which Nature seems most wisely to have prepared them by the greater or less profusion of fur, with which she has clothed them.

It is very evident that, as high North as Lake Winnipeg, seven or eight hundred miles North of this, the buffalo subsists itself through the severest winters: getting its food chiefly by browsing amongst the timber, and by pawing through the snow, for a bite at the grass, which in those regions is frozen up very suddenly in the beginning of the winter, with all its juices in it, and consequently furnishes very nutritious and efficient food; and often, if not generally, supporting the animal in better flesh during these difficult seasons of their lives, than they are found to be in, in the 30th degree of latitude, upon the borders of Mexico, where the severity of winter is not known; but during a long and tedious autumn, the herbage, under the influence of a burning sun, is gradually dried away to a mere husk, and its nutriment gone, leaving these poor creatures, even in the dead of winter, to bask in the warmth of a genial sun, without the benefit of a green or juicy thing to bite at.

The place from which I am now writing, may be said to be the very heart or nucleus of the buffalo country, about equi-distant between the two extremes; and of course, the most congenial temperature for them to flourish in. The finest animals that graze on the prairies are to be found in this latitude; and I am sure I never could send from a better source, some further account of the death and destruction that is dealt among these noble animals, and hurrying on their final extinction.

The Sioux are a bold and desperate set of horsemen, and great hunters; and in the heart of their country is one of the most extensive assortments of goods, of whiskey, and other saleable commodities, as well as a party of the most indefatigable men, who are constantly calling for every robe that can be stripped from these animal's backs.

These are the causes which lead so directly to their rapid destruction; and which open to the view of the traveller so freshly, so vividly, and so familiarly, the scenes of archery—of lancing, and of death-dealing, that belong peculiarly to this wild and shorn country.

The almost countless herds of these animals that are sometimes met with on these prairies, have been often spoken of by other writers, and may yet be seen by any traveller who will take the pains to visit these regions. The *"running season,"* which is in August and September, is the time when they congregate into such masses in some places, as literally to blacken the prairies for miles together. It is no uncommon thing at this season, at these gatherings, to see several thousands in a mass, eddying and wheeling about under a cloud of dust, which is raised by the bulls as they are pawing in the dirt, or engaged in desperate combats, as they constantly are, plunging and butting at each other in the most furious manner (Fig. 105). In these scenes, the males are continually following the females, and the whole mass are in constant motion; and all bellowing (or "roaring") in deep and hollow sounds; which, mingled altogether, appear, at the distance of a mile or two, like the sound of distant thunder.

72

105

106

G. Catlin.

During the season whilst they are congregated together in these dense and confused masses, the remainder of the country around for many miles, becomes entirely vacated; and the traveller may spend many a toilsome day, and many a hungry night, without being cheered by the sight of one; where, if he retraces his steps a few weeks after, he will find them dispersed, and grazing quietly in little families and flocks, and equally stocking the whole country. Of these quiet little herds, a fair representation will be seen in Fig. 106, where some are grazing, others at play, or lying down, and others indulging in their "wallows." "A bull in his wallow" is a frequent saying in this country; and has a very significant meaning with those who have ever seen a buffalo bull performing *ablution,* or rather endeavouring to cool his heated sides, by tumbling about in a mud puddle.

In the heat of summer, these huge animals, which, no doubt, suffer very much with the great profusion of their long and shaggy hair or fur, often graze on the low grounds in the prairies, where there is a little stagnant water lying amongst the grass, and the ground underneath being saturated with it, is soft, into which the enormous bull, lowered down upon one knee, will plunge his horns, and at last his head, driving up the earth, and soon making an excavation in the ground, into which the water filters from amongst the grass, forming for him in a few moments, a cool and comfortable bath, into which he plunges like a hog in his mire.

In this *delectable* laver, he throws himself flat upon his side, and forcing himself violently around, with his horns and his huge hump on his shoulders presented to the sides, he ploughs up the ground by his rotary motion, sinking himself deeper and deeper in the ground, continually enlarging his pool, in which he at length becomes nearly immersed; and the water and mud about him mixed into a complete mortar, which changes his colour, and drips in streams from every part of him as he rises up upon his feet, a hideous monster of mud and ugliness, too frightful and too eccentric to be described!

It is generally the leader of the herd that takes upon him to make this excavation; and if not (but another one opens the ground), the leader (who is conqueror) marches forward, and driving the other from it, plunges himself into it; and having cooled his sides, and changed his colour to a walking mass of mud and mortar; he stands in the pool until inclination induces him to step out, and give place to the next in command, who stands ready; and another, and another, who advance forward in their turns, to enjoy the luxury of the wallow; until the whole band (sometimes an hundred or more) will pass through it in turn; each one throwing his body around in a similar manner; and each one adding a little to the dimensions of the pool, while he carries away in his hair an equal share of the clay, which dries to a grey or whitish colour, and gradually falls off. By this operation, which is done, perhaps, in the space of half an hour, a circular excavation of fifteen or twenty feet in diameter, and two feet in depth, is completed, and left for the water to run into, which soon fills it to the level of the ground.

To these sinks, the waters lying on the surface of the prairies, are continually draining, and in them lodging their vegetable deposits; which, after a lapse of years, fill them up to the surface with a rich soil, which throws up an unusual growth of grass and herbage; forming conspicuous circles which arrest the eye of the traveller, and are calculated to excite his surprise for ages to come.

Many travellers who have penetrated not quite far enough into the Western country to see the habits of these animals, and the manner in which these *mysterious* circles are made; but who have seen the prairies strewed with their bleached bones, and have beheld these strange circles, which often occur in groups, and of different sizes—have come home with beautiful and ingenious theories (which *must needs be made),* for the origin of these singular and unaccountable appearances, which, for want of a rational theory, have generally been attributed to *fairy feet,* and gained the appellation of *"fairy circles."*

Many travellers, again, have supposed that these rings were produced by the dances of the Indians, which are oftentimes (and in fact most generally) performed in a circle; yet a moment's consideration disproves such a probability, inasmuch as the Indians always select the ground for their dancing near the sites of their villages, and that always on a dry and hard foundation; when these "fairy circles" are uniformly found to be on low and wet ground.

As my visit to these parts of the *"Great Far West"* has brought me into the heart of the buffalo country, where I have had abundant opportunities of seeing this noble animal in all its phases—its habits of life, and every mode of its death; I shall take the liberty of being yet a little more particular, and of rendering some further accounts of scenes which I have witnessed in following out my sporting propensities in these singular regions.

The chief hunting amusement of the Indians in these parts consists in the chase of the buffalo, which is almost invariably done on horseback, with bow and lance. In this exercise, which is highly prized by them, as one of their most valued amusements, as well as for the principal mode of procuring meat for their subsistence, they

73

107

G. Catlin.

108

become exceedingly expert; and are able to slay these huge animals with apparent ease.

The Indians in these parts are all mounted on small, but serviceable horses, which are caught by them on the prairies, where they are often running wild in numerous bands. The Indian, then, mounted on his little wild horse, which has been through some years of training, dashes off at full speed amongst the herds of buffaloes, elks, or even antelopes, and deals his deadly arrows to their hearts from his horse's back. The horse is the fleetest animal of the prairie, and easily brings his rider alongside of his game, which falls a certain prey to his deadly shafts, at the distance of a few paces.

In the chase of the buffalo, or other animal, the Indian generally "strips" himself and his horse, by throwing off his shield and quiver, and every part of his dress, which might be an encumbrance to him in running; grasping his bow in his left hand, with five or six arrows drawn from his quiver, and ready for instant use. In his right hand (or attached to the wrist) is a heavy whip, which he uses without mercy, and forces his horse alongside of his game at the swiftest speed.

These horses are so trained, that the Indian has little use for the rein, which hangs on the neck, whilst the horse approaches the animal on the right side (Fig. 107), giving his rider the chance to throw his arrow to the left; which he does at the instant when the horse is passing—bringing him opposite to the heart, which receives the deadly weapon "to the feather." When pursuing a large herd, the Indian generally rides close in the rear, until. he selects the animal he wishes to kill, which he separates from the throng as soon as he can, by dashing his horse between it and the herd, and forcing it off by itself; where he can approach it without the danger of being trampled to death, to which he is often liable by too closely escorting the multitude.

In Fig. 107, I have fairly represented the mode of *approaching,* at the instant the arrow is to be thrown; and the striking disparity between the size of a huge bull of 2000 pounds weight, and the Indian horse, which, it will be borne in mind, is but a pony.

No bridle whatever is used in this country by the Indians, as they have no knowledge of a bit. A short halter, however, which answers in place of a bridle, is in general use; of which they usually form a noose around the under jaw of the horse, by which they get great power over the animal; and which they use generally to *stop* rather than *guide* the horse. This halter is called by the French Traders in the country, *l'arrêt,* the stop, and has great power in arresting the speed of a horse; though it is extremely dangerous to use too freely as a guide, interfering too much with the freedom of his limbs, for the certainty of his feet and security of his rider.

When the Indian then has directed the course of his steed to the animal which he has selected, the training of the horse is such, that it knows the object of its rider's selection, and exerts every muscle to give it close company; while the halter lies loose and untouched upon its neck, and the rider leans quite forward, and off from the side of his horse, with his bow drawn, and ready for the deadly shot, which is given at the instant he is opposite to the animal's body. The horse being instinctively afraid of the animal (though he generally brings his rider within the reach of the end of his bow), keeps his eye strained upon the furious enemy he is so closely encountering; and the moment he has approached to the nearest distance required, and has passed the animal, whether the shot is given or not, he gradually sheers off, to prevent coming on to the horns of the infuriated beast, which often are instantly turned, and presented for the fatal reception of its too familiar attendant. These frightful collisions often take place, notwithstanding the sagacity of the horse, and the caution of its rider; for in these extraordinary (and inexpressible) exhilarations of chase, which seem to drown the prudence alike, of instinct and reason, both horse and rider often seem rushing on to destruction, as if it were mere pastime and amusement.*

I have always counted myself a prudent man, yet I have often *waked* (as it were) out of the delirium of the chase (into which I had fallen, as into an agitated sleep, and through which I had passed as through a delightful dream), where to have died would have been but to have remained, riding on, without a struggle or a pang.

In some of these, too, I have arisen from the prairie, covered with dirt and blood, having severed company with gun and horse, the one lying some twenty or thirty feet from me with a broken stalk, and the other coolly browsing on the grass at half a mile distance, without man, and without other beast remaining in sight.

For the novice in these scenes there is much danger of his limbs and his life, and he finds it a hard and a desperate struggle that brings him in at *the death* of these huge monsters, except where it has been produced by hands that have acquired more sleight and tact than his own.

With the Indian, who has made this the every day sport and amusement of his life, there is less difficulty and less danger; he

* The reader will be further instructed on this subject, by referring back to Fig 9, in the beginning of the book.

74

109

110

G. Catlin.

rides without "losing his breath," and his unagitated hand deals *certainty* in its deadly blows.

In Fig. 108, I have represented a party of Indians in chase of a herd, some of whom are pursuing with lance and others with bows and arrows. The group in the foreground shows the attitude at the instant after the arrow has been thrown and driven to the heart; the Indian at full speed, and the *lasso* dragging behind his horse's heels. The lasso is a long thong, of rawhide, of ten or fifteen yards in length, made of several braids or twists, and used chiefly to catch the wild horse, which is done by throwing over their necks a noose which is made at the end of the *lasso,* with which they are "choked down." In running the buffaloes, or in time of war, the *lasso* drags on the ground at the horse's feet, and sometimes several rods behind, so that if a man is dismounted, which is often the case, by the tripping or stumbling of the horse, he has the power of grasping to the lasso, and by stubbornly holding on to it, of stopping and securing his horse, on whose back he is instantly replaced, and continuing on in the chase.

In the dead of the winters, which are very long and severely cold in this country, where horses cannot be brought into the chase with any avail, the Indian runs upon the surface of the snow by the aid of his snow shoes, which buoy him up, while the great weight of the buffaloes, sinks them down to the middle of their sides, and completely stopping their progress, ensures them certain and easy victims to the bow or lance of their pursuers, as in Fig. 109. The snow in these regions often lies during the winter, to the depth of three and four feet, being blown away from the tops and sides of the hills in many places, which are left bare for the buffaloes to graze upon, whilst it is drifted in the hollows and ravines to a very great depth, and rendered almost entirely impassable to these huge animals, which, when closely pursued by their enemies, endeavour to plunge through it, but are soon wedged in and almost unable to move, where they fall an easy prey to the Indian, who runs up lightly upon his snow shoes and drives his lance to their hearts. The skins are then stripped off, to be sold to the Fur Traders, and the carcasses left to be devoured by the wolves. This is the season in which the greatest number of these animals are destroyed for their robes—they are most easily killed at this time, and their hair or fur being longer and more abundant, gives greater value to the robe.

The Indians generally kill and dry meat enough in the fall, when it is fat and juicy, to last them through the winter; so that they have little other object for this unlimited slaughter, amid the drifts of snow, than that of procuring their robes for traffic with their Traders.

The snow shoes are made in a great many forms, of two and three feet in length, and one foot or more in width, of a hoop or hoops bent around for the frame, with a netting or web woven across with strings of rawhide, on which the feet rest, and to which they are fastened with straps somewhat like a skate.* With these the Indian will glide over the snow with astonishing quickness, without sinking down, or scarcely leaving his track where he has gone.

The poor buffaloes have their enemy *man,* besetting and besieging them at all times of the year, and in all the modes that man in his superior wisdom has been able to devise for their destruction. They struggle in vain to evade his deadly shafts, when he dashes amongst them over the plains on his wild horse—they plunge into the snow-drifts where they yield themselves an easy prey to their destroyers, and they also stand unwittingly and behold him, unsuspected under the skin of a white wolf, insinuating himself and his fatal weapons into close company, when they are peaceably grazing on the level prairies, and shot down before they are aware of their danger (Fig. 110).

There are several varieties of the wolf species in this country, the most formidable and most numerous of which are white, often sneaking about in gangs or families of fifty or sixty in numbers, appearing in distance, on the green prairies like nothing but a flock of sheep. Many of these animals grow to a very great size, being I should think, quite a match for the largest Newfoundland dog. At present, whilst the buffaloes are so abundant, and these ferocious animals are glutted with the buffalo's flesh, they are harmless, and everywhere sneak away from man's presence; which I scarcely think will be the case after the buffaloes are all gone, and they are left, as they must be, with scarcely anything to eat. They always are seen following about in the vicinity of herds of buffaloes and stand ready to pick the bones of those that the hunters leave on the ground, or to overtake and devour those that are wounded, which fall an easy prey to them. While the herd of buffaloes are together, they seem to have little dread of the wolf, and allow them to come in close company with them. The Indian then has taken advantage of this fact, and often places himself under the skin of this animal, and crawls for half a mile or more on his hands and knees, until he approaches within a few rods of the unsuspecting group, and easily shoots down the fattest of the throng.

The buffalo is a very timid animal, and shuns the vicinity of man with the keenest sagacity; yet, when overtaken, and harassed or wounded, turns upon its assailants with the utmost fury, who

* The reader will look forward to Figs. 240 and 243, in the Second Volume, for snow shoes.

75

111

112

G. Catlin.

have only to seek safety in flight. In their desperate resistance the finest horses are often destroyed; but the Indian, with his superior sagacity and dexterity, generally finds some effective mode of escape, as in Fig. 111.

During the season of the year whilst the calves are young, the male seems to stroll about by the side of the dam, as if for the purpose of protecting the young, at which time it is exceedingly hazardous to attack them, as they are sure to turn upon their pursuers, who have often to fly to each other's assistance (Fig. 112). The buffalo calf, during the first six months is red, and has so much the appearance of a red calf in cultivated fields, that it could easily be mingled and mistaken amongst them. In the fall, when it changes its hair, it takes a brown coat for the winter, which it always retains. In pursuing a large herd of buffaloes at the season when their calves are but a few weeks old, I have often been exceedingly amused with the curious manœuvres of these shy little things. Amidst the thundering confusion of a throng of several hundreds or several thousands of these animals, there will be many of the calves that lose sight of their dams; and being left behind by the throng, and the swift passing hunters, they endeavour to secrete themselves, when they are exceedingly put to it on a level prairie, where nought can be seen but the short grass of six or eight inches in height, save an occasional bunch of wild sage, a few inches higher, to which the poor affrighted things will run, and dropping on their knees, will push their noses under it, and into the grass, where they will stand for hours, with their eyes shut, imagining themselves securely hid, whilst they are standing up quite straight upon their hind feet, and can easily be seen at several miles distance. It is a familiar amusement for us accustomed to these scenes, to retreat back over the ground where we have just escorted the herd, and approach these little trembling things, which stubbornly maintain their positions, with their noses pushed under the grass, and their eyes strained upon us, as we dismount from our horses and are passing around them. From this fixed position they are sure not to move, until hands are laid upon them, and then for the shins of a novice, we can extend our sympathy; or if he can preserve the skin on his bones from the furious buttings of its head, we know how to congratulate him on his signal success and good luck. In these desperate struggles, for a moment, the little thing is conquered, and makes no further resistance. And I have often, in concurrence with a known custom of the country, held my hands over the eyes of the calf, and breathed a few strong breaths into its nostrils; after which I have, with my hunting companions, rode several miles into our encampment, with the little prisoner busily following the heels of my horse the whole way, as closely and as affectionately as its instinct would attach it to the company of its dam!

This is one of the most extraordinary things that I have met with in the habits of this wild country, and although I had often heard of it, and felt unable exactly to believe it, I am now willing to bear testimony to the fact, from the numerous instances which I have witnessed since I came into the country. During the time that I resided at this post, in the spring of the year, on my way up the river, I assisted (in numerous hunts of the buffalo with the Fur Company's men) in bringing in, in the above manner, several of these little prisoners, which sometimes followed for five or six miles close to our horses' heels, and even into the Fur Company's Fort, and into the stable where our horses were lead. In this way, before I left for the head waters of the Missouri, I think we had collected about a dozen, which Mr Laidlaw was successfully raising with the aid of a good milch cow, and which were to be committed to the care of Mr Chouteau to be transported by the return of the steamer, to his extensive plantation in the vicinity of St Louis.*

It is truly a melancholy contemplation for the traveller in this country, to anticipate the period which is not far distant, when the last of these noble animals, at the hands of white and red men, will fall victims to their cruel and improvident rapacity; leaving these beautiful green fields, a vast and idle waste, unstocked and unpeopled for ages to come, until the bones of the one and the traditions of the other will have vanished, and left scarce an intelligible trace behind.

That the reader should not think me visionary in these contemplations, or romancing in making such assertions, I will hand him the following item of the extravagances which are practised in these regions, and rapidly leading to the results which I have just named.

When I first arrived at this place, on my way up the river, which was in the month of May, in 1832, and had taken up my lodgings in the Fur Company's Fort, Mr Laidlaw, of whom I have before spoken, and also his chief clerk, Mr Halsey, and many of their men, as well

* The fate of these poor little prisoners, I was informed on my return to St Louis a year afterwards, was a very disastrous one. The steamer having a distance of 1600 miles to perform, and lying a week or two on sand bars, in a country where milk could not be procured, they all perished but one, which is now flourishing in the extensive fields of this gentleman.

as the chiefs of the Sioux, told me, that only a few days before I arrived (when an immense herd of buffaloes had showed themselves on the opposite side of the river, almost blackening the plains for a great distance), a party of five or six hundred Sioux Indians on horseback, forded the river about mid-day, and spending a few hours amongst them, recrossed the river at sun-down and came into the Fort with *fourteen hurdred fresh buffalo tongues,* which were thrown down in a mass, and for which they required but a few gallons of whiskey, which was soon demolished, indulging them in a little, and harmless carouse.

This profligate waste of the lives of these noble and useful animals, when, from all that I could learn, not a skin or a pound of the meat (except the tongues), was brought in, fully supports me in the seemingly extravagant predictions that I have made as to their extinction, which I am certain is near at hand. In the above extravagant instance, at a season when their skins were without fur and not worth taking off, and their camp was so well stocked with fresh and dried meat, that they had no occasion for using the flesh, there is a fair exhibition of the improvident character of the savage, and also of his recklessness in catering for his appetite, so long as the present inducements are held out to him in his country, for its gratification.

In this singular country, where the poor Indians have no laws or regulations of society, making it a vice or an impropriety to drink to excess, they think it no harm to indulge in the delicious beverage, as long as they are able to buy whiskey to drink. They look to white men as wiser than themselves, and able to set them examples—they see none of these in their country but sellers of whiskey, who are constantly tendering it to them, and most of them setting the example by using it themselves; and they easily acquire a taste, that to be catered for, where whiskey is sold at sixteen dollars per gallon, soon impoverishes them, and must soon strip the skin from the last buffalo's back that lives in their country, to "be dressed by their squaws" and vended to the Traders for a pint of diluted alcohol.

From the above remarks it will be seen, that not only the red men, but red men and white, have aimed destruction at the race of these animals; and with them, *beasts* have turned hunters of buffaloes in this country, slaying them, however, in less numbers, and for far more laudable purpose than that of selling their skins. The white wolves, of which I have spoken in a former epistle, follow the herds of buffaloes as I have said, from one season to another, glutting themselves on the carcasses of those that fall by the deadly shafts of their enemies, or linger with disease or old age to be dispatched by these sneaking cormorants, who are ready at all times kindly to relieve them from the pangs of a lingering death.

Whilst the herd is together, the wolves never attack them, as they instantly gather for combined resistance, which they effectually make. But when the herds are travelling, it often happens that an aged or wounded one, lingers at a distance behind, and when fairly out of sight of the herd, is set upon by these voracious hunters, which often gather to the number of fifty or more, and are sure at last to torture him to death, and use him up at a meal. The buffalo, however, is a huge and furious animal, and when his retreat is cut off, makes desperate and deadly resistance, contending to the last moment for the right of life—and oftentimes deals death by wholesale, to his canine assailants, which he is tossing into the air or stamping to death under his feet (Fig. 113).

During my travels in these regions, I have several times come across such a gang of these animals surrounding an old or a wounded bull, where it would seem, from appearances, that they had been for several days in attendance, and at intervals desperately engaged in the effort to take his life. But a short time since, as one of my hunting companions and myself were returning to our encampment with our horses loaded with meat, we discovered at a distance, a huge bull, encircled with a gang of white wolves; we rode up as near as we could without driving them away, and being within pistol shot, we had a remarkably good view, where I sat for a few moments and made a sketch in my note-book (Fig. 114); after which, we rode up and gave the signal for them to disperse, which they instantly did, withdrawing themselves to the distance of fifty or sixty rods, when we found, to our great surprise, that the animal had made desperate resistance, until his eyes were entirely eaten out of his head—the grizzle of his nose was mostly gone—his tongue was half eaten off, and the skin and flesh of his legs torn almost literally into strings. In this tattered and torn condition, the poor old veteran stood bracing up in the midst of his devourers, who had ceased hostilities for a few minutes, to enjoy a sort of parley, recovering strength and preparing to resume the attack in a few moments again. In this group, some were reclining, to gain breath, whilst others were sneaking about and licking their chaps in anxiety for a renewal of the attack; and others, less lucky, had been crushed to death by the feet or the horns of the bull. I rode nearer to the pitiable object as he stood bleeding and trembling before me, and said to him, "Now is your time, old fellow, and you had better be off." Though blind and nearly destroyed, there seemed evidently

113

114

G. Catlin.

to be a recognition of a friend in me, as he straightened up, and, trembling with excitement, dashed off at full speed upon the prairie, in a straight line. We turned our horses and resumed our march, and when we had advanced a mile or more, we looked back, and on our left, where we saw again the ill-fated animal surrounded by his tormentors, to whose insatiable voracity he unquestionably soon fell a victim.

Thus much I wrote of the buffaloes, and of the accidents that befall them, as well as of the fate that awaits them; and before I closed my book, I strolled out one day to the shade of a plum-tree, where I lay in the grass on a favourite bluff, and wrote thus:—

"It is generally supposed, and familiarly said that a man *'falls'* into a rêverie; but I seated myself in the shade a few minutes since, resolved to *force* myself into one; and for this purpose I laid open a small pocket-map of North America, and excluding my thoughts from every other object in the world, I soon succeeded in producing the desired illusion. This little chart, over which I bent, was seen in all its parts, as nothing but the green and vivid reality. I was lifted up upon an imaginary pair of wings, which easily raised and held me floating in the open air, from whence I could behold beneath me the Pacific and the Atlantic Oceans—the great cities of the East, and the mighty rivers. I could see the blue chain of the great lakes at the North—the Rocky Mountains, and beneath them and near their base, the vast, and almost boundless plains of grass, which were speckled with the bands of grazing buffaloes!

"The world turned gently around, and I examined its surface; continent after continent passed under my eye, and yet amidst them all, I saw not the vast and vivid green, that is spread like a carpet over the Western wilds of my own country. I saw not elsewhere in the world, the myriad herds of buffaloes—my eyes scanned in vain for they were not. And when I turned again to the wilds of my native land, I beheld them all in motion! For the distance of several hundreds of miles from North to South, they were wheeling about in vast columns and herds—some were scattered, and ran with furious wildness—some lay dead, and others were pawing the earth for a hiding-place—some were sinking down and dying, gushing out their life's blood in deep-drawn sighs—and others were contending in furious battle for the life they possessed, and the ground that they stood upon. They had long since assembled from the thickets, and secret haunts of the deep forest, into the midst of the treeless and bushless plains, as the place for their safety. I could see in an hundred places, amid the wheeling bands, and on their skirts and flanks, the leaping wild horse darting among them. I saw not the arrows, nor heard the twang of the sinewy bows that sent them; but I saw their victims fall!—on other steeds that rushed along their sides, I saw the glistening lances, which seemed to lay across them; their blades were blazing in the sun, till dipped in blood, and then I lost them! In other parts (and there were many), the vivid flash of *fire-arms* was seen—*their* victims fell too, and over their dead bodies hung suspended in air, little clouds of whitened smoke, from under which the flying horsemen had darted forward to mingle again with, and deal death to, the trampling throng.

"So strange were men mixed (both red and white) with the countless herds that wheeled and eddied about, that all below seemed one vast extended field of battle—whole armies, in some places, seemed to blacken the earth's surface;—in other parts, regiments, battalions, wings, platoons, rank and file, and *'Indian-file'*— all were in motion; and death and destruction seemed to be the watch-word amongst them. In their turmoil, they sent up great clouds of dust, and with them came the mingled din of groans and trampling hoofs, that seemed like the rumbling of a dreadful cataract, or the roaring of distant thunder. Alternate pity and admiration harrowed up in my bosom and my brain, many a hidden thought; and amongst them a few of the beautiful notes that were once sung, and exactly in point: *'Quadrupedante putrem sonitu quatit ungula campum.'* Even such was the din amidst the quadrupeds of these vast plains. And from the craggy cliffs of the Rocky Mountains also were seen descending into the valley, the myriad Tartars, who had not horses to ride, but before their well-drawn bows the fattest of the herds were falling. Hundreds and thousands were strewed upon the plains—they were flayed, and their reddened carcasses left; and about them bands of wolves, and dogs, and buzzards were seen devouring them. Contiguous, and in sight, were the distant and feeble smokes of wigwams and villages, where the skins were dragged, and dressed for white man's luxury! where they were all sold for *whiskey,* and the poor Indians lay drunk, and were crying. I cast my eyes into the towns and cities of the East, and there I beheld buffalo robes hanging at almost every door for traffic; and I saw also the curling smokes of a thousand *Stills*—and I said, 'Oh insatiable man, is thy avarice such! wouldst thou tear the skin from the back of the last animal of this noble race, *and rob thy fellow-man of his meat, and for it give him poison!'" *   *   *

*   *   *   *   *   *   *

Many are the rudenesses and wilds in Nature's works, which are destined to fall before the deadly axe and desolating hands of cultivating man; and so amongst her ranks of *living,* of beast and human, we often find noble stamps, or beautiful colours, to which our admiration clings; and even in the overwhelming march of civilised improvements and refinements do we love to cherish their existence, and lend our efforts to preserve them in their primitive rudeness. Such of Nature's works are always worthy of our preservation and protection; and the further we become separated (and the face of the country) from that pristine wildness and beauty, the more pleasure does the mind of enlightened man feel in recurring to those scenes, when he can have them preserved for his eyes and his mind to dwell upon.

Of such "rudenesses and wilds," Nature has nowhere presented more beautiful and lovely scenes, than those of the vast prairies of the West; and of *man* and *beast,* no nobler specimens than those who inhabit them—the *Indian* and the *buffalo*—joint and original tenants of the soil, and fugitives together from the approach of civilised man; they have fled to the great plains of the West, and there, under an equal doom, they have taken up their *last abode,* where their race will expire, and their bones will bleach together.

It may be that *power* is *right,* and *voracity* a *virtue;* and that these people, and these noble animals, are *righteously* doomed to an issue that *will* not be averted. It can be easily proved—we have a civilised science that can easily do it, or anything else that may be required to cover the inquities of civilised man in catering for his unholy appetites. It can be proved that the weak and ignorant have no *rights*—that there can be no virtue in darkness—that God's gifts have no meaning or merit until they are appropriated by civilised man—by him brought into the light, and converted to his use and luxury. We have a mode of reasoning (I forget what it is called) by which all this can be proved, and even more. The *word* and the *system* are entirely of *civilised* origin; and latitude is admirably given to them in proportion to the increase of civilised wants, which often require a *judge* to overrule the laws of nature. I say that *we* can prove such things; but an *Indian* cannot. It is a mode of reasoning unknown to him in his nature's simplicity, but admirably adaptea to subserve the interests of the enlightened world, who are always their own judges, when dealing with the savage; and who, in the present refined age, have many appetites that can only be lawfully indulged, by proving God's laws defective.

It is not enough in this polished and extravagant age, that we get from the Indian his lands, and the very clothes from his back, but the food from their mouths must be stopped, to add a new and useless article to the fashionable world's luxuries. The ranks must be thinned, and the race exterminated, of this noble animal, and the Indians of the great plains left without the means of supporting life, that white men may figure a few years longer, enveloped in buffalo robes—that they may spread them, for their pleasure and elegance, over the backs of their sleighs, and trail them ostentatiously amidst the busy throng, as a thing of beauty and elegance that had been made for them!

Reader! listen to the following calculations, and forget them not. The buffaloes (the quadrupeds from whose backs your beautiful robes were taken, and whose myriads were once spread over the whole country, from the Rocky Mountains to the Atlantic Ocean) have recently fled before the appalling appearance of civilised man, and taken up their abode and pasturage amid the almost boundless prairies of the West. An instinctive dread of their deadly foes, who made an easy prey of them whilst grazing in the forest, has led them to seek the midst of the vast and treeless plains of grass, as the spot where they would be least exposed to the assaults of their enemies; and it is exclusively in those desolate fields of silence (yet of beauty) that they are to be found—and over these vast steppes, or prairies, have they fled, like the Indian, towards the "setting sun;" until their bands have been crowded together, and their limits confined to a narrow strip of country on this side of the Rocky Mountains.

This strip of country, which extends from the province of Mexico to Lake Winnipeg on the North, is almost one entire plain of grass, which is, and ever must be, useless to cultivating man. It is here, and here chiefly, that the buffaloes dwell; and with, and hovering about them, live and flourish the tribes of Indians, whom God made for the enjoyment of that fair land and its luxuries.

It is a melancholy contemplation for one who has travelled as I have, through these realms, and seen this noble animal in all its pride and glory, to contemplate it so rapidly wasting from the world, drawing the irresistible conclusion too, which one must do, that its species is soon to be extinguished, and with it the peace and happiness (if not the actual existence) of the tribes of Indians who are joint tenants with them, in the occupancy of these vast and idle plains.

And what a splendid contemplation too, when one (who has travelled these realms, and can duly appreciate them) imagines them as they *might* in future be seen (by some great protecting policy of government) preserved in their pristine beauty and wildness, in a *magnificent park,* where the world could see for ages to come, the native Indian in his classic attire, galloping his wild horse, with sinewy bow, and shield and lance, amid the fleeting herds of elks and buffaloes, What a beautiful and thrilling specimen for America to preserve and hold up to the view of her refined citizens and the world, in future ages! A *nation's Park,* containing man and beast, in all the wild and freshness of their nature's beauty!

I would ask no other monument to my memory, nor any other enrolment of my name amongst the famous dead, than the reputation of having been the founder of such an institution.

Such scenes might easily have been preserved, and still could be cherished on the great plains of the West, without detriment to the country or its borders; for the tracts of country on which the buffaloes have assembled, are uniformly sterile, and of no available use to cultivating man.

It is on these plains, which are stocked with buffaloes, that the finest specimens of the Indian race are to be seen. It is here that the savage is decorated in the richest costume. It is here, and here only, that his wants are all satisfied, and even the *luxuries* of life are afforded him in abundance. And here also is he the proud and honourable man (before he has had teachers or laws), above the imported wants, which beget meanness and vice; stimulated by ideas of honour and virtue, in which the God of Nature has certainly not cur tailed him.

There are, by a fair calculation, more than 300,000 Indians, who are now subsisted on the flesh of the buffaloes, and by those animals supplied with all the luxuries of life which they desire, as they know of none others. The great variety of uses to which they convert the body and other parts of that animal, are almost incredible to the person who has not actually dwelt amongst these people, and closely studied their modes and customs. Every part of their flesh is converted into food, in one shape or another, and on it they entirely subsist. The robes of the animals are worn by the Indians instead of blankets—their skins when tanned, are used as coverings for their lodges, and for their beds; undressed, they are used for constructing canoes—for saddles, for bridles—l'arrêts, lassos, and thongs. The horns are shaped into ladles and spoons—the brains are used for dressing the skins—their bones are used for saddle trees—for war clubs, and scrapers for graining the robes—and others are broken up for the marrow-fat which is contained in them. Their sinews are used for strings and backs to their bows—for thread to string their beads and sew their dresses. The feet of the animals are boiled, with their hoofs, for the glue they contain, for fastening their arrow points, and many other uses. The hair from the head and shoulders, which is long, is twisted and braided into halters, and the tail is used for a fly brush. In this wise do these people convert and use the various parts of this useful animal, and with all these luxuries of life about them, and their numerous games, they are happy (God bless them) in the ignorance of the disastrous fate that awaits them.

Yet this interesting community, with its sports, its wildnesses, its languages, and all its manners and customs, could be perpetuated, and also the buffaloes, whose numbers would increase and supply them with food for ages and centuries to come, if a system of non-inter-course could be established and preserved. But such is not to be the case—the buffalo's doom is sealed, and with their extinction must assuredly sink into real despair and starvation, the inhabitants of these vast plains, which afford for the Indians, no other possible means of subsistence; and they must at last fall a prey to wolves and buzzards, who will have no other bones to pick.

It seems hard and cruel (does it not?), that we civilised people with all the luxuries and comforts of the world about us, should be drawing from the backs of these useful animals the skins for our luxury, leaving their carcasses to be devoured by the wolves—that we should draw from that country, some 150 or 200,000 of their robes annually, the greater part of which are taken from animals that are killed expressly for the robe, at a season when the meat is not cured and preserved, and for each of which skins the Indian has received but a pint of whiskey!

Such is the fact, and that number or near it, are annually destroyed, in addition to the number that is necessarily killed for the subsistence of 300,000 Indians, who live entirely upon them. It may be said, perhaps, that the Fur Trade of these great western realms, which is now limited chiefly to the purchase of buffalo robes, is of great and national importance, and should and must be encouraged. To such a suggestion I would reply, by merely inquiring (indepen-dently of the poor Indians' disasters), how much more advantageously would such a capital be employed, both for the weal of the country and for the owners, if it were invested in machines for the manu-facture of *woollen robes,* of equal and superior value and beauty; thereby encouraging the growers of wool, and the industrious manu-facturer, rather than cultivating a taste for the use of buffalo skins; which is just to be acquired, and then, from necessity, to be dispensed with, when a few years shall have destroyed the last of the animals producing them.

It may be answered, perhaps, that the necessaries of life are given in exchange for these robes; but what, I would ask, are the necessities in Indian life, where they have buffaloes in abundance to live on? The Indians' necessities are entirely artificial—are all created; and when the buffaloes shall have disappeared in his country, which will be within *eight* or *ten* years, I would ask, who is to supply him with the necessaries of life then? and I would ask, further (and leave the question to be answered ten years hence), when the skin shall have been stripped from the back of the last animal, who is to resist the ravages of 300,000 starving savages; and in their trains, 1,500,000 wolves, whom direst necessity will have driven from their desolate and gameless plains, to seek for the means of subsistence along our exposed frontier? God has everywhere supplied man in a state of Nature, with the necessaries of life, and before we destroy the game of his country, or teach him new desires, he has no wants that are not satisfied.

Amongst the tribes who have been impoverished and repeatedly removed, the necessaries of life are extended with a better grace from the hands of civilised man; 90,000 of such have already been removed, and they draw from Government some 5 or 600,000 dollars annually in cash; *which money passes immediately into the hands of white men,* and for it the necessaries of life *may be* abundantly furnished. But who, I would ask, are to furnish the Indians who have been instructed in this unnatural mode—living upon *such* necessaries, and even luxuries of life, extended to them by the hands of white men, when those annuities are at an end, and the skin is stripped from the last of the animals which God gave them for their subsistence?

Reader, I will stop here, lest you might forget to answer these important queries—these are questions which I know will puzzle the world—and, perhaps, it is not right that I should ask them.   *

        *   *   *   *   *   *   *

    *   *   Thus much I wrote and painted at this place, whilst on my way up the river: after which I embarked on the steamer for the Yellow Stone, and the sources of the Missouri through which interesting regions I have made a successful Tour; and have returned, as will have been seen by the foregoing narrations, in my canoe, to this place, from whence I am to descend the river still further in a few days. If I ever get time, I may give further Notes on this place, and of people and their doings, which I met with here; but at present, I throw my note-book, and canvas, and brushes into my canoe, which will be launched to-morrow morning, and on its way towards St Louis, with myself at the steering-oar, as usual; and with Ba'tiste and Bogard to paddle, of whom, I beg the readers' pardon for having said nothing of late, though they have

been my constant companions. Our way is now over the foaming and muddy waters of the Missouri, and amid snags and drift logs (for there is a sweeping freshet on her waters), and many a day will pass before other Letters will come from me; and possibly, the reader may have to look to my biographer for the rest. Adieu.

END OF VOL. I.

PRINTED BY OLIVER AND BOYD, EDINBURGH

Other titles from George Catlin offered by *Digital Scanning, Inc.*

The North American Indians (2 Volume Set)
As Published in 1903

Volume 1:
ISBN #s
Tradepaper: 1-58218-212-4
Hardcover: 1-58218-273-6

Volume 2:
ISBN #s
Tradepaper: 11-58218-213-2
Hardcover: 1-58218-274-4

$27.95 Tradepaper, $39.95 Hardcover (per volume)

The Adventures of the Ojibbeway and Ioway Indians
(2 Volume Set) As Published in 1852

Volume 1:
ISBN #s
Tradepaper: 1-58218-494-1
Hardcover: 1-58218-495-X

Volume 2:
ISBN #s
Tradepaper: 11-58218-498-4
Hardcover: 1-58218-499-2

$17.95 Tradepaper, $29.95 Hardcover (per volume)

The Young Reader's Catlin: My Life Among the Indians
As Published in 1909.

Tradepaper ISBN #: 1-58218-478-X
Hardcover ISBN #: 1-58218-479-8

$19.95 Tradepaper, $31.95 Hardcover

To order any of the above titles:

* Contact your local bookstore and order through *Ingram Books.*
* Contact the publisher directly (for general information or special event purchases):

Digital Scanning, Inc.
344 Gannett Rd., Scituate, MA 02066
Phone: (781) 545-2100 Fax: (781) 545-4908
email: info@digitalscanning.com
www.digitalscanning.com

Printed in the United States
3001

9 781582 182735